The Ring of Services
The Story of a Very *Indian* British Raj

Amar Maini

Copyright © 2018 Amar Maini

All rights reserved.

ISBN: 0-646-99132-9
ISBN-13: 978-0-646-99132-0

Cover Image: Minister for Home Affairs Vallabhbhai Patel arriving at Nagpur, December 1947. Courtesy of Photo Division, Ministry of Information & Broadcasting, Government of India.

VIKSITH

MUMBAI SYDNEY

CONTENTS

	Introduction	iv
1	A Middle Class Quest	12
2	Insurmountable Distinctions?	49
3	A Declaration of Intentions	82
4	New Sahibs	113
5	War Veterans	171
6	Braving the Consequences	235
7	High Traditions	286
8	An Immovable Bloc	348
9	A Little Parliament	395
10	An Idea of India	440
	Afterword	510
	Notes	518
	Index	529

Introduction

When the Indian National Congress began its practice of non-cooperation after World War I it ran head on into the steel frame of the British Raj, the Indian Civil Service. As Mohandas Gandhi launched campaigns of satyagraha and civil disobedience against the Raj and began to challenge the centuries old relationships of co-operation between Indians and the British rulers, the Indian Civil Service had to step in and enforce the writ of the state. The elite bureaucracy engaged in constant intelligence work to undermine the Congress, attempted to stifle its growth with the help of Indian collaborators, and in the last resort directed the police and army in the violent repression of its political agitations. From 1920 until 1942 the Congress and the Indian Civil Service were thus in constant conflict at all levels of Indian society. During this period Congress rhetoric changed from pleas for the greater inclusion of Indians in the service, to threats to tear it down once Independence was achieved.

So when Independence came and an article guaranteeing the rights of those Indians who had served in the Indian Civil Service and Indian Police during the days of British rule was brought before the Constituent Assembly finalising the Indian Constitution on 10 October 1949, it was no surprise that many Congressmen objected. The most vocal among them thought it ludicrous that the Indian Civil Service, particularly its Indian officers, should be given any special privileges in the new order. Some of the Congress rank and file felt that the service should be wound up and replaced with something new. Rohini Chaudhuri reminded the chamber that Indians in the Indian Civil Service had never made any sacrifices for Independence, which meant that they should not enjoy any guarantees of remuneration under the new state. M. Ananthasayanam Ayyangar railed against any guarantees for the service, warning that those who had been rulers under the previous regime would continue to be so under the new one. He reminded the Assembly that Indians in the Indian Civil Service had committed "excesses" against the Congress "thinking that this was not their country". Panjabrao Deshmukh joined the chorus, describing the Indian Civil Service as "a remnant of the days of our slavery". Ramnarayan Singh remembered; "we were maltreated, oppressed, and jailed by them".

Yet despite the condemnation of the Indian Civil Service and its Indian officers and the bitter memories which many Congressmen held of their time as political prisoners, guarantees were made for the old service in the new constitution and Indians in the service did continue and flourish under the new regime, largely as a result of Vallabhbhai Patel's intervention. Speaking as India's first home minister, he invoked the teachings of Gandhi to try to cool tempers and the desire for revenge. He pointed out that the Indians in the Indian Civil Service had served the previous regime ably, which was proof that they would do the same for the new regime; loyalty to the state was the essence of their job. Patel's speech on the floor of the Assembly stood against the tide of sentiments of his fellow Congressmen. He was a lone voice speaking for the continuity of the service at the core of the Indian state structure. His intervention may have seemed isolated, and even random. But like all seemingly random events Patel's speech that day in New Delhi was driven by history. In this case a historical process stretching back to the introduction of English education in India 150 years earlier, and the creation of a new and unique class of Indians which sought employment with the British Raj.

Indians had provided services to the British merchants of the East India Company from the time that they arrived in the country in the 17th century. They worked as middlemen, accountants, lenders and interpreters and their skills were crucial for the development of British trade in India. Indian soldiers also fought for the Company's armies, and by the end of the 18th century the British found themselves in possession of vast territories in the east, south and west of the subcontinent. It was in their effort to construct a government that they came to further rely on co-operation from Indians. A small group of Englishmen could not possibly staff every position in the government of such a huge land, and the cost of bringing Englishmen from England to fill every post would erode the balance sheets of what was still a commercial enterprise. Instead the Company bosses decided to promote a system of education which would instruct a small class of Indians in the English language. English education prepared Indians to staff the lower levels of government as clerks working under the supervision of British officers. The mundane work of processing paper would thus be speeded up, whilst the Englishmen would handle the more sensitive matters of state.

The numbers were small at first. In a population of over 100 million, English education only touched a few thousand Indians in the presidency capitals and centres of British administration. By the mid 19th century Indian university graduates only numbered in the hundreds. But as the 19th century progressed English education expanded much beyond what the British had planned for. Indians started to invest in English education for the prospect of government jobs and with higher education they were no longer content simply to remain clerks, they aspired to the higher positions of state such as those in the Indian Civil Service. These rising aspirations would hit a brick wall however. As a small group of Indians fully embraced English education and began to talk back to their colonial rulers, the British, at the height of their power, would claim that Indians could never be trusted with the senior positions of state on the grounds of race. The argument was made that no amount of book learning could bring an Indian up to the level of an Englishman; the two races were completely distinct and the old British officer-Indian clerk relationship which had built the Raj would remain in place.

Despite tensions between the Indian middle class and the British rulers that imperial relationship continued largely undisturbed until World War I. The Indian National Congress was formed in 1885 and the first and second generations of Congressmen remained resolutely moderate. Although sometimes frustrated with the pace of reforms, they largely accepted the small constitutional concessions handed out by the Raj every ten years or so when they could no longer be denied. These concessions were mainly in the form of representation in the legislative councils in Calcutta and in the provinces. However, a major transformation of the Raj would occur during World War I as authorities in London and Delhi finally came to accept a new goal for the Raj; the British would guide India to self-government. The Montagu-Chelmsford reforms included the expansion of the councils, the establishment of a system of 'dyarchy', or shared governmental responsibility between British officials and elected Indian ministers, and a vastly expanded franchise. However, embedded in the reforms was another process which would influence the shape that the Indian state would take after 1947, it was called 'Indianisation'.

Prior to World War I less than 5% of the officers of the heaven born Indian Civil Service were Indians, only a few Indian policemen had ever been promoted to senior posts in the Indian Police, and there was no way for Indians to rise as officers of the Indian Army. Each of the services had been comfortable in its role; the British officer of the Indian Civil Service would supervise the Indian clerk, the British officer of the Indian Police would direct the Indian constable and the

British officer of the Indian Army would lead his loyal Indian sepoys. However, the order came from above to induct Indian officers into the senior ranks of the services as a part of the new commitment to self-government and the 'Indianisation' of the state. That old imperial hierarchy would be broken as Indians joined British officers in the Indian Civil Service, Indian Police and Indian Army. Each service put up varying degrees of resistance, yet after a slow start in the 1920s the services did become Indianised throughout the 1930s and early 1940s to the point at which around half the elite officers of the Raj were Indians.

The prospect of a prestigious and lucrative career in the elite services of the Indian state proved a great attraction to educated Indian youngsters. The only catch was that they were entering the services in the 1920s and 1930s at just the time that the Congress was challenging the British Raj with its epic campaigns of non-cooperation and civil disobedience. Most of these young Indians would watch the protest meetings from a distance during their student days. Some had family members in the nationalist movement and even attended Congress sessions and met the great leaders of the time. But they were all middle class, and given the lack of employment options at the end of their education they chose a career in imperial services which could provide them with financial security, social prestige and professional fulfilment. They could not escape the fact that they were serving a foreign power, but they argued that they were, in practice, serving the people of India and that the independent India of the future would need trained government officers.

The process was known as 'Indianisation', however the British had designed it to produce young Indian officers who would be as close to their British predecessors in culture as possible. The Indian Civil Service had been shaped by English public school values and the gentlemanly culture of Oxford and

Cambridge. Many of the Indian officers who joined the service after World War I had been through these British institutions and besides excelling in the civil service examination they were well prepared to convince the British rulers that they too were gentlemen who could be trusted with the great responsibilities of state. Indian boys competed for ten cadetships to Sandhurst each year where they were transported into an alien environment at the centre of British militarism. Initially only a minority graduated, but those who did imbibed British military culture at its source. Indians who joined the officer cadre of the Indian Police were not sent to England but instead did their training at Police Training Colleges around India and had to navigate the 'Little Englands' of the Officers' Mess. The judiciary however, did not need any explicit policy of Indianisation, cultural or otherwise. It was not a service but an organ of the state in its own right and had been 'Indianising' since the late 19th century with the appearance of England-returned Indian barristers at High Courts across India.

Whilst young Indians were confident of their ability to perform their duties in the elite services of the state, the British were not so sure. During the late 19th century they had filled bookshelves with theories of Indian racial deficiencies. Indians were said to be both physically and morally weak, and unable to exercise leadership or project authority. When the Indianisation process began, the British treated it as an experiment rather than an irreversible change to the Indian state; young Indian officers would have to prove themselves. They would first be trained by senior British officers of the civil service, police and army before being given charge of their own districts, police stations, and army companies. Furthermore, Indian officers would be tested when they had to uphold law and order during Congress agitations, in communal riots, when representing India abroad and when fighting in World War II. In all those situations of conflict and governance they proved themselves to be just as capable as the British officers who trained them. But the success of the Indianisation experiment was most apparent when those young Indians who joined the civil service, police and army in the late 1920s and early 1930s came to be trained by senior Indian officers who had entered the services just a few years earlier.

Indianisation had arisen out of the Montagu-Chelmsford reforms and it was these reforms which opened up India's councils and turned them into legislatures with greater Indian representation and an expanded voter base. The issue of whether to co-operate with these new legislatures and the broad process of guidance to self-government which the British had announced divided the Indian political class and split the Congress. During the 1920s and 1930s the Party was torn between the followers of Gandhi who had included a boycott of the councils in their policy of non-cooperation with the government and other sections of the Party which either wanted to enter the councils to bring them to a halt or co-operate with them to advance the nationalist cause. A Swaraj Party broke away from the Congress on the issue and contested elections throughout the 1920s. By the mid 1930s Gandhi's opposition to 'Council Entry' had diminished somewhat and Congress members were given permission to contest elections. Despite the reservations of Mohandas Gandhi and Jawaharlal Nehru and Subhas Chandra Bose, the Congress contested provincial elections in 1937 and entered the legislatures to form governments from the United Provinces to Bombay, and from Madras to Assam. By the late 1940s Congressmen sat in all the legislatures across India as the 'government in waiting'.

Thus, Vallabhbhai Patel's intervention on the floor of the Constituent Assembly on behalf of the services was not so random after all. By the time of Independence the first generation of government officers from the Indianisation era, who had been trained at Oxford and Cambridge and Sandhurst and India's Police Training Colleges had risen to positions of authority in their respective services. They were cabinet secretaries, major generals and inspector generals of police. India's High Court benches, once very British institutions were now dominated by Indian judges. During the turbulent days surrounding Independence in August 1947 Patel worked with these Indian officers to restore order on the streets of Delhi and integrate the princely states into the new Union. So when he spoke on the floor of the Constituent Assembly in October 1949 and defended the Indian officers of the services he did so from experience, and confidence in their abilities.

The Ring of Services explores the period of the Indianisation of the elite services of the Indian state which occurred between World War I and Independence in 1947. It is an aspect of Indian history which has been little explored so far, but fortunately many of the Indian officers who served the British Raj and then went on to serve independent India committed their memories to writing for future generations to learn from. Their writings provide a fascinating insight into the twilight world which they inhabited during the last days of the Raj; trying to do their jobs whilst watching the vast political transformations reshaping the subcontinent. They take us into the inner workings of the Indian state, from the dusty courtrooms of small town India to the cabinet secretary's office in New Delhi, and from the battlefields of Burma to the battered capitals of Europe and China during World War II. Many of their stories are informative, some are gripping, others comical, yet each helps to explain the resilience of the independent Indian state, which, defying the doubters of its early years, continues standing strong.

One
A Middle Class Quest

The British merchants who arrived in India in the early 17th century established a chain of 'factories', or warehouses strategically located at sea ports and on river banks where they lived and developed a regular trade in Indian textiles. Forts were erected to secure these trading hubs, and as the British East India Company defeated Indian rulers, annexed their kingdoms and took control of the collection of land revenue, new official buildings began to appear. By the late 18th century revenue collection offices and civil and criminal courts were built in Calcutta, Bombay and Madras as the Company attempted to create a government to administer its newly acquired territories. Indians also came into these courts and offices, taking up roles as scribes and clerks and judges and revenue officials, beginning a long record of service to the new Indian state.

Whilst Indians worked in the Company's establishments from the start, there was no system of education which could prepare them for the full range of occupations in its little bureaucracy. The Company thus had no option but to bring young 'Writers' from England to keep its government functioning. These Writers were hugely expensive however, and their difficulties in adapting to life in India, and even their inability to do the work required of them were a perennial source of frustration for the men who ran the Company in both Calcutta and London. It was in this context that Company Directors began to urge their government to educate Indians in the English language. Indian clerks would be cheaper than the English Writers, require fewer amenities, and it was hoped that they would be more efficient, given that they could be employed closer to their own homes.

The Company's government was slow to react to proposals for English education, but the idea of educating Indians in English did capture the attention of a range of British and Indian ideologues. Christian missionaries thought that English education would prepare the Indian mind to receive the teachings of the Bible. Hindu reformers thought it would assist in ridding Hinduism of superstitious practices. British politicians claimed that the spread of English would create a more productive and lucrative colony for the Company. Utilitarian philosophers argued that English would help India to quickly rise from its state of backwardness. All made their contribution to the establishment of English education in India in the early 19th century and thus, whilst the Indian middle class was born of economic necessity, it was also, from the start, envisaged as a great cultural vehicle which would play a historic role in modernising India.

The economic situation which the Indian middle class found itself in remained unchanged throughout the 19th century. The middle class had been created to serve the state, and so it was to the state that middle class Indians first looked for a job. Whilst at the start of the 19th century the range of government jobs was narrow and the work quite simple, as the century wore on and the functions of government expanded the work of the bureaucracy became steadily more complex. Education also started to expand, and as universities were established and Indians studied for higher degrees their aspirations also began to rise. Educated Indians wanted to be able to compete for more prestigious and lucrative positions in the administration, particularly the elite Indian Civil Service.

The cultural role of the middle class, as the maker of a new India was much more difficult to realise. Wherever English and Christian education went it was experienced as a challenge to traditional Indian culture. The challenge was direct when it came from the missionaries, and more indirect when it came from English teachers of science and literature. In both cases

India's society and its spiritual traditions were projected as areas of darkness to be contrasted with England's dazzling modern civilisation. It was Hindu students who felt the attacks most acutely, and so it was they who turned inward and began to examine their spiritual heritage most intensely. During the 19th century educated Hindus began to search for a refined Hinduism with which they could meet the criticisms of their English teachers, and engage with the modern world with their heads held high. When viewed from above, this search looks like a century long middle class spiritual quest, one which spanned the length and breadth of India.

***

English was, as early as the 17th century, a language of trade in India. Everyone thought there was either some money to be made, or some money to be saved by using it. English eased the wheels of commerce for both British traders and Indian middlemen, helped the British to establish a more permanent administration, and provided Indians with a new range of jobs. It even allowed stranded English visitors the chance to make some money and earn a passage back home.

When John Fryer, a Company doctor arrived at Masalipatam in the south of India in June 1673 he noticed a number of Indians coming on board his ship.[i] They were obviously distinct from the boatmen who carried the British possessions on shore, stylishly dressed in calico turbans, light vests and loose flowing pants. They all spoke English, offered their services to the passengers for a small sum of money and then waited for instructions from their clients on the type of business they wanted to conduct. There were similar scenes across the country as Indians came into service with individual Company merchants, interpreting for them, advancing money on their behalf and even keeping their accounts. As trading relationships were formed and trade became more regular, the Company began to employ munshis and dobhashis to keep their records and act as interpreters. By the 18th century the Company's Surveyor-General, James Rennell estimated that there were 1000 interpreters whose services could be called on in Bengal alone.[ii]

The Company's political and commercial affairs grew steadily more complex after its defeat of the Nawab of Bengal, Siraj ud-Daulah on the battlefield at Plassey in 1757. British merchants needed help in keeping accounts, collecting revenue, managing household affairs as well as negotiating with the Mughal Court, and so they began to employ gomasthas to take care of such matters. The Company fixed the rate of revenue it would collect from landowners in Bengal in the Permanent Settlement in 1793 and with the subsequent enforcement of private ownership of property, litigation over land began to increase. At this time the Company's distrust of Indians had deepened, but the ever increasing volume of litigation over land meant that it still had to appoint Indian judges at the lower level to keep its courts running. The Company also had to employ Indians as revenue officials to implement the land policy which had arisen from its surveys and settlement procedures. The range of new jobs came to be filled by the upper caste, mainly Brahmin and Kayastha poor who had been eking out livelihoods in the villages around Calcutta.

Whilst the Company wanted to save some money, it had not yet brought itself to invest in the education of its new employees. English private enterprise thus stepped in to meet the demand for English education, and Englishmen and women struggling to make their own living started teaching shops in and around Calcutta. Broken down soldiers, ruined merchants, and those who had simply exhausted all their savings would set up day schools to try to repair their finances before returning to England. The advertising for these teaching shops emphasised English language instruction and the high fees which they were able to charge reflected the growing demand for English education in Bengal in the early 1800s. These schools rarely outlived their cash strapped founders, but whilst they lasted, and in the absence of government schools, they did offer an education which could lead to a job as a clerk or scribe or interpreter with the East India Company.

***

The people who did the most to build a system of English education in India in the early 19th century were not however, motivated by money. Christian missionaries tried to put some method into the teaching of English and received financial and practical support from wealthy Hindu benefactors. Hindu parents even tolerated it when the preaching became heavy handed. There were few other options for an English education at the time, and their sons needed to learn the language in order to advance socially and economically in the new colonial order.

Upon arrival in India most missionaries took to street preaching. They would try to catch the attention of any Indians whom they could get to stop and listen. Whilst some did stop and listen, few were persuaded to convert, and this hard grind and lack of success led them to other avenues to achieve their goal. It was thought that education would provide captive classrooms of upper caste children, and it was a long held missionary belief that if only the Brahmins could be converted, the rest of the caste order would follow.

A feature of early missionary efforts at English language education was the use of what they called the 'New British Plan'. This New British Plan however, had a circular history. The Reverend Andrew Bell had observed the methods of village schools on his travels in Madras in which the pandits instructed the brighter students, who then taught the rest of the class. This method was brought back to England where John Lancaster made some alterations and it became the Bell-Lancastrian system. Missionaries in England were then so impressed by the Bell-Lancastrian system and its potential for use in their Indian schools that they took it back to India, and it became known as the 'New British Plan'.

By 1817 the Church Missionary Society operated over 60 one room schools in Bengal with an enrolment of over 2000 boys and 20 girls.[iii] In 1818 Lieutenant Stewart, an official of the Company, devised the Burdwan Plan in which there were 15 grades of instruction starting with Bell's table for writing and erasing English letters in the sand and culminating in English medium classes. From grades 1 to 10 students would learn to read and write the English alphabet and form English syllables. In the 11th grade they would start to make words and form short sentences, and in the 12th they would memorise and write down selected moral sentences. Students would then begin to read books published by the Calcutta Book Society such as *Scientific Dialogues*, *Selections from the Beauties of History*, and *A Compendious History of England*.

Mission schools did not try to hide their purpose. A missionary teacher's success was measured by the number of converts they won. The Gospels of Matthew, Mark, Luke and John were the principle texts and whatever their caste or religion students would have to write out daily exercises for their teachers on some passage from the Bible. Annual examinations were often held in public halls, and prescribed homework, full of Christian references and allusions could be read by any of the student's family members who had themselves received an English education.

After 1810 Hindu benefactors started to make endowments for the establishment of English medium schools and colleges which drew on the British curriculum. In 1818, Jai Narayana gave £1800 to Daniel Corrie, a Company chaplain, to establish a school for the intellectual uplift of Indian students.[iv] Corrie used the funds on behalf of the Church Missionary Society and within four months he had over a hundred boys studying English and Indian languages.[v] Jai Narayana continued his support, adding ₹40,000 to the new school's endowment.[vi] In 1825 Raja Badrinath Rai gave ₹20,000 to the Central Female School.[vii] Two years later an anonymous Hindu donor gave ₹400 to Bishop's College, an institution with clearly stated evangelical aims.[viii] In 1830 Ram Mohun Roy provided Alexander Duff with a hall in which he started school lessons. Roy even encouraged the students to read the Bible which Duff would place in their hands. To the inevitable objections, Roy told the boys that he had studied the Bible as well as the Hindu scriptures and the Koran and still remained a Hindu.[ix] The hall housed 5 boys on the first day, and 200 on the fifth.[x]

Despite the fact that so many Indians were lining up to admit their children to missionary schools that many had to be turned away, there was apprehension, and tension. Given the Company's lethargy in meeting the demand for English education, most Indian families had little choice but to send their sons to the missionaries if they wanted them to learn English. Missionary institutions were free or charged modest fees and the potential gains from an English education were judged to be worth the risk by many Indian parents. When Lal Behari Dey was enrolled in Alexander Duff's General Assembly school in Calcutta his father told him that he would be withdrawn as soon as he had learnt English so that he would not have to sit through Duff's lectures on the superiority of Christianity.[xi]

Hindu attitudes to the missionary educational project would quickly change however when the missionaries achieved their long held ambition and actually converted one of their

Brahmin students. Narayan Sheshadri and his younger brother Shripat had come to Bombay from Purli to study at the General Assembly Institute. They lived under the care of the Scottish missionary Robert Nesbit, and it was Nesbit who baptized Narayan in September 1843. The boys were Desatha Brahmins and news of the conversion caused concern within the city's Brahmin community. Their father Govind rushed to Bombay, and whilst he left the elder boy to the missionary, he started a legal battle to regain custody of his younger son who had not yet been baptized. Govind's writ of habeas corpus was successful and the Supreme Court ordered Nesbit to return Shripat to his father.

Shripat's return to his family was just the start of a schism within the Brahmin community of western India however. During his time with Nesbit Shripat had breached many of the Brahmin codes of conduct; he had eaten meat, consumed alcohol and eaten with non-Hindus. Dhakji Dadaji led what came to be known as the Prabhu party which opposed Shripat's readmission to the Brahmin fold. Bal Shastri Jambhekar led his Shastri party which wanted to take the boy back in. They both took their cases to the scriptural authorities of western India, and the Shastri party won a victory in November and December of 1843 when the pandits of Poona and Nasik decided in favour of Shripat's readmission to his caste. They did hand down a 36 year penance however, which was reduced to 18 years on account of the boy's age. Shripat would have to be cleansed, observe a fast for one day, consume five products of the cow the next, eat sacrificial food for three days and three nights, live by alms for another three days, fast again for another three days, undergo another thread ceremony, and then undertake a pilgrimage to Benares by foot. Only then would he undergo the final rite of readmission to the Brahmin community.

Shripat's readmission continued to be challenged by the Prabhu party, but the matter was put to a rest when the pandits of Poona gave their final decision in December of 1844. Shripat's readmission would remain, but he and the leaders of the Shastri party and the pandit who had performed the rite of readmission would all have to undergo their own penances for their actions in bringing the boy back into the caste before a proper consensus among the community had been reached. It was not only the Brahmin caste which had been affected by the conversion case however. A meeting of all the Hindu castes of Bombay had agreed on a boycott of missionary schools; Hindu parents were forbidden to send their children to Christian schools and were urged to break off all social relations with the missionaries.

Similar anxieties were stoked across India in the middle of the 19th century as news of conversions spread. Missionary schools in rural Bengal were picketed, enrolments at schools in north India halved, and more court cases were started in Madras. Indian parents wanted the education that missionaries could provide but feared religious conversions, whilst missionaries were happy to provide that education if there was a reasonable chance that it might lead to conversions. The two groups would thus remain at cross purposes, and missionary education would remain a lingering source of tension until alternative means of English education became available across the country.

***

Whilst Christian missionaries were quick to set up schools across India, they were also the first to urge the Company to establish its own government run English medium schools. Yet Company bosses would always be able to ignore the suggestion as long as it was held up as a religious idea. They were men of commerce, many of whom were Orientalists with a high regard for India's classical culture, and they did not want to do anything to disturb Indian religious sentiments at a time when the Company's administration was still new and fragile. The idea of supporting English would thus have to come from other quarters, from public men with sound political and commercial credentials.

Charles Grant arrived in India in 1767, and amassed a fortune during the heyday of pillage and plunder in Bengal which followed the battles of Plassey and Buxar. Like many of his generation he was a heavy drinker and free spender who accumulated enormous debts. But in 1775 the trauma of the loss of his brother, uncle and two young daughters in quick succession made him turn to a more pious life. By 1780 Grant wanted to get away from the Company's authorities in Calcutta and indulge his new interest in evangelism and decided to take a post as Commercial Resident at the remote town of Malda on the Bengal-Assam frontier. He was able to both promote Christianity and remake his fortune in the silk trade, and it was in Malda that he fully convinced himself that Hinduism was evil and that its cure lay in education, more particularly, English education.

In 1786 Grant came into contact with David Brown, a Company chaplain, and George Udny of the Company Civil Service who encouraged his study of the Bible. He returned to England in 1790, and two years later completed a draft of a treatise entitled *Observations on the State of Society Among the Asiatic Subjects of Great Britain, Particularly in the Respect to Morals and on the Means of Improving it*. Grant thought that the Hindus were corrupt, dishonest and fraudulent, engaged in barbarous customs such as sati and sunk in ancient caste hatreds. He did not have a higher opinion of Muslims whom he depicted as untrustworthy, arrogant and given to lawlessness and debauchery. What was worse was that the interaction of Hindus and Muslims down through the centuries had only led to the degradation of both communities. Grant criticised the Company, arguing that it was under no obligation to encourage or even tolerate Indian religious practices. The only way to lift Indian society out of its state was complete conversion to Christianity, something which could only happen through the spread of European science and literature. The reception of western knowledge would open the Indian mind to the Bible, and Salvation by Jesus Christ. Grant went on to advocate replacing Persian with English as the official language and instituting English as the medium of education. He further argued that Indians educated in English would then go out and teach the new language to their fellow Indians.

Lord William Bentinck went to India as governor general in 1828 as a firm disciple of the other activists of the day, the utilitarians at East India House. James Mill had been advocating the introduction of western literature and science to India as the best means of regenerating its stagnant civilisation, and at a farewell dinner before departing for India Bentinck told Mill: "I am going to British India; but I shall not be Governor-General. It is you that will be Governor-General."[xii] Like the missionaries, Charles Grant, Ram Mohun Roy and the utilitarians, Bentinck thought that the English language was the key to all improvements in India. By the late 1820s the Company's revenue was just above its expenditure, yet it carried a huge debt and had difficulties in meeting its annuity payment. The Company Court of Directors had been arguing for expanding the employment of Indians to lower its salary bill, a position which Bentinck came to accept. Bentinck's ideological enthusiasm for English education was thus entwined with the practical need to repair the Company's finances.

Bentinck was fond of the bright and eager young students at Hindu College who were quick in picking up Western science and English literature. He held them up in contrast to the dull, lazy, expensive and undisciplined Writers who had been brought from England and studied at Fort William College. Bentinck would visit Hindu College with his wife Mary to observe the working of the classes, ask the students questions and hand out prizes. At one of the prize givings, two future members of the Bengali intelligentsia, Madhusudan Sen and Ramtanu Lahiri gave a performance of Shakespeare's *The Two Gentlemen of Verona*, in which they included some gestures from Indian classical dance.[xiii]

By the time that Bentinck arrived in India there was already a great demand for English education amongst Indians in Bengal, Madras and Bombay. However, the East India Company's official position on education was always held back by the General Committee on Public Instruction. The committee was dominated by old orientalists, Company officials who were also often amateur historians and linguists with an enthusiasm for Sanskrit literature. The orientalists would spend the ₹100,000 allocated to the General Committee each year on reviving institutions of ancient Indian learning and providing patronage to classical scholars. As governor general Bentinck created new posts such as principal sadr amin and deputy collector for Indians, however educational institutions like the Calcutta Madrassa and the Sanskrit College at Benares were unable to provide students with the English legal skills needed to do the new jobs. In June 1829 Bentinck wrote a letter to the General Committee advocating the gradual introduction of English for government business.[xiv] The committee did not go that far, but it did introduce an English class in the curriculum of the Benares Sanskrit College in 1830.

The General Committee on Public Instruction had also caught the attention of assorted liberals, utilitarians, evangelicals and missionaries in England and India. It came to be seen as a bastion of obscurantism obstructing their project of westernising and regenerating India. Even the Company's Court of Directors began to get frustrated with the old men on the committee, arguing that the purpose of its activities should be to encourage 'useful learning' rather than 'Hindu learning'.[xv] Between 1828 and 1835 Bentinck changed the composition of the committee, replacing the aging orientalists with anglicists. He even sent the stubborn orientalist Henry Prinsep to Australia for three years. The committee gradually came to be so evenly balanced between the two groups that it became unable to take significant decisions. Proposals in early 1833 to reorganise Agra College on the model of Hindu College in Calcutta, and in April 1834 to turn the Calcutta Madrassa into an institute of western learning brought matters to a head. Henry Prinsep managed to make his way back to Calcutta and present his objections to the proposed policies favouring English education and even raised a petition of 30,000 signatures against the threatened Calcutta Madrassa and Sanskrit Colleges at Benaras and Calcutta.[xvi] The anglicists and the orientalists debated the issue, but they were unable to reach a resolution and so they sent their positions up to the governor general in January 1835. By this time Bentinck had his man in place.

Thomas Macaulay addressed Parliament in July 1833 before departing for India. He asserted that the spread of European civilisation throughout India would raise the level of prosperity and the purchasing power of Indians, giving them greater disposable income for the consumption of England's modern manufactured goods.[xvii] Yet more important than such gains was the "sacred duty" which the British owed to Indians as a race which was blessed with knowledge and liberty owed to another which had been debased by 3000 years of despotism and priestcraft.[xviii] It was in the figure of Thomas Macaulay that decades of missionary zeal began to merge with contemporary utilitarian thinking.

Macaulay took up his position as Law Member on the Governor General's Council in June 1834 and spent his first seven months in India at the hill station of Ooty where Bentinck was also staying. In December 1834 he proceeded to Calcutta and immediately recognised the absurdity of the Company being forced to support scholars of Sanskrit and Arabic through their long years of study, and then having to meet their demands for employment and allowances after graduation when Indians were lining up to pay for an English education. As law member, Macaulay had been appointed President of the General Committee on Public Instruction and whilst he did not participate in the debates, Bentinck asked for his opinion when the committee reached a stalemate over the issue of English education at the Calcutta Madrassa and the Agra College. Macaulay's response took the form of his famous 'Minute on Education'.

Macaulay argued that the official language, Persian, should be replaced by English, that English should be the medium of instruction of all institutions of education, and that it would be futile to translate English texts into as yet underdeveloped Indian languages. Once a select group of Indians were well versed in English, they would seek to translate that knowledge into their own languages, and so a good store of knowledge would be built up in Indian languages over the ensuing decades. In a similar way, Indians educated in English would, in the course of time take care of the education of their fellow Indians, an assumption which came to be known as the theory of 'downward filtration'. Macaulay wanted to civilise the Brahmins of Calcutta with English just as Russian aristocrats had been by French in Moscow a hundred years earlier.

Macaulay threatened to resign if his views were not heeded, however Bentinck was eager to accept his Minute on Education and put into place his long-held agenda for English education in India. Bentinck, like Macaulay and Wood before him, felt that the Indian mind had to be cleared by the English language before it could receive the benefits of modern knowledge. Like Macaulay, he did not see any benefit in keeping Indians in a state of ignorance.[xix] If Company rule was harmful then Indians should have the knowledge and language with which they could express their dissatisfaction. Furthermore, the acquisition of Western knowledge would help Indians in realising that it was their culture which was standing in the way of their progress.

With the return to power of the Conservatives in England Bentinck began to contemplate his retirement. He wanted to ensure his legacy however, even if it meant earning the displeasure of the directors in London and so he issued his orders on English education without first gaining their approval. On 7 March 1835 Bentinck issued an Order in Council deciding "that all the funds appropriated for the purpose of education would be best employed on English education alone". He further sought a plan from the General Committee on Public Instruction on how best to accomplish this new policy. Bentinck did pay the price for his actions, and upon returning to England he had to withdraw from Company affairs and retreated into a life of seclusion. His order may well have been rescinded, and in the years after his return to England some Company officials did try. They even had a draft ready for despatch to India, but it was never sent as the new Governor General George Eden, the Earl of Auckland opposed any change. The debate had been decided, the Company began to catch up with the people, and English came to be the language of education across India.

***

Whilst the Company instituted English education as a means to regenerate India, and some Indians took an interest in the new and modern culture it projected, both were still motivated by more immediate financial concerns. The British wanted to save money in their administration. Indians wanted a share of the better paying jobs in that administration.

The most lucrative posts of all were those in the elite bureaucracy of the state, the Indian Civil Service. A system of open competition was created in the 1850s which meant that Indians were not officially barred, however practical impediments such as the need to cross the oceans and travel to London for an examination in English, competing against British university students in their own academic subjects, and the government's reluctance to admit Indians all stood in the way. Of those Indians who tried some simply failed at the first hurdle and were unable to clear the examination. Others cleared the examination but failed the horse riding test. Still others cleared the examination and the horse riding test but died soon after, and some of those who did survive to gain entry to the hallowed service were dismissed for minor misdemeanours.

The prospects in the other elite services of the British Raj were not much better. The Indian Army would only accept Indian sepoys, the officer class was reserved for the British. The British and Anglo-Indians held a monopoly over the higher posts in the Railways and dominated the technical and managerial positions in Indian industry. It was a similar situation in the Irrigation Department, the Posts and Telegraphs Department, and the Public Works Department. The Viceroy Richard Bourke, the Earl of Mayo, made an effort to alleviate the situation, and new rules were framed in 1879 which stipulated that only Indians were to be appointed to the higher salary grades of the Uncovenanted Service. This gradually forced the British out and turned the lower civil service into an Indian preserve.

With the Indian Civil Service out of reach for most, and the lower bureaucracy offering miserly pay, Indian students started to study for the professions. At Bentinck's initiative the Calcutta Medical College was established in 1835, and like earlier training schools aimed to produce Indian surgeons who would assist British surgeons at military and civilian stations. A medical school was sanctioned in the same year at Madras but it did not begin to function until 1852, whilst Grant Medical College was established in Bombay in 1845. Most British residents in India did not want to be treated by an Indian doctor however, and so despite their qualifications, Indian medical graduates initially remained excluded from the Indian Medical Service and instead had to find employment with wealthy Indian families.

Early attempts at establishing engineering colleges ran into similar difficulties. The Thomason College of Civil Engineering was established in 1847 at Roorkee to assist with the planned construction of the Ganges Canal and an engineering class was started at Elphinstone College in Bombay in 1854 but had to be abandoned due to a lack of suitable candidates. It was only in 1856 that a separate engineering institute was started at the Writer's Building in Calcutta. The construction of the railways gathered pace during the 1850s, however opportunities for Indian engineers remained scarce as senior positions were filled by engineers brought out from England and the lower grades of railway engineers were dominated by Anglo-Indians.

Legal education was also slow to develop, and most Indian lawyers initially struggled to make a living in the Company's lower courts. The language of Indian lawyers was Persian, and English law classes only came to be organised on a permanent basis at Hindu College in Calcutta in 1855. However, the legal profession did begin to grow with the complexity and volume of new government regulations and the increase in litigation over land; the number of civil suits tripled in the three decades after 1857. More than one-third of these cases were in Bengal, which came to support the largest legal profession in India.[xx] Most Indian lawyers were pleaders and mukhtars plying their trade in the lower courts, whilst some worked as vakils who handled appellate work from the districts in the higher courts. Yet from the 1860s Indian lawyers with degrees from Indian universities started to travel to England to study at the Inns of Court in London and await a call to the Bar. When they returned to India Indian barristers initially faced difficulties in receiving case work from British solicitors, but by the end of the century some had built lucrative practices representing wealthy Indian merchants and landlords.

Teaching was the profession in which Indian graduates most easily got a job, but it was also the one in which they were most miserably paid. Positions ranged from jobs in the Department of Education, to professors and principals in government schools and colleges and the modest post of village schoolmaster. Many graduates returned to schools as teachers, and those without degrees but with enough English satisfied the demand for the new language by providing tuitions. In Madras the Department of Education carried the load of graduate recruitment, taking in more than half the province's university graduates.[xxi]

The employment situation was manageable up to the middle of the 19th century when the graduates numbered in the hundreds. The practice in Madras was not unusual, initially governments in each of the provinces employed about one-third to one-half of those graduating from the new universities.[xxii] However, as the 19th century progressed and the number of graduates went from the hundreds, to the thousands, and then tens of thousands, and English education spread wider and farther than the British had anticipated, the government simply could not keep up and offer every B.A. Pass a job.

British educational policy responded to the political climate of the times. Before English speaking Indians began to express their political aspirations, the Educational Dispatch of 1854 aimed to popularise English education and made a departure from the policy of 'downward filtration' from the Bentinck era. Rather than passing responsibility for education on to Indians, the government sought to expand it through the establishment of high schools, universities and encouragement to missionary institutions. By the time of the Education Commission of 1882 however, the responsible, loyal Brown sahibs of Macaulay's imagination had become opinionated Bengali babus, and so the commission recommended a shift from public control of education back to the encouragement of private enterprise. The new policy even sought to hand over some government schools and colleges to Indians who would manage them as aided institutions. As a result, government expenditure on education began to decline and popular endowments and local taxation soon met three-quarters of the expenditure on education.[xxiii] But this government withdrawal from education had an unintended consequence; the number of colleges and student enrolments tripled.[xxiv]

Viceroy George Curzon made his opinions on English education known at a conference in Simla in 1901: "There exists, a powerful school of opinion which does not hide its conviction that the experiment [of English Education] was a mistake, and that its result has been a disaster...They think that it has given birth to a tone of mind and a type of character that is ill regulated, averse from discipline, discontented and in some cases actually disloyal."[xxv] He began to act on this school of opinion and immediately applied a check on the policy of free enterprise in education started in the 1880s. Curzon introduced a system of control and reduced the number of colleges as well as overall government expenditure on university education. He abolished many intermediate colleges and brought higher education under the provisions of the Higher Education Act of 1904. His measures seemed to have the intended effect; there was a decrease in the rate of growth of the number of colleges in the first two decades of the 20th century. Yet despite Curzon's best efforts, the government could not control the increasing number of students at the existing colleges.[xxvi]

It was in this context that Curzon developed an enthusiasm for primary education and Indian languages. He felt that English education was thoroughly elitist and led only to the advancement of a small and noisy minority of Indians and embraced the idea that Indian languages were the life blood of India. Furthermore, basic education in Indian languages would lift the masses out of that state of ignorance in which they could be whipped up by anti-government hysteria.[xxvii] He also began to champion the cause of Indian languages at the university level and gave encouragement to technical education by establishing state scholarships for Indians to train in engineering abroad. The viceroy wanted Indians as far away from the classic works of English political philosophy as possible.

***

As Curzon had understood, English education was not just vocational. It did not simply prepare Indian students to work diligently in government offices. It also opened up a world of new ideas. Indians however initially felt as much threatened as empowered by the ideas projected by Christian and English teaching. Wherever English education spread Hindus gathered to find a way to reconcile their ancient spiritual culture with the modern western ideas which they had been taught in their classrooms. Hindu reform movements appeared in Calcutta, Lahore, Bombay and Madras, producing new 19th century interpretations of Hinduism, reassuring middle class Hindus of the greatness of their spiritual heritage despite the intellectual and physical domination which they were experiencing under the British Raj.

The first to take up the challenge posed by English education was Ram Mohun Roy. Roy was from a Bengali Brahmin family which had served Bengal's Muslim rulers in the 18th century, and as a young man he had started to work as a banker. Some of his clients included officers of the British East India Company, he began to study English, and like many of his caste in Calcutta he went on to work for the Company.

After a decade in service of the Company, Ram Mohun Roy retired to focus his energies on reforming Hindu beliefs and customs. He was deeply influenced by the Christian Unitarianism of his time which believed in the oneness of God rather than the traditional Christian trinity of the Father, the Son and the Holy Spirit. Like the Unitarians Roy dedicated himself to social reform and amongst his first targets was the custom of sati. Roy pointed to scriptures which supported his argument that sati was not required according to Hindu law and was merely a later perversion of true Hinduism. He sought to return Hinduism to a rational and ethical religion, one which had been debased through the centuries by his own Brahmin caste. For Roy, God was manifest in the complexity of reality and the social evils of the day were based on ignorance of the Vedas, Upanishads and the Vedanta Sutra. He translated and printed the Hindu scriptures in Bengali and English and started journals such as *Brahmmunical Magazine* which initiated dialogues within the Hindu community as well as with Christian missionaries. Roy claimed that Christianity, like Hinduism was riddled with error and superstition, and that if each was stripped back to an ethical core then they were as good as each other.

Roy organised a Brahmo Sabha which held its first meeting on 20 August 1828. The Sabha would meet on Saturday nights in Calcutta, and the gatherings seemed to replicate the form of Christian church services. Brahmins would recite the Vedas, there would be readings and teachings from the Upanishads and the singing of hymns in honour of the Supreme Being. Whilst the Sabha was open to all, it was mainly made up of Bengali Brahmins and in its early days had no creed or formal organisation. In 1830 Roy did file a Trust Deed which provided a list of principles for the Sabha, which was to worship "the Eternal, Unsearchable and Immutable Being who is the Author and Preserver of the Universe". This Higher Being was not to be called by any names of particular Gods or Goddesses, there were to be no sacrifices of animals or offerings or worship before idols, and criticism of other sects or religions was also prohibited. The Brahmo Sabha lost its founder however when Roy died in 1833 whilst in England campaigning against sati.

Debendranath Tagore, the scion of a wealthy landowning Brahmin family experienced a crisis of faith in 1838. The following year he formed the Tattvabodhini Sabha which began to hold weekly discussions on religious matters and gathered for monthly prayers. Like Roy, Tagore based his beliefs on Vedanta. However, rather than drawing equivalence with Christianity he emphasised the superiority of Hinduism. Unlike Roy, Tagore was not going to help the missionaries, in fact his favourite target was Roy's old friend Alexander Duff.

Tagore decided to revive Roy's Brahmo Sabha which had been dormant throughout the 1830s. He and his friends joined the Sabha in 1842 and set out to give it some coherence in the form of the Brahma Covenant. The Brahmo Sabha was renamed the Brahmo Samaj and in 1850 Tagore released a volume of scriptures, the *Brahma Dharma*. The principles which emerged from the work were that no scriptures, including the Vedas, were infallible, that there was no distinction between people, all were equal, there was only one higher power and there was no salvation or means to achieve it, a person could simply live a good life by doing good works. The resemblance of the new Brahmo Samaj with

Protestant Christianity started to become clear, and it was at this time that the body began to stand apart from the mainstream of Hinduism. Nonetheless, through the 1850s and 1860s the Samaj expanded out of Calcutta into the interiors of Bengal and Assam attracting Bengali students eager for a new spiritual life.

Keshab Chandra Sen, an English educated banker of the Baidya caste stood out among the younger followers of the Samaj as an impressive speaker and potential leader. He became a confidante of Debendranath Tagore and in 1860 started Sangat Sabhas or small discussion groups which met each week. These Sabhas soon took to radicalism, abandoning caste and sacred threads, giving up alcohol and working for women's rights. They drew on both Hindu and Christian writings and started something of an evangelical programme of their own. Sen and his young followers started to celebrate inter-caste marriages, the remarriage of widows, and went on to tour Madras and Bombay spreading the Brahmo message among the new Indian middle class. However, Sen split with the older sections of the Samaj when Tagore continued to allow members conducting Brahmo services to wear their sacred threads.

In 1866 Sen organised a breakaway faction, the Brahmo Samaj of India, whilst Tagore maintained the Adi Brahmo Samaj. Sen's Brahmo Samaj of India seemed initially to move closer again to Christianity with the introduction of ideas like sin, repentance and the power of prayer. Tagore however wanted to preserve the Samaj as a religious body concerned with theology and ritual rather than crusade for social reform and preferred to spend his time defending Hinduism from the attacks of Christian missionaries. With this more conservative position the Adi Samaj began to make its way back towards mainstream Hinduism and eventually faded away when Tagore died in 1905.

The Brahmo Samaj of India experienced its own split when its Sri Durbar missionaries began to follow Bijoy Krishna Goswami. Goswami wanted to emphasise the spiritual role of the Samaj and include traditional ceremonies and public displays of faith and his followers began to move away from Sen's group. Sen remained committed to social reform for a time and started the Indian Reform Society to educate and improve the life of the Indian peasant. However, after heated conflicts over the Special Marriages Act and the position of women in Brahmo temples, he started to shy away from social action and returned to spiritual matters. Sen turned towards Shaktism and met with Ramakrishna Paramhansa who deepened his worship of the female deity. Dissent amongst his followers came to a head when Sen married his very young daughter to the Maharaja of Cooch Behar in a ceremony which included idol worship. The young radical had turned old conservative and his followers felt it was time to start a new Samaj. And so the Sadharan Brahmo Samaj was founded in 1878.

Sen continued along the road of spiritual devotion, leading processions through the streets of Calcutta, singing hymns and playing musical instruments in the style of Vaishnav devotees. Sen felt he was being called by the Lord to bring all of humanity together under "the Holy City, or the New Dispensation" and in 1881 founded the 'Nava Vidhan'. He created a new festival, a pilgrimage to the saints, and a service to honour the great philosophers, spiritual figures and scientists from all the world's traditions and cultures. He also created a flag ceremony and combined it with a traditional aarti in which five lamps were lit to the sounds of ringing bells and blowing conch shells. Sen told his followers, whom he now called 'Apostles', to go out and work under the flag of the New Dispensation which bore the symbols of Hinduism, Christianity, Buddhism and Islam. Sen's attempt at a new universal religion did not survive his passing however, and the future of the Brahmos lay with his early rationalist followers who had started the Sadharan Samaj and put their efforts into shelters for untouchables, schools for girls, hospitals, leper asylums and orphanages.

Unlike the Brahmo Samaj which was founded by an English speaking banker, the Arya Samaj took its inspiration from a more traditional source, a religious ascetic named Mul Shanker from Gujarat. Mul Shankar, in the way of young Brahmins, was educated at home in Sanskrit to prepare for life as an orthodox Shiva devotee. However, he ran away, took to the life of a wandering mendicant and was given the name Dayananda upon initiation into the order of Saraswati Dandis. In 1860 he became a disciple of Swami Virajananda who led him to his life's new goal; to cleanse Hinduism and rebuild it from its state of decay.

It was on a visit to Calcutta in 1872 that Dayananda met Debendranath Tagore and his Brahmos who persuaded him to abandon his sadhu robes and Sanskrit in favour of a more modern approach. He began to preach in Hindi to the new middle class and published his thoughts as *Satyartha Prakash* in 1875 in which he elaborated on the roles of parents and children, the ideal diet, engaged in systematic criticism of Jainism, Buddhism, Christianity and Islam, and gave his opinions on government and the history of Hinduism. At the end of the work he stated over 50 principles of his beliefs, the most challenging of which for Hindus was that society should be ordered by merit rather than birth, and that much revered scriptures like the Bhagavat were not true Puranas, but a corruption of initially pure Vedic teachings. The realisation of Swami Dayananda's vision would have meant the end of the caste system as it was known, as well as the demise of much of popular Hinduism as it was practised around India.

An Arya Samaj was founded in Bombay in 1875, but it was in Lahore that Swami Dayananda attracted a group of followers amongst the young Hindu students and graduates of the government colleges. They came together to form the Lahore Arya Samaj in 1877 and Swami Dayananda's teachings were reduced to a universal creed based on ten principles. Unlike *Satyartha Prakash*, the ten principles were largely uncontroversial and seemingly easily acceptable to all. They did not make too many demands, or prohibitions, and upheld the sanctity of the Vedas, and ideals of dharma and selfless social service. Yet Swami Dayananda did not live to see the realisation of his vision; he died of poisoning in Ajmer in 1883 after becoming involved in the palace intrigues of princely Jodhpur. Shortly after his death the Lahore Samaj began to draft plans for a school to honour the Swami's memory and propagate his vision of Vedic Hinduism. Funds were raised, but the initial enthusiasm began to fade until Lala Hans Raj, a graduate of the Lahore Government College offered to serve as principal of the new school without a salary.

Lala Hans Raj had experienced the difficulties which middle class Indians faced in maintaining their self-esteem in the everyday life of the British Raj. Indians were reminded of their inferiority in every aspect of colonial life; Englishmen were in superior positions in the Railways, the Telegraphs and in factories where they applied their knowledge of technology to bring material progress to India. The administrative structure of the Raj displayed the Englishman's talent for organisation, and his character and patriotism:

> *"What wonder is it that in the company of Englishmen we feel ourselves conquered and humiliated? Just at this moment the missionary comes to us and whispers that the superiority of the European over the Indian is a gift of the Son of God, whom he has acknowledged as his King and Saviour,*

and that our countrymen can really become great if they come under his banner."[xxviii]

For Lala Hans Raj, Swami Dayananda equipped educated Indians to answer the daily criticisms of Hindu culture which they would hear from British officers and missionaries. He reminded them that in religion and philosophy the British could still not match the ancient glories of Vedic Hinduism. The Swami had even greater claims; that India's ancient rishis were well aware of the principles of modern science which created the steam engines and railways and telegraphs which the British had brought to India.

With Lala Hans Raj at the helm a school was opened in June 1886, attracting 550 students within its first month.[xxix] The school had no government support and no Englishmen served as teachers. Yet after its initial success the school became a source of conflict among the different ideological wings of the Samaj. Pandit Guru Datta took Swami Dayananda to be a rishi who opened up an intensely religious experience. He wanted the school to be a gurukul in the Hindu tradition, teaching Sanskrit and the Vedas, a revival of the universities of ancient India. The more moderate followers of the Samaj, the College Wing, simply wanted an English medium school in which Hindu children could receive a modern education without having to listen to preaching by Christian missionaries. The moderates led by Principal Hans Raj were able to keep control of the school, but the Gurukul Wing went on to gain control over most of the local branches of the Samaj.

The followers of the Gurukul Wing also became something like missionaries themselves, taking the preaching of the Vedas deeper into the districts of Punjab. Worried by the fall in Hindu numbers recorded in the 1881 Census they came up with a conversion, or reconversion ritual called 'shuddhi'. The Gurukul

Wing stepped up its shuddhi campaign in the 1890s, focussing on group rather than individual conversions, and besides seeking the return of converts from Christianity shuddhi was also used to bring outcastes into the caste order. In addition to reconversion campaigns, the Gurukul Wing branched out into education, particularly female education, founding the Arya Kanya Paathshala, the Kanya Ashram and the Kanya Mahavidyalaya whose graduates started their own small girls' schools. Pandit Guru Dutta's vision of the revival of ancient Hindu education also became a reality when the Gurukul Kangri opened in Haridwar in 1902.

Despite its efforts in promoting education, the Arya Samaj was never able to expand beyond its following amongst the Hindu middle class of Punjab. The pure religion which they preached was stripped of many of the elements by which Hindus recognised Hinduism; the Puranas, idol worship, the Brahmins and their rituals, pilgrimages to holy shrines, and the many forms of God. Similarly, the Brahmo Samaj never gained any great following beyond the Bengali middle class. Many Indians who encountered it thought it might just be the Bengali version of Christianity. Neither the Arya Samaj nor the Brahmo Samaj were thus able to bring all of India into their visions of a Hinduism for the modern world. It would take the energy of some spiritual seekers from further afield to keep the quest alive.

The Theosophical Society was formed in New York in 1875 by Colonel Henry Olcott, an American Civil War veteran and Helena Blavatsky, a Russian emigre related to one of the Czar's Great Ministers. The Society developed out of the spiritualist movement of the time and concentrated on what was known as 'scientific mysticism'. It had universalist ideals; it wanted to show that the same principles and ideas provided the foundation for all the ancient religions and sought to bring religion and science closer together. A chance meeting between Henry Olcott and Moolji Thackersey of the Arya

Samaj had led to a correspondence between the two, and the mistaken idea that the two societies shared the same goals. The Council of the Theosophical Society then voted to merge with the Arya Samaj and renamed itself 'The Theosophical Society of the Arya Samaj'.

Olcott and Blavatsky set sail for India to better acquaint themselves with the home of the 'Mother of all Religions'. They were warmly received by the Arya Samajis and their act of bowing and kissing India's sacred soil upon disembarking at Bombay made them instant celebrities amongst the Indian middle class. The Theosophists settled down and lived amongst Indians in Bombay and began lecturing and promoting the study of Sanskrit. With the help of the Arya Samaj they quickly created over 100 branches of the Theosophical Society across India and started a magazine, *The Theosophist,* which propagated their ideas amongst educated Indians and liberal Britons.

On a trip to Ceylon however, Olcott and Blavatsky decided to convert to Buddhism and when they returned to India they began to attack Swami Dayananda for installing himself as a 'Hindu Pope'. The Theosophists still believed that the Vedas were the source of all wisdom but claimed that Theosophy was not supposed to be a religion but merely a society for the study of ancient religions; their goal was to form a Universal Brotherhood of Humanity. Blavatsky then proceeded to write a scripture, *Isis Unveiled*. Its central doctrine was that humanity was just one stage in divine consciousness which had to return to its origin in Godhead by evolving through matter. The leaders of humanity were the mahatmas of the Himalayas who were perfect beings from different races who through thousands of years of birth and rebirth had honed their spiritual powers to break free of the bondage of karma. They formed the Great White Brotherhood, not white skin, but white light, and sought to work on inner and outer planes to lead humanity forward.

The Theosophical Society's annual conventions began in 1881 and brought together English educated Indians and liberal British residents from across India. Formal discussions initially ranged from scholarly approaches to Indian languages and culture to more general exchanges over the compatibility of religious ideas with modern European civilisation. A favourite theme was the materialism and growing decadence of the West and the timeless spirituality of India. In fact, one of the few points of agreement amongst such diverse gatherings was that India's spirituality would have to come to the rescue of a Western civilisation which was heading for destruction. Moreover, the Theosophical Society's message that all the world's religions taught valuable ancient wisdom made it a forum which could attract educated Parsis, Sikhs, Christians and Muslims in addition to Hindus from all over India.

During the 1884 Theosophical Convention in Madras a demand arose for the discussion of social and political matters. Raghunath Rao, a former Diwan of Indore put forward such a proposal only for it to be defeated by Blavatksy. Rao found another way however, calling all those Theosophists interested in political matters to a meeting in his home. These meetings led to the formation of the Madras Mahajana Sabha which in turn sought to form an All India political organisation. In Calcutta, Nurendranath Sen, the proprietor of the *Indian Daily Mirror* and a leading Theosophist who had been present in Madras also began to urge Surendranth Banerjea to use the Indian Association of Calcutta to push for an All India political body.

The Theosophists had taken the middle class spiritual quest as far as it would go. Unlike the Aryas and their austere, remote vision of a pure ancient Hinduism, or the Brahmos and their assimilation of Christianity, the Theosophists had established a pan Indian organisation for the discussion of all spiritual traditions. Yet whilst spiritual matters could be discussed with much enjoyment and without any need for urgent resolution, the Indians drawn to Theosophy from across the country found that their common education had stirred an interest in their political position, something which needed more immediate attention.

The man who would bring spiritual and political India together was a British officer of the Indian Civil Service with a mystical streak and an abiding faith in mahatmas. Allan Hume began his career with the East India Company in 1849. He had been the district magistrate in Etawah in northern India during the Mutiny of 1857 and whilst he was decorated for his bravery during the conflict, he came to be viewed with suspicion by his fellow Englishmen due to his liberal ideals. Hume continued his career in the Indian Civil Service but it was only when the liberal George Robinson, the Marquess of Ripon became viceroy in 1883 that he became a viceregal adviser on native affairs.

Hume had joined the Theosophical Society in 1880, and became President of the Simla Branch in 1881. It was a rare opportunity for someone in his position to mix with like-minded Englishmen and educated Indians. Hume however was most deeply attracted to Theosophy's spiritual doctrines, particularly the one about the mahatmas of the Himalayas who were waiting to lead the renewal of India. Blavatsky would place letters in little wooden shrines from which they would disappear only to be transported to the mahatmas. The mahatmas' replies would come falling from the sky into the same shrine, or even appear under the lucky Theosophist's pillow. Hume would receive his responses in this manner, and they would educate him on the outstanding qualities of Helena Blavatsky and instruct him not to question her leadership. Hume did begin to have his doubts however, and tried to open up a direct channel to the mahatmas, something which led to violent outbursts by Blavatksy. The Society began to divide over the authenticity of the mahatma letters and Hume was among the minority which distanced itself, but did not split from the Society on the issue. Blavatksy then left India, but Hume held true to his faith in the mahatmas and continued his efforts at the political awakening of India under their guidance.

Hume's distance from Blavatsky and the Theosophical Society had led to some strain in his relationship with Nurendranath Sen in Calcutta. Yet he continued to foster links with Behramji Malabari in Bombay and Raghunath Rao in Madras, and with the help of Malabari and Dadabhai Naoroji he was able to form the Bombay Presidency Association. During 1885 he travelled to Madras to meet with Raghunath Rao and his associates but was unable to persuade Surendranath Banerjea in Calcutta to take part in his plans for an All India political conference. Hume's efforts eventually did bear fruit however, when on 28 December 1885, 72 delegates from across India gathered at the Gokuldas Tejpal Sanskrit College in Bombay. They formed an Indian National Congress, one which would begin to shape India's modern history.

***

The Indian lawyers who dominated the early sessions of the Indian National Congress were the products of British liberalism, of a cultural project to impart English education and create a class which would work toward the renewal of India. They had been inspired by the ideals of British political history and philosophy which they had read in their college text books, and were reassured of Britain's good intentions when they heard its formal proclamations of equality of opportunity for all. The beginnings of a political conflict would emerge however, when Congressmen began to hold the British rulers to their promises.

On 2 August 1858 Queen Victoria became the Queen of India, and later Queen Empress of India. The days of the East India Company were over, the British monarch had assumed control of the British Raj, and the new regime sought to bring Indians along on a path of 'moral and material progress' which they could claim as subjects of the Empire. On 1 November 1858 the Queen issued a Royal Proclamation addressed to "the princes and people of India", declaring that Indian "subjects of whatever race or creed, be freely and impartially admitted to offices in our service, the duties of which they may be qualified by their education, ability and integrity to discharge." The prospect of equality of opportunity in the Raj proved a powerful lure for the Indian middle class which would benefit most should the higher reaches of the government services be opened up. Early Congressmen would harp on the Queen's Proclamation, which had seemingly opened all aspects of the administration of the Raj to Indians, claiming that they wanted nothing more than for the British to fulfil their noble promise. For Surendranath Banerjea, the Queen's Proclamation was the Gospel, and for Dadabhai Naoroji its fulfilment was everything Indians could hope for, translated versions would be on the tip of every Indian child's tongue.[xxx]

With the Queen's Proclamation justice came to be embodied in the British monarch and appeared to be a product of her mercy and benevolence. For the first generation of Congressmen political justice need no longer be restricted to natural law or common law but to the idea of equity which was grounded in the compassion and discretion of Queen Victoria. If they thought of political discourse as something like a courtroom, and the British Government as an unsympathetic judge, then they needed a court of appeal, the Queen Empress herself. In fact, annual Congress meetings included much homage to the Queen; Congressmen would swear loyalty, speak of her magnanimous and benevolent nature, and conclude their meetings with three cheers for Her Majesty.

The political language of the early Congressmen was incremental and constitutional. Congressmen would never dare to demand anything from Her Majesty's government. They would only suggest, or urge a course of action. They would never condemn the government's actions, they would merely express regret. Congressmen also had a particular fondness for long and winding quotations of British officials who had promised some concession to Indian interests. The early Congressmen simply wanted to reform the administration of the Raj by increasing Indian participation at its higher levels. More specifically, participation by themselves and their sons and nephews and grandsons in the Indian Civil Service and provincial and central legislative councils. Surendranath Banerjea, whilst addressing the Oxford Union argued that it was Providence which had entrusted representative institutions to Britain and as such it was Britain's role to spread liberty rather than hoard it.[xxxi] But he was careful to reassure the British that he was not demanding anything like democracy, or even Home Rule. What he wanted was "something much less than an English House of Commons".[xxxii] Pherozeshah Mehta echoed this in his presidential address to the 1890 Congress; Congressmen were not so naïve to think that British institutions could be imported wholesale into India. They did not demand universal franchise, in fact they thought that anyone who did would condemn their movement to ridicule. Representation was only for the middle and upper classes who were sufficiently familiar with the English language and British institutions and would be able to cast a vote responsibly.

The moderate nationalists of the early Congress thus raised moderate demands. They wanted to introduce elected members to the legislative councils and expand their legislative powers, to separate the judiciary and the executive and enlarge the scope of trial by jury. They wanted to have the annual Indian Civil Service examinations held in India, a reduction of the Home Charges, and reform of the income tax laws. They also sought an extension of the Permanent Settlement, a reduction in the salt tax, a repeal of the forest laws and reform of the police. According to the Congress view, with Indians in more positions of power in the districts and the legislatures the concerns of the administration would be re-oriented to the economic welfare of India and issues like poverty would be addressed with greater vigour.

Congressmen would be quick to proclaim themselves to be the loyal beneficiaries of British rule. As the educated elite of Indian society it was they who could most fully appreciate the blessings of the British Raj; the schools and universities, the railways and telegraphs, the post offices and law courts. In his presidential address to the second Congress in 1886 Dadabhai Naoroji pointed out that meetings of the Congress could not have been called under Vikramaditya or Akbar. It was the security of people and property and maintenance of law and order which allowed Congress delegates to travel from all corners of the country with the peace of mind that their families and property would be safe at home. Early Congressmen cherished an ideal of England which they had learnt from English political philosophers; the home of Parliament, constitutional liberties and free institutions. Specifically, they learnt from Edmund Burke the importance of moderation in the political history of nations and took British constitutional evolution rather than French revolution as their guide to political action. Their main criticism, far from being seditious, was that British rule often failed to live up to its own stated ideals. They took the word 'British' to be a synonym for justice and fair play, liberalism and modernity, and so anything which did not measure up to that standard, much of the everyday administration of the Raj, was labelled 'un-

British'. The British had brought English education, the common law, a civil service and legislative councils, but suddenly seemed hesitant to take these institutions to their logical ends and open them up to Indians.

***

By the end of the 19th century the lawyers of the Indian National Congress claimed to speak for all of India. That claim was still an ambitious one, but at the very least they could speak for a small but diverse Indian middle class. It was a class created by English education and the needs of the state, and it was to the state that middle class Indians continued to look for employment. Whilst a few barristers had grown wealthy, and Indian doctors found employment with landowners and princes, most middle class Indians remained more modestly employed as clerks and teachers. They worked in schools and government offices across the land, usually as subordinates to British principals or civil servants, processing paperwork or teaching a new generation of students who also aspired to a secure job with the government.

English education did not however, simply equip Indians with the skills to fill a new range of occupations. It created a cultural class as much as an economic one. During the course of an English education Indian students were exposed to a new world of philosophical, religious and political ideas. This was at the heart of Curzon's concern. But rather than political action against the British Raj, English education had first prompted middle class Indians to look within and attempt to reconcile a modern education with an ancient spiritual heritage. It was only when that attempt had exhausted itself, when a resolution seemed illusive, that educated Indians turned to politics and started a new body, one which would slowly develop a new Indian creed, modern Indian nationalism.

English education had not led the lawyers of the Indian National Congress to revolt, but just the opposite- to enthusiastic statements of loyalty. They were the educated elite of Indian society and the chief beneficiaries of British rule. They had gained the most from the imposition of the British legal system and the boom in litigation which it brought with it. They saw the state as the bearer of material progress and guarantor of security. As the spokesmen of their class they simply wanted greater participation and representation in the higher reaches of the state. Specifically, they wanted places for themselves in the legislative councils, and positions for their boys in the Indian Civil Service. They felt that their education and perspective meant that they had much to offer the British administration, and their expertise could help it to solve many of the pressing problems of the time.

Thus, Curzon's concern was slightly misplaced. It was not English education which had led Indians towards disloyalty. Many turned within and spent their time re-examining their spiritual inheritance, whilst others offered their services to the state. What did sow the seeds of growing dissatisfaction was that middle class Indians were increasingly told that the British Raj had no need for their services, and had little interest in their opinions. In the late 19th century the Congress plea for greater inclusion at the apex of the state, in the councils and in the Indian Civil Service would come to be seen as a threat to the racial hierarchy upon which the British Raj was built. It was not enough to have learnt the English language, it's literature and science, Indians would be told over and over that simply by virtue of being Indian they were born to be ruled, just as Englishmen were born to rule.

Two
Insurmountable Distinctions?

The Indian Civil Service was the elite corps of carefully selected bureaucrats who held the key posts in the British Raj. They were never more than 1200 at total strength, some of whom would be on leave at any given time. Those who were on the job advised the viceroy, held specially reserved posts in the secretariats and the provinces, and were the men on the spot, the district collectors overseeing the daily functioning of government in the 250 districts of the British Raj. Such was the competition and prestige of the elite bureaucracy that the Englishmen of the Indian Civil Service, with their large salaries and comfortable pensions were said to be worth '£300 dead or alive' on the marriage market. In fact it was over the question of just who could become an officer of the Indian Civil Service that the most hotly contested debates over race and class and education took place throughout the Raj during the last decades of the 19th century.

British liberals had put as much effort into reforming the institutions of the British state as they had into reforming Indian education. The old system of patronage which controlled appointments to the Indian Civil Service attracted their attention in the 1830s and 1840s, and by the 1850s liberals had successfully instituted a new system of competitive entry to the service based on an open annual examination held in London. During the late 19th century this annual Indian Civil Service examination was considered one of the most competitive in the world, with many of the best and brightest young Englishmen vying for a chance to become the head of an Indian district which might be the size of a small

European country. Indian students were eligible to compete, and so it seemed that a new opportunity had been provided for them to occupy higher positions in the state and share power and responsibility with the British rulers.

Initially the prospect of Indians succeeding in open competition with British students in an examination in London for entry to the Indian Civil Service seemed so remote however, that liberals could be satisfied with the system they had created, and conservatives need not be alarmed by it. Yet the problems for British policy makers started when the first Indians actually began to succeed; liberals had all along maintained that it was culture which distinguished the Englishman in India, and so the appearance of Indians who had imbibed that culture through education and could match Englishmen in their own academic examinations in their own language created some concern. Indian students had received an English education in India, travelled to England and scored high enough marks in one of the toughest examinations in the world to win a place in the hallowed service and so conservatives stepped in to declare that the assimilation of English culture by these young Indian scholars was not real, that it could never be learnt from books, because blood was blood, and it was in fact race which set the Englishman apart in India. This new conservative strain of thought based on racial difference would become the rising ideology of the British Raj at the height of its power.

When Indians started to make their way in to the Indian Civil Service in the 1860s and 1870s, secretaries of state in London and viceroys in Calcutta tried to bend the rules and create new ones to restrict their entry. Any attempts to increase their chances at the examination or ease their conditions of service were resisted by officials of the Raj and the British community across India. The matter which had been creating such concerns for two decades would finally come to a head in 1883 with the introduction of a bill to allow Indian magistrates in the civil service the right to preside over trials of British settlers in the districts. The proposed law was simply meant to give Indian officers the same rights as their British colleagues in the service and had significant official support, but it caused hysteria amongst the British community and even stirred talk of a 'White Mutiny'. The dilemma had sharpened and British officials were forced to decide on the pressing issues of their time; whether educated Indians would be allowed in the elite services of the state, and whether the rule of law, or the rule of a race would prevail.

***

From the days of Bentinck and Macaulay in the 1820s until the Mutiny of 1857 a spirit of liberalism dominated the high tables of the Raj. For liberals, it was the enormous distance between British culture at the top of the civilisational pyramid and Indian culture at its bottom that helped to explain Britain's domination of India. Their efforts were thus aimed at lifting India up by making both a new type of Indian, and a new India.

The liberals of the Raj worked with a well-defined view of the world. They believed that human nature was universal and that it could actually be improved, if not by the spiritual awakening which the missionaries sought, then by the working of laws, trade and education. They sought to free people from their traditional bondage to priests, landlords and despots so that they could become free individuals leading a life of public engagement and rational choice. What they sought was a society which rewarded good character, self-reliance and merit rather than status and patronage. The complete reform of any society was not just an ideal, it could actually be attained with the right liberal policies.

The contemporary liberal view of India was found in James Mill's *The History of British India* of 1818. Mill's measure of social progress was utility, and by that measure India's civilisation had little to boast of. Mill began the second book of his *History*, entitled "Of the Hindus" with a warning to his readers not to be taken in by any extravagant claims to how ancient India's civilisation was; it was the standard defence of "rude nations" to excuse how low they had sunk. Mill's work could be read as an elaborate rebuttal to the Orientalists of an earlier generation, men like Sir William Jones, President of the Asiatic Society, who were Sanskrit scholars and had grown to an appreciation for ancient Indian learning. *The History of British India* joined with the missionaries in their criticism of Hindu theology, but it was India's government, legal system, tax system and social structure which Mill was most interested in. Whilst the Kshatriyas were portrayed as typical Oriental Despots outsourcing the collection of land revenue to minor feudal lords, it was the Brahmins who were the enduring villains of Mill's *History*. The Kshatriyas were allowed their land revenue and armed forces, but it was the Brahmins who controlled the bureaucracy, judiciary and spiritual life of India. The result was a society which was unequal, unjust and cruel, something like Europe of the feudal period overlaid with a chaotic pagan religion.

John Mill's *On Liberty* was published in 1859, and his view on Indian society was largely shaped by his father's writings. He maintained that whilst representative government was ideally the best polity, it was only for those societies which met certain standards. For the rest it was necessary to have benevolent, autocratic rule. The world's cultures were to be placed into a clear hierarchy, and it was Britain's duty to pull all the other lower cultures up to its own level as best it could. For the younger Mill India had stagnated in a cruel, negligent despotism in ancient times. British rule, with its modern institutions and technology would be able to carry Indian society swiftly up the levels of civilisation in a way in which no Indian ruler had done or could ever do. The British would so transform Indian society that eventually its claim to self-rule would be undeniable.

It was this cultural imperialism advocated by the Mills at East India House which most interested Thomas Macaulay. He influenced British policy at a time when India was still an expanding set of military garrisons of a trading Company and not yet a colony supporting Britain's global economic and military expansion. In Macaulay's mind, India would one day achieve political independence from England, but it would be so deeply colonised that "the imperishable empire of our arts and our morals, our literature and our laws" would live on.[xxxiii] Yet given that the liberalism coming from England had neither racial nor environmental theories to sustain it, reformers like Macaulay took to ridiculing Indian culture to establish the necessary cultural distance between the Englishman and the Indian. His Minute on Education of 1835 was a warning against trying to relate to Indian culture, creating comedy by placing Indian science in a British context for his audience; the history found in Sanskrit works would not measure up to a few abridgements of good English texts kept in an English junior school, Indian medical doctrines would not be good enough to treat an English horse's feet, girls at English boarding schools would burst into laughter should they hear the theories of Indian astronomy, Indian history maintained that giant sized kings ruled for tens of thousands of years, and Indian geography claimed that seas were made of syrup and butter.

The inescapable endpoint of liberals' thinking was the end of their own empire. But at the time Indian self-rule was merely an abstract idea, it could not be drawn from the Indian society which they knew, it would have to wait for "some future age", possibly hundreds of years away. The idea of an independent India was considered so futuristic that it was almost a matter of fantasy. Thus, liberal efforts in education and law and trade could all continue without affecting the expansion of British rule for centuries to come.

***

Since the earliest days of Company rule appointments to the Indian Civil Service had been made through a system of patronage run by the Company directors in London. It was a system which threw up well connected public school boys, tough and full of energy, but not always of the highest intellectual calibre. It was also a system which offended the sensibilities of British liberals who believed in more modern ideas, like merit and competition.

The popular image of the Indian Civil Service officer in the 19th century was that of the lone, dutiful Englishman in boots and breeches riding on horseback through his district dispensing British justice to a humble and grateful Indian peasantry. Up at sunrise, he would settle minor legal disputes before breakfast, cast his eye over the village land records, and make the necessary corrections before taking lunch. The harsh Indian climate meant little to him, for he would shoot a couple of tigers in the afternoon, have some dinner, write a bit of Latin verse recalling his days studying classics at Oxford, and then take a cool bath as his loyal Indian servants prepared his camp bed.

But earlier, at the end of the 18th century, civil servants had alarmed the men who ran the British East India Company. A few had abandoned their posts and 'gone native'. It was thought that the influence of Orientalism, the immersion of young Englishmen in Indian languages and customs had led them astray. Rather than Fort William in Calcutta, Indian Civil Service probationers would be trained at a purpose built institution, Haileybury in the English countryside. Besides the necessity of learning Indian languages, law and political economy, they would be trained in Christian morality and the Greek and Latin classics to reduce the risk of seduction by Indian culture. East India Company officials would nominate young men to Writerships, after which they would have to pass an elementary examination and then attend Haileybury before departing for India.

Teachers at Haileybury found it difficult to expel students for breaches of discipline, or enforce academic standards. In the early days they could not even grade their students' papers or compel them to attend classes. Days began with breakfast parties flowing with beer and claret. There were a couple of hours of classes in the mornings, and then sports like cricket and rowing after lunch. The evenings were rounded out with singing and billiards and some more drinking. Secure in their nomination, the young men knew that there was little to stop them from signing the covenant and sailing to India when the time came. John Beames captured the Haileybury approach to India when he recalled, "All we knew was that it was 'beastly hot' and that there were 'niggers' there, and that it would be time enough to bother about it when you got out there."[xxxiv] He added that Haileybury was "a happy place, though rather a farce as far as learning was concerned. In fact you might learn as much or as little as you liked."[xxxv] Having completed his time at Haileybury the young Englishman was sent out to India where he would have to pass further tests to prove his proficiency in Indian languages before being able to take up his appointment.

By 1832 James Mill had begun to argue for recruitment to the civil service by public examination. Colonial officials Charles Trevelyan and Robert Lowe did not think it right that a service as important as the one which ran India should be made up of a random selection of English gentlemen.[xxxvi] A competitive examination would provide for selection on merit and would ensure both character and ability. The self-discipline and initiative which it took to master academic subjects and emerge at the top of merit lists spoke of the moral qualities and character of the scholar. Macaulay asked, "Has it not always been the case that the men who were first in the competition of the schools have been first in the competition of life?"[xxxvii] Patronage was held up as corrupt and degrading to the moral fibre of English society. Yet the motive for reform was not entirely egalitarian. It was thought that the emphasis on a university education, particularly one focusing on the classics would only prove the merit of the English upper class and strengthen its bond with the elite Indian service.

The British East India Company directors' powers of patronage were abolished by the Government of India Act 1853. Moving forward appointments to the Indian Civil Service were made on the basis of an open competitive examination and the following year the Macaulay Committee recommended that Indian Civil Service recruits be tested in Latin, Greek and mathematics, drawing heavily on the curriculum of the 'Greats' course at Oxford. Liberals had won their battle, and nomination by social connection would become an oddity associated with the improvised methods of governance of the early days of British rule in India.

***

When the Indian Civil Service was a British bastion and the prospect of the entry of Indians did not seem quite so serious, it was this concern with class rather than race which gave the British rulers in Calcutta and London a great deal of worry. The British Raj was not just the rule of the British race, but of its highest class, which gave it strength, shaped its values and provided its prestige. The new system of open competition however, had some unintended consequences. Smart English boys from the lower classes began winning places in the service.

Murmurs of discontent began to be heard in the British aristocracy in the 1870s as the results of the new system of open competition became evident. An anonymously written article in the *Edinburgh Review* in April 1874 attacked the new system. The writer's criticism reflected the prevailing aristocratic opinion that young Englishmen of low social origins, without the elevating influence of a university education were eroding the moral and cultural foundations upon which the Indian Civil Service was based. The writer made the case that if recruits could not be gained from the upper classes, then these 'competition wallahs' from London's 'crammers', or examination preparation institutes, should at least do a compulsory period at a university to absorb the culture of the English Gentleman.

Yet English aristocrats had never been a majority amongst the officers of the Indian Civil Service. The impact of open competition was to reduce them from one-third to one-tenth of the service.[xxxviii] In addition, the lower middle class recruits who so worried the anonymous writer only came to represent about 15% of the service intake in the two decades after the introduction of competition.[xxxix] However, graduates of Oxford and Cambridge who made up two-thirds of recruitment at the start of the competition era were reduced to less than one-tenth by 1874, which meant that many of the new middle class recruits of the 1860s and 1870s had not attended a university.[xl]

The English aristocracy saw the competitive system as a failure and the new recruits as socially inferior upstarts who had eroded the prestige of service in India. This attitude went all the way up to the Royal family and Queen Victoria herself. Any association with India seemed to carry a stigma in late Victorian England, something evident in the elite institutions of English society. Oxford tutors had begun to look down on Indian careers. Law Members returning from India were shunned by the legal fraternity. And perhaps most disheartening, English girls would forget their dances with English officials from India on furlough. It even became difficult to persuade English aristocrats to take up the viceroy's post.

In fact, all the viceroys of the period expressed the prejudices of their class. A familiar complaint was that if running India was not hard enough, then it was made more difficult by having to do so with such mediocre men from the Indian Civil Service. Senior Indian Civil Service men would then echo the viceroys' concerns; they too were stuck with mediocre officers who did not make their jobs any easier. It was even claimed that the lowly English competition wallahs were responsible for the new Indian criticisms of British rule; the Indians, with their subtle eye and sense for social hierarchy, knew that the British were sending out their lower class men to rule India. The older generation of British officials from the halcyon days of the service were supposed to be more at ease in dealing with Indians. In addition, the competition wallahs were blamed for the red tape and slow pace of work of the government. Being of British race was thus a necessary, but not a sufficient condition to rule India. The young officer had to be a Gentleman, if not by birth then by a specific type of academic and social education.

***

If the British establishment had reservations about its own smart boys whose only fault was that they had not attended an ancient university, then its reaction to the coming of young Indians might be anticipated. British liberals had created an open, merit based system for entry to the elite service of the state, but it was one which gave successive viceroys and secretaries of state a dilemma which they would never be able to fully resolve.

With his usual enthusiasm Thomas Macaulay told the House of Commons that Indian candidates "would, in the most honourable manner, by conquest, as a matter of right, and not as a mere eleemosynary donation, obtain access to the service."[xli] However, the President of the Board of Control, Sir Charles Wood was more circumspect, saying that "...we have arranged our matters so that they may come here and be admitted. But I cannot say that I either expect or wish them to do so to any extent."[xlii] British officials maintained a measured public tone until 1863 when the first Indian, Satyendranath Tagore actually won a place in the service. In 1859 the weighting for Sanskrit and Arabic had been raised to give Indians a better chance in the examination. After Tagore's success they were lowered again.

George Trevelyan, who as the author of *The Competition Wallah* mocked the new generation of English recruits to the service, went into some detail on the subject of Indians in the service on 5 May 1868 in Parliament during a debate on a motion proposing simultaneous Indian Civil Service examinations in India and England:

> "And if Sir, five percent of the English competition wallahs were found wanting the vigorous and manly virtues, indispensable to the members of a ruling caste, what will be the percentage among Hindoo competition wallahs. Why, many times as great, Sir: and everyone who thinks for a moment will see it must be so....We are there because nine Englishmen out of ten were born to rule, and 99 Hindoos out of 100 are born to be governed; because we are manly and they are effeminate: because

we as a nation always speak the truth and never take bribes."

Sir Stafford Northcote, the Secretary of State for India supported Trevelyan's line, arguing that the majority of Indians were weak in morale and integrity and pointed out that even amongst those officials who favoured taking in more Indians very few would say that Indians as a people had the qualities needed to rule.[xliii]

The Government of India refused to entertain Indian demands for an examination in India or a fixed quota for Indians in the service, yet in 1868 it did attempt to address Indian opinion by providing for nine scholarships a year for Indians to study in England for the professions or to prepare for the Indian Civil Service examination. The scholarship scheme was hardly in operation long enough for the first recipients to set sail from Bombay however, when the new Secretary of State George Campbell, the Duke of Argyll suspended it. He told the Government of India that the scheme was no longer needed because he was introducing a new bill by which Indians could gain admission to the Indian Civil Service at the viceroy's discretion without any need to sit the examination in London.[xliv] The Duke of Argyll's Bill which put an end to the government's scholarship scheme was passed as an Act of Parliament in 1870. Argyll outlined three principles to guide the Act; a high proportion of the top posts in the service needed to stay in British hands, Indians would be able to take up senior judicial, but not executive posts, and they should receive less pay than British officers.[xlv]

Four Indians had been successful at the examination of 1869. Three of them were accused of falsifying their age to appear for the examination. Sripad Thakur and Surendranath Banerjea managed to get their disqualification overturned by the issue of a writ of mandamus against the Civil Service Commissioners. Yet having survived the age controversy, Banerjea earned a severe governmental censure which ended his career less than two years later.

Banerjea's first posting was to Sylhet in Bengal where he was assistant magistrate, in effect an understudy to the District Magistrate Henry Sutherland.[xlvi] Sutherland was born in India, and Banerjea recalled him initially making a show of how cordial he could bring himself to be with his Indian underling. Banerjea rapidly passed his departmental examination and became a first class magistrate, something which he felt contributed to his downfall. He thought the fact that his senior in the service, Joseph Posford failed the same examination caused some amount of chatter in Sylhet's small community of government officials. Sutherland, who was "embued with a strong racial feeling", was said to have taken Banerjea's success and Posford's failure as an affront to the ruling race. In the meantime, Banerjea befriended James Anderson, the Joint Magistrate of Sylhet. Anderson was Sutherland's enemy, which Banerjea thought compounded his trouble. Sutherland then began to make life difficult for Banerjea, calling him for explanations over details of every minor case. In Banerjea's account it was racial feeling, combined with the petty jealousies and rivalries of small town officialdom which set the scene for his demise.

A case of a theft of a boat had been transferred to Banerjea, but he kept postponing it due to his heavy workload. Eventually he initialled an order which placed the accused on a list of absconders, when the man in question had never done so. Banerjea thought of it as a way to mask his delay in seeing to the file and maintained that in most cases this would be deemed the fault of the peshkar, or office advisor who would have guided the young officer in how best to handle the procedure. Banerjea then got his cases confused, and the district magistrate got involved and wrote to the district judge who then sent the matter to the High Court and a Commission of Enquiry was established to look into the matter. Banerjea was found guilty all along the way. The Government of India came to the conclusion that he had dishonestly fabricated his judicial record, attempted to shift the blame onto others, and then used his judicial powers to try to shield himself.[xlvii] The Government of Bengal also wanted to make an example of him to show that the standards of integrity of the Indian Civil Service applied to all its officers.[xlviii]

After an enquiry into the competition system in 1875, the Secretary of State Robert Gascoyne-Cecil, the Marquess of Salisbury reduced the maximum age for competition from 21 to 19. The measure was aimed at British candidates in the hope of catching them young, but it did impact Indians disproportionately and was seen as another measure designed to stifle the chances of Indian students. Having cleared the Indian Civil Service examination at a younger age, English competition wallahs could then spend time in the elevating environment of an ancient university. In fact the measure was likely initiated to favour Salisbury's alma mater Oxford; the university wanted to take on the successful Indian Civil Service candidates for their mandatory university residence.

James Stephen, a former law member in Calcutta who had returned to England managed to grasp both the essence and importance of the issue of Indians in the Indian Civil Service. He realised that upon the question of the suitable employment of educated Indians "lies practically the fate of the empire".[xlix] Educated Indians could not be uneducated. But to employ them in the highest reaches of the civil service would undermine one of the foundations of the British Raj; the almost magical aura of the Englishman and his exclusive racial claim to possess all the qualities necessary to rule.

***

The persistent ideological conflict between liberalism and conservatism in the Raj continued throughout the 1870s and 1880s. It found expression in the experiences of two Viceroys, one who wanted to rule as a conqueror and keep Indians in their place, and another who wanted to rule by co-operation and prepare Indians for self-government. Both departed India in defeat, and it would be left to the viceroy who followed them to conjure a middle path to satisfy both the needs of the British rulers, and the aspirations of middle class Indians.

Robert Bulwer-Lytton, the Earl of Lytton, was appointed Viceroy of India in 1876. He had an instinctive distaste for liberalism which he shared with the Secretary of State Salisbury, the Finance Member John Strachey and the former Law Member James Stephen. They felt burdened with Macaulay's legacy and thought that English education had only created political aspirations which could not be met. Unlike the liberals who saw India as a field on which they could apply their ideas on a grand scale, Lytton saw India as "the practical confutation of so many Liberal fallacies."[i] The viceroy was quite clear that Queen Victoria's Proclamation would have to be ignored in order to maintain the essence of imperial rule:

> "We all know that these claims never can, or will be fulfilled. We have to choose between prohibiting them or cheating them. And we have chosen the least straightforward course...both the governments of England and India appear to me, up to the present moment, unable to answer satisfactorily the charge of having taken every means in their power of breaking the heart of the word of promise they have uttered to the ear."[ii]

Lytton's plan to address the issue of Indians in the Indian Civil

Service was to divide the service into two parts, one a British preserve which Indians would not be able to aspire to, and another lower service which they would have to be content with. He claimed that it was foolish for British liberals to "...ignore the essential and insurmountable distinctions in race qualities, which are fundamental to our position in India."[liii] He further argued that it was imperative that the British realise that they held India by conquest and they needed to rule in a befitting manner. Lytton wanted an Indian Service in which he could transfer some of the lesser judicial posts from the Indian Civil Service as well as some of the better paid posts from the lower services. He did not want the Bengali babu, nor did he think that the graduates of Bombay or Madras were sturdy enough to serve outside their own province, whilst the martial races of northern India would not submit themselves to education. All the viceroy wanted were a few loyal young Indian men of good aristocratic stock to staff a service positioned clearly below the elite Indian Civil Service.

In Lytton's scheme Indian graduates would then be excluded from both the Indian Civil Service, which would be the preserve of the British, and the lower service, which would be the preserve of Indian aristocrats. However, this would mean breaking the Queen's Proclamation, failing to honour pledges, and amending Acts of Parliament. In addition, Lytton's proposal would require new legislation and it would be impossible to push such a bill through the British Parliament. The new Secretary of State Gathorne Gathorne-Hardy, the Earl of Cranbrook refused to introduce the proposed scheme. Thus, Lytton's tilt at ruling as a conqueror was defeated by Britain's constitutional system. What London did suggest was that Calcutta follow the 1870 regulations and implement the Duke of Argyll's principles; allow a few Indians to enter the Indian Civil Service but keep them out of the top offices.[liii]

William Gladstone led the Liberal Party to power in 1880 and immediately recalled Lytton from Calcutta. The new Viceroy George Robinson, the Marquess of Ripon had been an Under Secretary of State for India 20 years earlier and held liberal ideas about the need to include educated Indians in the administration. He argued that unless the British were willing to open up positions for Indians in keeping with their aspirations, the colleges and universities may as well be closed down, for graduates would only become enemies of British rule.[liv] He saw his path as that of progress and Lytton's as that of repression.

Ripon hoped to re-open the Indian Civil Service issue, however he was rebuffed by London. He then wanted to introduce an elective principle into the councils to get a better understanding of Indian opinion. Ripon's plan was to have larger municipalities elect Indians to the legislative councils, ten in total, one each from Madras, Calcutta and Bombay and the others from the seven other major towns. He thought that this would advance the political education of the people and be a measure towards giving them a major say in their own affairs.[lv] When Ripon put his plan forward he had to wait a year for a reply from London. The India Office saw it as the viceroy advancing a plot for Home Rule, much before Indians had even thought of it.

Most of the British community in India were instinctively conservative and found the new viceroy's ideas positively dangerous. Sir James Fergasson, Governor of Bombay, Rivers Thompson, Lieutenant Governor of Bengal, Grant Duff, Governor of Madras and Sir Alfred Lyall, Lieutenant Governor of the North Western Provinces made up a solid group of conservatives. Viceroy Ripon's circle of liberals included Evelyn Baring, the Finance Member, Courtney Ilbert, the Law Member and Sir Charles Aitchison of the Indian Civil Service. Ripon also had to deal with the Old India Hands of the India Council in London whom he saw as aged, overpaid and out of touch. The likes of Sir Henry Maine, General Richard

Strachey and Sir Ashley Eden on the other hand thought that the viceroy was only slightly less of an enemy than Prime Minister Gladstone. Their job was to stop both of them from damaging the grand edifice of the British Raj which had been built on the basis of sacrifice and toil down through the generations.

Ripon's grand plans did not make much progress and so he had to turn to a more modest field of endeavour, local government. Local self-government had been in a moribund state across the country, but he thought it would be useful in associating Indians with the administration and giving them some political training; Ripon's Resolution on Self Government of 1882 stipulated that Municipal and Rural Boards be established where feasible. He wanted elected members from outside the government with minimal interference from government appointed chairmen. Rural Boards would be given control of local rates and taxes, collect the license tax, and be able to propose and direct the construction of public works. Still, the viceroy reserved extensive discretionary powers for the government and gave it ample scope to shape the details of local schemes. The Finance Member Evelyn Baring supported him; he thought Ripon's measures would distract the Bengali babus from the big political questions of the day with more mundane concerns, like schools and drains.[lvi]

***

The event which took concerns over the entry of Indians into the Indian Civil Service from feisty but reasoned conversations amongst the senior officials of the British Raj, to mass hysteria amongst the British community in India was a seemingly innocuous piece of legislation, the Ilbert Bill. At issue were questions of race and education and law. Would the Indians who were making their way up the ranks of the Indian Civil

Service be able to act as officers of the service in all circumstances, like their British colleagues? Or would they too have to submit to the racial hierarchy which ruled colonial life in the districts of the Raj?

Until 1872 judicial officers in the districts did not have the power to try British subjects for anything beyond some minor offences and were restricted to committing them for trial by a higher court. The British tea and indigo planters appreciated this provision as they moved deeper into the interiors of eastern India. In 1872 the Criminal Procedure Code was amended to give justices of the peace, sessions judges and first class magistrates limited powers to fine or imprison British residents in the districts, but the planters retained the right to a trial by a British magistrate. As Indians began to enter the Indian Civil Service some went into the judicial branch and became district judges and sessions magistrates and the anomaly of not being able to try British subjects like their British colleagues became apparent. So one such Indian Civil Service officer, Behari Lal Gupta proposed an amendment to the law to give Indian officers the same powers as British officers. His proposal was supported by the Bengal Government. Administrators in the other provinces also lent their support, as did the Viceroy's Council. The home member thought that outrage would be limited to "the more bigoted Europeans".[lvii] It was only with the presentation of the Ilbert Bill that the storm arrived.

The British planters and merchants of Bengal and the British lawyers of Calcutta all united to condemn the idea that Indians, no matter what their level of education, could sit in judgement on White men and women. There was talk of a White Mutiny, forming a European and Anglo-Indian Defence Association, sending the viceroy to Australia, and even the establishment of a White Settler Republic. At a Town Hall meeting organised by the Bengal Chamber of Commerce in Calcutta on 28 February 1883 the President of the Chamber asked: "Do you think a native will become so Europeanised that he will be able to judge false charges against a European...Can the leopard change his spots, or the Ethiopian his skin colour?"[lviii] Speakers warned the gathering that lone British women in the districts would be in danger from conspiracies between zamindars and Indian judges. James Branson, a Calcutta barrister went into some detail on the possible scenarios which could occur were the Ilbert Bill to be passed:

> "What the stiletto is to the Italian, the false charge is to the Bengalee...Picture the position of an English lady in a remote district who has been brought before a District Magistrate on a charge fabricated by a wealthy zemindar who has designs upon her, and there subjected to an examination at his hands with all the insolence that cowards are capable of... Many of you have brought from afar some English girl for your wife who was entrusted to you by a loving father or a trusting brother...If you give in now, you are betrayers of that sacred trust...(Indignant cheers, cries of no! no!) Do not forget that the wily native is creeping about like a snake."[lix]

The dominant theme in the British press was that the lowering of the prestige of British residents in India would lead to their harassment, particularly those isolated planter families who would have to live at the mercy of the Indians around them. An additional economic argument was advanced that should the legal protections for British settlers be revoked, the necessary capital for the indigo, tea and coffee plantations would be scared away. Overlaid with all this hostility was an attack against Prime Minister Gladstone's Liberal Government and his Roman Catholic Viceroy Ripon.

James Stephen, although nominally a Liberal, led the charge against the bill. He argued that because India was so diverse everyone needed their personal laws. He had to stress the idea that the British Raj was not based upon consent, but upon conquest, and reduced the debate to its essential point when he stated: "If the Government of India have decided on removing all anomalies from India, they ought to remove themselves and their countrymen."[ix] He went so far as to say that British rule was not based on law but on "the superiority of the conquering race".[xi] For Stephen, the principles of the Ilbert Bill were inconsistent with the foundations of British rule; the British Raj was not based on the generosity of a fair and just law giver, but self-evident racial superiority.

As the controversy raged on, the government asked its officers, including Indians, for their opinions on the bill. Brajendranath De, the Joint Magistrate at Hughly supported the bill, seeing no reason why Indians and Britons should not be tried by the same magistrate.[xii] He thought that the British had little to worry about, given the enormous prestige they enjoyed in India. In his experience magistrates, Indian and British, acted conscientiously, and Indian magistrates would be too afraid of the repercussions from their superiors to show any bias in cases involving British settlers. In response to the argument that Indians were insufficiently acquainted with British manners and customs, he countered that manners and customs had little to do with criminal trials which were decided on the facts of the case, according to the principles and procedures of law. Indians had become well acquainted with English literature and the culture it projected, whereas the number of British magistrates who had any similar knowledge of Indian languages and culture was limited. John Beames, the old Haileybury man, and by now Commissioner of Burdwan Division forwarded De's note to the government. He claimed that it supported his case against the Ilbert Bill. De's lack of deference, and his uppity, know-it-all manner were just the reason why Indians should not sit in judgement over the British. Beames detected a "tone of dislike to Europeans and almost disrespect towards Government".[lxiii]

Coming up against the conservatism of the British community in India, Viceroy Ripon took the Queen's Proclamation quite literally and thought that it either had to be put aside or be respected. The real issue for Ripon was whether Indians were going to continue to be admitted in any great number to the Indian Civil Service, and if they were then the law would simply have to be amended. The fate of the Ilbert Bill would thus decide whether the liberal declarations and promises of the Raj were genuine, or whether they were in reality a sham. In this instance though, there was no clear resolution. The controversy over the Ilbert Bill ended in a compromise. Eventually British subjects accused of crimes were able to claim the right to a trial by jury, at least half of which would be made up of their countrymen.

A new viceroy, without the ideological commitments of Lytton or Ripon made his way to India. Frederick Hamilton-Temple-Blackwood, the Marquess of Dufferin was to go back to basics and be the protector of the Indian peasant against the babu and the zamindar. In addition, he brought with him a new strategy to keep educated Indians on side; he would offer them a few 'loaves and fishes'. The loaves would be more places in the Indian Civil Service, and the fishes would be greater representation in the legislative councils.

Dufferin wanted to put the raging controversy over Indians in the Indian Civil Service to rest and come to a lasting settlement on the issue. A Public Service Commission was set up in 1886 and instructed to produce a scheme "which may reasonably be hoped to possess the necessary elements of finality, and to do full justice to the claims of natives of India to higher and more extensive employment in the public service".[lxiv] The commission ended up recommending the creation of two services, both open to Indians. One, a smaller Indian Civil Service recruited only by open competition in England, and another provincial service which would be recruited in India and would receive some posts from the Indian Civil Service and some higher executive and judicial posts from the lower service. The commission also recommended that the maximum age for the Indian Civil Service examination be raised to 23 and some more marks be allocated for Sanskrit and Arabic. By an elaborate maze of transfers and reallocations the commission's recommendations amounted to a net gain of one post for Indians.

Dufferin also wanted to reform the legislative councils as part of a 10-15 year political settlement with the Indian middle class. Small legislatures, more akin to committees had been created across India in the middle of the 19th century. Most of the members were British government officials, and the Indian members were mainly large landowners and princes appointed by the viceroy. Unlike Ripon, Dufferin did not see his suggestions to open up these legislatures to greater Indian participation as a step on the path to self-government, but simply as a better mechanism for seeking Indian opinion on legislative matters. He thought that support for government measures from Indians brought onto the councils would popularise them and the government would appear less isolated than in the prevailing practice of passing legislation without consultation.[lxv] Dufferin did meet with opposition however from the Secretary of State John Wodehouse, the Earl of Kimberley, who wanted to improve the administration rather than reform the councils.[lxvi] Sir Henry Maine was also opposed to the expansion of the councils for its forebodings of representative government and claimed that such a vast land and population could never govern itself.[lxvii]

The viceroy did not persist with the issue, but then Richard Cross, the Viscount Cross took over from Kimberley in London. It became clear that some form of election would be necessary, but it would be indirect; the universities and municipalities would send a few Indian names to the government for nomination to the councils and the government would keep a majority of official votes. In 1888 Dufferin put his views to his Executive Council and directed a committee of Sir Charles Aitchison, James Westland and Sir George Chesney to report on the issue. Dufferin's plan however, found few supporters in London and only came into law in a diluted form as the Indian Councils Act of 1892.

***

By the end of the 19th century it seemed as though the liberal ideal of reform and opportunity for all races had reached a limit. Its fulfilment had become too imminent, too dangerous, and so whether in Parliament or the Calcutta Town Hall or the Viceroy's Council it had to be held to ridicule. But unlike the liberals' mockery of Indian culture, a more conservative strain of satire became fixated with race. The idea that Indians could fill their heads with textbooks and pass as many examinations as they liked but that they would, by virtue of some incurable racial defect, never be fit to govern themselves came to be a recurring theme in the period's English literature about India.

Calcutta was the capital of the British Raj, and so it was the Bengali babu who became a favourite target for British satire. The term 'babu' was, of course, a term of respect and affection in Bengali society used to address a man of learning and culture. However, the British began to use it as a term of disrespect for any English educated Bengali who expressed disruptive opinions. The Bengali babu came to be seen as a danger because he had so imbibed English culture that he could engage in reasoned English argument, threatening the Englishman with similarity when he constantly wanted to emphasise difference. It was after all difference, and in the last resort racial difference, which provided the foundation for British rule.

For English writers the Bengali male's racial deficiency was most evident in his effeminate nature. Bengali men's dhotis looked something like a long flowing lady's dress, they were devotees of the Goddess Durga, and would sometimes dress as women in order to express their devotion. They were thought to lack manly self-control and indulged in sexual intercourse with young girls, further weakening their race. The result was that Bengali men were physically small and did not make for good sportsmen, or even show much enthusiasm for manly games like snipe shooting and pig sticking. According to the English gentlemanly code of the time a man's worth could be judged by his chivalrous treatment of women. The way that Bengali men treated their wives was viewed as another sign of their lack of a noble masculinity. For the British, the Bengalis were small, effeminate men who avoided the battlefield and so deserved their status as a subject race. The growing romance of the martial races of north India only made the disdain for the babus of Calcutta more intense.

In the literature of Victorian England Indians remained in a permanent state of childhood. The British knew what was best for their Indian subjects and it would be dangerous to allow them authority over themselves or others. Indians lacked self-discipline, which was why they were good soldiers when commanded by British officers but were inevitably led to defeat by their own men. They were ruled by their emotions, were untrustworthy, cruel, lacked empathy and were given to hysteria. They were stubbornly conservative. And surprisingly happy despite their circumstances. Muslims however, were not portrayed as such irredeemable people. They were people of the Book and Muslim rulers had controlled vast swathes of India prior to British rule. They were active and manly, fought a spirited fight and had a code of honour. The towering Pathan of the North West Frontier was an especial figure of romance. Muslims at this time were not so threatening to the British, slower as they were to take to English education, more representative of the timeless rural India of humble peasants and brave soldiers and strict zamindars.

The British who settled in India revered one writer above all others. They read the stories of Rudyard Kipling and would be delighted when they found the situations he described in their daily lives. The civil servant and novelist Leonard Woolf found that "the white people were also in many ways astonishingly like characters in a Kipling story. I could never make up my mind whether Kipling had moulded his characters in the image of Anglo-Indian society, or whether we were moulding our characters accurately in the image of a Kipling story."[lxviii]

Kipling shared the British disdain for Bengal and Bengali culture of his time and so he started his book *The City of Dreadful Night* with a description of the Big Calcutta Stink. The smell in Calcutta beat anything that Benaras, or Peshawur, or Bombay could throw up. There was no escape from it; it was on the maidan, it blew into the Great Eastern Hotel, it swirled into the Bengal Club. It was on the streets, and in the morning breeze. The foul odour had a surprising cause however. It was local self-government. Indians had been allowed on the Calcutta Municipal Corporation which had come to be dominated by Bengali property owners who liked to talk, but did not like to be taxed. For Kipling freedom had got out of control, just as the smell had. The natives needed to be taxed and Englishmen needed to come in and have the mess cleaned up. Most damningly, Indians were oblivious to good governance "which they cannot, by the nature of their birth, understand." Things were much better in the districts where if such a smell pervaded the air the district magistrate would just take all the Indians off the District Board until sanitation had been restored "and men are kept clean despite themselves, and may not poison their neighbours."

In *The Head of the District* Kipling put the idea of Indians in the Indian Civil Service to the test on India's turbulent North West Frontier. His short story opens with Yardley-Orde, the much loved and respected deputy commissioner dying of fever. He had been stretchered by some loyal Pathans and began to talk quietly to his assistant Tallantire. Yardley-Orde did not mind dying, but he did not want to leave his wife and the district behind. Even unto his last breath he could not keep his mind off his work and reminded Tallantire to look into details of the land revenue and canal construction. He then spoke to his loyal Pathans in Pashtu and gave them some final moral instruction; be good men, pay your taxes, do not lift cattle, do not listen to the mullahs, do not sack caravans, and leave your arms at the police post when you come into town. He told them that Tallantire was now their sahib, and to go to him and follow his advice.

But in a sudden comic turn, Yardley-Orde's replacement on the Frontier was not Tallantire or Bullows, but one Grish Chunder De M.A. of the Indian Civil Service. He had been appointed on the recommendation of a viceroy with a particular sympathy for Indian aspirations. As for the matter of race, it would not make much difference, for Grish Chunder De was "more English than the English"; he was a university graduate who had won his place through competition in London, charmed drawing rooms in England, written pamphlets and already administered a crowded district in south east Bengal. The British Head of the North West Frontier agreed with the principle of De's appointment, but decided to put some precautions in place; he would be surrounded by strong deputy commissioners, be given the best assistant in the province, and the fear of God would be stamped into the Pathans before he even arrived.

Tallantire and Bullows discussed the new appointment and what it would mean for them and for the district. They had heard of Grish Chunder De; he knew his case law, was good at routine and desk work and pleasant enough to talk to. He had been kept in his home district amongst his sisters and aunts and turned the place into a "family preserve" where all his relations could make some money. But how would they explain his appointment to the Pathans? And if they dare objected to it they would be accused of prejudice. Bullows told Tallantire that the only solution was to run the district himself, keep the Pathans under control, show De the ropes along the way, and telegraph him if needed.

Grish Chunder De then arrived in the district, and the Pathan Khoda Dod Khan mistook him for a clerk. When De addressed a public meeting and attempted to hand down an order the gathered landowners burst out laughing. The District Superintendent of Police Curbar, who was waiting to one side, briefed Tallantire on the tribal raids which had broken out. He then had to take Grish Chunder De aside and explain that an armed uprising had started as the locals did not approve of him and thought that they could now do as they pleased. De's response was to insist that he had not yet taken charge of the district. He then feigned an illness and fled town with his brother, a lawyer who had come along hoping for some business.

De was "a terrified man" and spent his time sending telegrams of exaggerated accounts of the violence to all the authorities he could remember. Meanwhile Tallantire, who knew the district blindfolded was already at work, out on horseback, riding past Yardley-Orde's gravestone to seek his blessings before pacifying the Pathans once again. With some helpful intelligence from trusty Khoda Dod Khan, he led a night time cavalry charge of a tattered Baloch regiment and did put the fear of God into the Pathans once again. Tallantire had probably exceeded his authority, but Bullows did not "think the authorities will dare make a fuss about it. They've had their lesson."

If the comedy of *The Head of the District* was to remind readers that 'a Babu will always be a Babu', then Kipling's novel *Kim* was a more studied explanation for why 'a Sahib will always be a Sahib'. Kimball O'Hara was a little orphan boy, the son of an Irish soldier who had died in India. His skin had been "burned as black as any native", he spoke English hesitantly, was most at home speaking Hindustani, played with the Indian boys of the bazaar and knew all the ins and outs and strange men of the walled city of Lahore. He would creep about, running errands at night and eat from the same dish as the holy men just returned from their begging rounds. His guardian, an Anglo-Indian woman, insisted he wear European clothes, but much of the time he preferred Indian dress. He tagged along behind marriage processions, attended festivals and ate with his Indian friends. The guards and water carriers, sweet vendors and carpenters all knew him. He was even a protege of Mahbub Ali, an Afghan who worked for the British in the Great Game, the shadow war fought with Russia for control of the Afghan Government. Kim seemingly befriended everyone he encountered, and even became a disciple of a Tibetan Lama travelling through northern India on a spiritual quest. He kept doing small jobs for Mahbub Ali in exchange for hot meals, but what he really wanted was to travel with the Lama to the holy town of Benares.

Kim did go out from Lahore with the Lama, and on their

journey his restoration to his race began. Heading east through Punjab past Umballa Kim and the Lama spotted some White soldiers across a plain. They were an advance party of a regiment preparing the ground for a camp. The Lama wanted to leave, but Kim wanted to take a closer look and sneaked into the soldiers' camp. He was caught, mistaken for a thief, and a debate ensued between a Church of England chaplain and a Roman Catholic priest over what to do with the boy. Normally he would have been scolded and let go, but Kim spoke some English and had a charm around his neck and carried some papers with him. The papers were his baptismal certificate, and some scrawled instructions from his father to look after him. The Church of England man thought it was probably all a trick. The Roman Catholic felt it might just be a miracle. Kim then translated for the chaplain and the priest as they explained to the Lama that they would take Kim into their care and educate him, for they thought that "once a Sahib is always a Sahib".

Kim was thus suddenly delivered into the company of hundreds of White men of the Mavericks Regiment; a world of pickets, bugles, marches, military bands and lime washed barracks. The priest then put the boy on a train for Lucknow, to attend St Xavier's school, sending him on his way with the parting words "They'll make a man o' you, O'Hara, at St Xavier's - a white man, an', I hope, a good man." Xavier's did do that, but to start with Kim would be punished for smoking, using abuse never heard of within the confines of the school, and breaking out of the school boundaries. He was among the sons of the low ranking British officials from the Railway, Telegraph and Canal Departments and he had to learn how to conduct himself amongst his fellow White boys; he would stop himself from telling tales from his days in the old city of Lahore so that his class mates would not think that he had gone "native altogether". He enjoyed the new physical comforts of school life and the chance to apply his mind to academic work, and went on to excel in mathematics and geography, play cricket for the school's first eleven, and get vaccinated against small pox. He still had to be punished occasionally for skipping school to go out with beggars and for speaking with "improper persons", but by the end of his school days Xavier's had done its job.

When Kim later met Mahbub Ali, who had known him since he was a bazaar boy in Lahore, Ali adopted the tone he would normally reserve for Europeans. Kim had become a chotta sahib. He would go into government service and become a minor player in the Great Game on India's frontiers, and whilst he never fully reconciled his Irish ancestry with his Indian upbringing, he was at least restored, both by education and vocation, to his role as a White man in the British Raj.

***

It was the liberalism of Viceroy Ripon that Kipling was holding up to ridicule in *The City of Dreadful Night* and *The Head of the District*. Although based on well-meaning ideas it had disrupted the racial hierarchy upon which the Raj was built, whether in the city of Calcutta or on the distant North West Frontier. This official liberalism had little support amongst the British policy establishment, and even less within the British community settled throughout India. In Kipling's stories it only ended in disaster. But the type of conservatism which Kipling approved of also had its limits. When Viceroy Lytton tried to rule as a conqueror, he was defeated, not from Indian resistance to his plans, but from Britain's own constitutional system.

Viceroy Dufferin had to chart a middle path, meeting the aspirations of educated Indians with a policy of 'loaves and fishes'. It was a policy which still upheld the British racial claim to rule, and the British would remain in control of the levers of power and decide on the pace of change, yet it also acknowledged the need to bring educated Indians into higher positions in the state. Dufferin's solution was to do so exceedingly slowly. Indians did not realise just how slow the process would be however, and the loaves and fishes were effective to start with. The round of constitutional concessions which Dufferin initiated took form in the Indian Councils Act of 1892. That settlement would last 17 years before another round of reform became necessary under a new Indian Councils Act of 1909. The reforms of 1909 would last another decade until a new Government of India Act came into being in 1919, and so Dufferin's policy of 'loaves and fishes' served the British Raj in managing India's elite politics for close to 30 years.

This period between the viceroyalty of Dufferin in the 1880s and the outbreak of World War I in 1914 would mark the height of British power in India. British interests in India had hardened, India was no longer simply a source of valuable textiles and land revenue but came to be Britain's largest export market for its manufactured goods. British authorities were also able to export Indian labour to facilitate their economic expansion in Asia, Africa and the Caribbean, and by the late 19th century the British had come to depend on India for a vast pool of military manpower which could be used for the protection of British territories around the world. Given the seemingly impregnable position that the British held in India during this period they could afford to retreat into their clubs and cantonments, read Kipling and consciously or unconsciously emulate his characters. The Indian middle class and the Indian masses had also seemingly accepted their place in the British Empire, neither yet questioned what they had been taught from childhood; 'Angrez raj ki barkatein', that British rule was a blessing.

Symbolic of Britain's military and economic might and Indian acceptance of British power were the Delhi Durbars. The Durbars were an invented tradition, elaborate ceremonies which culminated with the installation of the British King or Queen as the Emperor or Empress of India. Although Queen Victoria did not attend her Durbar in January 1877, she was proclaimed Qaiser-i-Hind at a Coronation Ground not far from the Red Fort, the old seat of Mughal power. Some 68,000 Indians attended along with 15,000 British and Indian troops and 63 maharajas and nawabs. They all paid homage to the Queen Empress during two weeks of feasting, gun salutes, and exchanges of banners and medals. The pomp and splendour reached a peak during the Durbar of 1903 for the coronation of Edward VII. Neither did he attend his Durbar, but that did not dampen the festivities. A large tent city was erected complete with a temporary light railway, fireworks displays, exhibitions and dance recitals. Maharajas and nawabs arriving on the back of elephants all wore their finest jewels, making it possibly the greatest collection of jewels in one place in history. When a new British monarch, George V assumed the throne in 1911 he also became the first to travel to India for his installation as the Emperor of India. The 1911 Durbar was considered slightly smaller than the Durbar of 1903, nonetheless when the King made an appearance from the balcony of the Red Fort he did so before half a million people who had gathered for the event. The Durbar of 1911 however, would be the last, and the end of the Durbar ritual would also be symbolic of the decline of British power in India. World War I broke out three years later, and rather than planning more displays of pomp and pageantry, British officials spent the last days of the war remaking the Raj as a much more modest enterprise.

Three
A Declaration of Intentions

By the early 20th century the Government of India, the central government of the British Raj had grown so large that the need to devolve greater autonomy to the provincial governments in Bombay, Lahore and Madras had come to dominate thinking about the future of governance in India. Visiting officials complained of the 'slow moving machine' of Simla and Delhi producing reams of the Raj's famous red tape. It was thought that the Government of India was bearing a greater burden of work than it could carry. This impaired its efficiency, whilst the provincial governments were being prevented from developing the capacity to perform the basic functions of everyday governance. The Decentralisation Commission of 1909, the transfer of the capital from Calcutta to Delhi and the King's Message of Hope in 1911 all pushed the issue of decentralisation further up the policy agenda.

Indians were largely absent from these policy musings. It was, as yet, simply a matter of administrative reform. The Government of India wanted less work, the provincial governments wanted more, and London wanted to see governance in India move at a much quicker pace. The need for reform was even thought to extend to the armed forces. When the Indian Expeditionary Force suffered a humiliating defeat on the road to Baghdad at the start of World War I, in what came to be known as the 'Mesopotamian Debacle', British officialdom was quick to blame the excessive centralisation of command in the Indian Army. Centralisation seemed to be at the root of all problems, and it appeared as though decentralisation was an idea on which all members of the British policy establishment could agree.

Leisurely bureaucratic discussions on the need to reform the structure of governance in India were interrupted by the formation of Indian Home Rule Leagues during the middle of World War I. Indian politics suddenly became much less moderate, and the viceroy and his governors looked to London to provide them with some substantial constitutional concessions with which they could retain the support of the Indian political class. The correspondence between Delhi and London on the issue of reform of the British Raj lasted for the duration of the war and provides a glimpse into the way that decision making on India occurred at the highest levels of the British Government. When the matter was not so urgent the secretary of state in London would urge the viceroy in Delhi to show more boldness in his proposals for reform. When politics started to heat up in India the viceroy would try to persuade the secretary of state of the urgency of a statement which would cool tempers in India, rather than wait for a complete reform package. A new secretary of state would take over and bring the matter to a busy War Cabinet and after much debate over the precise wording, he was able to make a declaration before Parliament. He then visited India and together with the viceroy had to convince the central and provincial governments of the need for reform. They then co-authored a report charting a new structure for the Raj, and it was left to the secretary of state alone to see a new Government of India Bill through the British Parliament's houses and committees and joint committees.

The result of the viceroy and secretary of state's work in the corridors of power in Delhi and London was the most far reaching set of reforms in the history of the British Raj. The old debate between liberals and conservatives over the need to rule by conquest or by co-operation was settled once and for all. The British Government declared as early as 1917 that its aim was to guide India to self-government and include Indians in all sections of the colonial administration. After decades of conservatism based on theories of racial hierarchy, the Raj had come full circle and returned to the vision of its early liberals, who, before India had become such a valuable possession, spoke quite earnestly of a distant day when Indians would achieve self-rule.

***

Frederick Thesiger, the Viscount Chelmsford was appointed Viceroy of India in March 1916. At his first Executive Council meeting he put forward two issues which needed to be resolved; the ultimate goal of British rule in India, and the steps needed to achieve it. After a century long conversation about the nature of British rule, the viceroy was asking for a definitive statement. Indians also wanted to know. In his presidential address to the Indian National Congress in December 1915, Sir Satyendra Sinha had called for a "declaration of intentions" by the British in relation to their plans for self-government in India.

There was more consensus among members of the Viceroy's Executive Council than expected, and they agreed that the goal of the British Raj should be to "endow India...with the largest measure of self government compatible with the maintenance of the supreme authority of British Rule".[lxix] It was the supreme authority of British rule which was included in the formulation rather than the supreme authority of the King; India would thus remain a colony, rather than develop into a constitutional monarchy and achieve Dominion status like Australia or Canada. Self-government here meant a gradual and ordered transfer of power to Indians under British control and supervision. The initial formulation of the council was tempered however, and the road to self-government was made conditional on the spread of education, the development of political experience, and the easing of religious tensions. Having resolved the goal, the next stage was to gain a clearer idea of the first step towards achieving it. There was a consensus on providing commissions and benefits and increases in pay to Indians in the army and addressing specific grievances of the Congress relating to indentured labour, the Arms Act and cotton excise duties. There was also agreement that there should be more Indians in the Indian Civil Service and further development of local self-government.

The Viceroy's Executive Council however, was divided on the issue of expanding the powers of the legislative councils in the provinces. Sir Reginald Craddock wanted to continue with the system which had been in place for the previous 25 years in which council members represented classes and interests, rather than territories, and opposed increasing the powers of the councils.[lxx] He wanted to maintain the status quo; any provision for territorial constituencies would only lead to a little Indian Parliament, something which British officials had been trying to avoid for decades. Sir William Meyer and Sir Claude Hill however, wanted to increase the administrative and financial powers of the councils and enlarge the franchise.[lxxi] They argued that in order for the councils to have more powers they needed to be more truly representative, which required large majorities of members from outside the government, territorial constituencies and consultations on the budget. Viceroy Chelmsford was also in favour of bigger territorial constituencies, but did not want the powers of the councils to be expanded.[lxxii] He thought that the constituencies of the elected members should be further developed before any real power was devolved.

The Government of India's Despatch based on the deliberations of the Viceroy's Executive Council was released in November 1916. The Despatch did not advocate any expansion in the powers of the legislative councils; it just wanted to work within the existing framework by providing for elected majorities in the councils on the basis of a greatly enlarged franchise. Chelmsford left the matter of the type of constituency, based on class or territory, to be decided by the provinces. Although he did provide his views in favour of bigger territorial constituencies in a memorandum attached to the Despatch so that no one would be in doubt as to the viceroy's preference. The Despatch did not meet Indian demands. However, at the time, conciliating Indian opinion was not a high priority for the Government of India. Chelmsford and his council were discussing reform almost as a matter of administrative routine, something which came up every ten years or so, in this case driven along more by the need to provide the British establishment with clarity of purpose than by the demands of Indian politicians.

***

Something which would change the leisurely pace of discussions was the emergence of the Home Rule Leagues, led by a British lady long resident in India and a firebrand Indian nationalist from the Konkan. The Leagues seemingly sprang up overnight, attracted tens of thousands of members and disturbed the sleepy routines of Indian politics. The Congress would be stirred to action rather than more resolutions, and the British Government would also be forced to turn its attention from a broad goal for British rule, to a more far reaching change to the structure of the Raj.

The most energetic leader on the Indian political scene at the start of the war was a British woman of Irish origin, Annie Besant. Besant had been a free thinker, feminist, and socialist during her younger days in England. It was her attraction to Theosophy however, which brought her to India. Besant founded the Central Hindu College, fought against child marriage, and sought to put an end to the difficulties of Hindus who travelled abroad. She would tour India giving speeches imploring Indians to take pride in their civilisation, which though it had fallen on hard times under British rule, was based on the timeless wisdom and morality of Hindu philosophy. She was elected President of the Theosophical Society in 1907 and thought that an open and inclusive Theosophy could provide a springboard for Indian nationhood. Her books such as *Nation Building*, *India: A Nation* and *Wake Up India!* would drive home her message.

As Besant started to move from efforts in the field of education toward nationalist political action she came to realise that the Theosophical Society was not the ideal vehicle for her movement. The Congress was, and she started to wake it from its annual routine of passing long, polite and carefully worded resolutions. Besant thought that the occasional incremental reforms offered by the British were mere "scraps of paper", and found a kindred spirit in Bal Gangadhar Tilak who had just been released from jail. Tilak had spent decades as a leader of agrarian movements, political protests and religious revivals and had been sent to jail in Mandalay in Burma for six years in 1908 for sedition. Besant and Tilak each started their own Home Rule League and between them they soon had over 60,000 members. Both leaders began to exert pressure on the resolutely moderate Congress to demand more, sooner from the British Government, and the Congress then began to jolt the British Government out of its slow and dreary discussion of administrative reforms. As the Congress became less moderate, the British would have to entertain the prospect of wider ranging political reforms.

In June 1916 Major Freeman Freeman-Thomas, the Lord Willingdon and Governor of Bombay began to press for a statement of British policy which would take the energy out of the Home Rule movement. Such a statement would provide some clarity and reassurance of British good intentions but also announce the limits of their tolerance. Willingdon thought of it in the old style of concession to Indian opinion which would cool tempers and prevent the moderates from being marginalised in the Congress. Initially Viceroy Chelmsford in Delhi and Secretary of State Austen Chamberlain in London however, did not want to issue another announcement without having anything substantial to say. Yet Chelmsford did start to become more apprehensive in November 1916 as the spectre of the moderates getting swept away at the approaching annual Congress session became more serious.

As was anticipated, the moderates were marginalised at the Congress Session in Lucknow in December 1916. The radicals decided to form a pact with the Muslim League for a reform scheme and a proposed amendment to the Government of India Act. They planned to undertake a large scale propaganda drive in India and England, start a National Fund, and send a deputation to petition Parliament in London. The Congress President Ambica Mazumdar called for a formal proclamation from the British authorities stating a commitment to self-government.

Then, at the beginning of 1917 Besant and Tilak's Home Rule movement gathered pace. Chelmsford knew that his Despatch of the previous year would seem quite inadequate to Indian politicians in the prevailing political climate. He also knew that obtaining the consensus required to announce specific reforms would take some time. Yet with the political atmosphere becoming heated, a declaration seemed increasingly necessary. By the end of January 1917, Chelmsford began to take on Willingdon's concerns and was writing to Chamberlain in London for a statement of policy as early as possible.[lxxiii]

An India Office Committee chaired by Sir William Duke reported to Chamberlain in March 1917. Whilst agreeing with the general sentiment of Chelmsford's Despatch, the committee pointed out that it did not provide a coherent plan for reform; there would be no point in trumpeting reforms which were vague and would not even be very useful in furthering political development in India. Leaving the functions and responsibilities of the councils unchanged meant perpetuating a system in which narrow class interests were represented without the elected members having to take any additional responsibility. According to the committee, the councils needed to be given some responsibility to prevent them from being mere debating chambers or platforms for political rhetoric. In the existing system Indian members were indirectly elected by a tiny franchise, something which made them so unrepresentative that they could not feasibly be given any real power or responsibility. The Viceroy Chelmsford thought this needed to be fixed; constituencies needed to be developed before responsibilities could be devolved.[lxxiv] At this point Secretary of State Chamberlain argued that whilst it was a good idea to train Indians as bureaucrats and municipal administrators, they also had to be trained as legislators.[lxxv] Legislators would need to be able to deal with financial matters, and so they had to be given some involvement with the budget.

Chamberlain's stress on the need to devolve some power to Indians made Chelmsford reconsider a novel idea which had been circulating in London. The Round Table group, a think tank on Indian policy had floated the idea of 'dyarchy'; the division of the government between reserved and transferred subjects. Reserved subjects were to be kept under the governor's control, whilst the transferred subjects would be handled in a more fully parliamentary way with the legislature exercising direct control. It had been an idea spoken of in hushed tones by Lionel Curtis, however when fellow Round Table member and now India Office Committee Chairman Sir William Duke advocated the idea, dyarchy gained the support of Chamberlain and the War Cabinet.

Discussions between Delhi and London continued, but it was only in May 1917 that the matter became more urgent. Chelmsford started to press for a statement, regardless of whether there was any programme of reforms to accompany it.[lxxvi] He knew that London was unimpressed by his Despatch and it would be some time before any concrete proposals would be worked out between the two governments. The viceroy did not want more committees in London but wanted the secretary of state to visit India to expedite the matter. Chelmsford pointed to the Home Rule Leagues in India, the spirit of the Russian Revolution and the rising ideal of national self-determination around the world to urge London to make some sort of Declaration. The more urgent need to rally moderate opinion amidst rising political tensions in India eventually influenced Chamberlain to take the matter to a busy War Cabinet.

In June 1917 the Madras Government arrested Annie Besant, and moderates like Madan Mohan Malaviya and Tej Bahadur Sapru joined the Home Rule League. There was also an important development in London. Austen Chamberlain left the India Office and was replaced as secretary of state by Edwin Montagu. Upon taking charge at the India Office, Montagu circulated a draft within the War Cabinet which aimed for "the gradual development of free institutions in India with a view to ultimate self government within the Empire." He had a viceroy in Delhi eagerly awaiting a Declaration. But he would first have to deal with an old viceroy in the War Cabinet trying to scribble 'self government' away.

From an early stage in the discussions Arthur Balfour, the Foreign Secretary wanted to be clear about what 'self government' would actually mean in practice. On 14 August

1917 Cabinet proceeded to debate the definition of the term. Montagu argued that without 'self government' any declaration would be pointless; if it were left out then it would be better not to make any announcement at all. The former Viceroy George Curzon was concerned that Cabinet not offer something that it did not mean to, only to have it repeated back in the years ahead. The Prime Minister Lloyd George wanted the Cabinet to stop quibbling and said that Curzon had already defined 'self government' and that definition stood. Curzon had written the previous month that self-government did not mean that all of India would become one political unit in which Indians would replace the British in administration, but that after a period of tutelage Indians would have "a predominant influence in the administration of the country".[lxxvii]

Curzon had started writing "self government" out of the Declaration by referring to "self governing institutions", "with the object of responsible government" and that "India may enjoy responsible government within the Empire".[lxxviii] Chamberlain stressed that they did not want to get boxed into a corner by the term 'self government' and exactly what shape it would take, but rather convey the idea that with the growth of power there should come responsibility. Both Curzon and Balfour were concerned that Indians would interpret 'self government' to mean just that; the withdrawal of the British from India's administration, turning India into a self-governing constitutional monarchy like Australia and Canada. 'Self-government' had become 'responsible government', however Montagu could not understand the difference between the terms.[lxxix] Yet 'responsible government' was not being used in a technical constitutional sense, just as something more measured than 'self government'. The ideal was for Indian members of the councils to be elected by, and be more responsible to a broader constituency, one which would break the dominance of the Indian barristers in the legislatures.

When the wording was finally agreed upon, the Declaration which would shape the last 30 years of British rule in India was quietly slipped into a reply to a prepared question at the end of the parliamentary session:

> *"The policy of His Majesty's government with which the Government of India are in complete accord, is that of the increasing association of Indians in every branch of the administration and the gradual development of self-governing institutions with a view to the progressive realization of responsible Government in India as an integral part of the British Empire."*[lxxx]

***

Montagu arrived in Bombay on 10 November 1917. He and Chelmsford had to work out how to put the Declaration into action. The Government of India in Delhi was less than enthusiastic about reform at the Centre and the viceroy and secretary of state would spend much of their time trying to convince their own reluctant provincial governors of the need to share power with Indian politicians. By the time that their recommendations were published and found form in a new Government of India Act two years later however, a new force in Indian politics had arrived.

On 11 December the Government of India issued a circular arguing in favour of dyarchy. By January 1918 the provinces were actively arguing against it. The only province which did not oppose the idea was Bengal. The provinces were only willing to go as far as elected majorities and limited control of budgets by the inclusion of legislators on standing committees. The governors had to be coerced by Chelmsford and Montagu just to accept a compromise whereby dyarchy would be started in some provinces earlier than others and the right to recall transferred subjects would be guaranteed. Governor Willingdon in Bombay even went back on the compromise and stuck to his original position, cursing "Montagu's rotten dyarchy idea".[lxxxi] Chelmsford maintained that his scheme for dyarchy was the best fulfilment of the August Declaration; without it there could be no clear division of responsibility with Indian politicians.[lxxxii]

In June 1918 the viceroy and the secretary of state released a report which provided their blueprint for reform of the British Raj. The Government of India, Chelmsford and Montagu were all in favour of, or resigned to, some element of dualism in governance and so they needed to create a system which would allow it to work with the fewest problems. The Montagu-Chelmsford Report detailed the steps to be taken to create this system of dyarchy in the provinces. The report recommended that provincial governments would be conducted by an Executive Council of one Indian and one service member and ministers appointed from the legislature. The two halves of the government, one dealing with reserved subjects and the other with transferred subjects would deliberate and work as a whole, but then divide at the time of voting. The entire government would decide on the budget, with the governor intervening if necessary. The report recommended that a Legislative Assembly replace the Legislative Council in Delhi and that it have 100 members with large elected majorities. A Council of State or Upper House would be a much smaller chamber with 4 nominated members from outside the government, 21 elected members, 25 nominated government members and the viceroy as president. Both houses would have full legislative powers, contention could be resolved by a joint session, whilst the government could send bills or amendments to the Council of State if necessary. The budget was not yet to be opened to a vote, however there would be standing committees associated with the finances of key government departments. The report also recommended expanding the representative character of the legislatures by introducing the principle of direct election from territorial constituencies.

The report had been in circulation for a year during which time a Cabinet Committee had been drafting a new Government of India Bill based on its recommendations. On 14 May 1919 Montagu gained approval from Cabinet for the introduction of the bill to Parliament. The bill did not meet any substantial opposition in Parliament and was referred to a joint committee. As the joint committee began to examine the bill a point of contention arose over the authority of the secretary of state, the member of British Parliament responsible for Indian affairs; it was the supervision by the British Parliament through the secretary of state which kept India from achieving Dominion status. Chelmsford argued against the relaxation of supervision by the secretary of state.[lxxxiii] This would imply something unacceptable; the transfer of control from Parliament to the Indian Legislature, or possibly an increase in the powers of the Government of India. In addition, the Government of India wanted British authority maintained at the Centre. It did not want more Indian members on the Viceroy's Executive Council, or any voting on the budget. Keeping control at the Centre would make reform viable in India, and acceptable in London. Furthermore, questions over how finances should be managed, whether a government bloc should be maintained in the legislatures, whether the central legislature should be bicameral, and whether a ratio should be established for the Indianisation of the services were all discussed. The idea of dyarchy at the Centre, popular control of government budgets, and changes to the role of the secretary of state were all rejected at the committee stage. Much of Montagu and Chelmsford's vision did survive and find a place in the Government of India Act 1919 however; a new bicameral legislature was established in Delhi, power began to be shared in the provinces and millions of new voters came onto electoral rolls across India.

Elections were held in November 1920 and the new Indian Legislative Assembly was inaugurated in Delhi on 9 February 1921 by Arthur Albert, the Duke of Connaught. The franchise had been greatly enlarged, but was still quite restricted. Electoral qualifications varied according to the province and religious community of the voter; generally voters had to be male property owners, pay income tax, own land or be a member of a recognised local body. The new rules meant that there were around 1 million eligible voters across the country for the Assembly in Delhi, whilst the total number of voters for the provincial councils reached over 5 million. A new arena of electoral politics had been opened up across India, but the big question for Indian voters and Indian politicians alike, was whether they should co-operate to make the new system a success.

From the time of the circulation of the Montagu-Chelmsford Report in June 1918 to the holding of elections in November 1920 the Congress had come full circle on the big question. At its 1918 Bombay session, the Congress declared the Montagu-Chelmsford scheme unacceptable unless it handed over full responsibility for government departments in the provinces and partial responsibility at the Centre and wanted the British to commit to allowing full responsible government by 1933. The following year, although dissatisfied with the reforms, the Congress then asked the Indian people to co-operate with them as a step towards full responsible government. Mohandas Gandhi had returned from South

Africa and by this time he was taking a more active role in Congress politics, and it was at his insistence that the Congress issued a resolution thanking Montagu and Chelmsford for their efforts. However, by the time the Congress met in Calcutta in September 1920, the mood had changed in the wake of the uproar over the Rowlatt Acts, the massacre at Jallianwala Bagh, and the emergence of the Khilafat movement. Gandhi had spent the year developing a new programme of non-cooperation with the government and it was in Calcutta that he managed to persuade the Congress to boycott the reformed councils.

Whilst Gandhi had won the day and the Congress resolved to extend its policy of non-cooperation to the councils, there were still many Indian politicians, both within and outside the Congress who preferred to take the new political opportunities which were on offer. In fact, the very most moderate members of the Congress found they no longer had a place in the Party and left to contest the elections of 1920 under the banner of the National Liberal Federation. Another slightly less moderate group within the Congress would stay inside the Party and offer some resistance to Gandhi's leadership and argue in favour of entering the councils, not to make them a success, but to 'wreck them from the inside'. Unable to convince a majority within the Congress to adopt their tactic, this group formed another party of their own, the Swaraj Party which contested the elections of 1923 and livened up legislatures across the country with a more confrontational style of politics. Others who had stood apart from the mainstream of Congress politics would also join the electoral fray; landlords, merchants, labour leaders, Muslims and Christians, the 'depressed classes', and Independent lawyers. The issue of co-operation with the councils had split the Indian political class, but there was enough support for the new legislatures to keep them running and allow the budding institutions of parliamentary democracy to grow.

***

The controversies over race and class in recruitment to the Indian Civil Service at the end of the 19th century were really a problem of plenty. At the time there were as many as three or four or five candidates appearing at the world's stiffest examination for each place in the heaven born service. The British could afford to be choosy and occupy themselves in debates about the need for candidates to have attended one of the ancient universities. However, the arrival of World War I changed the terms of the debate entirely. By the end of the war almost a million British soldiers had died and another 2 million had been permanently disabled. Britain would no longer have an abundance of bright young men who were willing and able to serve in India, and the efforts of the British Government became mired in an ever more difficult attempt to maintain a regular supply of high quality recruits to the elite service through which it ruled India.

During the ten years prior to World War I, 501 out of the 528 recruits to the Indian Civil Service were British.[lxxxiv] The outbreak of the war in July 1914 ended the predictable routine of the annual Indian Civil Service examination. By the time the results of the examination had been announced, out of the 47 candidates who were selected, 11 had already gone into military service.[lxxxv] Six more candidates were selected to make up the deficiency, but by the time the new candidates had been selected three more had gone to war.[lxxxvi] Of the 14 who went in for military service, 9 were sent to serve in territorial units in India and 8 went on to serve in the Indian Civil Service. The remaining five all fought in Europe and died there.[lxxxvii]

As the conflict dragged on and recruitment dried up, Indian

Civil Service officers were denied leave and officers from the provincial services were brought in to fill vacant posts. The competitive examination continued to be held in London, however the number of candidates declined rapidly. At the end of the war there was an urgent need to make up a shortage of over 200 appointments, or one-sixth of the service.[lxxxviii] An Act of 1915 had made provision for the appointment of war veterans, not on the basis of competitive examination but by selection after passing a qualifying test. Under this provision 136 British and 2 Indian candidates were appointed between 1919 and 1922.[lxxxix] Many carried war injuries, something which damaged the image of the dashing British officer galloping through the districts of the Raj.

During the early 1920s the challenge before the India Office was how to attract a sufficient number of British university graduates to staff the Indian Civil Service despite the lower numbers required due to the Montagu-Chelmsford reforms. Speakers were sent to try and inspire students, yet confidential letters were being sent from Oxford and Cambridge detailing the general lack of interest amongst undergraduates in a career in India. At some Oxford colleges candidates had dried up and it seemed that the situation would remain that way for the foreseeable future:

> "(1) 'I have consulted my tutors, and our candidates will be a negligible quantity, if indeed there are any in August 1921'; (2) 'I shall not be sending any I.C.S. competitors next year'; (3) '... we have no candidates from this college, and I do not think it likely that there will be any in the immediate future'; (4) '... there appears to be a widespread disinclination among men of

> *the sort which used to gain most places in the Indian Civil Service to compete at all . . .'; (5) '. . . Balliol will have only one European candidate likely to sit for Competitive Examination for the Indian Civil Service in August 1921.' '*[xc]

The situation became so dire that the India Office did not want to appear desperate by reducing the examination fee. This state of affairs alarmed the Secretary of State, William Peel, the Viscount Peel who formed a committee headed by Lord MacDonell to advise him privately. The committee focused on career issues such as amenities, promotions, job security, financial prospects and the reduced power of the district officer rather than the effect of the Montagu-Chelmsford reforms and the general political tumult in India.

Whilst the Indian Civil Service represented a lucrative career for British students in the late 19th and early 20th century, once the rupee crashed and the cost of living rose British officers began to complain of not receiving a living wage. In addition, Indian Civil Service salaries were not keeping up with salaries in the private sector and there were promotional blockages in the provincial cadres holding up young officers. At the same time, the British officers of the Indian Civil Service had become a favourite target of the Indian politicians in the new legislatures, for the extravagance of their salaries and benefits. In addition to the lack of interest in the Indian Civil Service amongst students in England, many British officers in India took the opportunity to retire early given the offer made by the government to do so if they were unwilling to serve under the new constitutional scheme. As many as 97 retired between 1922 and 1924 alone.[xci] After five years of the scheme about one-tenth of the service had retired early. For many their sense of purpose, identity and security had been diminished as they saw responsibility being handed over to Indians throughout the Raj.

Service morale had become a public issue in the early 1920s, taking up space in the newspapers and in Parliament. London started to become more receptive to the demands of the Indian Civil Service for better pay and security, whilst Delhi was sensitive to the mood of the new Indian Legislative Assembly. Indian students were coming through in greater numbers with the establishment of an examination in Allahabad, and Delhi simply did not have the money for the Indian Civil Service given the weakness of the post-war economy. In fact, in 1922 enquiries were made with the provinces as to whether British recruitment to the services should be reduced or ended completely. A resolution seeking an end to the recruitment of British officers was even supported by a British government member in the Central Provinces Assembly.[xcii] Delhi was enquiring about winding up British recruitment to the Indian Civil Service much to the frustration of London which had to print denials in *The Times*. It was in this situation that the Prime Minister, Lloyd George intervened and made his famous 'steel frame' speech in Parliament:

> 'This small nucleus of British officials in India they are the steel frame of the whole structure. I do not care what you build on it, if you take the steel frame out, it will collapse ...There is one institution we will not interfere with, there is one institution we will not cripple, there is one institution we will not deprive of its functions or of its privileges, and that is that institution which built up the British Raj, the British Civil Service in India.'[xciii]

At this time the Viscount Peel wanted to increase British recruitment, correcting for under recruitment from previous years, but Delhi remained sensitive to Indian opinion which saw British officers as an unnecessary expense. What complicated the matter was that in the prevailing system if British candidates were unsuccessful in London then Indians could not be recruited beyond a certain number, leading to a shrinking in the overall size of the already small service which administered India. The Lee Commission was appointed in 1923 to look into the grievances of the services and recommend measures to boost recruitment. A report was published in 1924, and the British Government accepted its recommendations which largely addressed the financial grievances which were thought to be holding up recruitment. Implementation of the recommendations would cost over ₹12 crore however, and came to be labelled 'Lee Loot' by Indian politicians.

As service conditions improved there was a brief rise in the numbers of British candidates appearing in the late 1920s.[xciv] However, Indian Civil Service pay was cut during the Depression years, Indian income tax was raised, a surtax was imposed, and customs duties were increased. Because the number of Indian recruits had to be reduced due to the decline in the number of British recruits, key posts in the bureaucratic structure were being abandoned. Recruitment fell away again during the early 1930s and there came a point when the secretary of state in London became satisfied just to be able to fill the British allotment. Sir Samuel Hoare wanted to take more British recruits whilst he could get them, unsure as he was of future prospects.[xcv]

Problems of recruitment reached a crisis point by the middle of the 1930s. Although British students continued to top the examinations, successful candidates would often opt for the Home Civil Service or just decline the offer even if they did not have another one. In the 1935 London examination only five British students made the grade and their academic ranking was poor.[xcvi] No candidate who could secure an appointment to the Home Civil Service would accept the Indian Civil Service. Of the 12 who did not qualify for the Home Civil Service but could gain entry to the Indian Civil Service 10 refused to go to India.[xcvii]

The Secretary of State, Lawrence Dundas, the Marquess of Zetland had to resort to boosting the number of British recruits to the service by bypassing the examination and recruiting suitable candidates with good honours degrees. This produced another spike in 1936 with the number of British candidates for the examination rising to 145 from 83 the year before, whilst 208 put themselves up for selection.[xcviii] Of these, 16 British students won a place through the examination and 24 were selected.[xcix] Another World War began, the London examination was not held in 1940, and the recruitment of British candidates dried up completely after 1942.

***

After World War I English literature about India began to take a different turn. Whilst there were plenty of writers ready to write in the same old Kiplingesque way about the same old India, a new generation began to question just what the British were doing in India. For these writers, the Bengali babus were not the cultural oddities made for mockery, the British were. These new English writers were not romantics however, there was no great tendency to idealise Indians or Indian culture. The old criticisms remained. In fact, there was less concern for what British imperialism was doing to Indians, than for what it was doing to the British themselves.

The everyday practice of imperialism, based as it was on racial arrogance, was thought to be degrading the British people. The haughty, rude manner of the British on the railways, the eagerness of army officers to open fire on Indians, and the determined ignorance of the memsahib and her rudeness to her servants all became the objects of comedy. At a deeper level, the ravages of World War I led many to question the worth of western civilisation, whether it was having or would have any lasting impact on India, and whether maintaining the Empire was worth the effort given the growing nationalist opposition to the Raj.

This new mood of self-mockery and melancholy was captured in E.M. Forster's *A Passage to India*. Forster spent his time in India at the start of the Montagu-Chelmsford reforms, his novel was published in 1924, and he became something of a poet laureate for the ambiguous position of the British in a reformed Raj. During the 1920s *A Passage to India* replaced *Kim* as the standard reading for the British making their way to India. A new generation of British men and women in India would have a different cast of characters to emulate and identify with, and would begin to see themselves in a very different light to generations past.

Forster's novel is a long enquiry into the possibility of middle class Indians and British officials ever meeting as friends and working as equals under British rule. *A Passage to India* begins with the arrival of Adela Quested, a young Englishwoman in Chandrapore, an unremarkable small town on the banks of the Ganga somewhere in north India. Adela had come to India to see her prospective groom, Ronny Heaslop who was the town's magistrate. Mrs. Moore was Ronny's mother (Ronny was her son from her first marriage), and like her prospective daughter-in-law she was curious about India. Life in Chandrapore had been rather dull after the romance of their passage to India through the Mediterranean and the sands of Egypt. They wanted to see the 'real India' and so Ronny asked Cyril Fielding, the Principal of the Government College sarcastically: "Fielding! how's one to see the real India?". Cyril replied, "Try seeing Indians." Adela hadn't seen much of them since she reached India, but she was keen to meet the type of Indians whom Ronny might know socially as friends. Ronny explained that no such thing happened, but that he would arrange a Bridge party which would include some of the town's prominent Indian officials and professionals.

The Bridge party did not go well but Adela met Cyril, a kindred spirit who would spend his time with Indians and "talked to anyone and ate anything". Cyril found it refreshing to meet an English person interested in Indians, and he offered to introduce Adela to some he knew. Adela and Mrs. Moore then attended a little gathering which Cyril arranged and they met Dr. Aziz and Professor Godbole. Aziz invited the ladies to his home, and they accepted his offer. He didn't think they would, and the thought of showing them his home filled him with dread. So he created a diversion. He asked them if they had seen the Marabar caves. Thankfully they had not, and they all agreed to go on an excursion to visit the caves.

But a couple of weeks passed, and Adela and Mrs. Moore's excitement had time to cool. They arrived at the railway station early in the morning, still half asleep, and it turned out that they had all brought too many servants along. In addition, the caves were not particularly holy or scenic or even of much historical value. When Adela and Aziz walked together they had little to talk about, their minds were elsewhere. Adela decided to break the silence, and with her thoughts on her marriage to Ronny, she asked Aziz about his married life. Specifically, how many wives he had. Aziz was shocked by the question and had to go into a cave alone just to recover his balance. Things became more serious however when Adela experienced a hallucination whilst alone in a cave and returned to town accusing Aziz of having molested her.

News of an Indian doctor molesting an English girl quickly spread throughout Chandrapore stoking old British fears and anxieties. There was talk of the safety of "women and children" and the need to evacuate them to the hills. Adela was "an English girl fresh from England" and she quickly became the British community's "sister" and "darling girl", a symbol of English womanhood. The only person to instinctively come to Aziz's defence was Cyril Fielding. There was some circumstantial evidence against Aziz, he was found in possession of Adela's glasses, but Cyril knew Aziz's character and simply refused to believe that his friend was capable of such a thing. Cyril approached local officialdom, Aziz's Muslim friends, Professor Godbole and even took on the White Club defending Aziz's innocence. He resigned from the Club and was manhandled on his way out the door. All the while Mrs. Moore, who was present at the caves, like Cyril did not think that Aziz was capable of committing the act, but did not make her thoughts known and was packed off by her son Ronny who did not want to complicate the case. She died at sea on her passage back to England. Eventually the case came to court, Adela took the stand, and under cross examination she broke down. Aziz never followed her into the cave. It was all a mistake.

Cyril's defence of Aziz should have been the basis of an unbreakable bond between the two men. But when the question of Aziz suing Adela for compensation arose Cyril tried to counsel him against it and a new strain in the friendship emerged. He could not bear the thought of a "queer honest girl" losing both her money and her potential husband over a hallucination. Aziz on the other hand did not see the point in being gentlemanly after everything he had been put through. He did not care for British approval any more, in fact he had turned quite "anti-British" and thought he should have done so sooner to save himself his misfortune. Cyril continued to plead with him on Adela's behalf though; the girl had the whole of British India pushing her on, but she climbed down and eventually told the truth, and she should not be punished further. He even asked Aziz to behave like one of the benevolent Mughal Emperors he so loved to talk of. Aziz wanted an apology but the matter kept going until Cyril pulled out an unlikely trump card; it was what Mrs. Moore would have wanted. He knew Aziz had some respect for the old English lady, and so in her name he asked him to drop the law suit for damages. Aziz, seemingly powerless before the memory of the English mother, agreed.

Aziz and Cyril continued their strained friendship, but it all ended in an argument about politics. Aziz argued for Indian freedom, Cyril asked who among the Indians will rule, Aziz said the Afghans will come down like the old days, Cyril said the Hindus wouldn't like that, Aziz retorted that the matter would be settled at a Conference and India would be a nation of Hindus, Muslims and Sikhs. And so in politics, as in personal relationships, Aziz was given the last word; he wanted the Englishmen to clear out of India. Only then, he told Cyril, will "you and I be friends."

***

British civil servants also saw the writing on the wall. As early as 1917 Sir William Marris, who had joined the Indian Civil Service in 1896, told Edwin Montagu that "the Indian Civil Servants were very sorry that their day was done, [they] recognised that it was inevitable and were willing to go ahead."[c] But officers of the Indian Civil Service were English gentlemen, and so whether they returned to England or continued their careers in India, their disillusionment with the British Government found its place in gentlemanly forms; they wrote their own novels, and letters home, and published weighty books on Indian politics.

Hilton Brown was a civil servant in Madras, and despite continuing in the service he wrote a novel, *Dismiss!* in 1923. The protagonist Andrew Allen, an Indian Civil Service officer, whilst not quite a paternalist of the old school, came around to the familiar conclusion about Indians; they were petty, domestic people most at home in family and village affairs, and should they take to politics they were dreamers, other worldly, given to extravagant phrases without understanding hard realities. Yet Indians were capable of devotion to ideals, and all that was required was that they be led, and that earnestness be channelled in the right direction. But, alas, this prospect was becoming engulfed in the hate and bitterness generated by the nationalist movement.

Allen was made to serve under an Indian secretary as a result of the reforms. He thought that his Secretary Devadoss, an Indian Christian, was a fine man, something which made him completely unrepresentative of the majority of Indians. He was unimpressed with the intellectual calibre of most of the Indians he worked with but thought that "If the Progressive Party were made up of Devadosses we could hand over India-with reservations-tomorrow." The situation came to a head when he was posted to Yelrud in the south of India where a nationalist agitation was threatening. Allen wanted British troops called in to establish some order and project authority but his request was denied and in a small distant outpost some policemen were burnt alive by a violent mob. He then decided, perhaps as the author wanted to do, to leave the Indian Civil Service and retreat to the hills.

An Indian Civil Service officer writing under the alias A.L. Carthill thought of India as *The Lost Dominion*. Whilst England had lost other possessions on the battlefield, or through negligence, bartered some away and surrendered others once they had become useless, the loss of India was unique; it was the abandonment of a valuable territory for purely moral reasons. The Indian Civil Service officer's purpose was, in 1923, to write a history explaining the reasons behind the fall of British power in India.

Carthill was adamant that India was not and had never been a nation and that it had been let slip from England's firm grasp by the 'mugwumps', or woolly-headed liberals who had begun to exert growing influence over British imperial policy at the start of the 20th century. He created the character of 'Panditji', who was an archetype of the wily Brahmin politician who had absorbed English culture, but hated it. Panditji resented England's intrusion into India, his millennia old spiritual and political possession. He transcended space and time, hovering in the Indian political sky, searching and sensing for weaknesses in Britain's civilisation by which he could bring its presence in India to an end. Panditji took his opportunity when the liberalism ran out of control in London, resulting in the accursed Montagu-Chelmsford reforms. He was able to strike a final, fatal blow to the foundations of British power in India.

Alexander Tottenham, who like Hilton Brown had served in Madras, wrote letters to his sister at home in which he was dismissive of the idea that self-government could be applicable to all races.[ci] He thought that only the chosen few were fit for it and that the Oriental races were not among them. He pointed to the chaos in China since it had become a republic and ridiculed the idea that the Indian people were hapless and downtrodden under the British yoke. The British were in India to keep the peace amongst Indians and to defend its frontiers from external aggression. The Indian masses were primitive and ignorant, which accounted for the lack of any coherent public opinion. It would be farcical to hand over India in the name of democracy to an Indian oligarchy whose outlook was positively archaic and who were oppressive and selfish beyond belief. The 'Indian oligarchy' he was referring to were the Brahmins of Madras, and he thought of himself as the protector of the peasant against the tyrannical landlord and greedy moneylender.

Michael O'Dwyer, who had been Governor of Punjab at the time of the massacre at Jallianwala Bagh, maintained a position of defiance in *India As I Knew It: 1885-1925*. He argued that the Montagu-Chelmsford reforms had been a rash concession to the tiny class of English speaking Indians. He had been in India since the late Victorian age and he, like Alexander Tottenham had imbibed the central creed of the Indian Civil Service; the protection of the Indian masses who merely wanted good government from whoever was best able to provide it.

O'Dwyer began *India As I Knew It* by citing the Queen's Proclamation of 1858; not the part about equality of opportunity for Indians, but the one about the British administering government in India for the benefit of all their subjects, whose gratitude would be their best reward. O'Dwyer thought that all the reforms had done was to stir up the racial and sectarian violence which was inherent in Indian society. He repeated the common complaint about the theorists in London making policy for an India they barely knew. He wanted to bring them out to rural Punjab, to Lyallpur, to his India, and show them how the administration really worked in the villages.

But unlike Carthill who was already intent on explaining the reasons behind the fall of the British Raj, O'Dwyer would remain in denial. The liberalism driving imperial policy in London was not rooted in the British character and was just a post-war fad. India was inherently unsuited to democracy, oppressed by caste tyranny, riven by racial and sectarian hatreds, divided between martial and non-martial races, and was being conspired against by Indian nationalists and English socialists. Indian political parties were hopelessly divided amongst themselves, and Indian minorities and communities which had been loyal to British rule felt abandoned. Most English writers did not know anything about India and mistook the opinions of India's English speaking class for the opinion of all Indians. Sedition was being taught in schools and Indian politicians had not even done a good job of working the reforms which had been designed for them. In O'Dwyer's account, this imperial nightmare could be brought to an end by winding the reforms back and putting the Indian politicians and the microscopic minority they represented in their place and ruling once again for the humble Indian peasant.

***

The old British racial claim to having all the attributes necessary to govern India was dependent on an abundant supply of British men willing to do so. In that sense, Michael O'Dwyer was amongst the last of a dying breed. When O'Dwyer joined the Indian Civil Service in 1885 competition for places was still stiff, service in India had some glamour attached to it, and he and his colleagues were prized catches on the marriage market. When O'Dwyer returned to England after World War I he had the disheartening task of travelling to English universities to motivate a new and unenthusiastic generation of students to serve in India. Yet no amount of stirring speeches could reverse the structural changes which had led to English students losing interest in the Indian Civil Service. And although O'Dwyer held the Indian middle class in contempt, its support had been crucial to the maintenance of the British Raj for decades. O'Dwyer had arrived in India in the year that the Indian National Congress was founded and another pillar of the Raj at the height of its power was a resolutely loyal and moderate Congress. The Montagu-Chelmsford reforms which O'Dwyer and his colleagues so detested had come about because the old 'loaves and fishes' policy which had managed elite Indian politics for much of O'Dwyer's career would no longer work in buying the loyalty of an increasingly assertive middle class. The India that Michael O'Dwyer knew was, in reality, gone forever.

The Montagu-Chelmsford reforms could not be turned back. They were the most far reaching reforms of the state in the history of the British Raj. From August 1917 British rule in India became a more formally liberal enterprise, with a stated goal of guiding India to self-government and bringing Indians into all reaches of the administration. For the first time the principle of direct elections based upon territorial constituencies was introduced and half the government departments in the provinces were handed over to elected Indian ministers who began to manage key portfolios, work with the bureaucracy, and dispense patronage. Although the Indian members of the new Indian Legislative Assembly in Delhi did not exercise any government responsibilities, the Assembly became a debating chamber for national political issues and did manage to exert influence on what was still a highly autocratic Government of India. Perhaps most importantly, the reforms greatly increased the number of Indians eligible to vote. Rather than just university senates or chambers of commerce sending their candidates to the viceroy for his approval, a section of the Indian middle class began to send its own candidates to legislatures across India.

For the British, the early 1920s was the 'beginning of the end'. Indian Civil Service officers voted with their feet; they knew that the halcyon days of Britain's Indian empire were over and many decided to leave early rather than remain for the slow decline. Although they lamented the change, few sought to turn back the clock like Michael O'Dwyer. Most were content to engage in criticism of British policy and expose its intellectual flaws, hold firm to old creeds and predict a dire future for India without British rule. A generation of Indian Civil Service officers had lost its identity and sense of mission and it was this disruption to the small social world of British officials in India that E.M. Forster explored in *A Passage to India*. He was able to view the scene as a visitor and a novelist, exposing the futility of old ways, the disorder which occurred when Britons and Indians met as equals, the looming conflict between Hindus and Muslims, and came to the conclusion that a reformed Raj would not last for long.

One element of the reforms which had yet to fully take shape in Forster's Chandrapore was the 'Indianisation' of the elite services of the British Raj. British district collectors, police superintendents and army colonels had been the officers projecting authority throughout the Raj, comfortable in their roles supervising Indian clerks and constables and sepoys. However, the order would come from above that young Indians were to be inducted into the services as officers in greater numbers, and those British officials who stayed on would have to train them to take their place. Targets were set for the pace of Indianisation, and middle class Indian students eagerly took the new opportunities for a career in the elite imperial services. Selected Indians were sent to London to train as civil servants, some would attend the Royal Military College at Sandhurst, and many more entered Police Training Colleges around India. During the 1920s and 1930s, it was these young Indian officers who became the New Sahibs of the Indian state.

Four
New Sahibs

The figure of the Indian Civil Service officer which had provoked such heated debates in the late 19th century no longer stirred passions in the early 20th century. By the time of World War I it was recognised that more Indians should be inducted into the Indian Civil Service and the principle was accepted as a part of the Montagu-Chelmsford reforms. The debate had progressed to how it should happen and the pace at which it would proceed. Delhi seemed to accept the new situation and began to argue for a reduction of the number of Englishmen in the service given that they were increasingly difficult to recruit and may not even be required as the Raj continued to reform. London however put up some resistance and took every measure to maintain a British presence in the elite bureaucracy through which it administered India.

Just as the British Government had erected a system in the 19th century to attract its ideal Englishman to the service, so it erected one after World War I to attract its ideal Indian. The examination in London had been the centrepiece of the system of recruitment to the Indian Civil Service since the 1860s. It was thought to be one of the world's most competitive examinations, but right from the start there were reservations over whether an academic test would throw up the type of officer with the requisite moral and physical strength to rule India. The concern became more acute when the examination was brought to India in 1922. Students from Indian universities began to sit the examination and so the officials of the Raj put some additional restrictions in place; Quota Committees were formed to try to reduce the number of students appearing, and security clearances and character certificates became mandatory to ensure that the new recruits came from the right class of Indian society.

Those Indian students who cleared the hurdles and made the grade travelled to England for a period of probationary training where they were taught Indian languages, Indian law and Indian history by retired British officers of the Raj. Then when they took up their first assignment in their allotted district they trained under old British collectors who guided them through the workings of a government office, the codes and the files and the paperwork, and also the more intangible values and standards of the service. This transfer of technical knowledge and culture was quick however, before long the young Indian officers would climb a couple of notches in the service hierarchy and they would have to train their own young officers in the service codes and culture which they had only recently been taught themselves.

It was not certain that young Indian officers coming into the Indian Civil Service in the 1920s would succeed. In fact, Indianisation was considered an experiment from the start, one which would only be accelerated if it proved to be successful. But the process was successful, and during the 1930s and 1940s Indian officers took up increasingly senior positions in the state. In the districts they would be the 'Man on the Spot', the district collector responsible for law and order, overseeing the local police, acting as a judge and supervising the collection of land revenue. They would also rise to more senior positions in the Indian Political Service and act as agents to the princely states in India, and diplomats in Europe, China and Africa. Indian officers would have to ensure law and order on the North West Frontier and control communal riots across India, but their most severe test would come when the Congress engaged in political protests against the government. During the civil disobedience movement of the early 1930s and the Quit India movement of 1942 Indian officers of the Indian Civil Service would have to enforce the writ of the state, against their fellow Indians seeking freedom from British rule.

****

Even before the ravages of World War I began to take their toll on the British Raj, the Islington Commission had recommended that a separate competitive examination be held in India and become the main source of recruitment of Indians into the service. There was no longer any objection to an examination in India from Delhi or London, and the Government of India accepted the proposal and incorporated it into the Government of India Act 1919. As the rules for the competitive examination had not yet been framed however, the government began recruiting Indians into the Indian Civil Service through nominations to vacancies which had accumulated during the war. The nominations were made in October 1919 for the Indian Civil Service batch of 1920, and another batch was nominated in 1921. This measure supplemented the number of Indians which was successful at the London examination.

Amongst the political turbulence in India in the early 1920s, the Home Member in Delhi, Sir William Vincent wrote a note on 9 May 1921 arguing for a reduction in the number of British officers in the imperial services.[cii] Sir William suggested that their recruitment be lowered and they be allowed to retire on favourable terms. He accepted that such a course of action would affect the efficiency and integrity of the services, but argued that it had become a political necessity. He was not confident that the constitutional scheme envisaged in the Montagu-Chelmsford reforms would last for even a decade, and so did not want to recruit young Englishmen who would be told that they were no longer required just a few years into their careers.

In the meantime, the Government of India received notice of

two resolutions which had been brought for debate before the new Indian Legislative Assembly in Delhi in September 1921. The first sought the complete Indianisation of the Indian Civil Service within ten years, and the second urged that recruitment for the imperial services take place solely in India. The government gave assurances that it would consult with the provincial governments and departments concerned and consider the matter before announcing its decision.

The Finance Member, Sir Malcolm Hailey wrote a Minute on 19 November 1921 supporting Sir William Vincent's argument. He described the distrust British officers felt in the future of the new constitutional scheme.[ciii] The British officers saw the increased power of the Indian legislatures only working to reduce their numbers and erode their service conditions. Sir Malcolm argued that the government should accept the situation and move to reduce the British element before the Indian legislatures were able to do so. He wondered whether India needed the Indian Civil Service at all or would retain it given the choice. He also saw that Indianisation would have to be accompanied by some measure of provincialisation of the service; some posts which were held by the Indian Civil Service would have to be passed over to the provincial services and the number of posts in the Indian Civil Service to which provincial officers could be promoted would need to be increased. Sir Malcolm also wanted to pay Indians Indian rates and at least save some money in the process.

The Viceroy Rufus Isaacs, the Earl of Reading sent a telegram to the Secretary of State Edwin Montagu on 1 January 1922 informing him of the resolutions which had been moved in the Legislative Assembly in Delhi during the previous September.[civ] Accepting Vincent and Hailey's suggestions, he recommended both a reduction in British recruitment as well as a provincialisation of the service. He further urged Montagu to review the entire policy of Indianisation given the difficulty of obtaining British officers, the expense of their salaries, the apprehensions of the current British officer cadre, the difficulties under which they served, as well as the role which the Legislative Assembly would continue to play in trying to reduce their numbers. Delhi, now more responsive to Indian opinion in the new constitutional framework, was urging London to reduce the British involvement in the administration of India.

Montagu was unhurried by the suggestions and recommendations coming from Delhi. The secretary of state in London was under pressure from the British public and Parliament not to be seen to be bowing to Gandhi and his non co-operation movement. Montagu reminded the viceroy that Indianisation was bound by the principles of his August Declaration of 1917 and the Government of India Act 1919.[cv] He did not want to make any announcement which would further damage Indian Civil Service morale or harm the recruitment of British officers. Montagu's advice to Reading on replying to the Legislative Assembly resolution was simply to point to the preamble of the Government of India Act which referred to the gradual and contingent nature of Indianisation. That is, it would happen with the retention of British officers and in a way in which the efficiency and integrity of the Indian Civil Service would be maintained. London, answerable to British political opinion, was telling Delhi that there was no need to hurry, and the British role in the administration of India would remain.

The viceroy accepted the secretary of state's argument, but he was still worried that should the government's response be too vague, it would lose the support of moderate Indian opinion and the Legislative Assembly may go along and proceed towards a resolution all its own.[cvi] Montagu's position prevailed however, and the Assembly in Delhi passed a much more moderate resolution on 11 February 1922, simply urging further Indianisation in line with the August Declaration and the provision of better educational facilities to allow Indians to compete and enter the imperial services.

Edwin Montagu departed the scene and his replacement, the Viscount Peel appointed the MacDonnell Committee to examine grievances related to the cost of living, pensions and insufficient pay in the Indian Civil Service, rather than ways to accelerate Indianisation. The committee pointed out that whilst Indianisation could not be scaled back without a breach of faith, any acceleration would only discourage recruitment of British officers. It recommended recruiting from the surplus of British Army officers and wanted an emphatic statement from London supporting British officers in their efforts to uphold law and order in the districts of the Raj. The matter was settled however with the implementation of the recommendations of the Lee Commission. After 1923 a convention arose whereby 40% of recruits to the service would be Indian, 40% British and the remaining 20% would be promoted from the provincial services. Then, in 1925 Sir Alexander Muddiman pledged that one-third of all appointments to the imperial services would be reserved for candidates from minority communities who were adequately qualified.

The first examination for the Indian Civil Service in India was held at the Law College in Allahabad in February 1922. A quota system initially stipulated the maximum number of candidates who could appear for the examination from each province, and Quota Committees worked to keep the total number of candidates to less than 200. By 1928 the quota system was ended and the examination was moved to Delhi. The students appearing for the examination were now Indian rather than English, but the authorities in Delhi in the 1920s held the same concerns as their predecessors in London in the 1870s; they feared that the young men appearing for the examination were 'crammed' rather than educated. The Public Service Commission even wanted to establish Advisory Committees at Indian universities to give students a frank assessment of their chances in the examination and discourage those who were unlikely to succeed.

The examination was just one part of the system of selection to the Indian Civil Service however. Screening of each Indian candidate for the Service was undertaken by their provincial government and required both a security clearance and a character certificate. The security clearance was intended to discern whether the young man could be trusted politically, whilst the character certificate was supposed to gauge whether he could assimilate into the social world of the Indian Civil Service. All successful candidates from India were then sent to England for a two year probationary period during which they would study Indian law and languages at a designated university and learn to ride a horse. At the end of their training they would have to pass the Civil Service Commission's tests on their coursework before being allowed to sign their covenants with the British monarch.

***

The system of examinations and security clearances and character certificates and probationary training had been put together for a specific purpose. The British Raj wanted young Indian recruits who would be able to conform to the century old culture of the Indian Civil Service. That culture was one of upper middle class Victorian England, and its values had been shaped by the rugged masculinity and moral ethos taught at the English public schools.

Relatively few Indian boys had attended a public school in England. Those that did belonged to families with generations of English education and a culture of Anglophilia. The men of these families were amongst the earliest Indians to receive an English education, reaching the highest levels an Indian could for their time, enamoured of English culture and the possibilities for advance which it provided. In many cases the women of the family were highly educated, pioneers of their day, breaking social norms and taboos, as much at home speaking English as any Indian language. Indian boys would thus be sent to England by their parents for a proper public school education, and would find themselves in the strange position of being taught, like their English classmates, all the values, habits and codes of conduct with which generations of Englishmen had gone out and conquered India, and much of the world.

Neil Bonarjee traced his ancestry to Kulin Brahmins who were amongst the earliest scribes of the East India Company.[cvii] Bonarjee's grandfather Shib Chunder came under the influence of the missionary Alexander Duff as a boy and converted to Christianity in 1847. Shunned by his family, Shib Chunder relied on Duff for financial support and was in time given a post in the Finance Department by the Bengal Government. He went on to become a minister of the Christian Church of Bengal and devoted his last years to charitable work. Shib Chunder married a Sikh woman who was orphaned early in life and had been taken in after the Anglo-Sikh wars by a British Army officer. She was later placed under the care of missionaries in Calcutta and converted to Christianity. Bonarjee's father Debendranath tried for the Indian Civil Service but failed, and then took to journalism. Bonarjee's mother, from a Christian family of Chandernagore, had been amongst the first Indian girls to go to England for her education. Unusually for such an Anglicised and urban family, Bonarjee's parents decided to make the most of their inheritance of some land in Rampore and spent over a decade trying to develop an estate. But then in 1904, tired of the hard life and isolation, the family set sail for England to educate the next generation of Bonarjees.

On reaching England, Bonarjee, just three years old, was put into Miss Roberts's kindergarten before entering Dulwich Preparatory School. Dulwich was a relatively cosmopolitan

London school with a famous art gallery, a history of service in India, and students from around the world. Be it winter or summer the boys would start their day with a cold plunge. Brutal bullying had died out by Bonarjee's time, however the boys did engage in 'sheep washing'; a new boy would be tossed about by the other boys after his first cold plunge. Yet schoolboy fights could not be avoided, and when an English boy called Bonarjee a "Bengali babu" he, hardly knowing India, was not sure what the boy meant. But he did sense an insult and the two boys exchanged blows. On the academic front Bonarjee was marked out as a bright student, which for better or worse meant that he would come to concentrate on the classics, which still held higher prestige at Dulwich than modern languages or sciences.

Bonarjee became a little English patriot after reading Shakespeare, Dickins, Scott, Stevenson, *Tales From Ancient Greece*, and *Deeds That Won the Empire*. He learnt that the English had conquered India for the benefit of Indians, almost against their own wishes, read tales of the loyalty and self-sacrifice of Clive's Indian sepoys at the siege of Arcot, and came to the understanding that Indians were an awful people who burned their widows and locked Englishwomen in black holes. Bonarjee accepted the proposition that the British ruled India by God's will, and like the English boys he cheered on King George and Queen Mary as they drove past the school grounds after their coronation in the summer of 1911. Nonetheless, Bonarjee praised his Principal Arthur Gilkes's spirit of equality in allowing Indian boys to become prefects in what was, after all, a training ground for empire builders. Towards the end of his days at Dulwich Bonarjee started to find himself conflicted with the prevailing public school ethic which taught the acceptance of a situation rather than a critical questioning of it. As he prepared to leave for Oxford he even began to question Britain's civilising mission, and its aims in World War I.

Jayavant Shrinagesh's grandfather was a soldier from Mhow in central India who fled to Hyderabad after the Mutiny of 1857.[cviii] He took up service with a local Nawab who saw his son through school. Shrinagesh's father came to the notice of the British Resident and was sent to Edinburgh to study medicine. He qualified with an MD and then travelled to Berlin to study with the renowned bacteriologist Robert Koch. Upon returning to Hyderabad Dr. Mallanah began the search for an educated wife, which led him to the social circle around the prominent social reformer Mahadev Ranade. He made the acquaintance of the Kevalkars who were known to be advocates of English education and matrimonial discussions began. Things took a peculiar turn however, when the chosen Kevalkar girl refused to marry Dr. Mallanah, because he was too dark. So he had to take the next Kevalkar girl who was willing, a mere 13 year old, of quite modest education. Nonetheless, Dr. Mallanah took his child bride home and educated her. Shrinagesh's mother went on to obtain an arts degree from Edinburgh, found a girls' school and take part in the International Council for Women. When it came time to educate his son Dr. Mallanah visited 40 different public schools all over England, judging the teaching ability, reputation and principal of each school before deciding on West Buckland in Devon. He wanted his boys to be educated in one system; the British system under which they would have to advance in India. In 1914 Shrinagesh and his elder brother Satyavant set sail for England with their parents.

School life did not start well however, as Shrinagesh had to follow a rite of initiation and get up on a platform on the first Sunday of the new term and recite a poem in front of the whole school. The little Indian boy, in the Devon countryside during World War I decided to recite *Casabianca*, a poem of a son's loyalty to his father taught to him by his mother. However, "it only served to bring the house down with derision."

Like Bonarjee at Dulwich, Shrinagesh and his brother realised that they would have to stand up for themselves and fight and were given plenty of opportunities when they were called 'niggers' and treated with contempt by the English boys. But it was Shrinagesh's brother who did most of the fighting, for which his reputation in the neighbouring village grew. Whether it was in the school yard or on the football field, Shrinagesh learnt the lesson that the ability to fight his own battles depended on his will to succeed. And this, in the final analysis, was what earned a public school boy the respect of his peers.

For Shrinagesh the purpose of an English public school was to teach a boy to reconcile the need for self-reliance with being a member of a team. He admired his Principal Reverend Harries, who like Principal Gilkes at Dulwich, had the moral courage to make Indian boys prefects at a time when "colonials were treated as dependants, and Indians regarded as incompetent". At West Buckland prefects could enforce discipline and had the freedom to use the cane on younger boys. Shrinagesh saw this as a unique privilege; whilst the prefect would be placed above the other boys, he would have to give up his previous friendships and associations, appear unbiased in his judgements and win the respect of his peers by setting a good example. The prevailing culture meant that the boys would not tell tales on each other, and if a culprit did not own up to a misdemeanour on his own the whole class would accept a punishment. 1923 was a good year for Shrinagesh; he excelled in academics, shooting, cricket, football and athletics and won the Fortescue medal. Principal Harries then made him prefect of the under-performing Fortescue House. He took it as a challenge, calling a meeting of the boys of the house and motivating them to contribute. Fortescue's performance turned around and the boys made many of the school's honour boards, something which secured young Shrinagesh the head prefect position by the end of his West Buckland days in 1924.

***

The officer of the Indian Civil Service was not just a grown up public school boy however, he was also ideally a gentleman, and it was Oxford and Cambridge which provided the necessary finishing of the scholar and the gentleman and raised the intellectual level of the service. Indians had been attending both universities in greater numbers since the late 19th century, but most of the Indian students who attended Oxford and Cambridge after World War I found the little social world of the Oxbridge colleges much more absorbing than the academic instruction they had travelled to receive. They, like generations of English officers before them, had largely come to benefit from the 'elevating' atmosphere of the ancient universities, rather than their system of lectures, tutorials and examinations.

Kumar Padma Sivasankar Menon arrived at Christ Church, Oxford from Christian College, Madras towards the end of World War I.[cix] Far from dreaming spires, his first impression of Oxford was of an empty town with a few wandering drunks, squalid lanes and butchers' shops. The colleges were deserted with the able bodied men having left for the war. Menon quickly settled down to academic work under the guidance of his tutors however, and began to cultivate the airs and graces of an Oxford Man. He would only wear grey flannels and tweed coats, and despite his well learnt Indian academic discipline would not attend too many lectures. Attending every lecture was something only the weaker students had to do.

Menon would go out to Devonshire or the Lake District and spend his summers studying there. He would speak in Oxford slang, and thought it proper to cultivate a contempt for the female scholars who were a recent intrusion at the university. Tom Tower, Tom Quad, Peckwater Quad, the tudor staircase to the dining hall, the lovely meadows of the college, Menon would spend decades after his return to India speaking proudly of his college's fine history. But despite his love for Oxford, he did not make many English friends during his years there, for he was not good at games.

Menon did however become President of the Indian debating society, the Oxford Majlis. During his time as President, Rabindranath Tagore came to address the students. Menon remembered that "with his long beard, flowing robes and silvery voice, he looked like a being from another planet." Tagore had fallen out with the British after renouncing his knighthood in the wake of the massacre at Jallianwala Bagh, but given his moderate philosophical bent and the emergence of Gandhi's non- cooperation movement he had come back into favour. The Oxford Union and the Majlis held a combined meeting to honour Tagore and in his speech Menon welcomed him "not merely as a poet, not merely as a patriot, not merely as a philosopher but as an honorary member of the Oxford Majlis."

Menon graduated from Oxford in 1921. After the written examination he appeared for the viva voce, which he thought was meant to pull a student up rather than bring him down. A short viva would mean that the examiner had already decided a mark based on the written examination, a long one meant the student was a marginal case. Menon recalled that his own viva lasted less than a minute. The examiner said that his written work had brought credit to the college and university and he received that most coveted of honours, a First at Oxford. The excitement caused a rush of blood to his head however, and he suffered a headache all that afternoon.

After his experience at West Buckland, Jayavant Shrinagesh was surprised to find the 'colour bar' at Cambridge in the 1920s.[cx] At West Buckland he could put it down to the ignorance of boys, but at Cambridge it was cultivated with the intent of men. He found that "Englishmen prepared to look upon their coloured fellows as equals were still few and far between." This started to fan the flames of nationalism in the young Shrinagesh, and he was "certain that many of the extremists on the political scene of the British colonies were born there [Cambridge]." Neil Bonarjee observed something similar at Oxford.[cxi] He thought that British racial arrogance was enhanced by their victory in World War I. It confirmed their self-image as indestructible Englishmen striding the world stage, bearing the White Man's Burden whilst having to suffer Indian wogs and niggers at their universities.

Shrinagesh found the tutorial system at Cambridge colleges to be laissez faire, the assumption being that the student was an adult, who in consultation with his tutor could select which subjects to study and which lectures to attend. This would only amount to 10-12 hours per week, but he would have to attend five dinners a week at his college hall. In fact, he found it harder to avoid the college dinners than the lectures, for some of the professors would only mark the attendance roll at the start or finish of the term, many did not know their students by name and others were only interested in payment of their fees.

Shrinagesh thought that the best way to overcome the colour bar was to excel in college activities. Despite earning two Trinity College colours he was barred from entry to the 'Hawks Club' and instead had to settle for the separate Indian sports club called the 'Crocodile Club'. He tried his hand at athletics and then rugby, but ended his Cambridge career in disappointment, not being able to represent the university in his final year. Shrinagesh did not get entangled with any English girls at Cambridge and his one attempt to woo an Indian girl ended in failure as she became enamoured with his dashing elder brother.

Like the other Indian students Shrinagesh considered himself a firebrand at the Majlis and the college debating society the "Magpie and Stump". The catchword at the time was "Home Rule for India", but having been away from India for so long he did not feel he had any political line to hold on to. He was even almost convinced when the Secretary of State for India Frederick Smith, the Earl of Birkenhead "who was known to be at his best when had had a few whiskies", arrived at the college late one evening and spoke eloquently of "the sacred duty of the British" in India and "the lack of experience of Indians in governing".

As late as the mid 1930s Rabrindra Dutt experienced the little disciplines of undergraduate life at Corpus Christie, Cambridge.[cxii] If a student were to return to his room late, it would be reported to the tutor. Frequent late nights were a sign that the student was not focused on their studies, something which might result in them being "sent down" from the university. Dutt remembered that the students would have to wear the gown appropriate to their status at lectures, at dinners and whilst out after dark. The Proctor would be accompanied by burly porters, and would start prowling the surroundings after dusk for undergraduates without their caps and gowns. If caught, the undergraduate could either run for his life, or pay a fine. Little cat and mouse games would ensue, with undergraduates looking for safe houses to run to should the necessity arise. In addition, Cambridge was still considered a "man's university" and women were only admitted to Girton and Newnham Colleges. They were not members of the university or formally admitted to the degree which they were studying for, although they could attend lectures and appear for examinations. When Dutt planned to invite two female students from Girton College to tea in his room he thought it best to ask the hall Porter whether there were any restrictions. The Porter stood to his full height, puffed up his chest and replied: "No, Sir, Corpus trusts its men."

Edward Mangat Rai arrived at Keble College, Oxford from St

Stephen's, Delhi in 1936.[cxiii] Keble was not thought to be a very brainy college. It was one which the Church of England would recruit its priests from. But the college was good for rowing and rugby and produced many fine sportsmen. Mangat Rai recalled that Oxford was something of a shock coming straight from the Indian system. He felt he got very little out of Oxford intellectually, much less than he received from St Stephen's. But he thought the fault for his lack of intellectual engagement at Oxford might have been as much his own as the university's. He had not attended an English public school and came from the Indian system in which students were led rather than having to lead themselves. The social atmosphere had changed since K.P.S. Menon's days however, and Mangat Rai would recall that his time at Oxford in the late 1930s was most valuable for the friendships he made. He became friends with Paul Weatherly, later a colonial civil servant and business leader and Ronald Sampson, an eccentric who would go on to become a radical academic at Bristol University and write books such as *Equality and Power*. On the eve of World War II they would spend their college nights talking about God, and Nehru, and Indian Independence, and women, and the future of the British Empire.

***

For those Indian students who had been to English public schools and Oxford and Cambridge the question of what to do at the end of their degree was the same as for students around the world and in all times. They were middle class, and after their parents had made such a large investment in their education they would have to find a suitably lucrative and prestigious career. For most, the Indian Civil Service examination seemed like the perfect solution to their graduate dilemma.

Ambitious fathers sent Hiralal Patel and Vadakke Kurupath

Ramunni Menon to England with the specific objective of trying for the Indian Civil Service.[cxiv] For Patel, it had already been decided whilst he was studying in Bombay that he would travel to England for further studies with a view to sitting the Indian Civil Service examination in London. The exchange rate was favourable to rupee holders, his father had the cash to spare, and so he decided to set aside the whole amount for his entire period of study in England. Menon's father had been at Cambridge himself, and wanted his son to follow in his footsteps and take the Natural Sciences Tripos and then sit the Indian Civil Service examination.

For Ronald Noronha it was parental pressure, particularly an insistent mother, who sent her son all the required forms to appear for the Indian Civil Service examination, pre-filled. In addition, Mrs. Noronha threatened to cut off Ronald's allowance should he not appear.[cxv] Nagendra Baksi from Faridpur in east Bengal had wanted to be a surgeon, but his mother was also adamant, and rather dramatic in insisting that her son compete for the Indian Civil Service.[cxvi] Mrs. Baksi told Nagendra that if an independent India would need able administrators, and that if he had drunk his mother's milk, then nobody would be able to purchase his character and so he should take her blessings and start studying for the examination.

Jayavant Shrinagesh made his way to the service by a process of deduction.[cxvii] He did not feel that business, medicine, law or politics were his line, but he did have an interest in administration and so decided to sit for the Indian Civil Service examination. Dharma Vira recollected himself as a rather aimless young man moving between Allahabad University and Lucknow University and back to Allahabad, starting courses and not finishing them when a chance encounter with Sir Ganga Ram, a self-made millionaire and pioneer of lift irrigation in Punjab led him to the Indian Civil Service.[cxviii] Dharma sounded out Sir Ganga in Lahore about the possibility of using his position as a director of the Imperial Bank of India to secure him a job. Sir Ganga advised the young man to earn a job himself by facing the open competition of the Indian Civil Service. Triloki Kaul from Baramulla in Kashmir had taken a law degree from Allahabad and was similarly uncertain about his future.[cxix] He was trying to decide whether to go to the Bar, sit for the Indian Civil Service examination in India, or go to England for further studies and sit the examination there. He approached Sir Tej Bahadur Sapru and Kailash Katju for a place in their chambers but both advised him to first sit the Indian Civil Service examination. Kaul's father gave him the same advice, and even accused him of being a coward, fearful that he would not pass the examination.

Neil Bonarjee found that his history degree from Oxford would only qualify him to teach in an English school.[cxx] He then proceeded to apply, but found that these schools were not clamouring for his services. He did manage to find a temporary vacancy at his old prep school Dulwich though, and taught history, English and mathematics for a time. Bonarjee tried to pull a string with Sir Norcot Warren for a place with the Imperial Bank of India but he too was advised to try for the Indian Civil Service. In the end it was a sense of debt to his parents for the enormous investment they had made in educating him in England, combined with a desire to prove himself as good as other students in a competitive examination which led him to the service. He compared the examination to Mount Everest: "The ICS, like the mountain, was there."

Rabindra Dutt had a family tradition to live up to.[cxxi] His grandfather, Romesh Dutt was one of the first Indians in the Indian Civil Service. Besides his official duties, Romesh was one of the leading public intellectuals of his time, publishing translations of Hindu epics, writing *The Economic History of India* and presiding over the Indian National Congress in 1899.

Rabindra's father was also an Indian Civil Service officer, but despite his family connections to the service he cited peer pressure as his main motivation for clearing the examination; he had failed at his first attempt whilst all his friends had succeeded. Irrespective of whether he was keen on a career in the Indian Civil Service he did not want to be branded a failure.

Mangat Rai was immersed in the nationalist politics of St Stephen's College in the early 1930s.[cxxii] However, the romance ended when the question of a job at the end of the degree arose. The story had not changed much since the 19th century and the government remained the biggest employer of educated young Indians. Mangat Rai was studying during the depression years, and even in good times there were limited openings for Indians in industry or private companies. The other major option, the legal profession was a risky proposition in which a young man would either sink or swim. He saw his seniors with good degrees floundering; those who could not clear competitive examinations for the services would spend years struggling to get a job as a clerk on less than ₹100 a month. "Government as an employer was thus an inescapable conclusion" which created a "duality of purpose" between the desire for Independence and the need to work for the British Government. Mangat Rai was middle class, and unlike his rich friends he had to "catch as catch can", despite his inner convictions.

Even Braj Nehru did not face much resistance to his Indian Civil Service ambitions.[cxxiii] His father was Jawaharlal's cousin and he had grown up in Anand Bhavan in Allahabad with the rest of the Nehru clan. When he finished his studies in Allahabad in the late 1920s it was decided that he would go to England and compete for the Indian Civil Service. The non-cooperation movement was in a lull, the family already had two members in the Indian Civil Service, and Nehru recalled that "There was no prejudice of any kind against these 'collaborators'." Jawaharlal did not oppose his plans, and although Motilal had lost his enthusiasm for the service he did not raise any objections either. It was only from his distant aunt, Jawaharlal's mother Swarup Rani that he had to accept some remarks about training to become a "slave of the British".

***

Whilst students would study furiously for the Indian Civil Service examination, there was another test embedded in the system of selection which they would have to clear in order to win a place in the service. Marks were allocated for a viva voce, and given how stiff the competition was, a candidate's chances could be made or broken by their performance before a board of government officials. The interview was a particularly intimate form of social screening, designed to ensure that the young man could hold his own in the company of high officials of the state. It could even be thought of as 'the gentleman test'.

When K.P.S. Menon went for his interview, he was questioned about his home and antecedents.[cxxiv] However, the conversation got stuck on the word 'native' in a question about the 'Native State of Travancore' and a discussion on the pejorative nature of the term ensued. He was asked about the Maharaja of Travancore, the matrilineal practices of the Nair community, and then asked what he thought Britain should do about its Irish problem. He replied that it was a domestic matter for Britain, whereas India was an imperial issue.

V.K.R. Menon was particularly nervous before his interview, for it was his first time before an all British panel, and his first experience of a viva voce.[cxxv] His interviewers put him at ease however, and asked him if he had any interests outside of his studies. He replied that he was an amateur mechanic. Sir

Frank Sly, a former Governor of the Central Provinces was sceptical, knowing the upper caste Hindu reluctance to perform manual labour. He asked whether young Menon just meant that he could drive a car. But Menon was insistent, and when asked why he liked to tinker with cars, he replied: "Just to have an idea of practical life." Menon ended up doing well in the interview and scraped into the Indian Civil Service.

During his interview Triloki Kaul managed to demonstrate his grasp of the English sense of humour whilst weaving in his Oxford connections.[cxxvi] The interviewers asked him what he thought of the standard of debate at British universities. He said that he was most impressed by the sense of humour at Oxford debates, and then related Lloyd George's address at the Oxford Union on Liberalism, after which an undergraduate had quipped: "We have heard funeral orations before, but never seen the corpse itself deliver one!" Kaul also had to hold forth on the agrarian situation in the United Provinces, the difference between the Australian and Canadian Constitutions, and the Statute of Westminster. He scored the maximum 300 marks for the interview.

Braj Nehru made the Indian Civil Service on his third attempt.[cxxvii] By the time he appeared for his third and last interview the civil disobedience movement of the early 1930s had broken out and he was questioned on why, with half his family in jail for campaigning against British rule, he would want to join the Indian Civil Service. He replied that he wanted to prove himself capable of clearing the world's stiffest examination, and then wanted to know more of how the Indian Civil Service worked. If he found it worked for the national good he would continue serving, if not he would resign.

***

Those candidates who ranked high enough after the

examination and interview were selected and put on probation for a period of specialist training in Britain. They were sent to Oxford, Cambridge, or London, which were recognised as 'centres of excellence' for training officers for the Indian Civil Service. The probationers were able to express their preferences for the province they wanted to serve in, however very few were accommodated given that most British recruits chose Punjab or the United Provinces. At the end of the course the probationers would sit the Civil Service Commission's tests in Indian law, Indian history and their Indian language. Each probationer was also issued with a booklet titled *Hints on Riding*. He would have to arrange and pay for his own course of equestrian training at an approved stables and it was the riding test rather than law, history or language which usually gave Indian cadets the most cause for concern. Having cleared their tests, when October came the probationers would proceed to the India Office to sign their covenants with the Crown, pledging to serve the British monarch and his heirs and successors loyally and faithfully, following all orders and service rules and regulations and forswearing engagement in private trade. They would then sail first class on the P&O to Bombay, and from there they journeyed to their assigned districts.

Neil Bonarjee did not strain himself too much during his probationary year, in fact the only test he took seriously was the one for horse riding.[cxxviii] Mangat Rai also recalled that the courses in Indian law, history and languages were not too strenuous and that the teachers were usually retired British officers who had served in India.[cxxix] They were taught Indian history by an Oxford Don, Urdu by retired Colonel Edric Harcourt and Indian Law by retired judge Sir Benjamin Lindsay. Braj Nehru remembered a lecture by a retired Indian Medical Service officer on public health.[cxxx] The officer emphasised that it was important to look after the health of the Indian people; should plague break out like it had in Bombay, famine would ensue and the people would not be able to work the land, and the government would not be able to collect its revenue. Nehru spent his spare time reading Indian and English history and playing bridge, badminton and tennis. Rabindra Dutt thought that the probationary year was basically designed for the British probationers in order to give them some familiarity with the strange new country they would be heading out to rule.[cxxxi] He felt it had little to offer Indians besides a knowledge of Indian criminal and personal law. But Dutt had studied at Cambridge, whereas for Indians selected through the examination in India the probationary period was their introduction to British life, something which they had only previously read about and heard of.

Triloki Kaul made friends with three of his English colleagues; Philip Adams, Alan Flack, and Thomas Sharpe during his probationary period in London.[cxxxii] Together they decided to travel to India overland by car rather than the customary P&O journey by sea. In fact most of their probationary period at the School of Oriental Studies was spent drinking beer and planning the journey. The India Office was not keen on the idea, but the young men put up some of their own money, purchased a second hand Ford V-8 30 and fitted it out with a reclining seat for sleep. They packed a tent and some sleeping bags and bought the Automobile Association's *Furlong-by-Furlong* guide map.

Kaul and his colleagues set out for India from London in September 1937. The young men drove in light and dark and shared four hour driving shifts during the day and two hour shifts at night. One passenger would sit with the driver, whilst two would sleep in the back. On the way they ate and drank and made merry in German beer gardens, and even followed the cars to Munich to watch a meeting of Hitler and Mussolini. They started to notice more poverty as they journeyed east from Budapest to Belgrade however; the locals were poorly dressed and lived in shabby huts and Kaul felt some connection with the Slavs, whom he recognised as people more of the East than the West. As they moved closer to Istanbul Kaul started to feel more at home, and his English colleagues further away.

After taking in a sunset on the Bosporus the young civil servants then crossed over to the Asian side of Turkey. But the roads became worse and the journey tougher; it started to rain, the mud built up, they started to have tyre punctures, were robbed by some bandits dressed as policemen, their compass did not work properly and they lost their way. In the middle of nowhere they received help from some village urchins who led them to a tea house where the proprietor offered them some bread, tea and eggs and directions onward to Eregli. There the English speaking manager of a textile factory offered to put them up in a guest house.

At Alexandretta the four officers had to build their own makeshift bridge to cross a river, a feat they celebrated with pineapple juice, cheese and biscuits. After an accident on the road to Damascus the Ford suffered a broken radiator and front lights and Timmy Sharpe had to sit on the bonnet filling the leaking radiator with water. They then decided to engage a local driver across the desert towards Baghdad, who managed to lose the way. There were, after all, no roads in the desert. The rear springs broke near Karmanshah in Iran, and given that there was no local supplier of Ford parts, Kaul managed to persuade a local cobbler to improvise springs from some old ones he had lying around.

The group took some rest in Tehran, and were dissuaded by the British Ambassador of their idea of travelling into the Soviet Republic of Georgia via the Caspian Sea; the Indian Civil Service officers might be tainted as communists for the rest of their careers. They also had to abandon their plan for travel to Afghanistan due to "unsettled conditions". Kaul, Sharpe, Adams and Flack finally reached the frontier post past Zahidan at Qila Safed and received a warm welcome by

British Army officers at Quetta. They were treated as guests of the Officers' Mess, lodged in comfort and entertained lavishly. Quetta was a cantonment town and home to the Staff College and Kaul remembered being impressed by the 'unity of India' which was on display at the institution; almost all the races, creeds and castes of India were represented in the army establishments in the town.

***

Journeys back to India, whether by P&O or by Ford V-8 complete, the new Indian Civil Service officer would travel to his allotted province. He would go there to learn the Raj, both from the dusty manuals he would have to master, and the words of wisdom he would receive from old British district collectors. Before long he too would be called on to hand down advice and instruction to a younger generation of officers entrusted to him for training in the workings of the service.

Astad Gorwala had entered the Indian Civil Service in 1924 and during his 1952 R.R. Kale Memorial Lecture at the Gokhale Institute of Politics and Economics in Poona he reflected on what he called the "unofficial training" which occurred through social contact between the young officer and his seniors in the service.[cxxxiii] Gorwala presented an ideal in which the Old Collector would never be too busy for a few words with his young Assistant. He would suggest that the new class II magistrate have tea once a week and bring his cases or judgements in which points of evidence might be troubling him. The assistant collector would arrive at 4:30 pm sharp with his bundle of cases, and seated in the drawing room and plied with tea and cakes the bright young officer would have to shed his pride and give his work for examination, talk freely with his senior officer, and be pleased with praise but not hurt by warning and advice.

The junior officer would thus imbibe service standards, without having to be told things explicitly. He learnt in this way never to lie, no matter how difficult the circumstances. He had to do his duty and stand firm and never show his personal fears. He had to maintain probity in personal dealings, prioritise work over everything else, and never just throw tasks onto a junior officer. He had to respect his seniors but not quake in fear of them and express his views frankly. The commissioner would make time for the young man once or twice on a visit to the district. He could bring his problems to the commissioner and be called a "damned young fool", but be encouraged to sort the matter out by taking the difficult path. It was this "unofficial training" which prepared the young officer to go and work out of a sense of self-realisation and pride in his service.

Braj Nehru's recollection of his time as assistant commissioner to his Deputy Commissioner Ivan Jones most closely fits Gorwala's ideal.[cxxxiv] Jones was an Irish Protestant from Trinity College, Dublin, and in Nehru's estimation he was one of the minority of British officers which was devoid of racial feeling. Nehru recalled Jones educating him with "tender understanding and infinite patience". He taught Nehru that the duties of a civil servant were for the public good rather than personal credit or publicity. For Jones the life of a civil servant was devoid of self-interest, like that of a monk. But the civil service officer served humanity rather than God.

As in Gorwala's ideal, Jones was not shy in reprimanding young Nehru should he transgress the rules, written or unwritten. Nehru recalled that the only time that Jones was harsh in his tone was when he had allowed a naib tehsildar to pick off a melon whilst they were inspecting some village fields. Jones explained that as assistant commissioner Nehru's actions were watched closely by everyone in the district. If he was seen to take one melon it would be taken as a licence for the tehsildar to take 5, the naib 10, the kanoongo 20 and the patwari 100. After Jones's lecture Nehru felt as though he had committed a theft. But he never forgot the lesson in appropriate behaviour for people in authority.

As time passed however, Indians started to learn less from British officers, and more from senior Indians in the service. Indian officers who had begun their careers in the early 1920s were on hand to teach new Indian recruits the ways of the Indian Civil Service in the late 1920s. There came a time when a young Indian officer training in a district was just as likely to receive his education in the codes and culture of the Indian Civil Service from a fellow Indian, a demonstration of the assimilation of the service culture and the distance it had travelled from its exclusive racial origins. Another account which resembled Gorwala's ideal was one provided by Hiralal Patel.[cxxxv] In 1927 Patel served as a supernumerary assistant collector to the assistant collector in the Larkana subdivision in Sind. During this training period he was attached to none other than Astad Gorwala. Patel described Gorwala as "an officer of outstanding ability, drive, and initiative".

Patel gave an account of Gorwala's work schedule in which he would leave for his field inspection on the back of a camel at sunrise. The assistant collector would be expected to carry out an on-the-spot physical verification of the village officer's field book in which he had to record the type of crops sown in each survey area of the village for which he was assigned. The assistant collector would pass through several villages, halting briefly to meet local leaders and discuss any problems and measures which may need to be taken. He would visit village schools, inspect encroachments of government land and return to camp at 1 pm. After bathing and lunch Gorwala would proceed to do his files. The head clerk would read the last file note and any other relevant note and Gorwala would then dictate his recommendation or order. After that he would proceed to deal with complaints and applications from the people of the subdivision. He would instruct the appropriate action on each application, sometimes fixing another date for the respondent to be called for a hearing of his side of the case.

For Patel "It was remarkable to see the large number of disputes which got settled in that manner. The number of applicants each day used to be quite phenomenally large." He watched Gorwala closely, asked questions and sought clarification, accompanied him on his morning field inspections and observed how he spoke with landowners and cultivators. He soon believed that this was the best training possible; watching the senior officer at work and developing initiative, responsibility, and judgement of character. Gorwala had become Patel's first role model in the service, for he was "not merely an officer with an extraordinarily high sense of values and a very strict code of conduct. He was exceptional in as much as he worked with only one objective, how best to serve the people." Patel admired Gorwala's championing of the downtrodden, which made him unpopular with land owners and money lenders, "caring neither for popularity nor for promotion, doing what he considered to be the right thing to do."

***

There was a specific reason that Astad Gorwala and Hiralal Patel went out on camel back through Larkana district in Sind. The revenue systems of the Raj depended on a detailed knowledge of the agricultural society of each district as well as the relationships between landlords and their tenants. This necessity led the Indian Civil Service to place such importance on the need for regular tours of the villages and checking of land boundaries and soil conditions. These tours and inspections were a matter of routine, but every 30 years each district would be inspected and surveyed field by field. Land tenure, titles and occupation were all cross checked, soils were classified and the government's revenue demand was then set once again. This task of district revenue settlement was carried out by settlement officers, usually Indian Civil Service officers especially deputed for the task.

Sankara Chettur had done his district training at Tanjore and was selected for settlement work in the early 1930s.[cxxxvi] The settlement officer would write a Scheme Report and Chettur was told to study Benjamin Holdsworth's Report on the Godavaris and the Krishna district which was thought to be a classic of the genre. Chettur took his assignment to be an opportunity to learn all about the revenue of the district and he thought that preparing his own report would give him the chance to show off his administrative abilities.

Chettur was sent to Nellore to be special assistant settlement officer in Party No. 1. However, Party No. 1 did not have a head settlement officer, so Chettur had to learn the work from another Indian Assistant Officer for six months before taking over the Party and heading to Tirunelveli and completing the resettlement there. Chettur stayed at the Vinukonda Travellers' Bungalow and ended up doing 'remnants work' on the settlement of Guntur District. From his base at the bungalow Chettur inspected the surrounding villages, going out on horseback to inaccessible villages, sending his settlement staff of chainmen, karnams and field supervisors a day ahead. Upon arrival at the village he began inspecting the fields and classifying the soil, occasionally having a rest under the shade of a five foot high thorn bush. He toured nearly every tulak in the district and inspected the fields and irrigation sources of over 100 villages.

Later, as an assistant collector Chettur went to his first Survey and Settlement Camp at Poonamallee. He lived in tents and went out each morning with a ten foot chain and a theodilite and learnt the triangular survey method. Once the Poonamallee Camp was over, Chettur and his fellow assistant collectors were sent to a small village in Salem District called

Thalaivasal where they pitched their tents and were instructed by Mr. Humayun, a special assistant settlement officer. The crucial part of the training was the classification of the soil. The officers would go into the field with a servant who carried a pot of water and a crow bar. With the crow bar they would dig a hole nine inches deep, take the soil, mix it with water and bring it to a fine consistency and determine the sand or clay content, or whether it was loam, a mix of sand and clay.

At the other end of India Triloki Kaul had to 'settle' the district of Gonda near Nepal at the start of World War II.[cxxxvii] His first lesson in settlement came from Jai Kirat Singh, who went on to write the Final Settlement Report for Gonda in 1944. Jai Kirat showed him how to classify the soil and demarcate the fields according to fertility and productivity. The fields ranged from those closest to the villagers' habitation which were rich and fertile and called 'Goind' and marked with a 'G' on a map, to portions of land marked D_1, D_2, D_3 and lastly D_4 which were barren or made of ravines. Kaul had to go out and visit each and every field, examine the soil and produce, speak with the villagers and then either approve or change the chak tarash, or soil classifier's tentative demarcation from the day before.

Kaul thought that the settlement work was fascinating for it brought him into contact with the tiller of the soil and gave him a chance to talk to him in his own language about his land, his family and his problems. Kaul and his settlement team would have to detail the history of each village, its population and composition of castes and professions, the number of brick houses and mud houses, and the number of bicycles, bullock carts and cattle. They would then fix a rough family budget for each class in the district, estimating their income, expenditure and savings. Each tenant would then have to pay the landlord 20% of their gross income, and the land revenue which the landlord would then pay to the government would be assessed at 8-10% of the net rent which they received from their tenants. A remission of 6-12% would then be given back to the Brahmins, Thakurs and Sayeds, whose status meant that they would not work the plough and would instead have to hire labour for the task.

Kaul did what he could to reduce the rent but could do little to stop the practice of begar, or the forced extraction of labour. He thought settlement work gave him an insight into the "deep poverty and abject misery of the village folk and the intolerable conditions in which they lived." He described the collusion of the village patwari, the local policeman and the village bania, who would work together to take the humble cultivator's earnings. Money lenders would charge between 24 and 48% interest and so the cultivators of eastern U.P. were most often born into debt, and would die in debt. Kaul thought it was a "pitiable sight" to see the lean, thin figures of the poor hard working villagers just eking out their marginal existence, "yet they would smile and laugh, smoke their little hookahs and try to be friendly and hospitable."

***

Besides knowing how to classify soil, mark maps and fix revenue demands the civil servant would also have to know the law, because he was also a local judge. The everyday administration of justice would in many cases be quite difficult; witnesses were unreliable, police prosecutions were riddled with errors and local lawyers knew all the tricks of their trade. The law had to be followed, but often judgements would be left to the intuition of the judge, something which made that old emphasis on the character of the Indian Civil Service officer so important in the distant outposts of the Raj.

Mangat Rai found the work of a magistrate in Lyallpur, Punjab quite frustrating.[cxxxviii] He recalled sitting in court and meticulously recording a series of lies told by prosecution witnesses, and then another series of lies told by witnesses for the defence. The record of lies would have to be kept in both English and Urdu. He thought that proving or disproving a case was largely a matter of putting together corroboration for a thesis through "suitably tutored witnesses, relations and friends". At the end of the process he would have to rely on instinct. Generally the ahlmad would keep a record in Urdu and the magistrate would keep the English record, but to relieve the boredom and to improve his Urdu Mangat Rai started to keep a single record in Urdu himself. The English record was only needed for cases which would go up to the High Court and the simple cases he dealt with were unlikely to travel so high on appeal.

Braj Nehru was gazetted as a third class magistrate and assigned a courtroom in the kaccheri in Hissar, Punjab.[cxxxix] He could hear criminal cases and award punishments of up to one month in jail or a fine of up to ₹50. As a matter of routine he would hear cases of 'simple assault' which usually amounted to no more than shoving, pushing and slapping. Nehru thought that the object of the work was to enable him to learn the procedures to be followed in criminal cases and acquaint him with the Indian Penal Code, the Criminal Procedure Code and the Law of Evidence.

Nehru had a staff of two chaprassis, a munshi and an ahlmad. He remembered that he was "putty in the munshi's hands", who was fully aware of the fact and took advantage of his ignorance. In one case when he acquitted an accused the complainant flew into a rage, created a scene in the court and shouted at the munshi that he had given him ₹2 to ensure that the sahib would convict the accused. The munshi denied the allegation and then threw ₹2 on the floor and said "here are the two rupees, if you think you gave them to me." Nehru took the matter to the deputy commissioner who suggested he make a written report, which he did, but the munshi continued serving in the court for as long as Nehru was there.

In Hissar the testimony of the witnesses was given in Haryanvi. As in Lyallpur, the munshi would record it in the Urdu script, and the magistrate would write a translation in English. The result was a record in two languages, neither of which the witnesses understood. The law directed that the witness either sign or put a thumb impression on a record of the statement which said "Read over and acknowledged correct". The statement was almost never read over, and in most cases the witness's thumb would but caught, pressed on ink and then placed in the appropriate spot. The magistrate would however, write his own record which was read aloud before the lawyers who could check its accuracy.

Nehru would listen to opposite versions of events from witnesses on either side of the case, not knowing which to believe, and would be even more confused when lawyers for each side presented their cases. He thought he might as well have tossed a coin at the end of proceedings. However, he felt that over time he was "to some extent" able to discriminate between truth and lies, and after a few months became a better judge of witnesses, learnt the tricks of the lawyers and thought his judgements "were reasonably correct".

Nonetheless, Nehru remained an acquitting magistrate, much to the disgust of the local superintendent of police. He thought that the procedures for criminal investigations and the rules on admissibility of evidence were so complex and unsuited to India that the only way that a criminal could be convicted was through the introduction of some falsehood by the prosecution. He had been trained as a barrister and was taught that it was better that 99 criminals go free rather than a single innocent person be convicted. And so in his court the slightest falsehood introduced into the prosecution's case would be grounds for an acquittal. The tragedy was however, that Nehru thought that in nine cases out of ten the accused was not just a criminal, but a habitual one at that.

***

Indian civil servants had to be trained in the workings of government offices by their British superiors and Indian clerical staff alike. The workings of the Raj depended on it. Work as a class III magistrate in a small town courtroom was usually the young officer's introduction to this maze of government offices and files which came to be known as 'Kagazi Raj', or the 'Rule of Paperwork'. But beyond just learning to clear the files and write reports, many Indian officers steadily grew to feel something like love for the codes and manuals and legislation which came to order their working lives.

Braj Nehru had the basic structure of the government's system of files explained to him when he was called to the Department of Finance in New Delhi in September 1940.[cxl] It was the office superintendent and the stenographer who showed him how each file was divided into two parts; one with a red cover and the other with a green cover. The correspondence was contained in the red cover, whilst the note was contained in the green cover. The note had to be written on a specific type of light blue paper and required a wide margin. It would start with an 'office note' which summarised the case and presented the points requiring a decision and provided the relevant references and precedents. Files which contained precedents would be placed below the current papers and the relevant rules and regulations would be placed above them. The papers were always kept in this order, placed on a file board and tied in white tape. As a relatively junior officer Nehru was expected to either pass orders himself, or send the case up to the next highest level of decision maker. Delays would ensue when another department had to be consulted and the whole bundle of papers would have to be sent on, getting stuck along the way. The note explained the reason for a decision, and given the civil servants' easy access to official information, they could engage in long and elaborate internal debates. Nehru remembered that "being the product of highly trained minds these notes were usually impressive and it was a matter of pride for them to be expressed in elegant language. Some of them could well have qualified as masterpieces of literature!"

V.K.R. Menon gave an account of the instructions and expectations of his British senior officer as he trained in the workings of a government office.[cxli] His superior, William Brett gave him clear guidelines regarding his work; he should familiarise himself with the main codes, manuals and rules of the Finance Department, besides those of other departments, and when submitting a case he should ensure that attention was drawn to the appropriate rule or regulation and a suitable precedent was cited and that all the facts were correct. He had to bring out all valid objections, but measure as a yardstick of his success the number of cases agreed to by the finance secretary rather than the number rejected. Yet Brett also preferred that his office and the under secretary remain "rigid" to avoid the risk of financial control growing slack.

Menon became enamoured with the codes, manuals, and compilations of rules and regulations relating to the important subjects to be handled by government departments. He praised legislative enactments such as the Indian Evidence Act 1872. Unlike Braj Nehru, Menon thought it was "acclaimed as one of the most perfect pieces of legislation in the world". He recalled that the *Fundamental Rules*, the *Bihar and Orissa Code*, the *Civil Service Regulations* and the *Bihar and Orissa Account* were publications on financial matters which were his "constant companions".

Menon felt that the most important feature of the system in which he served was that "The Rules had to be followed whether the case was big or small and whether it concerned a Member of the Executive Council or a peon." He thought that rigid adherence to rules by the British contributed to good administration because it removed all scope for arbitrariness and the whims of individual officers. Junior officers had the satisfaction of knowing that however harsh a rule may be when applied to them, it would be applied equally to senior officers. The existence of such rules gave officers a measure of protection. Menon thought that even if there was a delay in the various stages of processing files as a result of study and the application of rules, a much greater wastage of time would be avoided later on should irregularities be detected.

Sankara Chettur had his first taste of secretariat life in 1945 when he was appointed Secretary in the Local Administration Department in Madras.[cxlii] The Local Administration Secretary was known to have the lightest workload in the Secretariat. Office hours were from 11 to 5, with lunch being taken between 2:15 and 3. The secretaries would lunch together, with the chief secretary sitting at the head of the table. 'Talking shop' was taboo, and conversations were kept to 'general topics', but Chettur enjoyed the camaraderie of the lunch room.

Chettur recalled that in secretariat life everything was done for the officer. The files which came to him were all but finished, he would simply have to write a summarising note and push the file up to the Advisor for an order or pass an order himself in matters within his own competence. Chettur would read the administration reports of the municipalities, assess their work, review their budgets and write confidential reports on their commissioners. The files were not too complicated, and the flow of work was light and smooth.

Beyond perusing files, Chettur did get down to some practical work in pushing for a scheme to build bridges over the railway line at local level crossings. Not only had the public been demanding it, but Chettur himself had been held up for 15 to

20 minutes at the level crossings on several days. He even walked from his own desk to the Public Works Department Secretary's room and proposed a scheme to finance the construction of the bridges. Chettur wrote a note on the relevant file outlining a plan to finance the building based on a loan, grant and self-funding formula. The file kept going around and around the Secretariat for years, and Chettur had to be content with a small victory when one out of the three proposed bridges was finally built and opened "triumphantly" by the Governor of Madras in 1960.

***

Even in the late 19th century when the entry of Indian officers into the Indian Civil Service was so hotly contested, it was never Indians' ability to process paperwork which was at issue. A concern of the British rulers was that they would not be able to exercise the authority of their office. That ability to project strength and stay firm under pressure was said to be a uniquely British quality. So when an Indian officer took the place of a British one, all would be watching to see whether the new sahib could cope when law and order was challenged and he had to enforce the writ of the state.

In 1937 the Government of India transferred K.P.S. Menon to Zhob in Baluchistan as political agent.[cxliii] Everyone wondered whether Menon would be able to rule over the tribesmen of the frontier with a firm hand, or whether he, like Grish Chunder De in *The Head of the District* would drop his codes and case law and run for his life at the first sign of danger. Sir Herbert Metcalfe was sceptical and asked Menon: "Do you think you will be able to put it across to the Pathans?" Sir Girija Bajpai thought Menon would soon be in line to become a Joint Secretary or Secretary to the Government of India and there was no need for him to forge his bond with the British Empire in his own blood.

The main apprehension of the local British community was however, that by custom the new political agent would be the president of their club at Fort Sandeman. The locals of Zhob were apprehensive for different reasons. Not only was Menon an Indian, but a Hindu and a 'down-country Hindu' or 'Madrasi' at that. They thought that his appointment was designed to lower their prestige and had taken a delegation to Menon's predecessor to express their reservations. However, they were told that Menon had already served on the frontier and acquitted himself well and to wait and watch his progress. The Pathans were relieved when Menon arrived and did not wear a lungi or paint any caste marks on his forehead, and even spoke reasonable Pashtu.

Menon took up residence at 'Windsor Castle', the highest hillock at Fort Sandeman and immediately encountered some service rivalry with the Area Commander, Brigadier Alfred Ross. The political agent had precedence over the army commanders and a small stand-off ensued when Ross summoned Menon to the Inspection Bungalow. Menon interpreted this as an order, and so issued one of his own for the area commander to meet him at Windsor Castle. Ross then broke off all relations and did not allow army horses to participate in the races the following week. Menon did receive support from the rest of the military officers at Fort Sandeman however, and appreciated the encouragement of Sir Arthur Parsons, the Agent General of Baluchistan.

The political agent had an irregular force called the Zhob Militia at his disposal for maintaining law and order in the Agency. The militia was manned by specially recruited and trained tribesmen who were commanded by British officers. The commandant of the militia was Major Alastair Scotland, somewhat reminiscent of Tallantire from Kipling's story; "a bluff, hearty big built individual who was ready at a moment's notice to go out and chase raiders." Both Menon and Scotland received the most trouble from an outlaw named

Pale who struck terror throughout the Zhob countryside. Pale would fight with the maliks, leave for the hills between Zhob and Afghanistan, and then descend back into Zhob to commit some outrage in order to attract the government's attention and force them to put pressure on the maliks to address his grievances. In one instance Pale held up the government mail truck near Kapip with two accomplices and shot eight of its passengers. Menon decided to appoint a jirga, or council of tribal elders to look into the case, and in keeping with their findings he imposed a heavy fine and enforced collective responsibility on the villagers of Kapip for not preventing Pale from committing the attack.

This method of maintaining law and order through the jirgas was necessary given that Baluchistan was ruled through an 'indirect system of administration'. This system had been pioneered by Colonel Robert Sandeman and much of the actual administration was left to the maliks who would have to enforce respect for the government amongst the tribes people of the region and maintain law and order. The government's direct authority was restricted to the cantonments and the lines of communication, for the protection of which they also relied on the maliks. Tribal custom prevailed, and the British Raj's system of land revenue collection and criminal laws such as the Indian Penal Code and Criminal Procedure Code never made it as far as Baluchistan. So when a murder took place Menon would appoint a jirga of three or four 'respectable individuals' from the tribe and frame the issues on which they had to take a decision. He would then withdraw from the proceedings and the jirga would speak with the accused and the complainant and anyone with a knowledge of the crime and then announce its verdict. If the jirga gave a guilty verdict Menon could still convict or acquit the accused, however if a not guilty verdict was reached then he was bound to acquit. If Menon thought the accused deserved to be convicted he would simply appoint a new jirga to look into the case.

Menon recalled that he could generally rely on jirga verdicts in cases which concerned land or money but he would have to tread more carefully in cases which involved women. Tribal law decreed that a man could kill his wife for 'siahkari' or 'secret business', which could amount to something much less than adultery. A simple smile at a neighbour or a glad eye could lead to murder. Menon came across cases in which a man would murder another man in the heat of the moment and then come back and murder his own wife in order to try to set up a defence of siahkari. Jirgas were favourably disposed to these pleas of siahkari, and even in cases in which Menon thought the accused was guilty he could not simply issue a verdict himself, and so as in other cases he would keep appointing jirgas until one returned what he thought to be the right verdict.

In keeping with the policy of non-interference in tribal matters the government did little to improve the standard of living of the tribal people and instead put as much money as possible into the pockets of the maliks. Each malik would be given a monthly allowance and would also receive a present whenever he came calling on the political agent. Menon would hold a little durbar twice a week, on Mondays and Thursdays between 10 am and 1 pm, sitting in his room with a bag of money which he would dole out to maliks who came to pay their respects. It was in these durbars that he was supposed to talk to the maliks and keep himself informed of events throughout Zhob.

Problems arose when the maliks were paid for the provision of services such as road protection which were not always carried out as well as they should have been. The maliks were expected to maintain a specified number of levies, or road protection units. However, they would most often just pocket the money provided to them, and the levies would only turn out to do their duty when a high official like the political agent came visiting. Sir Arthur Parsons wanted to reform the system and have the levies live in their levy posts and patrol the roads every day for which they would be paid directly rather than through the maliks. Not only would such a system affect the maliks' income, but it would also lower their prestige amongst the young men of their tribes who looked to them for a job. The maliks were coming to the brink of non-cooperation with the government when Menon stepped in to mediate. He persuaded Parsons to raise the maliks' regular allowance, and also explained to the maliks that there would be fewer grievances amongst their tribesmen over the embezzlement of levy salaries and the new system would work in their long term interest.

Menon's work in mediating the dispute over the levies was appreciated, but in the end he was lucky to leave his posting in Zhob alive. Under the traditional system the levies were led by jemadars, daffadars and havildars who passed their posts down to their sons. Parsons disrupted this system, insisting that these posts be chosen on the basis of merit rather than birth. One jemadar's son, Sher Jan was thus demoted to havildar and would often come to Menon to complain of the injustice done to him. Menon recommended that Sher Jan be appointed daffadar, but the boy was not satisfied and still wanted his father's jemadari back. Even after Menon left Zhob he would continue his complaints before the new agent, Major Humphrey Barnes, and one day during an interview in an office in Windsor Castle his patience ran out; he drew a revolver and shot the major dead. Major Barnes was not the first agent to be assassinated, two others had lost their lives before him and Menon also had a couple of close calls; he avoided an attempt on his life at Gul Kach where an outlaw was lying in wait for him, and in another instance a peon quickly disarmed a tribesman approaching Windsor Castle on horseback with the intent to kill the agent. Menon's children were also lucky to escape kidnapping when some tribesmen kidnapped the wrong Hindu children.

Menon would leave Fort Sandeman in October 1939, and held a durbar before he left. He recalled: "I put on my uniform, with helmet, sword and the King Jubilee medal all complete, made a speech in Pashtu and gave sanads and rewards to deserving Maliks and admonition to others." He then gave a farewell party which all the British officers of the town attended and thought "the British officers were sorry to see us leave" and "The Sardars and Maliks were equally sorry." He even recalled Jogizai Nawab and his rival Zarghun Khan escorting him and his family to the border of Zhob, embracing them in Pathan style, and bidding them goodbye with "tears in their eyes".

***

Keeping the restive Pathans of Baluchistan under control, or preventing Hindu-Muslim riots in small towns across India could be thought of as a standard part of a civil servant's job. These threats to order challenged their administrative skill in working within the law and judiciously using the force available to them, yet they did not create quite the moral dilemma that the political agitations of the Congress did. Most Indian officers were sympathetic to the nationalist cause and gave accounts of handling the civil disobedience campaigns with tact and good humour and a minimum of force. Typical of these accounts was one left by Dharma Vira; he had to deal with the satyagraha movement at the start of World War II as the jails overflowed with large numbers being imprisoned for what seemed to be technical offences.[cxliv] He thus suggested to his commissioner that it would be better not to arrest the satyagrahis and make martyrs of them. Vira's suggestion was met with some scepticism, and so he took the matter up to the Chief Secretary Frank Mudie, winning him over with the argument that if the protesters returned without being arrested they would only look ridiculous in the eyes of their followers. Congress leader Govind Pant was unimpressed, accusing Vira of "killing the movement". A compromise was then reached in which only "important people" were arrested.

One Indian officer however, left a more detailed and frank account of his role in propping up a British Raj on the brink of collapse.[cxlv] On the day that the Congress issued its 'Quit India' resolution in August 1942 Nagendra Baksi was sitting on the verandah of his collector's bungalow at Monghyr, Bihar trying to visualise the repercussions which the arrest of the Congress leadership would have around the country and the administrative steps which would need to be taken to maintain law and order. He sat down and began to work out an emergency scheme for the protection of essential communications and strategic installations. Anticipating that supplies of essential commodities could be cut off for an extended period, he formed a Council of Economic Affairs to ensure supplies for hospitals and jails and the public at large for at least one month.

Baksi then called an urgent meeting of the top officials of Monghyr, including his Joint Magistrate James Walmsley and his Superintendent of Police Chandra Jha. He put his apprehension that a serious state of affairs could develop quite quickly before the meeting and outlined the tentative emergency scheme which he had drawn up. The gathered officials did not seem to think there was much to worry about; the top Congress leaders were in jail, the Congress rank and file appeared demoralised and there was no sign of organised protest against the government. Baksi thought the country would not take the situation lying down however, and argued for putting the emergency scheme in place for a few days as a precaution. Colonel Leonard Brewester from the Ordinance Depot and Chandra Jha came to his support; they thought there would be no harm in some precautionary measures for a few days if Baksi so wished. Baksi had already made up his mind to implement the measures with or without the support of the officials, but was happy to have the key men on side.

Colonel Brewester released some officers and troops from guard duty at the Ammunition and Ordinance Depots, some military vehicles and Bren guns for Baksi's use. The Monghyr railway station, the jetty, and the power house were all put under armed guard. However, Baksi thought the best way to avoid using force on unruly crowds was to stop them from gathering in the first place and so he promulgated an Order under Section 144 of the Criminal Procedure Code; assemblies of more than five people were banned, a curfew was imposed between sunrise and sunset, and armed pickets prevented crowds entering the town during the day. It was war time and so street lights had been shaded and house owners had been instructed to keep their windows covered to not throw light out onto the street. But these orders had not been complied with, and so Baksi passed an order that any home owners who defied the order would be rounded up and placed under arrest at the town police station near the fort. There was an element of the old civil servant's bluff in Baksi's actions. The number of armed police and troops was completely inadequate in the town and armed patrols had already been sent to distant parts of the district. If residents were kept indoors during the day and darkness was enforced at night, the few vehicles doing the rounds of the town might create the impression of a larger force than the collector actually had at his disposal.

Baksi then drove out in the middle of the night beyond the town limits and saw a sign of things to come. Telegraph posts had been uprooted and wires had been tied to trees on either side of the road to prevent the movement of traffic. Baksi rushed back to the collector's bungalow but the telephones had gone dead. He then went to Chandra Jha's house and managed to call the members of the Emergency Council. They met the next morning and decided to further tighten up the precautionary measures. Between the 10th and

12th of August most of the railway tracks in Bihar had been dismantled, engines had been derailed, railway stations set on fire and signal towers destroyed. Railway wagons containing food supplies and ammunition for the war effort on the eastern front were broken open and looted. Police stations were also set on fire and policemen fled for their lives. Communications with the Sub Divisional Officers in North Bihar, the Commissioner at Bhagalpore and the Bihar Government at Patna had broken down leaving the administration on the verge of collapse.

British military officers were particularly furious with the disruption to the war effort and Baksi started to receive reports that British troops were burning villages near railway tracks and shooting Congress workers and villagers. As he was completely cut-off from his commissioner and the Bihar Government at Patna, Baksi issued a proclamation assuming all powers of the government and issued a series of ordinances for the safety of communications, collective fines and the evacuation of villages. Two mechanics of the Posts and Telegraphs Department were given the task of repairing the phone and telegraph lines connecting officials of the district, but no sooner would they repair a line than Congress workers would cut them elsewhere. A secret plan was then put into effect to repair some of the telephone wires from the uprooted posts at night and then connect them with the telephones of key government offices. During the day a show of repairing the regular telephone lines along the Monghyr-Jamalpur Road would continue to keep the Congress workers busy in cutting them.

In order to counter the Congress propaganda machine, the government printed the *Monghyr News* in English and Hindi. The English copy would be prepared at the collector's bungalow around midnight, whilst the Editor, Kedar Goenka would prepare the Hindi copy. Baksi tried to explain his position as district magistrate, and appealed to the citizens of

Monghyr for their support and co-operation. He mentioned his acquaintance with the Congress leaders Rajendra Prasad and Sri Krishna Sinha and stated that he was sure that they would agree with him that even under a National Government the district magistrate would have to do his duty to maintain law and order. He would leave it to the people to decide whether he had done so, but reminded them that not a single shot had been fired in Monghyr since the political movement had started.

Baksi then received a coded message from his Commissioner Bhalchandra Gokhale in Bhagalpore. The message had been carried by a constable who had taken two days to reach Monghyr and when decoded it read- "All District Headquarters isolated. Hooliganism uncontrollable approaching the Kacheri. Send for assistance from Patna at once." The constable told Baksi that the British men and women of Bhagalpore had taken shelter in the commissioner's bungalow and the 700 constables at the Police Training College had fled or actually joined the mobs which were threatening to burn down the kaccheri and loot the treasury. Baksi decided to call a late night meeting of the Emergency Council, but none of the civil or military officers were in favour of sending soldiers or police from Monghyr to Bhagalpore; there were already so few in Monghyr, besides which it did not reflect well on the administration at Bhagalpore that with their bigger armed police and 700 constables they could not even protect their own town. Baksi acknowledged the soundness of their reasoning but argued that his commissioner had asked for help, and as there was no chance of reinforcements from Patna he decided to send an armed force in a steamer to Bhagalpore the next morning.

Baksi telephoned Colonel Brewester later that night about his decision to send an armed force, accompanied by a magistrate who would provide civilian supervision, on a steamer to Bhagalpore. Early the next morning Baksi sent for the young magistrates of the district, told them the nature of the mission to Bhagalpore, and warned them that any who volunteered would have to face grave risk and attempt to keep 200 yards clear in the event of the armed force using their Bren guns to shoot any threatening mobs or boats. There were enough volunteers, and it was Muni Singh who was chosen for the task. The force reached the commissioner's bungalow without any resistance and helped to stabilise the situation before troops arrived from Patna a few days later.

A brief civilian-military stand-off did occur however, as news arrived of British troops from neighbouring Muzzaffarpur entering North Monghyr without Baksi's knowledge or permission. One group had set fire to the house of a senior Congress leader and another had shot some villagers and burned houses down near Barauni. Baksi consulted with the Monghyr station Commander Major Hope and then sent some troops lent by Colonel Brewester to North Monghyr with instructions to disarm the Muzzaffarpur troops if they did not leave Monghyr immediately. Baksi then met the Sub Area Commander of Muzzaffarpur, a brigadier, who objected to his interference in the troops' work in helping to suppress riots. Baksi informed him of the steps which had been taken in Monghyr with the agreement of civilian and military authorities to disarm his troops. Baksi then told the brigadier that if he was not satisfied he could go to the state government in Patna and urge them to declare Martial Law, which would divest him of his powers and responsibilities as a district magistrate in regulating the movements of the military in the aid of civil power.

***

During the days of the British Raj most Indians who left India's shores did so as labourers. They went out from India to other British colonies where the colonial masters could not get the locals to work for them. Indian labourers worked the mines and plantations, and built harbours and railways from the Caribbean to East and South Africa, South-East Asia and the islands of the Pacific. The journey was one way. Most would never return to their villages, and so the modern Indian diaspora was born. A smaller number would continue an older Indian tradition and follow the British to their far flung colonies as merchants, trading and lending money and building local businesses as part of a developing imperial commercial network.

It had been a long time however, since Indians went out into the world as representatives of the Indian state. Indian officers got their chance as they moved up the levels of the Indian Civil Service, taking up assignments as far afield as Europe, Africa and China. Given that Britain ruled so much of the world, they were often representing the Government of India in negotiations with other British colonies in what were, in essence, internal imperial matters. Much of their work revolved around protecting the interests of Indian labourers and merchants around the world and making sure that India got the best deal possible from international political and economic agreements.

Hiralal Patel was appointed Indian Trade Commissioner for Northern Europe in 1937 and took up his appointment in Hamburg at an office located on Alster Lake.[cxlvi] It was a small office, with a deputy trade commissioner, a stenographer who doubled as his private secretary and one typist clerk. The trade commissioner had to deal with complaints brought to him by Indian businessmen as well as deal with requests for information from European businessmen. Patel also had to keep the Government of India informed of economic developments which would affect India's interests and suggest ways to deal with them appropriately. He recalled that it was the second of these duties which kept him most busy; he had to establish the necessary contacts which would give him the supply of information he needed to report back to the Government of India. Patel then started to establish contacts with German businessmen and officials and began travelling to France, Holland and Belgium where he met the Indian diamond traders of Antwerp.

But Patel was in Hitler's Germany on the eve of World War II, and political developments quickly overtook economic ones. He was in Vienna when the Nazis marched in and happened to be staying in the same hotel in which the Austrian Chancellor Kurt Schuschnigg had been detained. Similarly, he was in Prague as Czechoslovakia was overrun by Hitler's army, and he managed to get out of Warsaw just before the Nazi invasion. In Germany Patel witnessed the aftermath of many pogroms against the Jews and saw first-hand the way in which Jewish businesses were being throttled. Speaking to Germans he felt that their sympathies lay with the Jewish families whom they had known for generations, but they kept their mouths shut in public out of fear. The Brown Shirts and Black Shirts were on the streets, and according to Patel the average German citizen could only look on without being able to help.

Patel packed his young family off to England, whilst he remained in Hamburg as the political situation deteriorated. His brief was to boost trade relations between the nations of northern Europe and India, but in the absence of industrial development in India he did not think that there was much scope to improve the dormant trading relationships with European countries; India had little to export besides agricultural produce, and in the absence of any programme for industrial development in India there was little need for industrial imports. Patel met the British Consul General in Hamburg, who informed him of economic conditions in Germany and advised him to meet the British Ambassador in Berlin, who in turn set up a meeting with the German Commerce & Industry Minister. Patel worked off the notes of his predecessor, who was a senior Indian Civil Service officer, and continued his practice of sending a monthly report on commercial and economic developments in the region. He accompanied Sir Zafarullah Khan, Member of the Viceroy's Executive Council in a meeting with the Commerce Minister. He thought of Khan as "our Minister" and was impressed with his handling of his brief. The German minister had come similarly prepared and Patel was pleasantly surprised, it was one of the more fruitful meetings amongst the many he had attended.

In 1925 K.P.S. Menon became the first Indian officer of the Indian Civil Service to join the Indian Political Service, India's nascent diplomatic corps.[cxlvii] He had served in Hyderabad, the North West Frontier and Baluchistan, and represented the Government of India in Ceylon and Zanzibar before taking over as Agent General of the Government of India in China from Sir Zafarullah in 1943. Chungking was thought of as a hard post with an "execrable" climate, lacking in basic amenities and was likely a target of bombing during the summer time. It was, along with Washington one of India's first semi-diplomatic posts, and the Government of India had agreed to Menon's request to take his family with him. Menon flew from Calcutta to Chungking in September 1943; it was known as one of the most dangerous air routes in the world and he remembered it as "a thrilling experience". Menon and his family flew over the Brahmaputra river, the tea plantations of Assam, refuelled at Dinjon on the north eastern edge of India and then flew over the mountains and jungles of Burma, all the while sniffing at oxygen masks. They made one more halt at Kunming in south-west China before making their way through the fog and finally landing in Chungking.

In much the same way as Menon had been underwhelmed upon arriving at Oxford as a young man during World War I, Chungking did not present the colourful pagodas and wonders of Chinese architecture he had expected. It was, after all, an improvised war time capital, dark and grey, bombed and battered. Menon presented his credentials on 10 October 1943, the day that Chiang Kai-shek was sworn in as President of China. The inauguration ceremony took place at 10 am and the President and Madame Chiang received him at noon. At the reception in the evening his position of 'Agent-General' caused some confusion however. According to the Vienna Protocol he was neither an ambassador, nor minister nor charge d'affaires. It had not been envisaged that a colony would have diplomatic representatives abroad, and although he was given treatment equivalent to a minister, the Turkish charge d'affaires managed to push his way ahead of him to shake hands with President and Madame Chiang.

Menon started to gather his thoughts and impressions of war time China and wrote a dispatch to the Government of India about the influential Soong family entitled 'The Song of Soongs'. The Minister for Foreign Affairs, Soong Tse-ven invited Menon for lunch after he had presented his credentials. Menon thought that the lunch was excellent but the minister was lacking in manners. He kept his guests waiting, arrived without a word of apology and did not even ask his guests to sit down. The Norwegian ambassador had hardly finished his cup of coffee before he was hustled out by the vice minister. Menon thought that this could not be typical of Chinese behaviour and would have liked to put it down to the ways of a powerful political clan.

Accompanied by his wife and daughter, Menon then went to tea with Soong's sister, Soong Mei-ling, or Madame Chiang. He found her charm quite artificial but admired the way she could move with ease and grace in conversation on topics as varied as saris and international politics. He met Soong Ai-ling, or Madame Kung, another Soong sister the following day. Menon thought that she was "very worldly, with an altogether false sense of values" who had married Kung Hsiang-hsi for his wealth. He recoiled when she suggested that Gandhi was following a wrong path; Madame Kung thought it would be better to lift peasants up to the level of the elites, rather than have elites descend to the level of the peasants. Kung, who had been finance minister for a decade asked Menon about the Nizam of Hyderabad, and Menon thought that he might just be trying to compete with the world's richest man in the unbridled accumulation and display of wealth.

Menon noted that whilst the Soongs and Kungs wielded money and power, the ruling Party's ideology was shaped by the Chen brothers, Chen Ko-fu and Chen Li-fu. Menon viewed their ideology as an odd mixture of Confucius, Sun Yat Sen and Chiang Kai-shek. At a meeting Chen Li-fu explained to Menon that nationalism was like geometry; the nation was created at the intersection of the vertical line of history and the horizontal line of geography. Menon was not impressed with Chen, whom he dubbed a "party fanatic" who was overly proud of China's historical achievements; he claimed that Einstein's theory of relativity had already been discovered by ancient Chinese scientists.

Menon also had to revise many of his cherished ideals of Chinese civilisation. In India people would speak glibly of the spiritual affinity between the two cultures, but on experiencing China he felt that India actually had much more in common with European civilisation in spiritual matters. The Chinese were not other-worldly, they had put the question of another world to Confucius in ancient times but he declined to provide an answer. And so they preferred to focus on the facts of this life rather than theories of the next. Buddhism had passed through Chinese thought, but the continuum of Chinese philosophy was designed to ease human relationships in this world as much as possible. Unlike Indians, the Chinese were not obsessed with religion, and were, in the end, materialists. Menon did not think that most Chinese had any religion at all, but in some cases there could be three or four religions followed by members of the one family, and an individual could follow one religion in his personal life, another in his public life and a third in his family life.

When the war eventually ended, Braj Nehru was sent to a reparations conference in Paris in September 1945 which met to assess the German industrial installations which would be removed and relocated elsewhere.[cxlviii] Each of the representatives would make their claim to a share of the loot based on the damage their country had suffered during the war and their contributions to the war effort. Nehru went as a member of a three member Indian delegation led by H.V.R. Iyengar, the Joint Secretary of the Department of Commerce and Industry. It was his first experience both of an international conference and travelling abroad by air. When he got to Paris he was asked by New Delhi to represent India at a conference on refugees, but without any specific instructions he sat on the Indian seat for two days without any idea of what to do, besides enjoying a sumptuous lunch put on by the French foreign minister.

The reparations conference was presided over by Jacques Reuff, who later became Governor of the Bank of France. It was Nehru's first impression of international diplomacy and as expected the delegations stated their cases for their share of reparations. But Nehru was surprised by how leisurely the proceedings were; they would start late and were slowed down by the need for translations. He quickly picked up on the diplomatic practice of complimenting the previous speaker, emphasising agreement and then tearing their case to pieces. Details would be discussed in the committee room and after three months of discussions an International Reparations Agency was established. India was to send a team of engineers to Germany to select industrial installations to be relocated to India, but before the plans were put into place the Cold War had started and the consensus on returning Germany to a primitive agrarian economy had been reconsidered.

***

Whether at home or abroad Indians in the Indian Civil Service were finding it increasingly uncomfortable serving the British Raj whilst sympathising with the Congress, and so found ever more creative ways of reconciling the contradiction of their situation. In his autobiography Jawaharlal Nehru recalled the 'parlour firebrands' from his university days at the Cambridge Majlis who would use extreme language whilst discussing Indian politics and who even spoke in admiration of the political violence which was just starting after the Partition of Bengal.[cxlix] He noted how most went on to serve the British Raj as Indian Civil Service officers and High Court judges and how few took part in Indian political movements.

K.P.S. Menon was just the type of young man Nehru was referring to. Menon recalled being filled with indignation at events in India whilst at Oxford as a student, particularly the massacre at Jallianwala Bagh.[cl] He appreciated the irony of the situation though, and remembered that the forum for letting off steam was the Oxford Majlis, where the undergraduates would make patriotic speeches, seditious to the British, all the while studying for the Indian Civil Service examination, a situation which did not strike them as "particularly odd". Even after passing the Indian Civil Service examination Menon kept making vehement speeches and writing articles against British rule in India for which he received a summons from the India Office. He had written an article in *Indus* in which he argued that India should not remain within the Empire. When questioned by two members of the Secretary of State's Council in London he made the fine distinction between Empire and Commonwealth, arguing that India should remain within the Commonwealth as an equal partner. It was a sign of the times that the members allowed him to sign his covenant with the British monarch and begin his career in the Indian Civil Service.

Mangat Rai imbibed the ideals of the nationalist movement at St Stephen's College, Delhi.[cli] He remembered that "the national movement was the very air that every student breathed in the thirties". Mangat Rai's impression of the Indian Civil Service in the late 1930s was one of disloyalty, albeit discreet, among its Indian officers. None of those who were willing to talk about politics advocated the continuation of the British Raj, yet on the surface there was every indication of loyalty and silence on public occasions and in social contacts. According to Mangat Rai, the more educated the Indian officer, the greater the zeal for Independence and also the greater the discretion in political matters.

Ronald Noronha made no attempt to gloss over his service to the British Raj, calling himself a "mercenary" purely attracted to the salary, serving the Raj loyally "within the limits imposed by a robustly practical conscience."[clii] He began to witness the winds of change by 1940 however, for prior to the formation of the Congress Ministries in 1937 the practice for local elites was to show public respect for the Raj with the hope of an award or title. The Congress Ministries changed that, and local notables began parading their patriotism and any link, however tenuous, to the civil disobedience movement. Noronha observed that by the time the Congress Ministry had ended and the governor returned to rule, all of local society had realised that the end of the Raj was near, a situation in which Indian Civil Service officers had to "ride two horses with one bottom". By the early 1940s Indian officers were increasingly asserting their nationalist views in arguments with their British colleagues who expressed some surprise, but also sympathy, influenced as they were by the left wing politics of British universities in the 1930s.

***

By the 1940s a new Indian officer class had emerged which had been systematically Anglicised from the start. A few among these officers attended public schools in England, the training grounds of empire, and imbibed the public school ethic at the heart of the Indian Civil Service culture first hand in school houses and dormitories and on playing fields. Many more passed through the gentlemen factories of Oxford and Cambridge and went on to civil service probationary training, sitting in classes in which they were taught the British method of ruling India alongside their English colleagues. When they reached India the first among them were further instructed in the processes and procedures of the government office and duties of an officer by old British collectors. There are no accounts of rebellion against the system, all the young Indian officers knew what they had signed up for and eagerly absorbed both the culture and codes of the service. There was no snipe shooting or Latin verse in Astad Gorwala's daily routine in the Larkana district in Sind, however he was admired by his understudy Hiralal Patel for his embodiment of the values of the Indian Civil Service which had guided generations of British officers over the previous century. New Sahibs were being brought into the system, and they were supposed to be as much replicas of their British predecessors as possible, bearers of their spirit, their methods and their ways of working.

Just like their British predecessors, Indian officers of the Indian Civil Service would have to perform all the functions of the elite service of the state, keeping the British Raj functioning as it always had. They collected its land revenue, became masters of the government office, dispensed justice according to British penal codes, represented India abroad, kept the Government of India informed of developments around the world, and sat in ever expanding secretariats in the provincial capitals pushing files between departments. They even used all the techniques and resources available from the mighty state when law and order was challenged and Indians threatened the authority of the Raj.

It was when the threat to law and order came from the civil disobedience movements of the Congress that Indian officers would be reminded that they were, in the end, servants of the British Government. They had signed covenants with the British monarch and they reported to the Secretary of State for India in London, and so they had to find a way to justify their position to themselves and their fellow Indians. Most took the view that someday India would be independent, and the country would need trained and able civil servants and they would be those officers when the time came. Of course this assumed that other Indians would have to undertake the massive task of running a successful nationalist movement and wresting control from the British to achieve that Independence. Nagendra Baksi touched on this theme in the tense days of the Quit India movement. He appealed to the people of his district in Bihar, asking them to understand that even under a nationalist government the district collector would be expected to do his duty and maintain law and order and he had done so with a minimum of force. The only problem was, that by doing his duty, he was a key figure preventing a nationalist government from coming to power. Baksi was doing his duty, and what was often referred to as 'duty' in English could be interpreted as a modern English word used to communicate the older Hindu idea of 'dharma'. The Indian officers of the Indian Civil Service were doing their dharma, one different from that of the nationalists in the Congress. And just as in the ancient epics, if everyone did their dharma, the ideal state would prevail in the end.

As the 1940s progressed and British power in India declined, Indian officers began to occupy a political and social netherworld. Neither were their hearts with British rule, nor did they work with their fellow Indians in the nationalist movement. Yet they skilfully rode both horses with one bottom, never breaking from the service, nor fully reaching out and seeking an accommodation with the Congress. They just continued doing their jobs at increasingly senior positions in the state, uncertain about what might lie in store for them when the transfer of power came.

Five
War Veterans

Military might was the source of British power in India. A civil service which collected land revenue and maintained law and order could only be developed in the aftermath of British military victories across India during the late 18th and early 19th centuries. Those victories were made possible by the recruitment of Indian sepoys who were led into battle by British officers of the East India Company's armies. The Company began recruiting Rajputs, Bhumihars and Pathans from Bihar and Oudh into its Bengal Army as early as 1757. This new army was successful at the Battle of Plassey that year, and a similar force of Indian sepoys was raised in Bombay which fought in the first Maratha War from 1775 before defeating Tipu Sultan in Mysore in 1799. A Madras Army was also raised and put onto the battlefield during the Carnatic Wars in the mid 18th century before being used to suppress internal rebellions in Madras in the 1830s. These presidency armies went on to be deployed in key campaigns in Sind, Punjab and Afghanistan during the first decades of the 19th century as the British Raj expanded through the north and west of India.

By the eve of World War I the Indian Army was the largest volunteer army in the world. It was made up of 107 single battalion and 11 two battalion regiments of infantry, 38 regiments of cavalry, a joint infantry-cavalry unit, 12 batteries of mountain artillery, 3 regiments of sappers and miners, and could be reinforced with the armies of the Indian princes and the regiments of British volunteers.[cliii] Herbert Kitchener had been appointed Commander in Chief in 1903 and set about reorganising the old 19th century colonial army into a more modern fighting force. He renumbered the regiments from the Bengal, Bombay and Madras Armies in a single sequence, abolished the Indian Staff Corps, established a Staff College at Quetta, made regiments ready for service anywhere in India, made a tour of duty on the North West Frontier mandatory, and higher formations such as brigades and divisions were all maintained during peacetime, ready for action should war break out.[cliv] Although much reorganisation and modernisation occurred during Kitchener's time before World War I, the army, like the other elite services of the Raj remained unreformed in one crucial respect. The 200 year old structure of the Indian Army in which the British officer led the Indian sepoy had not changed in any significant way.

Between the Mutiny of 1857 and the outbreak of World War I, as the British Raj grew to the peak of its power, the racial ideas which floated about in the debates over Indians in the Indian Civil Service actually became codified in the recruitment of Indian soldiers to the Indian Army. A theory of the 'Martial Races' emerged which identified those Indian communities which could provide the most physically fit and loyal soldiers to the Indian Army. The theory was based on ideas about climate, geography, history and culture, and became a dogma of the British military establishment until the end of British rule and beyond. The martial race theory was most concerned with classifying Indian communities for their usefulness in providing soldiers to the Indian Army though; in the late 19th century the thought of inducting Indian officers into the army was not yet taken seriously.

World War I and the subsequent Montagu-Chelmsford reforms would force the issue of the Indianisation of the officer corps of the Indian Army higher up the agenda of the British policy establishment. Yet Indianisation of the Indian Army presented a conundrum for British policy makers. It could only, ultimately, mean the handover of their military power, the means by which Britain had conquered India in the first place and continued its rule, to Indians. In keeping with the customs of British bureaucracy, British authorities in Delhi decided to form a committee to look into the matter. The British Government formed its own committees in London. Subcommittees were formed and Delhi's committees could not convince London and London's committees did not impress Delhi and the 1920s passed by with the puzzle of finding a way to Indianise the Indian Army whilst maintaining British control of India remaining unsolved.

One small start to Indianisation did begin after World War I however. Ten cadetships to the Royal Military College at Sandhurst were reserved for Indian boys each year. These cadetships tended to attract upper middle class and aristocratic boys and the failure rates were high to start with. As the 1920s progressed the demand of moderate Indian politicians in the Indian Legislative Assembly in Delhi evolved into a call for the establishment of an 'Indian Sandhurst'. It was thought that a local institution would be able to train a larger number of Indian cadets who would have to undergo less financial and emotional strain than in the prevailing system in which they had to travel to England for their training. Eventually, after a decade of non-cooperation and civil disobedience, and much official reluctance, the Raj conceded an Indian Sandhurst at the Round Table Conference in London, and the Indianisation of the officer corps of the Indian Army began in earnest with the establishment of the Indian Military Academy at Dehra Dun in 1932.

***

The idea of the martial races came about in the aftermath of 1857 as the British sought to assess the causes of the Mutiny. The Peel Commission concluded that the British had recruited to the Indian Army indiscriminately, in that they had been unaware of which Indian communities possessed true martial attributes. The Brahmins were thought to be the culprits behind the events of 1857; scheming and dishonest, they had come to dominate the Bengal Army and disrupt traditional caste roles. The Sikhs, Gurkhas, Rajputs and Marathas on the other hand had all remained loyal, which demonstrated their martial culture. They accepted the military basis of British rule and understood ideas such as honour, loyalty and duty.

Three criteria came to be employed to determine which Indian communities were truly martial; climate, culture and physique. The sub-tropical climate of eastern and southern India was said to have a debilitating effect on the martial spirit, whilst years of prolonged peace had also softened the fighting qualities of once war like communities around India. The more temperate climate of north India where the traces of the Aryans could still be found was thought to produce both a better physique and a greater energy for combat. Army recruitment handbooks describing the different recruiting pools across India were full of references to sturdy builds, the length of limbs, fairness of skin, purity of descent, and the shape of noses. In the late 19th century 16 groups were classified as martial races and each group was attributed a collective personality; the Gurkhas were loyal and independent, hated Indians and looked up to the British, whilst the Jats were manly, unpretentious and jovial.

There did seem to be an element of making the story up as it went along however. The Rajputs were thought to be the descendants of the Kshatriyas, and something like the original ancestors of the martial races. During the Islamic invasions of India the Rajputs were said to have fled to Nepal where they married the local women to produce the Gurkhas. Others fled into the Punjab hills and became the Garwalis. Some accepted Islam and became Rangars and married Muslim women in the Punjab to make the Punjabi Musalmans. A different version of the story was that nomadic warriors from Central Asia had settled in India and fought against the Buddhists for which they were rewarded by the Brahmins with

Rajput status. Those who did not maintain their new caste duties were downgraded to the status of Jats. Later many of the Jats and Rajputs converted to Islam and became Punjabi Musalmans. Likewise, the Dogras were actually Rajputs who had taken to the Himalayas long ago. The British enjoyed the romance of Rajput folklore, whilst Rajput status was also held in high esteem in Indian society by Hindus and Muslims alike which meant that each of the martial races could be satisfied with their origin story.

The experiences of Field Marshal Frederick Roberts, the most famous British military hero of his time only seemed to support the emerging martial race theory. Roberts was born in India in 1832, the son of General Sir Abraham Roberts who had been commanding a British regiment of the Bengal Army. He was sent to England as a child and educated at Eton and Sandhurst and then returned to India in 1851 to follow in his father's footsteps and serve in the army of the British East India Company. At the end of his career he wrote a monumental account of his service entitled *Forty One Years in India*. It was a memoir in two volumes, the first of which provided a detailed account of Roberts's involvement in the British effort to put down the Mutiny of 1857. The second volume chronicled the emerging Russian threat to India's frontiers and Roberts's own audacious march from Kabul to Kandahar during the British victory in the Second Anglo-Afghan War in 1880. In both cases he relied on the loyalty, courage and soldierly skill of both the Gurkhas and the Sikhs.

Roberts was a household name in Britain in the 1890s and when his *Forty One Years in India* was published in 1897 it went on to become a best seller. Neither crude scientific theories nor fabulous origin stories were needed to prop up his theory of the martial races. It was Roberts's experience on the battlefields of Delhi and Lucknow and Kabul and Kandahar that gave him the authority to declare which Indian communities could fight and which could not. He had ended his Indian days as Commander in Chief in Madras, and his thoughts turned to how he could make his army "as perfect a fighting machine as it was possible to make it." He thought the first step towards achieving this goal was to alter the recruitment pattern to the army. Roberts wanted to reduce the intake of Hindustani soldiers in Bengal, the Tamils and Telegus in Madras and the Mahrattas in Bombay. He thought it was difficult to get his proposals accepted however, due to the prevailing belief amongst British officials that a balance needed to be struck between the three presidency armies. But more frustrating for Roberts was the belief that many British decision makers held that "one Native was as good as another for the purposes of war."

Roberts argued that with the doubling of British troops and the reduction of Indian sepoys over the previous decades there was no longer any danger from large scale recruitment from a smaller number of Indian communities. The chances of another mutiny had been reduced and the more pressing need was to recruit Indian soldiers who could be relied on to take on "a European foe". He explained to his British readers that whilst the English and Irish and Scots all shared a similar level of courage, which meant that the superiority of one regiment over another in the British Army was generally a matter of training, the same was not true in India. There could be no comparison between "the warlike races of northern India" and the "effeminate peoples of the south". He did not think the whole Indian Army as it was constituted could be relied on in a time of war. He also spoke for the sanctity of the British officer-Indian sepoy relationship and argued for more British officers to be given to Indian regiments in time of war. Roberts admired many qualities in the Indian soldier, but leadership was not among them; "history and experience teach us that eastern races (fortunately for us), however brave and accustomed to war, do not possess the qualities that go to make leaders of men."

Field Marshall Roberts's early difficulties in convincing his military and civilian establishment of the need to change the regional balance within the army were somewhat exaggerated however. He came to have great influence over military policy during his last days in India, and even for many years after. As a result, army recruitment saw a huge shift from the south and west and towards the north and north-west of India during the late 19th and early 20th century. The number of Gurkha battalions was quadrupled, the number of battalions from Punjab was doubled, battalions from Madras were reduced to just a quarter their former strength, and the number from Bombay was halved. By the eve of World War I roughly three-quarters of the Indian Army came to be recruited from the designated 16 Martial Races of India.[clv]

***

As on all the other high tables of the Raj, there were always a few British liberals who questioned the prevailing order and argued for greater Indian participation in the institutions of the state. In the late 19th century one lone British military bureaucrat tried to take on a British military hero and a sceptical establishment, arguing in favour of admitting Indians to the officer corps of the Indian Army. He, like liberals throughout the Raj, thought that English education could turn Indian aristocrats into officers and gentlemen fit for service in the Indian Army.

It was General Sir George Chesney, Military Secretary to the Government of India, who raised the idea of opening up the officer class of the army to Indians to the Commander in Chief General Sir Donald Stewart in January 1885. Chesney had been an army engineer and had spent much of his career in India on attachment to the Public Works Department where he worked closely with subordinate Indian engineers. With Indians beginning to enter the civil service and the higher judiciary, Chesney thought it natural to offer Indian aristocrats the opportunity for higher service in the military.[clvi] These Indian aristocrats were Indian royals and landowners of martial stock who had supported the British in military conflicts in the recent past. They were seen as a bulwark of support for British rule and crucial to the expansion of British interests in India. They had been marginalised in the government by the rising English educated middle class and they needed an outlet for service in keeping with their status and heritage.

Chesney suggested that Queen's Commissions in the army would be the best such outlet, but in preparation Indian aristocrats would have to be first educated in English and trained at one of the recently established Chief's Colleges.[clvii] Chesney realised that racial distinctions were much stronger in the army than in the other services and so he recommended that the Indian officer go in as the junior of his regiment to avoid the situation in which any British soldier would have to serve under him. If the initial experiment was a success more Indians would be inducted into a regiment until it was completely officered by Indians.

General Stewart supported Chesney's ideas and sent them up to the Viceroy's Executive Council which then forwarded them to the secretary of state in London. But in the process the Government of India altered Chesney's plan. Rather than a single regiment, two regiments, one infantry and the other cavalry would receive Indian officers, but these would be special units apart from the regular army. The Government of India argued that it was doing so to spare Indian aristocrats the caste indignity of serving alongside British officers. But the more delicate issue was the possibility of British officers shunning Indians on racial grounds.[clviii] In the Government of India's plan the Indian officers would be appointed on the basis of character, social standing, military fitness and personal qualifications rather than compete for places through examinations.

The Secretary of State John Wodehouse, the Earl of Kimberley, was cautious in approaching the Government of India's proposal, seeing it for the "organic change" to the army that it was. Kimberley sought the opinions of 22 senior members of the British military establishment and then sent an ambiguous reply to the Government of India. Whilst broadly supporting the sentiment behind inducting Indian officers, the special units scheme needed to be reconsidered in the light of the concerns which had been brought to his attention.[clix] With the events of 1857 still in living memory, there was a concern that any army units not under firm British control would be prone to revolt. It was thought that one of the reasons that the Mutiny had not been successful was the lack of trained Indian officers to lead the way. Moreover, British officers would always be needed to maintain the efficiency and discipline of any unit. Concerns were also raised over the prospect of any British soldier ever having to serve under an Indian. It was also unclear whether there was even any real demand among the Indian aristocracy for such a scheme. There were of course concerns over the scheme's potential cost. Kimberley then proposed his own plan. He suggested that the experiment start with the two regiments already approved to be raised by the Bengal Army, and that they be combined into a single corps under the command of a British officer and sent to the North West Frontier.

General Stewart had been succeeded as Commander in Chief in India by Frederick Roberts, who did not like the look of Kimberley's plan. Roberts argued that the true martial races, rather than Indian aristocrats, would make for better officer material in the distant future. But as yet the average Indian sepoy was unambitious and only wanted to serve without punishment from his British officer before collecting his pension and retiring to a quiet life in his village.[clx] Roberts also felt that he knew the mind of the British officer who thought that the Indian soldier was morally and physically inferior and who would never submit to an Indian in a position of authority.

In addition, Indian officers, with their caste sensibilities, would remain aloof from their British colleagues which would affect cohesion within their units. On the other hand, they might be inclined to socialise too much with soldiers of their own religion, blurring the officer-sepoy distinction. Roberts came up with his own plan: some of the best Viceroy's Commissioned Officers, the intermediate rank of Indians between British officers and Indian sepoys, would be appointed to security levies for patrolling duties on the North West Frontier.

Viceroy Dufferin suggested that honorary Queen's Commissions be granted to outstanding Viceroy's Commissioned Officers, something which Roberts was able to agree to.[clxi] In August 1887 Dufferin replied to the India Office explaining that Stewart and Kimberley's schemes could not be implemented due to financial constraints. Instead, he put forward his own proposal for honorary ranks for Indians which would have all the status of regular ranks, besides command.[clxii] The Viscount Cross, who was the new secretary of state in London objected to Dufferin's plan on the grounds that honorary ranks would only emphasise Indian inferiority rather than address Indian aspirations.[clxiii] He proposed that Viceroy's Commissioned Officers should only be granted honorary commissions extra-regimentally as orderlies or aides de camp. Cross also suggested that they be employed in the Indian Army Reserve as District Reserve and Recruiting Officers where their example would be beneficial to recruitment.

Chesney had become the Military Member on the Viceroy's Executive Council and thought that the pressure building up from the Congress and the Indian press had only made the necessity of his original plan more urgent.[clxiv] He came up with a new plan which would meet the aspirations of both the Viceroy's Commissioned Officers and the landed aristocracy; he called for the creation of a military college in India in which

Jamadars as well as Indian aristocrats would receive an English education. Cadets so trained would then receive Queen's Commissions in the Indian Army. In order to overcome the standard objections to Indians commanding British officers, rather than Indianising regiments gradually, a certain section of the Indian Army would be officered by Indians from the start. Chesney also thought that cadets should be selected on the basis of 'promise and character' rather than through examination.

Chesney knew that Roberts would oppose his plan and so he sneaked it into the Viceroy's Council meeting whilst Roberts was away and managed to get it approved. Roberts received news of the developments and made sure that Dufferin delayed deliberations until he could submit his own opinion. When Roberts did submit his opinion he accused Chesney of getting carried away by the seditious Indian press and failing to take into account the political and military implications of his proposal.[clxv] Chesney had not understood the intrinsic racial difference between the Englishman and the Indian; whilst the sepoy was no doubt brave, the Indian ultimately lacked leadership qualities. Roberts repeated his argument that British officers would never accept such moves as "The youngest British recruit thinks himself infinitely superior as a soldier to the highest born native in the land." British officers, being gentlemen, would be able to conceal their discomfort in times of peace but never under the strain of battle. British troops would revolt and the whole edifice of the British military in India would collapse. If Indians were found to be incompetent it would be difficult to remove them without a public backlash. Furthermore, if too high an educational standard was imposed on Jamadars the reliable martial races would start to avoid army service. Besides which, according to Roberts, staff training for Indians would give them access to the internal security workings of the Raj and they may end up selling British secrets to the Russians. Roberts managed to regain the support of the Viceroy's Council and Chesney's proposal was once again rejected. Chesney did make more attempts to institute English military education for Indians, only to be blocked by Roberts each time. In April 1893 he retired and returned to England.

In June 1900 Viceroy Curzon wrote a Memorandum on Commissions for Indians in which he raised the issue again after it had been lying dormant in British policy circles. He argued in favour of such commissions, but wanted to emphasise that the sons of the educated middle class were the last type of officer that the government would want to recruit under any new scheme. In the face of opposition, the following year he established the Imperial Cadet Corps at Meerut and Dehra Dun and in 1905 four graduates of the corps were awarded a modified commission in His Majesty's Indian Native Land Forces. Many more who were trained in the following years either abandoned plans for a military career or returned to their State Forces. As Curzon had envisaged, the commission was for aristocrats rather than middle class boys and was intended to be an outlet for a naturally loyal aristocracy for whom other types of service were felt to be demeaning. These officers were only appointed to supernumenary duty to avoid commanding British officers and when on regimental duty with the Indian Army they were only squadron or company commanders. Curzon had in fact advocated that Indians be eligible for King's Commissions in 1903 but Frederick Roberts, still fit and active, defeated his proposal.

Curzon's Imperial Cadet Corps was a failure. In 1904 not a single Rajput, that most idealised martial race, came forward for service. General Sir O'Moore Creagh began to call for further responsibility for Indian officers only to be opposed by General Herbert Kitchener; nobody should think that he was completely opposed to progress, but capturing the military establishment's sense of the issue Kitchener maintained "we must move slowly and on well considered lines."[clxvi] In 1911 the

Indian General Staff put down a tentative guideline for Indianisation of the army officer corps. The proposal suggested removing racial distinctions in rank or service matters between Indian and British officers. Selection would be by nomination on the basis of status rather than open competition and early education would be in England followed by the course at Sandhurst. On obtaining their commissions Indians would be assigned to a British regiment for one year and would be eligible to serve in all units of the cavalry and infantry rather than being relegated to special units. The scheme would start with the award of ten commissions a year. Robert Crewe-Milnes, the Earl of Crewe and Secretary of State for India largely accepted these recommendations, with the exception that separate native regiments would absorb the new officers so that Indians would not command British officers.[clxvii]

During the first half of 1917, Secretary of State Chamberlain, amidst his calls for a declaration from London on self-government in India repeatedly urged the War Cabinet to agree to the principle of admission of Indians to the commissioned ranks of the army.[clxviii] The War Cabinet then finally conceded the principle, and worked from the General Staff's 1911 guidelines, but it did insist that the appointments would have to be through an examination or nomination after service in the ranks. And so, after almost 40 years of internal debate, the first small step toward the Indianisation of the army's officer corps was taken and a new policy was implemented in which Indian boys would be able to compete for ten King's Commission cadetships each year to the Royal Military College at Sandhurst.

***

The performance of the Indian Army in World War I had been damaging the reputation of the Raj in both India and Britain. An Army in India Committee was established in 1919 under

Reginald Brett, the Viscount Esher to investigate the issues before the Indian Army with a view to serious reform. The Esher Committee would be just the first of over a dozen committees examining reform of the Indian Army throughout the 1920s and early 1930s, all of which would try to find ways to give the appearance of Indianising the officer corps of the Indian Army, without actually doing so.

The Esher Committee did touch upon the need for broad reforms of the Indian Army but ended up limiting itself to matters of service conditions which would keep British officers and Indian jawans content and loyal in the uncertain political conditions of the time. As in the Indian Civil Service, there was a sense of dissatisfaction among the British officer corps of the Indian Army over service conditions, and there was a growing reluctance of Sandhurst graduates to opt for a career in India. The trend was most noticeable among those British families which had a long history of service in India. The committee concluded that improvements in pay, allowances, travel, health care and accommodation were all necessary to attract British officers to the Indian Army once again. The experience of World War I had also altered the social and cultural horizons of Indian soldiers. When they returned to India rising prices began to hurt and so the committee recommended increasing pay for Viceroy's Commissioned Officers. The Esher Committee skirted the issue of Indianising the officer corps, largely maintained the ideology of the martial races and the recruitment patterns which it supported, and even baulked at abolishing corporal punishment. Indian members of the committee argued for the establishment of an Indian Sandhurst, but in the end agreed with the majority which came to the conclusion that the time had not yet come.

The fact that the two Indian members of the Esher Committee, Sir Krishna Gupta and Sir Umar Hayat Khan were so divided on key issues did not help in breaking new ground.

Sir Krishna, a former Indian Civil Service officer argued that Dominion status would be incomplete without Indian officers in the army. He wanted to do away with the dogma of the martial races and argued that the only way to achieve economy without impairing efficiency would be to gradually open up the superior ranks of the army to Indian officers. Sir Umar however, was a Punjabi zamindar, and represented the interests of the Muslims of Punjab, amongst the favourite martial races of the British. Sir Umar echoed the old British line that military tradition could not be compromised simply for the sake of reform, and the right type of officer could only be trained at Sandhurst. Drawing even deeper on British anxieties he warned of the threat of the Russians colluding with Indian revolutionaries to challenge the might of the Raj. According to Sir Umar, the time and tested formula of martial race sepoys led by British officers needed to be maintained to ward off both foreign aggression and domestic conspiracies.

The first Indian Legislative Assembly of the reforms era sat in Delhi in February and March of 1921, just as the recommendations of the Esher Committee were published. On 17 February 1921 Sir P.S. Sivaswamy Aiyer, a former Advocate General of Madras, led the charge of the Indian members who wanted to see the Indianisation of the army's officer corps, a reduction of military expenditure, control on the use of Indian forces for imperial purposes, a reduction in the number of British troops, and the establishment of an Indian Sandhurst. Sir Sivaswamy moved 15 resolutions in response to the Esher Committee Report and, invoking the spirit of Montagu's August Declaration, he questioned the government over whether it was committed to the "increasing association of Indians in every branch of the military organisation and administration." The Military Member, Sir Godfrey Fell then invoked the old British escape clause; the government was of course committed to such a policy, but "to the extent to which Indians show themselves to be qualified."

The Indian Legislative Assembly then formed its own committee to look into the report of the Esher Committee. The Legislative Assembly's committee was chaired by Tej Bahadur Sapru, a leader of the new Liberal Party, and it reported back to the Assembly on 21 March 1921. The committee detailed its recommendations in the form of 15 proposals which were then formally moved in the house by Sir Sivaswamy. The resolutions were a list of nationalist demands and focused on restricting the use of the army to the defence of India and maintaining internal order, increasing civilian control of the army and restricting the interchange of British officers between the British and Indian Armies. The committee also recommended that middle class boys be encouraged to enter the officer corps of the army, a minimum of 25% of King's Commissions each year be given to Indians and an Indian Sandhurst be established. Whilst moving the resolution Sir Sivaswamy spoke of the humiliation which Indians felt at being reduced by their own army to "hewers of wood and drawers of water". India had produced great generals in the past, and it was difficult to believe that such talent and capacity had been lost entirely. He complained that the army gave too much credence to aristocratic birth and martial race theory and until these grievances were removed Indians would not be able to "walk with their heads erect among the peoples of the earth." The resolutions were moved at the end of the legislative session when the government did not have a majority present in the chamber and had to be passed almost without modification. However, the government did manage to get the resolution relating to Indianisation of the officer corps altered with the help of a single vote from a member representing landed interests. They combined to make sure that selection of officers would be in proportion to those communities which had traditionally provided recruits.

The Government of India broadly accepted Sir Sivaswamy's resolutions, and so the Commander in Chief, General Henry

Rawlinson decided to chair a Military Requirements Committee to look into the details of a potential policy for Indianisation of the army's officer corps. In its broad outline the committee accepted that responsibility for defence was a natural outcome of the path toward self-government and recommended the early announcement of a clear policy on Indianisation. The Rawlinson Committee recommended broadening the base of recruitment, fostering self-sufficiency and envisaged the eventual replacement of British officers by Indians. All new commissions would go to Indians as British units in India would gradually be reduced. The committee further recommended that 25% of all Indian Army cadetships to Sandhurst be reserved for Indians and this level increase annually by 2.5%. After ten years Indians would receive half of all the commissions awarded.

The Government of India made no specific commitment to the recommendations of the Rawlinson Committee and the British Government thought that Rawlinson's proposals were too bold. Lieutenant General Sir Alexander Cobbe, Secretary to the Military Department put forward his own plan for Indianisation. Like many in the military establishment he did not think this new demand for Indian officers in the army was a popular one but a political one of the tiny class of educated Indians.[clxix] He repeated the familiar line of thinking that the efficiency of the army would be impaired for "few, if any, Indians having the natural aptitude for leadership possessed by the average Englishman." He worried that the King's Commission would not attract the virile martial races, and the weak and effeminate middle class boys would top the examinations. It was a fact of India according to Cobbe that the most capable fighting communities were the most backward in education, whilst the most educated lacked fighting ability. In this dire scenario the efficiency and morale of the Indian Army would be broken forever. Cobbe warned that no British officer would happily serve under a senior Indian officer.

Cobbe's solution was to set up a separate Dominion Army which would operate alongside the regular Indian Army. The Dominion Army would be led by Indian officers from the beginning, besides one or two British officers who would be attached for formation and training purposes. Indian officers would hold a Dominion Commission rather than a King's Commission and so would not be able to command British troops or officers. This new Dominion Army would be created from a base of demobilised soldiers and voluntary transfers from the Indian Army. Alternatively, brigades would be gradually Indianised and the number of British officers reduced until the fully Indianised brigades would be separated and the Dominion Army would be raised. If all went well the regular Indian Army would contract and the Dominion Army would come to be something of a National Army of India, and the problem would be solved. No British officer would have to take orders from an Indian.

Cobbe's plan was forwarded to the secretary of state in London, but when the viceroy in Delhi received news of it he expressed dismay. Viceroy Reading thought that Indianisation was a test of British sincerity in guiding India toward self-government.[clxx] In addition, a Dominion Army would cost the Government of India far too much money. Whilst a subcommittee of the Imperial Defence Committee examined the Dominion Army idea, the Government of India had convened its own committee in 1922 under Lieutenant General Sir John Shae, to examine the Cobbe Committee's recommendations. The Shae Committee did not accept the Indian Legislative Assembly's resolution which wanted 25% of King's Commission's to be awarded to Indians annually. Nor did it accept the recommendations of the Rawlinson Committee for an annual incremental increase. It also disagreed with Cobbe's recommendation for the formation of a Dominion Army on the grounds that the requisite development of "a conscious, mature and homogeneous national spirit" had not yet occurred in India.

Instead the Shae Committee proposed its own scheme for the complete, but exceedingly slow Indianisation of the Indian Army. The process would be carried out in three stages, each lasting fourteen years. If the first phase was successful then the second stage would be accelerated to nine years. The Indianisation of infantry battalions and cavalry regiments would start slowly and be accelerated as each phase progressed. During this second phase British officers would stop being commissioned in the Indian Army and any ongoing requirements would be met by loaned officers from the British Army. As Indian officers progressed in rank they would replace the existing strata of Viceroy's Commissioned Officers who, like the British officers, would be phased out. The Shae Committee was concerned that Indian jawans not be rushed into the potentially disturbing new territory of being commanded by Indian officers. On the other hand, it did recommend the appointment of Indian officers to units without regard to their class composition. The Shae Committee agreed to the demand for an Indian Sandhurst but maintained that its graduates should receive a lower rate of pay than King's Commissioned Officers trained in England. Overall the plan for Indianisation could be completed within 30 years if successful or 40 years if the going was slow. Viceroy Reading was pleased and wanted to place the Shae Report before the Indian Legislative Assembly, but the secretary of state in London was aghast. Edwin Montagu thought the Report lent "colour to the dangerous belief in a policy of retreat".[clxxi] The British Government, not the Government of India, would decide on the pace towards self-government.

The Military Requirements Committee then proposed that four units of the Indian Army be officered by Indians. This measure would be treated as an experiment, the result of which would determine the future pace of Indianisation. In so small a force it would be quite easy to find the required number of Indian officers, and any potential dangers could be contained. The Government of India then had the four unit scheme expanded to eight; six infantry and two cavalry units. This scheme effectively turned the selected eight units into a Dominion Army inside the Indian Army and it allayed the great British fear, for no British officer would have to serve under an Indian and the recruitment of young British officers to the rest of the Indian Army would not be hindered. Rawlinson announced the scheme in the Indian Legislative Assembly on 17 February 1923, putting the onus on Indian officers to prove themselves worthy of the new positions which were being opened up for them. The eight unit scheme came to be seen as a form of segregation by Indians however, and four of the five Indians who already held King's Commissions and were to transfer to the Indianised units refused to do so. Exceptions were made, but later Indian graduates from Sandhurst were commissioned as second lieutenants and upon reaching India were posted to a British regiment for a year and then served out their regimental careers in an Indianised unit.

In June 1923 Lieutenant General Sir Alexander Cobbe, who had become Commander in Chief appointed another committee. This one was headed by General Claude Jacob, the Chief of General Staff. He was to look into the progress made by the policy of Indianisation so far. The Jacob Committee found that both the British and Indians perceived the eight Indianised units as inferior, and not a single Indian Sandhurst graduate had opted for one of these units. The committee did not think that Indianisation had been a success and that it would be best to restrict it to a small section of the army. It was found that Indian officers were gravitating towards men of their own caste, something which confirmed doubts about their impartiality and ability to maintain the obedience and respect of their troops. The committee also pointed to a potential revolt amongst the jawans should the time honoured rank of Viceroy's Commissioned Officer be phased out. It was felt that the key to the success of Indianisation was the presence of the British officer. Indians would always look to the British for leadership, whilst the British would never trust regiments commanded by Indians. The committee concluded that Indian sepoys weighed down by centuries of tyranny were prejudiced against their own race and would themselves not want to serve in Indianised units.

Like the Shae Committee, the Jacob Committee noted that India was not yet a nation. Furthermore, the committee recommended that Indians should not be assigned to non-Indianised units so as not to disturb the recruitment of British officers from families with long records of service in the Indian Army. It was noted that the majority of Indian Sandhurst cadets had not lasted, with close to half failing the course. The reason for the high failure rate was thought to be the lack of Indian public schools which could adequately prepare Indian boys for the rigours of life at Sandhurst. A competitive examination was urged to select a group of cadets which would have a better chance of success in England. The committee ended with a warning; impatient Indian politicians did not understand that if Indianisation proceeded too quickly it would put the safety of India in danger, and the government had to keep them under control until it became clear that Indianisation could actually succeed.

Under the system of sending ten Indian cadets to Sandhurst each year it would take at least 200 years before the officer corps of the Indian Army was Indianised. Mohammad Ali Jinnah forced the issue in the Indian Legislative Assembly in March 1925 when he threatened a vote of censure on the government's Indianisation policy. The demand for an Indian Sandhurst would be a matter for the Cabinet in London, but the Viceroy's Executive Council in Delhi did not mind setting up another committee to look into the issue. Jinnah was castigating the government for being insincere and forever advising caution. His great victory however, was another committee.

The Government of India set up another committee under Chief of Staff Lieutenant General Sir Andrew Skeen in June 1925 which came to be known as the 'Indian Sandhurst Committee'. The committee was mainly made up of Indian members and included Mohammad Ali Jinnah, and for a time, Motilal Nehru. The terms of reference were quite narrow; the committee was not to look into stepping up the pace of Indianisation but instead restrict itself to investigating measures which would improve the number and quality of Indians coming forward for the King's Commission, and look into the possibility of establishing an Indian Sandhurst to train Indian cadets.

Since the time of the Jacob Committee the failure rate for Indian cadets at Sandhurst had come down from two-thirds to one-third. Like the Shae Committee, the Skeen Committee blamed the still high failure rates on the lack of public schools in India which could prepare Indian boys for Sandhurst. Committee members visited England, inspected public schools, were impressed by what they saw and characterised the lack of such schools in India as an abdication of British responsibility. Indian members pointed out that the Indian middle class was still not aware of the new opportunities for an army career and Indian parents had to bear a heavy emotional and financial burden in order to send their sons to Sandhurst.

The Indian members of the Skeen Committee implicitly accepted the British reservations about the cultural deficiencies of Indian boys which might prevent them from developing into effective army officers. Jinnah used an interesting word for these deficiencies; he called them 'angularities'. These angularities were communalism, provincialism and casteism, and the main concern of committee members was how best to get rid of them, and whether this could be done effectively in India. There was a general understanding that young Indians would have to be lifted out of their cultural environment and be trained at an Indian Sandhurst, followed by a short stint in England to familiarise them with the ways of the West in order to turn them into good officer material.

The report of the Skeen Committee went further than the Government of India was willing to go however. If its proposals were implemented, at least half the officer corps of the Indian Army would be Indian by 1952. The Skeen Committee wanted the number of Indians admitted to Sandhurst each year increased to 20, with an increase of 4 per year and an Indian Sandhurst established by 1933. The existing system was thought to be too much of a burden on both Indian cadets and Sandhurst itself. The Indian Sandhurst would initially take in 100 cadets for a 3 year course, with an additional 12 each year after that. In order to increase the pool of potential cadets the committee wanted to expand the Royal Indian Military College at Dehra Dun and another preparatory school be opened elsewhere in India. The Skeen Committee also wanted an end to the eight unit scheme which it branded a form of segregation, and to admit Indians into all branches of the army, including signals, artillery, engineering and tank units.

***

As the subject of Indians at Sandhurst and their lack of preparation for the course of instruction continued to be examined by committee after committee, a small number of Indian boys travelled to England each year to attend the hallowed military college. Those who passed out successfully generally had fond memories of their time as cadets. They received rigorous technical training from the British staff and managed to perform well in coursework and drill. Navigating the visible and invisible racial and social boundaries at the institution however, would take much greater effort both for boys educated in England, and those who came straight from school in India.

Shankarrao Thorat applied for the army on his father's suggestion.[clxxii] The total cost of a Sandhurst education was ₹20,000. Thorat's father deposited the amount and submitted an application to the Government of Bombay for permission for his son to appear for the Sandhurst examination. Thorat then received a call to appear for an interview before the Governor of Bombay, Sir Leslie Wilson, who then forwarded his name to the Government of India. Thorat was then chosen to travel to Simla to sit the written examination.

Having completed the examination young Thorat appeared before a Selection Board of army officers. He felt overawed, but tried his best to answer their simple questions which were followed by more exhaustive supplementaries. Thorat was then interviewed by the Commander in Chief Field Marshal Sir William Birdwood who chatted amiably with him, but had a bit of fun, pointing out Thorat's ancestry which included connections to the Maratha Army which rose against the British at Panhala in 1842. Finally, Thorat was interviewed by the viceroy himself, the Earl of Reading with whom he discussed Indian history, and said that he would try his best to make a good officer of the army. The viceroy replied, "I hope so."

Unlike Indian boys who had been to school in England, Thorat came to Sandhurst from India in 1925 with a distinct inferiority complex. He had not mixed with the British during his school days and was not confident of his ability to compete with them. However, he did well in his musketry course, and was one of only 12 cadets chosen to wear the marksman's badge of crossed swords which distinguished him as a good shot with a rifle. In addition, quite by accident, after taking control of his riding sergeant's Olympic show jumper horse, he impressed his instructor who awarded him spurs on the spot.

Besides the technical training, moral instruction was ever present. After the Passing Out Parade a regatta was held in the afternoon on the college lake and Thorat recalled that he and some of his fellow cadets, "out of sheer mischief", drowned the boat club's canoes. In the evening in the Mess the Commandant, Major General Charles Corkran commended the young men on the parade and the fine day they all had. He then asked them who had drowned the canoes. Thorat and his fellow cadets all put their hands up. Corkran then instructed them to go and remove the canoes from the lake, he thought "it should be rather jolly". It was not such an enjoyable experience for Thorat and the cadets however, as the lake had a thin surface layer of ice and a cold breeze had begun to blow.

Once the canoes had been removed from the lake, the commandant addressed the young men. He told them that he already knew exactly who was involved in the prank and if they had denied their involvement he would have "rusticated" them; not for drowning the canoes but for not having the courage to admit the truth. He continued, "Remember when you are commissioned you will be known not merely as officers but as 'officers and gentlemen' and never you forget the gentleman part of it. Remember also that a person who is afraid of telling the truth is a moral coward, and no coward can ever become a successful officer."

The following year Joyanto Chaudhuri, who had been at school at Highgate in London, started to examine his limited career options and read a notice in the newspaper calling for a King's India Cadetship to Sandhurst.[clxxiii] He had enjoyed the Officer Training Corps at school, and thought that a career in the army may be right for him. He wrote to the Military Department at the India Office, and the Department then wrote to Chaudhuri's Headmaster, Dr. Johnstone, informing him that it would be willing to consider the boy for an ordinary cadetship if his father could pay his way. Chaudhuri would be interviewed, and then the matter of fees would be settled. Dr. Johnstone thought that Chaudhuri might just be right for the army. His academic record had been less than stellar, and he was not a great athlete, but he had shown "independence of outlook" and character. As a prefect he had shown that he could be a just leader and get others to work as a team. Dr. Johnstone would speak well of his application should he be asked.

Chaudhuri arrived at the India Office in London to be interviewed by a panel led by Field Marshall Sir Claude Jacob, of the Jacob Committee. He recalled that the questions were general, and his responses were frank. He admitted to not being much of a scholar or an athlete but felt that the life of an army officer was an honourable one, and it was important that more Indians be trained as officers. He won the cadetship, and his father agreed to pay the fees. Chaudhuri's father was sceptical however of how he would be treated in the army, given that the British had always dubbed the Bengalis a seditious non-martial race.

Chaudhuri recalled that the first ten weeks at Sandhurst were all about "passing off the square", or becoming sufficiently adept at drill to be able to perform in public. In between the drill practice there were some academic lessons, equitation, running and physical training, and getting fitted out for the different uniforms required for each activity. Chaudhuri's first Drill Sergeant, Bill Manger asked him if he understood English, and then shouted at him to march off to see his company commander, the aristocrat Major Ronald Fellowes, the Baron of Ailwyn. Fellowes then decided that whatever he might be called in India he would be "Chawdree" in the army. Chaudhuri's servant Mr. Bartley, who was universally known as 'Uncle', was a foul mouthed but generous man who would often lend the young cadet a pound when he would end up without money at the end of the week.

Colonel Charles Stooks, a retired officer of the Indian Army acted as an official guardian to the Indian boys. He was responsible for keeping his cadets in order, supervising their finances, teaching them English manners and customs, and sending them to resorts in Britain and Europe during the holidays. But Chaudhuri thought that Stooks's unofficial role was to make sure that no young Indian cadet took an English wife back with him to India. Whenever Stooks had to introduce the Indian cadets to visiting VIPs he would either ignore Chaudhuri, or put him at the end of the line and say "And him. I know nothing about him."

The British cadets rarely mixed with non-British cadets and during the course of the decade that Indian cadets were trained at Sandhurst they had evolved certain social rules. The Indian cadet had to tip his servant twice the going rate, he would always have to take the more expensive balcony seats at the cinema, stay away from the pawn shop, and avoid the end of term ball unless he could bring an Indian girl. And an Indian could never cut in, or 'filch' another Indian cadet's Indian girl.

Chaudhuri did not think that the curriculum at Sandhurst was particularly complex. The main aim was to produce a young officer who would be able to competently command a platoon of 30 men. A social gaffe was thought to be a more serious mistake than a wrong command. The cadets received a fair idea of regimental life from the regimental officers who taught military subjects and military behaviour. Officers seconded from the Army Educational Corps taught the more intellectual subjects such as history and geography and chemical warfare, whilst weapons training, physical training, drill and equitation were all taught by warrant officers. Chaudhuri enjoyed equitation, or horse riding, aspired to a place in the Cavalry, and was one of the 16 cadets selected to compete for 'The Saddle'. The physical training was tough; contorting and twisting whilst getting screamed at by the stocky instructor. And more awkward for the Indian youngster was when the cadets would, exhausted, strip nude and plunge under a common shower at the end of a training session.

***

At the end of a decade of committees the demand of the moderate nationalists in the Indian Legislative Assembly had distilled into the creation of an Indian Sandhurst. The First Round Table Conference met in London in October 1930 and a Subcommittee of Defence was formed, with Indian delegates including Mohammad Ali Jinnah, Sir Tej Bahadur Sapru, Mukund Jayakar and Balakrishna Moonje. Jinnah pressed for a specific time frame for complete Indianisation but was outnumbered by the majority. The subcommittee did want action on an Indian Sandhurst however, rather than more pious words. Yet in order to translate words into action, another committee would need to be formed. The Government of India was thus urged to create a committee of British and Indian experts to work out the details of an Indian Sandhurst. This was a curious demand. Jinnah had travelled to London in 1930 to sit on a subcommittee which created another committee to implement the recommendations of the Skeen Committee which he had sat on in Delhi five years earlier.

The Government of India accepted the Subcommittee of Defence request and established a committee chaired by Commander in Chief General Sir Philip Chetwode in May 1931. Unlike earlier committees, the Chetwode Committee was encouraged by the progress in Indian education, the spread of public schools in India and the role of the Prince of Wales Royal Indian Military College at Dehra Dun in turning out Indian boys with a public school ethic who would be fit for command in the Indian Army. The committee wanted the institution expanded as a feeder for the new Indian

Sandhurst.

The Chetwode Committee recommended that the Indian Sandhurst, or the Indian Military Academy would run a three year course. Applicants would have to be between 18 and 20 years old and half the intake of 60 cadets would be from within the ranks of the Indian Army. Of the other half, 24 places would be filled by open competition based on an examination administered by the Public Service Commission, whilst 6 places would be reserved for nomination by the commander in chief for those who passed the examination but missed out in open competition. Graduates of the academy would be posted to British units for a year before joining their own Indianised units. The Government of India was advised to start Indianisation of a complete division immediately to accommodate the larger number of cadets which would graduate from the new institution. The committee settled on Dehra Dun as the location for the Indian Military Academy which was to be opened towards the end of 1932.

***

Whilst Sandhurst had attracted a small group of sons of the Indian elite during the 1920s, the intake of cadets to the new Indian Military Academy at Dehra Dun was drawn more from the middle of the middle class. They came into the Indian Army during the even more turbulent political times of the 1930s, as nationalist politics intensified and another civil disobedience movement challenged the Raj. In Dehra Dun they entered an institution which, like Sandhurst, gave them technical and social training, but proved to be a much less lonely experience than the one Indian boys had faced in England.

Harbakhsh Singh was at Government College, Lahore when the Congress met there on the banks of the Ravi in December

1929.[clxxiv] He and his friends went to listen to Jawaharlal Nehru deliver his speech and announce the Congress's new goal of purna Swaraj, or complete Independence, and recalled that Nehru was mounted on a white horse at the head of a huge procession to mark the momentous event. As the political agitation intensified the students would read reports of processions and police repression in the form of lathi charges in the newspapers. In Lahore, government educational institutions were picketed and political processions were led by Lala Lajpat Rai through Anarkali Bazaar. The youngsters would go down to watch the processions from the sidelines and witness the inevitable police lathi charges.

Government College was considered pro-British because of its mainly British staff and was a favourite target of the political protesters. Students from the Arya Samaj's Dayanand Anglo-Vedic College would picket Government College only to be taken away in a police lock-up and then released a little way down the road. Children would also enter the main gate and make a bonfire of foreign clothes and hats. Smaller children would even peep through the hedge on the hockey ground and shout out "Toady Bacha Hai! Hai!" Harbakhsh and his friends would read about the exploits of Bhagat Singh, Satguru and Sukhdev and get agitated. But beyond talk and feelings of agitation they did not take any action and focused on their education, which "was more important than anything else". Harbakhsh had his sights set on a commission in the Indian Army and so he prepared for the army entrance examination whilst continuing to study for his B.A.

Harbakhsh was selected after an examination and interview in Delhi and joined the Indian Military Academy at Dehra Dun in 1933. The course at the academy extended over 5 terms, or 2 ½ years and the cost to Indian parents came to about ₹8,000. Like Chaudhuri at Sandhurst, Harbakhsh spent his first few days in the tailor's shop getting fitted for an elaborate wardrobe for ceremonies (drill jackets and khaki ties), physical training (white drill shorts and vests), and trips to the town (grey and red striped blazers). The cadets were put through a tough routine; rising at 6 am, they were served tea by their servant, would get dressed for physical training, and then go for a run. During physical training they would do ground work and use wooden horse and parallel bars, followed by rope climbing and boxing and an hour long drill with and without rifles. When they became seniors they would also practice sword drills. The cadets would then proceed to academic work for three hours, studying military history, mathematics, geometry, general knowledge, English phonetics and accounting. Lunch was taken at 1 pm in the Cadets' Mess and by 2 pm they were playing cricket, hockey, football and athletics. In the evenings they would play tennis and squash. The cadets would then be expected to bathe and change into a white or blue jacket according to the season. They would then assemble in the ante room for the following day's orders, or to play more games like 'More Arty, where are you?', which was played under a blanket with a rolled up magazine to beat the opponent with, and the 'toppling game' in which the opponent was toppled with a tackle using the right leg. The British company commanders would join in and they would then proceed together for dinner in the Cadets' Mess.

Harbakhsh felt that the staff who were picked for the new academy were the best of the Indian Army. He thought that this was proof of the fact that the British wanted to make a success of the experiment, however small it was thought to be at the time. The Commandant, Brigadier Lionel Collins was popular among the cadets, as were most of the company commanders, with the exception of Colonel Arthur Bird of the Royal Engineers who was "very rough and gruff". Harbakhsh excelled at equitation and was awarded spurs in his first term and led his class in cross country riding. He also excelled at sports and held the army record for hurdles and long jump and was awarded academy colours for swimming, hockey and athletics.

Each of the company commanders at the academy was expected to invite the cadets to their home as a part of "social training". Harbakhsh recalled that he and the cadets of the second term were asked to tea by the commandant's wife. They all arrived punctually at 4 o'clock and after engaging in some polite conversation with Mrs. Collins and her young daughter, the group moved to the dining room where liveried servants served them sweets and the hostess was to serve them tea. However, one of Harbakhsh's colleagues, Makhan Singh did not think that she would be able to handle such a large pot of tea and tried to wrench it out of her hand, exclaiming "I can't let you do this, give it to me as it is too large for you to handle." Mrs. Collins insisted that it was her duty as hostess to serve the tea, but Makhan Singh did not agree and almost pulled the pot out of her hand before his colleagues intervened and advised him to leave her alone.

***

By the 1920s and 1930s the great expeditions into Afghanistan in which Field Marshall Frederick Roberts made his name had become a thing of the past. Instead, frontier columns consisting of a brigade composed of three or four infantry battalions with supporting arms came to be used to put down rebellion amongst the tribes of the North West Frontier. The British knew that a long term occupation of Pathan lands would be costly, whilst the Pathans were willing to accept restraint as long as their land was not permanently occupied. This meant that the army columns were the 'boots on the ground' maintaining the political status quo on the Frontier. Between the world wars, during the period of the Indianisation of the army, it was on the North West Frontier that young Indian officers like Shankarrao Thorat and Harbakhsh Singh had their first experience of fighting a well-armed and tenacious opponent.^{clxxv}

Thorat was not too keen on heading to the North West Frontier. He thought it was a land where bloodthirsty Pathans hated and hunted Indians. However, he had to go, and reached the Frontier at the end of 1927. When he arrived at the collection of tents at Manzai he found it desolate as his battalion had gone out on a column to Wana in order to discourage the local villagers from supporting sniping, hit and run raids and ambushes on army camps. Thorat was then given command of a Pathan Company of Cis-Indus and Trans-Indus Pathans. His second-in-command, Subedar Mir Dast explained the intricacies of mountain warfare and the tactics of the tribesmen; the troops had to cross gorges which were flanked by hills, and from these heights the tribesmen would open fire on them and raid their baggage column, snatching weapons and loot before escaping back to the safety of the hills. In one raid the Pathans attacked the Quarter Guard, killed every member and then fled with nine rifles, for which the brigade was fined ₹90,000 by Headquarters. As a result of the attacks the brigade's tented camp came to be protected by barbed wire, sentry posts and nightly armed patrols.

Harbakhsh Singh's first posting was to the British unit of his choice, the 2nd Battalion Argyll and Sutherland Highlanders at Rawalpindi. He was put in charge of a platoon and then departed for Hunza on the North West Frontier in 1935 to carry out Mohmand operations against the Pathan tribesmen. Harbakhsh and the troops marched from Peshawar railway station to the scene of the action at Ghalanai. They would have their breakfast at 1 am and carry out a night march to their pickets to be in a position to face the Pathans once they rose and had said their morning prayers. However, the Mohmand operations were called off after a disaster in which the Guides Battalion- 12th Frontier Force Battalion misjudged a halt, were caught by the Pathans, and had nearly all their

90 men wiped out. Harbakhsh watched the scene unfold through his binoculars at a neighbouring picket. The operations ended a month later with a jirga of local tribal chiefs and the Governor of the North West Frontier Province agreeing to revert to the status quo.

In 1936, Thorat's battalion was moved to Peshawar to take part in subsequent Ghalanai operations on the Khyber. Thorat's task was to organise and command a large scale ambush of Pathans who were sniping at the Force Headquarters. He selected an ambush hill over the most direct route between the tribesmen's village and Force Headquarters. No reconnaissance was done so as not to alert the tribesmen and anyone likely to cough or clear their throats was left behind. After silent marching Thorat and the troops reached their hill in the middle of the night. Four platoons were positioned for the ambush. The Pathans approached, and the troops opened fire. Surrounded, the Pathans reached for their knives to hack their way out and hand-to-hand combat ensued. Thorat used his kukri and drew blood. At the end of the fighting seventeen Pathans were dead or wounded, eight Indian troops were wounded and one died from a cut to his windpipe.

Later, in 1938 Harbakhsh's battalion headed back to the North West Frontier at Razmak under the command of Lieutenant Colonel Geoffrey Ford. Whilst he was used to picketing hills from Operation Mohmand, the focus had turned to road protection duties. The troops were given the task of protecting the road up to Alexandra picket and had to picket three main heights. However, at the end of each Road Protection Day the Pathans would climb up an unpicketed height, fire a few rounds and pick off a casualty or two. Harbakhsh's A Company came under fire whilst withdrawing from a picket, and one of its men was hit and left behind in the withdrawal. Later a counter attack was launched to recover the body, however the dead man's rifle had been left behind. Harbakhsh remembered; "on the North West Frontier losing the screw of a rifle was a big offence, and this was a rifle!" He wanted to tell his commanding officer the truth of what had happened but his Viceroy's Commissioned Officer, Subedar Attar Singh begged him not to do so and vowed that he would find the rifle before midnight. The subedar produced a havildar and two men to go out and look for the rifle but wanted to take their own rifles for protection. Harbakhsh did not want to risk losing another rifle and so allowed them to go out with a bayonet instead. Harbakhsh did not inform his commanding officer of the incident over dinner, but when he went to his cubicle to retire for the night he could not sleep from worry. But true to his word, Attar arrived just before midnight, and informed Harbakhsh that the rifle had been recovered.

***

It was on the North West Frontier that young Indian officers got to put their technical training to the test, but it was in the Officers' Mess that they were socialised into the traditions of the Indian Army. Both Shankarrao Thorat and Harbakhsh Singh would be fitted out for their elaborate mess kits specific to their battalions, and then on entering the inner sanctum they would have to quickly learn its intricate rules and regulations and customs relating to food, drink, conversation and games.[clxxvi]

Thorat's regimental dress was a red jacket with green facing and white piping, tightly fitted overalls of blue serge and red piping and Wellington boots with electroplated spurs. Harbakhsh had to call in at Rankins Tailors at Connaught Place in New Delhi to get fitted out for his battalion mess kit; a woollen red jacket with yellow facings, two chequered white cotton waist coats and a stretchable woollen navy blue overall with red piping down the sides. This outfit was to be worn with black leather boots up to the calves with a metal box behind each heel to hold enamelled spurs. A black leather strap held the overall under the boots and was fastened by a buckle.

Thorat recalled that the Officers' Mess was "not merely a place for drinking and eating, but a very well-regulated home were decorums and regimental customs were taught and observed." He remembered that whisky was seldom taken before dinner, rum was not served, and most of the drinkers would take gin, vermouth or madeira before their meal. The whisky drinkers would consume their quota in their quarters and then stick to short drinks when they arrived at the Mess. Thorat thought the public's perception of heavy drinking in the army was misplaced and only occurred on special occasions like Christmas and New Year. Dinner would always start on time and would never be delayed to allow an officer to sneak a "quick one". Smoking was banned in the dining hall during meals. For Thorat the "Mess was, as I believe it should be, a place where officers were groomed to behave as gentlemen."

Dinner in the Mess would be an official affair for the dining members who had to dress in their mess kit. Harbakhsh remembered that an officer was never to enter the Mess without a coat and tie, however if entering after sports a cravat in place of a tie would be permissible. The diners were led into the dining room by the senior member, sat together and were served their meal ceremonially by the Mess staff, who were supervised by the Mess Havildar, who himself was in ceremonial dress standing at the head of the dining table. Officers could not leave the Mess after a meal until the senior dining member had left, or they had taken his permission. Sunday dinners were a relatively casual affair; only dinner jackets were required, and diners could serve themselves from the dishes placed on the table. Ladies, whether alone or with their husbands, were prohibited from entering the Mess except if specially invited to the New Year's Banquet. And badminton, which was considered a 'sissy game' in the army, was prohibited in the Mess and Club.

***

World War II broke out in 1939 and as the fighting in Asia became more intense through 1940 and 1941 many more Indian officers were required than had been trained at Sandhurst and Dehra Dun. The unexpected expansion of the war necessitated the creation of a system of Emergency Commissions to train thousands more officers for the Indian Army at short notice. The training which these Emergency Commission officers received was short and sharp and technical and physical, only the social training meant to produce a gentleman cadet had to be cut out due to the urgency of the situation. For those young Indian men who came forward, an Emergency Commission provided a potential opening for a long term career in the Indian Army once the war ended.

K.V. Krishna Rao had been a student at the Maharajah's College, Vizianagaram during the early years of the war.[clxxvii] He responded to the calls in the media for young Indians to come forward for the officer class of the army and was first interviewed by the District Selection Board and then by a British military officer. He was interviewed again in front of a Central Review Board of British officers. Applicants were checked for mental and physical fitness, quizzed on their general knowledge and assessed for leadership potential. Rao was questioned on fighting in different theatres of conflict around the world as well as science, geography, history and sports. He was also asked to demonstrate cricketing techniques; how to bowl a leg break, play a late cut and show where gully stood. Rao managed to clear the interviews and was asked to report to the Officers Training School at Bangalore in February 1942.

Krishna Tewari studied at the Forman Christian College, Lahore and had his heart set on a career in the Indian Railways.[clxxviii] He wanted to follow in the footsteps of his favourite uncle who had risen to a high post as an Indian Railways officer. However, having passed the written examination but failing in the interview, he took the advice of Lieutenant Colonel Alan Kilroy of the Jullundhar Cantonment and applied for a commission to the army in 1940. He too was ordered to the Officers Training School at Bangalore in February 1942.

Tewari recalled that the training at Bangalore had been reduced to five months. It was tough and was conducted mainly by British officers and non-commissioned officers who took a no-nonsense approach. The physical training instructor taught Tewari to box, taking on a much taller opponent, telling him to just keep punching away above his opponent's belt. The regimental sergeant major would bark his orders of "quick march", making the cadets so nervous they would forget left and right. Some cadets were relegated and others withdrew on account of the physical rigour of the course, and then the final obstacle course and endurance test eliminated many. The trainees had been given flag and lamp signalling instruction as part of the course and were paired off and tested with one trainee reading the signals at one end of a field with the other sitting facing away and writing what was read by the other. Tewari's partner saved him and wrote down the right version of the signal even though he called out the wrong one. Tewari ended up scoring 100%, and went on to a fine career in the Signals Corps of the Indian Army.

Pessie Madan had actually fled from his childhood home in Burma upon the outbreak of the war.[clxxix] Back in India, poor vision disqualified him from his dream of a career in the air force, but he managed to pass the medical test for the army and was called to the Officers Training School at Mhow. The Training School placed an emphasis on infantry training.

Madan remembered the training in using gun cotton slabs with a seven second fuse as particularly nerve wracking. The trainees were to walk up to a slab of gun cotton ten feet from a trench, insert the fuse, light it, and then walk back and take cover from the explosion. They also had to storm an imaginary enemy position with live ammunition, providing overhead cover whilst crawling with bullets whizzing over their heads and crackers bursting to simulate fire. In November 1943 Madan and his fellow cadets were commissioned as second lieutenants in His Majesty's army and allowed to wear one star on the shoulders of their tunics.

***

Although manpower was not a problem, the Indian Army was ill prepared and underfunded on the eve of World War II. Defence expenditure had been in steady decline since the days of General Rawlinson in the early 1920s. The army was short of modern weapons and equipment and its men were not even trained in operating mechanical transport. When fighting broke out neither London nor New Delhi thought there would be any great need for Indian troops. The situation quickly changed however, and the first Indian divisions were sent to the Middle East and went on to contribute to campaigns in North Africa and Italy. The focus of military preparations remained to the west of India though, with little thought given to the defence of India's east in Burma and Malaya. The result was that as the Japanese moved swiftly down through South East Asia in 1941 and 1942 almost 70,000 Indian troops were taken as prisoners of war in Singapore, and Indian forces were pushed back to India's eastern border.

Harbakhsh Singh was one of those Indian soldiers who was captured by the Japanese.[clxxx] His World War II journey however, started from Quetta in April 1939. He was commanding a company travelling by train through Punjab and the British commanding officer feared that some of the soldiers might get off along the way. Harbakhsh thought that the British officer had little to worry about. He had a direct line to his troops, spoke to them in Punjabi, and they had given their word that they would not desert. He thought that this highlighted the fact that the British officer was completely dependent on reports which were submitted to him about the men under his own command.

Harbakhsh and his men eventually boarded a passenger ship at Madras. They did not know their destination; they could have been sailing to the Middle East or to Malaya, nobody was sure. They sailed for a day due south at which point the captain opened a secret envelope, and the ship turned east. They were heading to Malaya. The troops disembarked at Singapore a few days later and then boarded a train, travelling up the Malay peninsula to the town of Ipoh. After a month they were moved to Kuanton on the Malayan east coast.

Harbakhsh thought the British authorities never seriously anticipated the Japanese attacking the Malay peninsula. British generals would visit and mock the Japanese as bandy legged soldiers with poor eyesight who would not dare to attack British forces. When the Japanese invaded and took control of Indo-China the troops were told that was about their limit. When two convoys of ships were detected heading out of Indo-China escorted by the Japanese Navy, they were said to be heading to Thailand rather than Malaya. But then on 8 December 1941 the 3rd Garwal which had been stationed on the beaches of Kuanton sighted a ship on the horizon with a light on a high mast. A line of landing boats then appeared and the Garwalis opened fire. After half an hour the ship turned northward and the Japanese landed on an unmanned beach a few miles north of Kuanton. That same evening the Japanese landed at Kota Baru, overpowering a defensive brigade and also landed at Pitani, north of Kota Baru inside Thai territory. Harbakhsh recalled a few British officers still insisting that the Japanese were really intending to take Thailand and had landed on the Malay peninsula by mistake.

Harbakhsh provided a picture of the calamity which ensued when the Japanese started bombing the Kuanton airstrip. Prior to the attack the Australians boasted that they would blow the Japanese to pieces should they land on the Malay peninsula. But when they took off to engage Japanese landing crafts at Kota Baru only three of the nine bombers returned, with three wounded crew members. The next day when 50 Japanese bombers came to destroy the Kuanton airstrip the Australian crew of Hudson bombers refused to fly and fled in panic. In the afternoon the Japanese aircraft came down, bombing and strafing everything on the ground and set fire to the aircraft stationed on the strip. Harbakhsh's company tried to defend the airfield but their anti-aircraft Lewis guns malfunctioned.

On 3 January 1942 Harbakhsh's brigade major sent him to reconnoitre the next defensive position for what was left of the brigade. He got on a motorcycle with his batman Piyara Singh riding pillion and they went out to search for a place for defence on the withdrawal route. After inspecting a position which they did not like the look of, Harbakhsh and Piyara proceeded further down the road and were ambushed in a Japanese attack. Harbakhsh was hit on the head by a splinter from a hand grenade, lost consciousness and woke up 72 hours later in Alexandra Hospital in Singapore. A surgeon had inserted a silver plate to cover the gash in his cranium.

Piyara Singh later told Harbakhsh that the Japanese had lobbed the grenade from high in the trees, come down, kicked both of the them but thought that they were dead and moved on. Harbakhsh and Piyara were then picked up by a vehicle which was following them, taken to Battalion Headquarters, put on another vehicle, taken down the road and then put on a ferry which came under Japanese bombardment. Harbakhsh's vehicle was hit but he did not receive any further injuries. At the Jeruntut railway station a young army surgeon dressed his wound and put him on a train, which also came under Japanese bombardment. Many fled, but Harbakhsh was still unconscious. He was removed from the train on a stretcher and his identification card slipped out of his pocket in the process.

Harbakhsh spent January 1942 in Alexandra Hospital, during which time the Malay peninsula had been evacuated, the naval base on the north of Singapore had been abandoned, and the causeway connecting Singapore and the Malay peninsula had been blown up. He learnt that Japanese forces had landed on the north-west of Singapore in the Australian held sector and were heading towards Singapore town down the Bukitima Road. On the 10th of February Japanese forces entered Harbakhsh's hospital spraying gunfire in all directions. Staff and patients were left crouching for safety along a drainage channel and Harbakhsh managed to escape to Singapore town.

On the morning of the 16th of February Japanese aircraft dropped pamphlets which announced that the surrender of Singapore had taken place and Indian prisoners of war were to assemble at Tyrsal Park, a race course near town. Harbakhsh made his way to the park and when he arrived he met a Havildar wearing a band with the letter 'F' on his left arm. The Havildar told Harbakhsh that it stood for 'free' as he had joined Mohan Singh's Indian National Army. Harbakhsh knew Mohan from his days at the Indian Military Academy at Dehra Dun and tried to meet him, but his Military Secretary Mahabir Dhillon insisted on an appointment.

A British officer spoke to the Indian officers and troops over a microphone from the grandstand, handing them over to the Japanese as prisoners of war in the name of His Majesty's

British Government. A Japanese major general then handed them over to Mohan Singh of the Indian National Army. Mohan Singh implored the soldiers to join the Indian National Army and free India from British rule. He received a good response from the troops sitting at the back, but a more cautious one from the officers at the front.

Soon enough the prisoners of war began to be subjected to propaganda for enlistment in the Indian National Army. They would listen to Mohan Singh lecture them on his plans to free India from British rule. A Japanese intelligence officer would be standing behind him. Mahabir Dhillon would also address the prisoners of war and Harbakhsh would pose questions to him about the conduct of the Japanese Army in Manchuria. He was eventually persuaded against any further questions by his elder brother Gurbakhsh who was commanding the Jind Infantry; besides having power over their lives, Mohan and Mahabir were unlikely to be won over by reason.

Mohan and Mahabir tried to highlight the contrast between the lives of prisoners of war and the soldiers of the Indian National Army by placing an Indian National Army barracks in front of the prisoners' camp. In the mornings as the prisoners would be lined up in a work gang with a handful of boiled rice tied up in a piece of cloth and slung over their shoulders, the Indian National Army soldiers would be doing their morning physical training with hot tea and puris awaiting them. Propaganda teams would visit the prisoners everyday with enticements such as promises of promotion. But Harbakhsh recalled that he and his colleagues had accepted their fate and decided to remain prisoners of war. During their early days in captivity Harbakhsh and Gurbakhsh would insist that unless Gandhi or Nehru made an appeal over the radio for Indians to join the Indian National Army they would refuse to do so as they did not have any faith in its present leadership. Harbakhsh thought that Mohan Singh was a sincere man, but placed too much trust in the Japanese. In the end

Harbakhsh's work party, which had come to be made up of 'obstructionists', or those who refused to join the Indian National Army, totalled about 1500 men and they were moved to the wharfs to await a ship which would take them to the island of Rabal. The ship never arrived, and they were instead taken to a railway station to be sent to the infamous 'Death Railway' in Thailand. But they had some luck. Their train was stopped outside the Kluang airfield by the Japanese Air Force which needed a working party to help clear the airstrip.

The Kluang airstrip was dilapidated but had plenty of scrap metal, random parts, wires, abandoned vehicles and gasoline. The mechanics and carpenters of the Jind Infantry quickly set up their own workshops and besides cups and plates and scissors they managed to put together a car and a motorcycle which ran well. The work party was then ordered to take out stones from a quarry near where their train had been stopped for which they were given trucks and some assistance by Chinese labourers. Harbakhsh recalled that the Japanese had a shortage of manpower and so control of the working party was not very strict. In fact, they were largely left to themselves.

Despite their best efforts to smoke out mosquitoes and avoid water from the streams, both malaria and dysentery broke out in the camp. Men started dropping like flies and so the officers requested the Japanese to allot them some accommodation. They were allowed to search for some themselves and found wooden barracks near the airfield for the troops and three old British Warrant Officers' pre-fabricated houses at the other end of the airfield for the officers. Harbakhsh was appointed staff officer for the camp by Gurbakhsh.

Near the officers' quarters was a large tin shed on a wooden platform on which the prisoners would stage plays and hold musical concerts. Gurbakhsh wrote out dramas on social themes in Punjabi which would be directed by Ajaib Singh. Harbakhsh was a bathroom singer and so was appointed music director. For the female parts Ajaib would dress up young boys, mainly the barbers who followed the Jind Infantry, in Punjabi dress and Harbakhsh thought they "truly looked like girls". As the music director Harbakhsh collected some singers and they would start their performances with a rendition of 'Vande Mataram'. They would observe each 'national festival' and hoist the national flag and sing a suitable national song. The prisoners would continue to compose their patriotic songs, invite the local South Indians to their performances, reminisce about their near and dear ones back home, and fantasise about eating Indian sweets. In the evenings they would look up at the tropical sky and were actually thankful that they had been put to work under the Japanese Air Force. Harbakhsh remembered them as "on the whole considerate to us. They were more concerned about their work being done and other than that left us alone most of the time."

Harbakhsh had a wireless radio which he had picked up whilst cleaning the streets of Singapore shortly after being taken as a prisoner of war. He had kept it a secret, only his brother Gurbakhsh and his nephew Mohan Mukand knew of it. Through 1943 it proved crucial in keeping the morale of the prisoners up as news came in of Allied advances in Asia and Europe. The 6 volt battery which Harbakhsh had collected with the radio in Singapore ran out however, and so he needed a source of electricity. In his capacity as staff officer responsible for the troops' welfare he approached the Japanese for kerosene lanterns for lighting the way at night and an electric connection to which a high powered bulb could be attached. The bulb would be placed centrally to illuminate the camp, and the Japanese officer agreed that the prisoners could take an electricity connection from the main switchboard, but that they would have to use their own resources. An extra line was taken underground to

Harbakhsh's secret bunker not far from their living quarters. The radio set was placed in a large empty drum covered with a wooden board and buried under the floor of the bunker.

The set was tuned to pick up the All India Radio broadcast at 9 pm Indian time and the BBC broadcast at 9:30 pm, which came in the middle of the night in Malaya. Harbakhsh received news of the landing of American forces in Algeria, the landing of American and British forces at Normandy, the initial successes of the Japanese in Burma, as well as the raising of another Indian National Army under Subhas Chandra Bose. Unfortunately, some of the prisoners of war who also worked as boatmen for the Japanese divulged a bit too much knowledge of world events. The Japanese became suspicious, but the prisoners would claim that they had just heard some rumours from the Chinese labourers working in the camp. Prison guards would bring out clinometers mounted on tripods to bluff the prisoners into thinking that they would be able to detect the source of the radio. They even claimed to have found the radio, but when the prisoners offered to go to the spot and help with the search the guards backed off.

Harbakhsh recalled that as prisoners of war they always maintained "friendly relations" with the Indian National Army and whenever their detachments passed through the Kluang railway station they would go and meet them and share food and news. Jaganath Bhonsle, a senior figure in the Indian National Army even sent for Harbakhsh and Gurbakhsh to attend one of Bose's public meetings in Singapore. Harbakhsh accepted the invitation and recalled the meeting as a grand affair on the maidan in front of a municipal building. A map of India had been erected on a high stage with each province being highlighted by a different colour rose. Indian girls dressed in tri-coloured saris would stand behind microphones ready to sing the national anthem. Tri-colours were draped down each column of the municipal building "in real fascist style", reminiscent to Harbakhsh of images of Nazi Germany in the 1930s. Harbakhsh was however doubtful as to whether the real Bose would appear. But when a figure emerged out of a car in a white dhoti and kurta with spectacles and addressed the crowd with brilliant oratory in English and Hindustani, his doubts were allayed. Bose asked the gathering to contribute for India's Independence and they immediately started throwing cash, gold rings and ornaments onto a white sheet which had been laid out for collections.

In late 1943 Bose himself called Harbakhsh and Gurbakhsh from their prisoner of war camp at Kuanton to Airhitam about 20 miles west. The brothers were taken under Japanese escort to a house, and as they approached they saw tea and pastries, which they had not had for years, laid out on the verandah. Bose, who was addressing a conference of his workers, soon appeared in a khaki uniform with black boots and a cap with a leaping tiger on it. He started the meeting by saying that he had learnt that neither of the brothers had joined the Indian National Army and wanted to know their reasons. Gurbakhsh stated that no leader of any standing had led the army so far and that they were not patriotic enough to join a noble movement and lay down their lives for it. Were they so, why would they have joined the British Indian Army in the first place? In addition, it was becoming clearer that Japan was going to lose the war, which made them even less willing to throw their lot in with the Indian National Army. Bose appreciated their frankness and admitted they were "perhaps" correct in their assessment of the war. He wanted people who were willing to die for their country, and whilst they would never be compelled to join him, if they changed their minds they would be welcomed in with open arms. Bose invited the brothers to take tea, and that was the last they saw of him.

***

As the British Armed Forces were being defeated in Malaya, Singapore fell, and Harbakhsh Singh started his long years as a prisoner of war, the Japanese 15th Army had been moving with lightning speed through Thailand and into Burma. The Japanese took Rangoon, Burma's capital and main port in the south of the country in March 1942, and then began to advance north, destroying Chinese forces and compelling British and Indian forces to retreat in a state of disarray back into Assam. It was India's Eastern Army which suffered the worst defeat in Burma in 1942, and so in October 1943 the Eastern Army was renamed the '14th Army' and was placed under the command of General William Slim. General Headquarters India was then placed under Admiral Louis Mountbatten's South East Asia Command and plans to retake Burma gathered speed.

Like Harbakhsh Singh's earlier journey, when Krishna Tewari departed from south India in the middle of 1944 he was not initially aware of the direction of the journey or its ultimate destination.[clxxxi] From the south of India Tewari and the troops followed a zig zag route, driving 150 to 200 miles a day. They reached Calcutta in 12 days, crossing the river Mahanadi during the last stretch on the *Islami*, an old pilgrim ship. They disembarked at Chittagong at the river ghat reinforcement camp, before moving on to the Chirangha transit camp to join other soldiers who had arrived by different ships.

Tewari recalled his first night operations on the Maungdaw-Buthidaung Road in Arakan, the modern Rakhine state of Myanmar in the country's west which now shares a border with Bangladesh. His 25th Division had relieved another division and the Japanese, sensing that fresh troops had been moved in, sent in a few of their men to the 418th Royal Garwal Rifles on the first tunnel. Defensive firing started from a lone section post and then spread to their platoon companies and sections of the unit. Tewari was in the Brigade Headquarters next to the unit and was woken by the heavy firing. Artillery defensive fire also joined the action as did the Brigade Headquarters Defence Platoon and Divisional Artillery. No one slept that night. They expected a Japanese attack, and Tewari spent the night operating the telephone exchange from the brigade commander to the Garwali Company, the divisional commander and the Commander Royal Artillery. Their entire first line of ammunition was expended, but the next morning when the patrols were sent out to count the enemy dead they did not find a trace of blood. The troops had to learn to hold their fire until they were sure of live targets.

Indian forces looked to capture Hill 551 which overlooked a portion of the Maungdaw-Buthidaung Road. It had not been captured by previous divisions and the brigade had lost three or four vehicles in the first four days besides casualties. Tewari was able to watch the final successful assault on Hill 551 from nearby high ground as the Gurkhas stormed the position with their kukris, rifles and grenades. When the fighting ceased he and the troops went up the hill to lay a telephone line, but months' worth of dead soldiers had piled up causing a great stink. The Japanese would return to make a counter attack a couple of weeks later however, and two companies of Punjabis were targeted as they were changing over at night. Tewari operated the telephone exchange through the night until the Punjabis were successful in capturing the hill at 7 am the next morning. Seeing 50 Japanese dead and another 50 wounded the next morning put some spirit into the forces, who until then had thought that the Japanese were invincible.

Tewari had his first live battle experience when Japanese forces on a nearby hill opened fire with mortars and guns as he was crossing a narrow stretch with a cable. Tewari and his sergeant would dive every time they heard the scream of incoming shells. On the first dive the sergeant fell on top of

Tewari for which he screamed at him, but Tewari later realised that the soldier was a veteran of earlier wars and had fallen on him only to protect him. An infantryman coming up behind them was not so lucky and a shell which landed close to him blew him up. In the end most of the shells went overhead or fell short of Tewari and he and his sergeant only tore some clothes, strained a finger and had a few minor bruises. But he recalled, "Our Division had got bloodied in battle very fast and it brought on a great spirit of pride and confidence. We had become war veterans."

Tewari was a Signals officer however, and after the recapture of territory, he and his men were able to employ a new method of laying cable lines away from existing roads and tracks. Tewari was given two sections of infantry for the jungle clearing work and they managed to lay two pairs of telephone cables. They did come under Japanese sniper fire from the tree tops but the snipers were picked off by the leading infantry escort. The cable line came to be known as the 'Tewari Route'.

Tewari's brigade had to survive the monsoons during which there was a lull in operations. They started to live above ground under tarpaulins but seldom got to wear dry clothes. Leaches were a major problem and so they took to burning cigarettes, or applying salt or tobacco to the mouths of the leaches to remove them. Malaria was another more serious problem, with the army suffering more casualties from mosquitoes than from Japanese soldiers during the early days of the war. Besides mosquito nets the troops had to take yellow mepacrine tablets. A rumour had gone around that mepacrine caused impotence and officers actually had to supervise each soldier taking his tablet. The wet clothes caused skin irritations such as 'dhobi itch' and 'Burma foot' and the Corps Commander Lieutenant General Phillip Christison ordered a 'Free From Infection' inspection. Not a single man passed.

After the initial inroads into Arakan a plan was devised to capture the fort of Akyab, the capital of the province. Two brigades would advance on either side of the Mayu range whilst a third would support the movement along the ridge to assist in mopping up. Tewari's brigade would advance along the Kalapanzin river. They started training on small Burmese boats called 'sampans', a large number of which had been gathered for the operation and they were given training in watermanship, swimming with full equipment, riding and animal management, and travelled with mules for signals. Tewari remembered the training as being "great fun". The sampans would float down the river with the men marching along the bank and crossing the chaungs, or streams by swimming across them. Boat to boat communications were erected and the cables had to be kept taut to prevent them from sinking in the undergrowth. The brigade would also send out deep offensive patrols to gather information about the enemy.

Tewari's brigade started its advance down the Mayu Range as a part of Operation Romulus on 14 December 1944. Whilst advancing along the Kalapanzin river many of their sampans were sunk and the mules dropped their loads by kicking and screaming and supplies had to be replenished by airdrops. The forces then advanced south along the Kalapanzin River with the West African 82nd Division. Through Kwazon, Prinshe to Rathedaung they would float down the river under darkness. Kudaung and Rathedaung were taken together, being completely destroyed by shelling, and they were receiving reports that Akyab may be vacated by the Japanese without a fight. One of the battalions was ordered to undertake an opportunity landing on the northern tip of the island and a landing took place unopposed at 4 am on 3 January 1945. Tewari had accompanied the brigade commander in a motor launch and was given permission to go ashore and visit the unit. But he missed his ride back and had to hitch hike to Rathedaung without a hat or any shoes. An assault amphibious landing on Roywa to the south of Akyab was a success, however the next day there was an intense Japanese bombardment. Tewari was then promoted to captain and assigned to another brigade. On his way out he was flown by an American pilot over the battle of Tamandu. Circling over the airfield at Akyab he was dazzled by the sight of all the latest aircraft. Tewari then joined Kondandera Thimayya's Fighting 51st, taking over as Officer Commanding Signals from the British officer, Captain Hall.

Shankarrao Thorat's situation was very different to Krishna Tewari's. He was a Sandhurst graduate from a family with a distant history of military service, and by the middle of World War II he was more than 15 years into his army career.[clxxxii] He had hoped to be posted to a fighting formation in the Middle East, but had instead been sent to the General Branch Staff at Army Headquarters in Simla. He knew that future promotions and command of a battalion would be denied to him if he did not have sufficient operational experience and soon began to "agitate" to be posted to regimental duty. He "pestered" the Military Secretary's Branch so much that in 1944 he was posted to the 4/14th Punjab Regiment which was fighting on the Kohima Front on the India-Burma border.

The 4/14th Punjab had been trying to clear the Japanese from the Naga Hills. But the fighting had been such that no reinforcements could be sent and Thorat had to wait at a reinforcement camp until the Dimapur-Kohima road was safe for convoys. He then joined the rear party of the 9/14th Punjab and started to walk towards the Silchar track. The road was full of shell holes and mortar bombs and artillery shells had stripped the trees. Thorat's men took some long range fire from Japanese guns but little damage was done and the battalion held a defensive position on a much battered hill. Thorat had been posted as second in command but requested the commanding officer to give him command of a forward company to get to know his men and the terrain. The company was involved in a few small skirmishes and he then took up command of his battalion. He enjoyed the thrill of commanding a battalion in fighting; he felt it allowed him to give full scope to his tactical and administrative abilities and he had an awareness that thousands of soldiers now trusted his word.

The Japanese held a hill a mile or two away and Thorat sent out patrols. They were repeatedly beaten back and so he went out himself with his orderly Rahim Bux. The two dressed as stragglers and took dry rations, a sten gun and a kukri. If caught they would pretend to be soldiers of the Indian National Army. Thorat managed to get close to some Japanese sentry posts and a cook house before making his way back to the battalion. A successful attack was made a couple of days later and Thorat's men occupied the hill and destroyed the Japanese dug-in defences so that they could not reoccupy them. They had to spend an afternoon digging to consolidate themselves on the hill and only later realised that they had erected their temporary headquarters on top of a makeshift Japanese cemetery. Thorat was first given a dressing down by his British brigade commander for going out on his own, and then invited over for a drink.

In November 1944 Indian forces moved in three columns to the west of the Chindwin river for the final push into Burma. They had to march, and given the heavily mined fields and the lack of maps, they were worried about getting blown up along the way. Thorat was then given a signal to take over command of the 2/2nd which was fighting in Arakan. When he reached them they had been badly mauled. Thorat's second in command was Major John Montagu, and all the company commanders were British. He was apprehensive about how they would react to being commanded by an Indian; for the previous 179 years the battalion had been commanded by a British officer. He found the company commanders responsive, but felt he had to win their confidence by leading a successful action.

Shankarrao Thorat, Lionel Sen and Kondandera Thimayya each commanded battalions of what came to be known as the 'All India Brigade'. The brigade was tasked with establishing a road block on the route at Kangaw which would enable them to destroy the Japanese forces as they retreated into south Burma. They would have to gather at Akyab, proceed to Myebon by sea, and then capture Kangaw and penetrate Japanese territory. Initially they had to force their way through long and narrow mountains known as the Arakan Yomas which were defended by the Japanese forces. The brigade left Mangdaw in the last week of December 1944 and began its journey through the Kalapanzin Valley. They were moving on a pack basis, which meant that each soldier had to carry four days rations in his own pack. The troops were opposed by Japanese posts on the first day, skirmished their way to Akyab and waited for a ship to take them to Myeob. The commandos did however, have some trouble taking Hill 170. They landed on 25 January 1945 and disembarked unopposed, but began to dig in their defences and took some long range fire from the Japanese. With the incoming tide they had to move inland, and the battle of Kangaw ensued.

Brigadier Reginald Hutton gave his orders for an attack on the Kangaw position. Thorat watched from Brigade Headquarters as the Hyderabadis led by Thimayya launched an attack. But after a fierce counter attack they were forced to fall back. The Baluchis too had to fall back after an attack on Hill 170 and gloom began to descend on the camp. Hutton then told Thorat to "have a bang" at the hill. Thorat did a reconnaissance and then prepared to make a flank attack. The attack would not draw aimed fire from the entire length of the Japanese position, but only from one end of it. However, Thorat would have to move his battalion over 300 yards of open paddy fields. A conference of navy, army and artillery commanders was called and together they made a fire-plan. Whilst the three companies were moving around the hill, artillery had to silence the enemy machine guns and put up a smoke screen. Two companies would move forward, another in depth, and the fourth following in reserve. The move was to be preceded by artillery concentrations on selected targets and the air force was to bomb enemy positions for ten minutes prior to the attack. This would go on until the leading troops were within 200 yards of the enemy trenches. Thorat felt for his troops who would get shot down crossing the paddy fields.

When the time came the air support did not arrive, but they continued the attack nonetheless. Thorat evoked a stirring scene as he showed himself to his men and they shouted out "The Old Man has come!" and all let out cries of 'Sat Shri Akal' and 'Maro Nara Haidari Ya Ali'. The men charged forth with their bayonets, stabbing and slashing, screaming and yelling abuse as they cut down and shot their enemy, battering heads with rifle butts. Thorat thought the men had gone crazy with blood lust, "but what a grand madness it was!"

The Indian and Japanese forces were locked in such close combat that when the air force eventually arrived they realised they could not bomb the main positions but had to bomb the rear of the Japanese position and then strafe opportunity targets. The Japanese eventually fell back and the Indians began to chase them. The battle ended shortly thereafter and the Japanese began to withdraw in an orderly manner. But the Japanese withdrawal was so orderly that Thorat felt that he had not seen the last of them. In the past the Japanese had vacated a defensive position and allowed the Indians to occupy it, but before they could consolidate it the Japanese would return for a quick counter attack. Thorat issued orders to limit the exploitation to half the hill, the remainder could wait until they had consolidated their positions. To Thorat and his battalion the capture of Hill 170 was a great achievement and he did not want to risk losing it. As he was issuing his orders his Signal officer was standing beside him with a Verey light pistol to fire the success signal. Thorat turned to smile at him, and three gunshots went up into the afternoon sky.

Thorat then summoned his company commanders and issued them with orders not to occupy the trenches which had been vacated by the enemy; they could be subjected to accurate artillery fire as their range would be known to the retreating enemy. Instead they were to dig their own defensive positions ahead of those vacated by the retreating Japanese forces. Thorat also issued orders to erect improvised head covers over the trenches. Once the digging of the new trenches had begun, he issued additional orders to his administrative company to send grenades and mortar bombs and ammunition to replenish the depleted stocks. Thorat was expecting a counter attack so these supplies, along with food and water had to be brought quickly up the hill and casualties had to be cleared away. He had to prepare a fresh fire-plan to break up the anticipated counter attack and inspect the new defensive positions to co-ordinate their fire and boost their morale. He felt that no commander should be too busy for a word of cheer or a pat on the back for his troops. Thorat thought they had paid a heavy price to capture the hill, would defend it at any cost, and pushed his men to keep digging "without any mercy".

After the trenches had been dug and the weapons sited, Thorat issued orders for all the men except the sentries to lay down and relax, for he knew they would not get any rest once night came. The Japanese counter attack was delayed, as their original garrison had been so badly mauled that they needed to call for fresh troops. When it came, it did so with frightening suddenness. But despite waves of mortar bombing and artillery shelling, the Japanese were unable to do much damage as the Indians were well dug in and protected by their improvised head covers. The artillery lifted but the mortar fire continued; Thorat took it as a signal that the infantry would be coming up from behind. He issued orders not to fire until the enemy was in sight, and when they did open fire the Japanese were just 100 yards away. The Japanese crept forward, making "weird noises" and Thorat ordered the artillery to open pre-determined defensive fire. The Japanese had advanced enough for close combat, and the Indians came out of their trenches to meet them. The fight continued for 15 minutes after which the Japanese retreated for an hour only to return for a fresh attack. The cycle of battle continued throughout the night.

The next day with only a few jitter parties coming forth to create some nuisance, Thorat ordered half the officers and men to sleep for four hours at a time, something which he supervised personally. Thorat thought of himself as a mother who had to look after his men without regard for his own comfort. He then called a co-ordinating conference of all officers; he was standing in a trench and his officers were crouching in trenches and shell holes around him. As he began the meeting Japanese mortar fire came in, a bomb burst and Major Jack Cumber, who was a little outside of the trench threw up his arms and collapsed. Thorat jumped into his trench and took Cumber's head in his lap. He was rushed to the regimental aid post and despite initial fears he was operated on under a tarpaulin and managed to survive. Thorat was appreciative of the personal valour, administrative ability and loyalty of his officers, most of whom were British. He also thought he could not have served with a better group of jawans, who under the privations of battle never complained or deviated from the path of duty.

***

In order to be promoted to the higher command positions

Indian officers had to attend Staff College. At the start of World War II only 4 out of the 62 officers at the Staff College at Quetta were Indian.[clxxxiii] Under Field Marshall Claude Auchinleck's tenure the number of Indian officers steadily grew through the war years. But even by 1947 only 62 out of the 200 officers in attendance at Quetta were Indian.[clxxxiv]

Anant Naravane had passed out of the Indian Military Academy in 1938 and went on to serve in north Africa during World War II.[clxxxv] After returning from the war he moved to Quetta to join the Staff College course in July 1946. The course placed emphasis on the proper writing of orders and instructions for operations for war. Minor staff duties consisted of crossing Ts and dotting Is and correct numbering of paragraphs, sub paragraphs and punctuation marks. Once officers had mastered the paperwork they went on to an 'appreciation of the situation' and various war operations, followed by ground exercises with and without troops. Naravane recalled that officers were divided into syndicates in which they played roles such as staff officers and commanders in appointments in formation headquarters at levels including brigade, division and corps. Towards the end of the course the officers took part in a seven day camp in which they performed different command and staff appointments. The routine was relieved by cocktail parties and dinner functions for staff and students.

Onkar Kalkat was commissioned in 1942 and went on to serve in Burma. He passed the examination for the Quetta Staff College in December 1946 and in 1949 he received a message that he had been chosen to attend the first long course at the Defence Services Staff College at Wellington in Madras.[clxxxvi] General Thimayya told him that the college would probably not be able to teach him much about staff duties which he already knew, but that he would get the opportunity to form life-long associations with colleagues from the army, navy and air force.

During his year at Wellington Kalkat came into contact with the College Commandant, Major General Walter Lentaigne. He learnt a lot from him and found his summing up at the end of the exercises to be "quite brilliant". Kalkat thought that Lentaigne had great tactical insight and a good eye for the ground. He was the founder of the institution and devoted to it, and when there was nothing else going on he could often be seen weeding the gardens himself or checking on the construction work of the contractors. Lentaigne did not mind giving Kalkat his views on Indians' lack of patriotism and civic sense though, something which was evident in the filth of city streets and railway platforms. He would also hold forth on the medley of self-seeking groups all across India; although the colony had become independent, it would not become a nation until Indians could develop individual and collective discipline and dedication. Kalkat remembered the students branding Lentaigne "anti-Indian", but he admitted that "truth is bitter and we have to face it and meet the challenge."

Harbakhsh Singh returned to the Indian Military Academy after Independence as deputy commandant, and saw some evidence of Lentaigne's criticism.[clxxxvii] Besides his responsibility for general administration, he was also in charge of allotment of accommodation, and when he went to visit his own lodgings he found the house in a bad state with the grounds neglected and the pool choked with weeds. He moved into the bungalow and set about restoring it to its former glory. He also noticed that the grounds throughout the academy were no longer as well kept as they had been during his days as a cadet. During his time the cadets had not been allowed to walk on the grass, but the rule was no longer followed which resulted in both the cadets and the public leaving unsightly foot tracks all over the academy's lawns. Harbakhsh reinstituted the rule that the cadets were not to step on the grass and had the foot tracks dug and re-laid and notices put up warning passers-by to keep off the grass. He even reprimanded the academy's horticulture staff and instructed them to plant flowers and shrubs to beautify the grounds.

In addition to the deterioration of the academy's grounds, Harbakhsh also noticed that cadets were drinking hard liquor in secret. To combat the menace he instituted a system in which cadets could 'officially' pay for a bottle of beer each, on the condition that they only drink on the apron of the grass near the cricket ground on Sundays where they would be served a picnic lunch from the nearby Cadets' Mess. He wanted to give them some freedom as future officers of the Indian Army and thought the system was well received. He would often have meals with the cadets and also see that the standard of the Officers' Mess was maintained. Harbakhsh wanted to teach the cadets the meaning of punctuality and would set an example himself, arriving five minutes before the stipulated time for both official and unofficial events and dealt strictly with any late arrivals. He would also remain vigilant at the morning sick parade "to find out if there were any malingerers among them."

***

The army had always been recognised as the most stubborn of the services when it came to the racial attitudes of its British officers. These attitudes had often been held up as a reason to delay the Indianisation process; British officers would never be able to respect fellow Indian officers whom they viewed as racially inferior. They would never take orders from Indians, and in the end would stop serving in India were the racial hierarchy of the British Raj disturbed. It was a familiar argument used from the days of Frederick Roberts down to the generals who sat on each and every committee on Indianisation during the 1920s. Edwin Montagu had recognised the reticence of the army to reform, but argued that times were changing and the army would have to change with them.[clxxxviii]

Harbakhsh Singh found the 'colour bar' much stronger in Malaya than in India and one incident in particular stuck in his mind.[clxxxix] The Raja of Perak invited the British officers of Kuanton to a drinks and dinner party and Harbakhsh thought that his Commanding Officer, Lieutenant Colonel John Parkin would insist that the Indian officers also be invited or else refuse the invitation. Instead Parkin accepted the invitation and took all the British officers along to the party and the Indian officers were left behind. The Indians had thought of Parkin as a "bit of an Imperialist", but not anti-Indian, particularly as he had been an instructor to Indian cadets at the Indian Military Academy in Dehra Dun.

Shankarrao Thorat thought the attitude of some British officers towards Indian officers was not what it should have been; their social behaviour "was bordering on hostile".[cxc] They did not hide the fact that they did not want Indians as officers and it was forbidden for Indian officers to bring Indian food or even play Indian music in their own rooms. Some British officers would not allow their wives to dance with Indian officers at the Club, and Thorat thought they were being treated as "outcastes". However, there were notable exceptions and instances of kindness and courtesy and Thorat thought that whatever their social attitudes, the British were fair in their official dealings and took care in training the young Indian officers in their duties and responsibilities. Onkar Kalkat was an example of this; he was promoted to major, superseding three superior British officers in his battalion.[cxci] The three British officers marched the next day to the commanding officer to protest against the promotion. The commanding officer reprimanded them but they continued their protest, and were packed up and sent to the training centre at Ambala the same afternoon. Kalkat saw it as a victory for merit and one which left a lasting impression on all in the battalion.

Pessie Madan gave an account of the daily frictions over food and music between British and Indian officers.cxcii He thought that the British regular officers were more patronising to Indians than those who had been called up more recently on compulsory service. They would not lose an opportunity to criticise Indian eating habits and table manners or make fun of Indian accents. Lieutenant Reddy came to their attention for his habit of putting large amounts of tomato sauce on his fried eggs at breakfast. The English practice at the time was to only add tomato sauce to fried fish. Reddy then took the fight to the lounge and turned the radio to a station which was playing Carnatic classical music, only to be shouted down by the senior captain to "turn off that bloody radio". Reddy switched the radio off and left the lounge and took the matter up with the colonel the next day. The colonel skirted the issue of discrimination by instituting a rule that the majority in the lounge, which happened to be British, would decide on the music to be played.

***

Indianisation of the officer corps of the Indian Army only gathered pace in the 1930s when it could no longer be resisted. The conundrum which had baffled committee after committee during the 1920s of how to implement a programme of Indianisation in the army without letting go of the Indian state was enveloped by the passage of events. By the time the Round Table Conference of 1930 recommended setting up another committee to establish an Indian Sandhurst it was clear that self-government, or Dominion status or Independence was just a matter of time.

The Indian cadets who had been trained at Sandhurst in the 1920s had to make their way in an alien and hostile cultural environment. They were Indian boys who were a long way from home, trying to survive in the fountain of British military culture, knowing that the course had cost their parents a large amount of money. There were no special concessions for the Indian cadets, they were under strict supervision by British officers, their British instructors were tough, and they rarely mixed socially with British cadets. It was this type of culture and environment which moderate Indian politicians of the 1920s like Mohammad Ali Jinnah wanted to replicate in India. They thought it was necessary to take Indian boys out of their cultural environment and their religious and caste and provincial prejudices in order to turn them into officers of a modern national army. When the Indian Military Academy was set up it did largely replicate the technical training of Sandhurst, but the social training was relatively relaxed. Makhan Singh's struggle with the teapot in Dehra Dun was much less serious than all the unwritten rules which Joyanto Chaudhuri had to observe at Sandhurst. The establishment of the Indian Military Academy at Dehra Dun was also the beginning of an Indian institution, one which its cadets would return to as teachers after Independence.

The racial theories which had sustained the Indian Army for over a century were finally blown away during World War II. Both the sanctity of the British officer-Indian sepoy relationship and the theory of the martial races would die on the battlefields of Burma. One of the main objections to the entry of Indian officers had been that they would not command the obedience of their own Indian troops who would always look to a British officer for guidance. Another was that Indian officers simply did not have leadership qualities and could never earn the respect of British officers. As the war came to India's eastern frontier Emergency Commissions were opened up irrespective of race, and those Indian officers who had been trained at Sandhurst and Dehra Dun during the 1920s and 1930s finally took up positions of command. When the fighting started Indian officers disproved both of the old objections; Shankarrao Thorat's memory of standing in the trenches cradling an injured Jack Cumber, commanding British officers and ordering his Indian troops across the paddy fields of Burma showed what an Indian officer was capable of when tested in battle.

During the early 1940s the Congress began to place 'national control' of the army at the top of its demands for any transfer of power which might occur after the end of the war; it was thought that a transfer of power without Indian control of defence would be incomplete. The Congress did not have any plans for raising a new army, and so what it was referring to in its demand for 'national control' was a handover of the British Indian Army. However, by the time of Independence in 1947 the officer class of the Indian Army would be split into three separate groups; British officers would start to leave, as would Muslim officers for Pakistan, and as Indianisation of the army had started much later than in the other services Indian officers only made up a small section of the total officer corps. In the months after Independence it was this relatively small group of Indian officers who would have to step up and take command of one of the largest armies in the world.

Six
Braving the Consequences

The development of an efficient and effective system of policing was a relatively neglected aspect of state building in India during the late 18th century. Militias were created in Bengal, as were the posts of lieutenant of police and superintendent of police in Calcutta, yet they could do little to control the dacoits who roamed the interiors of the province. In 1774 the East India Company's Governor General, Warren Hastings even advocated the restoration of the powers of the old Mughal Faujdars who would be responsible for maintaining law and order on the land and report to a Company President in Calcutta.[cxciii] This broad policy of indirect policing and reliance on traditional Indian figures of authority continued for 70 years in Bengal and Bombay and Madras. The period was one of warfare and rampant violent crime throughout much of India, and it was from one of the newly annexed corners of the land that the first attempts to build a modern police force arose. Sir Charles Napier conquered Sind in 1843 and proceeded to establish a police force modelled on the Royal Irish Constabulary. Governments in Bombay, Madras and Oudh all followed his lead in the late 1840s and 1850s before a Police Commission finally established an Indian Police in 1861.

Whilst the Indian Civil Service and the Indian Army were the pride of the British Raj, the Indian Police was not held in quite the same high regard. The district officer of the Indian Civil Service was an archetype of rugged masculinity, galloping through the districts of the Raj, keeping the peace and collecting revenue, his strength and integrity unquestioned.

Likewise, the British officer of the Indian Army was known for his courage and daring, leading his loyal Indian sepoys, conquering new swathes of the subcontinent against the odds. They were the heroes of British imperialism found in stories and novels and children's books. But the Indian Police officer was nowhere to be seen in this imagery of empire. Even Rudyard Kipling found it difficult to create a heroic British police officer in his India, and no British parents wanted to marry their daughters into the service. Much of the derision that British officials held for the service was thus not on account of its Indian constabulary, but the calibre of their own British officers.

The Indian Police was based upon a similar racial hierarchy as the Indian Civil Service and the Indian Army however. The British police officer supervised the Indian constable, just as the Indian Civil Service officer supervised the Indian clerk and the British army officer led his Indian sepoy. Given that middle class Indian families held similar reservations about the force to the British, there was never any great demand for places in the Indian Police. In fact, Congressmen looked down on the service as much as the British rulers did. As in the Indian Civil Service and the Indian Army before World War I, any suggestions for the induction of Indian officers into the Indian Police were met with concerns about the security of the service, overlaid with familiar statements about Indian racial deficiencies. But like the other services the Indian Police was subjected to reform after World War I, and a framework was eventually established for Indianisation; the officer cadre would be Indianised at a slightly slower pace than the Indian Civil Service, but much faster than the Indian Army.

The first Indian officers entered the force and began their training in the early 1920s at just the time that the non-cooperation movement was gathering momentum. As their fellow Indians were challenging the state, these young men made their way into Police Training Colleges around India where they were taught to maintain law and order for the British Raj. They entered the inner sanctum of British police officers in India, the Officers' Mess, and were then instructed by British superiors in their first postings as assistant superintendents. They were not the last resort in the case of a breakdown of law and order like the army, nor were they directing operations behind the scenes like the officers of the civil service. Indian officers of the Indian Police were the men in uniform, on the street, waving lathis against Congress protesters, controlling crowds and enforcing the writ of the state. Most Indian officers missed the first non-cooperation movement of the early 1920s, but many had graduated to senior ranks by the time of the civil disobedience movement in the early 1930s. As the political campaigns of the Congress became more confrontational, they would have to find creative ways to maintain law and order whilst also maintaining their own personal safety and reputations in the towns and cities in which they would spend their careers.

***

The Indian Police was established with the passage of the Police Act of India 1861. Police officers were like the officers of the Indian Civil Service in that they were recruited by the Government of India which paid their salaries and pensions, however they spent their careers working for the provincial governments to which they were assigned. Thus, whilst the initial appointments were made on an All India basis, training, transfers and promotions of officers took place at the provincial level.

The officer cadre of the Indian Police maintained a relatively flat hierarchy. This meant that much like the Indian Civil Service officer, the Indian Police officer was, from a junior level allowed great autonomy and was expected to exercise huge responsibilities. The inspector general of police, the highest police officer in the province would, until the start of the 20th century be an Indian Civil Service officer who reported to the lieutenant governor. Next in the pecking order was the deputy inspector general who would report to the inspector general and be responsible for law and order in the districts within his range. Next came the district superintendents of police, the middle management of the police force. But whilst the district superintendent of police was the senior policeman in his district, he had to bow before the district collector from the Indian Civil Service who was technically in charge of maintaining law and order, for which the police was just one instrument. After the district superintendents of police came the assistant superintendents of police, the entry level for the Indian Police. The assistant superintendent of police would spend long years assisting the district superintendent of police, preparing to eventually take charge of a district.

Initially recruitment to the Indian Police was by nomination. Englishmen in India needed only to secure a nomination from the lieutenant governor of their province to gain a position as an assistant superintendent of police. They simply had to be between 18 and 25, of good character, and be able to furnish details about their education and background. Only once they were appointed would they have to pass examinations in criminal codes, police procedures and the language of their province. Many joined from the army and to start with they were put on probation as head constables and inspectors and then quickly promoted as assistant superintendents of police. The early British officers of the Indian Police were generally from poor backgrounds, did not take the job seriously, and in many cases just saw their position as a path to other appointments in the government. They were thought of as inferior to their colleagues in the Indian Civil Service in education and manners, often married local White women, and many were drunks who ran up large debts. The British ruling elite, the Indian press, and Indian politicians all characterised British police officers as rude and uneducated.

Given that most Congressmen came from the educated elite of Indian society, they did not hesitate in expressing their contempt for these ill-educated young Englishmen. Speaking at the annual Congress session in Calcutta in 1901 Hem Chandra Roy quoted *The Pioneer,* describing the Indian Police as "the favourite refuge for the European destitute- a peaceful haven where the examiner is unknown and the acquaintance with Chaucer and conic sections was at a discount." In addition to not having read *The Canterbury Tales* or mastered geometry, most of these Englishmen were born and raised in India. They were thought to be at least mildly corrupted by a boyhood in India and unlike civil servants and army officers they were thought of as "too of this country".[cxciv] They were looked upon by the British establishment in India as lacking the English character which could only come from a childhood in England.

***

By the late 19th century the Indian Police was recognised to be a blot on the British administration of India. Complaints came in from all parts of the country and bore similarities in their descriptions of an inept police force which harassed innocent people and brought disrepute to the British Raj. District officers gave a graphic account of a system of policing which was always let down by the quality of its people.

The Public Service Commission of 1886 noted that the practice of the appointment of police officers from amongst the officers of the army, whilst useful in the wake of the Mutiny almost 30 years earlier, had fallen into disrepair. The prevailing system of pure nomination to the police did not throw up a sufficient number of candidates with adequate educational qualifications or a good enough work ethic. The commission recommended that there should be limited competition among candidates in England for a portion of the total recruitment, another competition among candidates selected in India on the basis of physique, education, and knowledge of Indian languages, as well as promotion from the rank of inspector for exceptional ability or merit shown in service. It recommended that appointment to the rank of inspector should be made from the lower grades of the force rather than admitting outsiders. The commission concluded that most of the abuses within the police force were due to low pay at the lower grades and whatever other reforms the government may envisage, nothing would change as long as the man in-charge of the local police station was not paid well enough to withstand temptation.

According to the commission, the preservation of law and order and the security of property were considered to be pillars of British rule and so the entry of Indians to the higher posts of the police could not be allowed to damage them. The Public Service Commission argued that one of the most important qualities in a police officer was the ability to remain impartial and firm in the event of a religious clash, and it was unclear whether Indian officers would be able to do so. The isolated instances of Indians being appointed to the charges of district posts had not been completely successful. The commission held that whilst British officers would have to predominate in the higher ranks for many years to come, Indians should not be excluded altogether. In the way of Commissions of Enquiry, the question of whether to employ Indians in the higher ranks of the police was left to the Government of India.

The Government of India then initiated enquiries into the police in the six provinces in December 1888. The Bengal Government admitted that law enforcement by the police was inadequate and a large percentage of serious crime never came to its notice and so was never even enquired into.[cxcv] Of the cases which were investigated, many were challenged and acquitted in court. The Bengal Government blamed this on the regular police not being adequately assisted by the chaukidars. In addition, the lower police working on investigations were incompetent and untrustworthy and the criminal courts were biased in favour of the criminals. The Bengal Government did not want head constables to be in-charge of thanas or involved in investigations.

In the North West Provinces and Oudh it was found that there was a higher proportion of serious crime according to the population than in Punjab, the Central Provinces and Bengal.[cxcvi] The local administration blamed this on increasing population, poverty, rising prices, the decay of traditional industries, the desire for more opulent living, the lack of co-operation from the public, the loss of control of the peasantry by the zamindars, the workings of the courts, the work of Indian lawyers, the insufficient use of chains and whipping, the reduced diet in jail, and crooked police being exposed to bribes.

District officers made their opinions known: "In more serious cases the police, though they do not conceal the crime, if it is made worth their while, mismanage the investigation. This is another cause of the want of success in securing the conviction, and is only to be remedied by bettering the position of investigative officers."[cxcvii] Another officer wrote that "The condition of the police is beyond doubt gravely defective. The force is underpaid and its standard of honesty and intelligence is low. Service in the police is held in ill repute and offers hard work and no prizes."[cxcviii]

Senior officials joined the chorus of criticism. The

Commissioner of Lucknow wrote: "The police are a disreputable body, and they know it, they are, therefore, mistrusted and hampered even when they want to work openly and fairly."cxcix The Senior Commissioner said: "every year convinces me that the police is honeycombed with corruption. Facts constantly come to my knowledge which convince me of this, although it would be hard to prove it in a judicial enquiry."cc The Commissioner of Allahabad wrote: "The only suggestions for police reform which I desire to urge are based on the belief that the police is by far the most backward branch, and that the need for improving it is so urgent as to demand strong measures and much expenditure of thought and money."cci At the top of the provincial hierarchy Lieutenant Governor Sir Auckland Colvin stressed that much of the time the police could not properly understand the Code of Criminal Procedure with which they had to work, whilst the public was unhelpful and untruthful and the press, Bar and public opinion were not yet developed enough to prevent the police from abusing their powers.ccii

The Inspector General of the Central Provinces demanded a revision in the pay scales of the police to stop the influx of untrained men who were hampering the efficiency of the force.cciii A good agricultural year would mean an increase in wages and prices which would make just about any job other than police constable preferable for the Indian peasant. The district superintendent would have to take in anyone who presented himself as long as he was not a known bad character. Sooner or later the government would be left without a police force. In Punjab officials tried to pass the blame for the increase in crime. They reported that the accused had better lawyers, the district magistrates were not paying enough attention to criminal work, the number of British magistrates had fallen, and second and third class magistrates were doing most of the criminal work and were not keeping up with the load and complexity of the cases.cciv

In Madras the government also lamented that the rank and file received a coolie's pay which only encouraged corruption.[ccv] In a Memorandum prepared for Parliament, Secretary of State for India, the Viscount Cross tried to moderate the torrent of complaints: "Though the Police Department is now, as heretofore, a weak point in the administration, and though from time to time cases of extortion and oppression by the police come to light still there have been important improvements in the police system and practice in the past 30 years."[ccvi]

The enquiries which emanated from the provinces in 1888 led to more detailed investigations in Bengal and the North West Provinces. In Bengal, a committee was chaired by the Commissioner of Bhagalpore and Haileybury alumnus, John Beames. The committee submitted its Report in 1891, finding that First Information Reports were recorded carelessly, that there were delays in taking up investigations, omissions were made in sending up important evidence and there was undue reliance on confessions which led to a lack of confidence in the police from the courts.[ccvii] Another committee was appointed in the North West Provinces and Oudh in 1890 under William Kaye, a Member of the Board of Revenue.[ccviii] Kaye recommended that the police should be an imperial service and should be selected on the basis of competition in England. The committee wanted the martial races to be recruited into the lower levels of the service and for remuneration to be in cash rather than land grants.

***

A racial hierarchy ordered the relationship between British officers and Indian constables in the police as it did in the other imperial services. The entire edifice of policing in India was dependent on a watchful British eye; it was thought that Indians could make for good and useful subordinates as long as they were subject to British supervision. Left to themselves Indians lacked discipline and initiative and so could only learn under the guidance of others. Another argument precluding promotion of Indians to the higher ranks of the police was that they would not enjoy the social standing to deal with the other officers of elite services like the Indian Civil Service and members of the judiciary.

As early as 1860 William Robinson, the Inspector General of Madras and Member of the Police Commission wrote:

> "They [Indians] are deficient in those habits of discipline and command which are essential to the maintenance of an organised force. They are wanting in self reliance, resource and pluck to [unclear] emergencies, nor do they possess the strong will and determined energy and persistence which are indispensable for the constant and irksome work of personal inspection over a wide area without which a police force languishes and falls into confusion....To this may be added the grave risk of want of integrity in a post of exceptional temptation and of want of confidence and assurance on the part of the district magistracy and the people...the existence of caste feeling and other local influences weaken the confidence of subordinates in the impartiality of such superior officers."[ccix]

Views did not change as the decades wore on. Most of the

British officers who appeared before the Public Service Commission of 1886 opposed the appointment of Indians to the higher grades of the police. Indians were variously thought to be unwilling to engage in hard physical activity, lacked the capacity to supervise, were deficient in courage, lacked a sense of responsibility and would be unable to maintain discipline. John McAndrew, Deputy Inspector General Punjab argued that Indians were "wanting in energy, both physical and mental" and that they would not be able to maintain discipline or be impartial in religious disputes and in such events the government would not be able to rely on them for accurate information.[ccx] The Bombay Government did not think that Indians were qualified and the Resident at Hyderabad thought that Indians were corrupt and would be liable to conceal crimes committed by men of influence.[ccxi]

Whether Indians were fit to be officers of the Indian Police or not, there was an urgent need for a better class of British officer to improve the workings of the force and rescue its reputation from the depths to which it had sunk across India. With a view to reform, the recommendations of the Public Service Commission were circulated to the provincial governments in 1891.[ccxii] Madras wanted to recruit those who had just failed the Indian Civil Service or Sandhurst examinations. Bombay was not in favour of either selection in England or competition in India; candidates just needed a solid education and then be selected according to qualities like health, tact, discipline and shrewdness. Bengal wanted two-thirds of the recruitment reserved for those who missed out on the Indian Civil Service, and the other one-third held for limited competition amongst British residents in India. The Government of the North West Provinces did not want competition in England either, it thought there was enough good material in India. It recommended that there be competition among the nominees and a special proportion reserved for Indians. Neither did Punjab want competition in

England; 25% of the Punjab Police was reserved for army men. Only the Government of the Central Provinces was in favour of a system of open competition.

In 1893 the Viceroy Henry Petty-Fitzmaurice, the Marquess of Lansdowne advocated a competitive examination in England for the Indian Police modelled on the Indian Civil Service examination.[ccxiii] Lansdowne suggested that recruitment to the Indian Police take place from those boys who had sat for the entrance examination for Sandhurst but missed out on entry to the army; the India Office could save some money as it would not need to run a separate examination. As there were often ten candidates appearing for every place offered at Sandhurst, the Government of India would still be able to draw on a talented pool of applicants who could go on for further specific training at Sandhurst or at the Metropolitan Police before travelling to India.

Objections to Lansdowne's plan included the concern that the Indian Police would become formally, rather than informally associated with academic failure. Sandhurst would neither want to host rejected candidates nor would the rejected candidates want to train at Sandhurst having missed out in open competition. Most however agreed that some training should be completed in England and the remainder on arrival in India. The India Office then decided to progress with recruitment from those candidates who had passed the entrance examinations to Sandhurst and Woolwich. Later, at the start of the 20th century a separate examination for entrance to the Indian Police was established and administered by the Public Service Commission.

Much as in the Indian Civil Service before World War I, when Englishmen willing to serve in India were still abundant, the main concern in British Government circles was with drawing its police officers from the right class in English society. The Viceroy, George Curzon wrote of his concerns to the India

Office:

> *"I have seen enough of India to know that the greatest menace to the future of British Rule in this country is not, as has sometimes been alleged, the House of Commons, nor the Russian advance, nor the Indian Congress, nor the Indian character, but the attitude and passions of the inferior class of Englishmen who will be increasingly attracted to India by the lower grades of employment, or by industrial, mercantile and professional careers. If this class of man is let loose among the people as a Police Officer, there is no end to the mischief he may do."*[ccxiv]

In 1902 Curzon recommended setting up a strong commission to look into the shortcomings of the police. In making the recommendation to the secretary of state, he cited the fact that the improvements in the pay and prospects coming out of the 1888 reforms had not had the desired effect of controlling the increase in crime.[ccxv] The Indian Police did not offer Indians of a high enough class an attractive career, which meant that the British officers were not well served by their subordinates. Discipline and punishments were overly harsh, police on the railways were inadequate, and the organisation and pay at the district level was not as uniform as it could be. Curzon argued that whilst the government was doing a good job in other areas, a commission of enquiry was necessary to alleviate the derision which an incompetent police force had brought upon the British Raj across India. Sir Andrew Fraser was named President of the Police

Commission, and two of the seven members were Indians.

The Report of the Police Commission pointed to the fact that corruption in the lower ranks of the police resulted from the constabulary being paid less than a living wage. Even upright and honest constables would have to succumb to temptation given that they had families to support. Besides which, the public expected no better of them in the first place. Apart from the economic factors, corruption was supposed to be an organic part of Indian culture and British officers could only do their best to keep it under control rather than eradicate it completely. The Indian constables were also thought to possess the characteristics of the class from which they were recruited and the inspectors and sub inspectors were not much better given that they carried with them the habits they had learnt as constables. In addition, it was the all pervasive corruption of the force which then kept Indians from respectable backgrounds from joining the police due to objections from their families.

According to the Police Commission, the British officer's only redeeming quality was his integrity. Besides that he was ill-educated, lacked intelligence, was poorly trained and could barely speak an Indian language. He was often inundated with paperwork which he would then pass off to his Indian subordinates which would make him reluctant to take any disciplinary action against them should the need arise. The commission condemned the system of nomination, and competition among nominated candidates in India which co-existed with competition in England and the promotion of inspectors. It approved of the system of competition in England, but wanted the age limit lowered to 18 from 20, and recommended that successful candidates undergo a two year probationary period at an English university followed by a stint at a provincial training school in India. New entrants would be promoted to senior superintendent of police after seven years of service.

The Police Commission recommended that more Indians be promoted as long as they did not impair efficiency and that a certain number of superintendent posts be reserved for them. A new rank of deputy superintendent of police, which would be equivalent to assistant superintendent, was to be reserved for Indians; half the places would be for those already serving in the revenue, judicial or police services, and the other half would be drawn from the inspector rank. Viceroy Curzon was not in favour of the move and British officers saw it as a threat to their positions. Sir Rameshwar Singh Thakur Bahadur, the Maharaja of Darbhanga recorded a note of dissent in which he advocated open competition in England and India irrespective of race. The commission rejected his suggestion, stressing that the government needed to have different standards in order to control the proportions of the races better in the higher ranks of the service.

The Secretary of State William Brodrick, the Earl of Midleton was apprehensive about the publication of the Police Commission's Report, however Curzon and the Government of India thought it should be made public. The report had raised the touchy issue of corruption, but the Government of India argued that the matter of corruption in the force was common knowledge and that bribery was customary in India and not unlike money given in Europe to ease daily transactions. It was only a problem when it got out of control and it was worse amongst the police because of the powers which they held.[ccxvi] The Government of India highlighted the need to improve the qualifications of the British officers in the service but recommended that the recruits be trained in London and attached to Scotland Yard for a year rather than a university. It suggested that India born British officers should continue to be appointed as assistant superintendents by the viceroy, but that only one such appointment should be made in each province annually. All training for those selected from

England would take place in India for 18 months at one of the Police Training Schools.

A resolution was eventually published with the Report of the Police Commission in March 1905, almost two years after the Report had been submitted to the Government of India. The resolution argued that the failings of the police were partly due to the attitudes and habits of the Indian public as well as the low pay and poor prospects of the members of the force.[ccxvii] The Indian Police was untouched by English education and its traditions and culture which had raised the standard of the Indian Civil Service. Police traditions were Indian, and so were the traditional beliefs about it. In addition, the pay was pitiful compared with the skills necessary to successfully perform the work. According to the resolution, the shortcomings of the Indian Police were a display of just how difficult it was to govern India given the material that the government had to work with. It recommended that British officers be recruited exclusively in England, however the viceroy would still be able to appoint British residents in India in exceptional circumstances. Officers would be trained for 18 months in India and a new cadre of Indian deputy superintendents would be raised with functions similar to assistant superintendents. They would be eligible for promotion to the post of superintendent and would mainly be promoted from the inspector rank.

***

Despite reluctance from the Government of India, the new deputy superintendent rank was opened to both experienced Indian inspectors and educated Indians from outside the Indian Police. These Indian deputy superintendents would work alongside assistant superintendents who were brought out from England. The situation became awkward however, as most of the deputy superintendents were older, experienced Indian policemen whilst the assistant superintendents were English boys new to India and police work. The Indian deputy superintendent would also end up with much of the administrative paperwork and translation requirements whilst the British assistant superintendent would be groomed to take the superintendent's place.

One Indian deputy superintendent, Manmun Hasan Khan grew tired of translating case diaries from English to Urdu and decided to file a written complaint.[ccxviii] He argued that translation duties should be more evenly shared with the English assistant superintendent since it was he who needed to learn the language. Khan's superior, Henry Williams argued that Khan would be much more efficient in translation, and if he and other Indians wanted to rise in the service they would have to master the paperwork. The inspector general of police took Khan's side however and ordered a more equitable distribution of the work.

Those Indian deputy superintendents who were recruited from outside the Indian Police were often highly qualified and well educated, much more so than the English boys who could not gain admission to a university or to Sandhurst. Many Indian recruits were even physically sturdier than their English colleagues. Alakh Sinha, who had studied for an M.A. at the General Assembly Institution, Calcutta was among the first of the directly recruited Indian deputy superintendents.[ccxix] He was sent to the Training School at Bhagalpore in Bihar in February 1908, and a question about uniforms quickly arose. The uniform for the new deputy superintendents was the same as that worn by British superintendents and assistant superintendents prior to the creation of the provincial service. In order to maintain a distinction with the new deputy superintendents, the assistant superintendents' uniform was changed to an open collar tunic with a blue neck tie and a helmet with a blue pagri. Whereas the deputy superintendents would wear a closed tunic and a helmet similar to those worn by British sergeants, with a khaki pagri. The assistant superintendents would wear a shoulder badge with the initials I.P. for 'Imperial Police', whereas deputy superintendents would wear B.P. for 'Bihar Police'.

The uniform issue irritated Sinha and his Indian colleagues, and they finally lost patience when deputy superintendents were expected to salute assistant superintendents on parade. Sinha and the new deputy superintendents refused to do so. The principal of the Training School was displeased and asked them why they were refusing to salute the assistant superintendents. The deputy superintendents referred him to the relevant section of the Police Commission Report and the Orders of the Government of India under which deputy superintendents and assistant superintendents held 'similar status'. The principal argued that the deputy superintendents would have to salute the assistant superintendents once they became superintendents. But Sinha's colleague Saiyid Rizawi retorted that it was not clear who would reach superintendent rank first. After this the matter was put to rest and deputy superintendents would simply exchange a 'good morning' or 'afternoon' with assistant superintendents on the parade ground.

Months later, after a new principal had taken over there was another slight as the Lieutenant-Governor of Bengal visited the Training School and the British assistant superintendents were introduced to him individually by name and received handshakes. The Indian deputy superintendents were introduced as a group and missed out on the coveted handshakes. Sinha thought it may have been because the principal did not remember their names. He felt that this showed the assistant superintendents, "most of whom were boys in their teens", that the deputy superintendents were an inferior being. One of the assistant superintendents wanted the deputy superintendents to salute a senior subaltern of the army who had been appointed first grade assistant superintendent. They replied: "Nothing doing".

***

The principle of including more Indian officers in the Indian Police had been accepted by the Islington Commission during World War I. After the war it was bundled into the broader process of the Indianisation of the imperial services in the wake of the Montagu-Chelmsford reforms and the issue was taken up with some vigour by moderate Indian politicians in the Indian Legislative Assembly in Delhi. The customary correspondence between Delhi and London ensued and featured debates over whether the Indian Police was closer to the Indian Civil Service or the Indian Army in its security role, and the appropriate pace at which Indianisation should proceed.

The Islington Commission however still accepted the need for importing the majority of officers of the Indian Police from England. The commission recommended that competitive entry into the Indian Police be held in London, Dublin and Edinburgh. The age limit of the candidates was to be restricted to between 19 and 21 years and recruits were to remain unmarried until they reached India. The commission also advocated that Anglo-Indians and Indians educated in England for five years be able to appear for the London examination and the viceroy's discretionary appointments be used more often to appoint Indians. In a new formula it recommended that one-third of all recruitment to the assistant superintendent rank be reserved for Indians, of which two-thirds would be on the basis of competitive examination and one-third would be appointed from the deputy superintendent rank.

Madan Mohan Malaviya moved a resolution in the Imperial

Legislative Council in Delhi on 13 March 1918 recommending that the age limit be raised to between 21 and 23, that the Islington Commission's recommendation for raising pensions and salaries be rejected, the rule that candidates appearing for the Indian Police examination be of pure European descent be removed, and that there be simultaneous recruitment in India and England, and if not, then half the recruitment take place by open competition in India. The resolution was opposed by five British members of the Council. The Home Member, Sir William Vincent argued that the police did not need university men, but boys straight out of public school who were fit and could be trained. The police was closer to the army than the civil service in this respect. The British wanted character rather than book knowledge and the resolution was opposed.

The Government of India conveyed its views on the recommendations of the Islington Commission to the Secretary of State, Edwin Montagu.[ccxx] It opposed allowing Indians to appear for the London examination, citing the racial arrogance of the British in the Indian Police and the possibility that with open competition Indians may outrank British officers and the government would not be able to control the balance. There was also a concern that particular Indian castes and communities would be over represented. The government recommended that one quarter of recruitment be filled by Indians in India besides the North West Frontier Province and Burma. Two-thirds of this allotment would be filled by competitive examination among nominees from the provinces and one-third by promotion.

Sir Chettur Sankaran Nair attached a long minute of dissent to the Government of India's recommendation. Sir Sankaran argued against nomination, labelling it a system of patronage. He opposed the imperial/provincial distinction as there was no difference in the duties performed by the two services; the London examination was of a low standard and not difficult to pass, whilst the directly appointed Indian deputy superintendents were university graduates whose work was generally superior to their British colleagues. The London examination was closed to Indians which meant the imperial service was exclusively British, which amounted to racial discrimination. The Royal Commission and the Government of India were in favour of opening the London examination to Indians in 1918, and although recruitment of Indians would take place in India, the maintenance of two services, one higher and the other lower would exacerbate racial distinctions. Sir Sankaran went on to argue that the imperial and provincial services should be amalgamated. He also opposed the rule which mandated five years residence in England for Indians appearing for the London examination. He pointed out that the Indian Civil Service had not been overrun by Indians, besides which it was thought relatively few Indians would take the London option. Sir Sankaran wanted one-third of recruitment to take place in India with an annual increase of 1.5% over the ensuing ten years. He thought that it was the attitude of keeping Indians out which was fuelling the extremist political movement and when given the chance Indian officers had served ably and loyally.

The secretary of state's orders were then issued in a series of telegrams.[ccxxi] Indians would not be allowed to appear for the examination in London but would be recruited in India. Montagu recommended one-third of places for Indians, of which two-thirds would be chosen by open competition, and one-third by promotion of deputy superintendents. The Indian Police finally opened up a limited number of assistant superintendent positions to Indians on the basis of competitive examination in India in 1920 and 15 Indians were appointed to the Indian Police under the new rules that year. As it did for the Indian Civil Service, the Lee Commission settled the matter in 1923 when it recommended that 50% of officers coming into the Indian Police were to be British, 30%

were to be Indians, and 20% would come from the provincial services. Parity in recruitment between British and Indian officers would be achieved after 25 years. The Lee Commission also improved pay in order to attract better Indian candidates and made provision for the promotion of Indian deputy superintendents if the open competition quota was not filled.

Having decided on recruiting Indians in India, the Government of India prescribed the procedure to be followed in consultation with the provincial governments. The Provincial Selection Committee consisted of a member of the Governor's Executive Council or a minister, the inspector general of police, an experienced commissioner or officer of the Educational Service, three non-government members, and a member of the Public Services Commission. The district officers could nominate university graduates between the ages of 21 and 24 and the provincial governments had the discretion to nominate a boy with a First Arts pass who would have to pass physical requirements prescribed by the province, have a respectable background and provide character references. The examination was to be held at the end of each year and be run by the Central Advisory Board of Education. With the nomination process in the hands of provincial governments it was thought that they would maintain communal balance in sending their young men into the service.

***

The rules for the Indianisation of the Indian Police were being decided in the early 1920s during a time of political upheaval across the country. Whilst the Congress's non-cooperation movement was intended to be non-violent, it was nonetheless meant to challenge law and order. It had its roots in Ahmadabad in February 1919 where Mohandas Gandhi decided to start a campaign of satyagraha against the Emergency Regulations which had just been passed. In

March he announced a nation-wide hartal for a date which was yet to be fixed.

Mob violence started to break out in Punjab and in some cases the police were only saved by army reinforcements. Amritsar saw some of the worst violence in April 1919 after the deportation of Dr. Satya Pal and Saifuddin Kitchlew. The house of the deputy commissioner was attacked, crowds were fired upon, the National Bank was set on fire and its British managers were murdered. Amidst the mayhem the police went missing, the constabulary lay idle and the civilian administration had to be handed over to the army. The police did a better job in Lahore where news of Gandhi's arrest and the violence in Amritsar created further trouble. A crowd which had been turned back from the Mall and was gathered near the Lawrence statue challenged the attendant constables and on the orders of the deputy commissioner the police opened fire. The crowd would disperse and then regroup to challenge the superintendent of police and his small force which would incite another round of firing.

After Gandhi's call for non-cooperation at the end of 1920, 1921 saw over 60 major outbreaks of violence across India. In Punjab there were hundreds of assaults on the police. Congress policy was to wean Indian policemen away from government service and in Bengal the police faced a social boycott with attempts to cut off their supply of food. In some cases the children of policemen were denied medical treatment. In early 1922 there were mass demonstrations against the police in Bihar and Bengal and in February 1922 about 2000 villagers attacked a police station at Chauri Chaura in Gorakhpur, killing its policemen in a particularly brutal manner and burning the station to the ground. It was into this atmosphere of nationalism and violence directed against the police as the representatives of the British Raj that educated young Indians came forward to become officers of the Indian Police.

***

Those young Indians who came forward to serve in the Indian Police usually did so after having tried for the Indian Civil Service or Indian Army. They missed out for a variety of reasons; some scored well in the examination but did poorly in the interview, in some cases they had not studied the necessary subjects at school to be competitive in the examination, whilst others blamed their lack of social connections. Assessing their options, the newly opened places in the Indian Police provided another chance for a secure career in an imperial service. When Indians did gain entry to the Indian Police they would be sent to Police Training Schools across India, and their first and foremost challenge would be to navigate the social world of the Officers' Mess. A secondary challenge came once their training started and they would have to adapt to an unfamiliar culture in which they would receive both verbal abuse, and support, from their British principals, and both ragging and camaraderie from their British colleagues.

Bishwa Nath Lahiri sat the examination in India in December 1921 and joined the Indian Police in August 1922.[ccxxii] He received his orders to proceed to Moradabad and report to Robert Dodd, Principal of the Police Training School. Lahiri was the only Indian in his batch at Moradabad, but he thought he would "brave the consequences" as well as he could. He drove straight to Dodd's residence, who gave him a letter of introduction to the senior assistant superintendent of the Mess, George Reeves. Reeves was tinkering with his Model T Ford, rolled out from under the car, and greeted Lahiri quizzically. Lahiri was still something of a novelty, and Reeves took him to the Mess to make his introductions. The members of the Mess were having their morning meal and simply nodded and continued eating. Lahiri knew that he was being observed and felt the tension. He recalled; "I could feel it under my skin that I was the subject of close though unobtrusive observation by as many pairs of blue or grey eyes as made up their number." It was a relief when Masit, the Mess khidmatgar made a place for him and he took his breakfast.

After breakfast Lahiri adjourned to the Mess President George Parkin's room. Parkin took it on himself to get the young officer fitted out, and with the help of a local tailor a new summer outfit was sewn up and delivered within 48 hours. Parkin organised a personal servant for Lahiri and set about inducting him into the mysteries of the Mess. Whilst breakfast and lunch were casual, members had to be punctual for dinner. There was a bugle call after which everyone would march in to take their appointed place at the dining table. They all dressed up in the regulation kit of a peak cap and jacket with silver badges and overalls, with Wellington boots and box spurs. It was something like a parade, except for Wednesday and Sunday which were supper nights. On Ladies Guest Nights the Mess would be transformed into a "fairy land" and the dinner tables would be artistically laid out with all the silverware on display.

Looking back Lahiri at once found the mess kit "outlandish", but also remained nostalgic for it; it made a man feel important. When dinner was over the Mess President made sure that the decanters for claret or port had gone around and then made a light tap on the table. Everyone would stand to attention, the Mess President would say "Mr. Vice, the King" and the Vice President of the Mess would then say "Gentlemen, the King Emperor". If there was a band it would play 'God Save the King', and all in attendance would then drink and say "God Bless Him". Lahiri toasted with water. With access to the Mess being restricted, Lahiri thought of it as "a small corner of England". He felt the British were not too hostile to him because he did not chew paan or play Indian music on the gramophone, but he was not eligible for the post of Mess President when his time came.

Lahiri remembered his initiation into the Mess a few days after his arrival as "like a nightmare". He was asked by his British colleagues to either take an alcoholic drink or sing them a song. The problem for Lahiri was that he did not drink and did not know how to sing. An argument ensued until past midnight, in which time his colleagues had consumed many glasses of Johnnie Walker scotch whiskey. They eventually reached a compromise; Lahiri would have to stand on a table and sing a song. He tried to pass off some Bengali verse as a song and he recalled that his "inquisitors not knowing a word of this language looked on with wonder writ large on their faces." He thought they were suspicious because his performance did not feature the high notes they all knew from Indian songs which they would mimic back to him as "ee-ee-ee".

On Guest Nights at Moradabad much "merry making" would follow dinner. Lahiri recounted all the officers joining in community singing which would go on until the early hours of the morning. In one case some of the officers appeared for the morning parade late "by a fraction of a second" due to the previous night's celebrations and the new Principal, Sidney Gordon gave the late comers "a sound dressing down". Later another Principal, Richard Powell would give a young probationary assistant who had come to meet him without his lounge coat properly buttoned up a "severe reprimand for his negligence" and also threaten to have the young man expelled from the institution if he repeated his mistake. This sense of discipline and attention to detail was a side of the British character which Lahiri came to admire. But he thought just as highly of his British colleagues' capacity for "riotous gaiety". He felt it came from their "surplus energy" which also explained why they were so fond of "manly games" like pig sticking and hunting and polo.

Narayanrao Kamte's father had started as a police jamedar in Poona and rose to the rank of inspector in the Criminal Investigation Department.[ccxxiii] Kamte studied at Deccan College in Poona and then tried for one of the ten cadetships open to Indian boys for the Royal Military College at Sandhurst. He was not chosen, and his plans for further study at Cambridge also fell through. He had been successful in gaining entry to the Bombay Provincial Civil Service however, and also cleared the examination for the Indian Police.

Kamte reported to the Police Training School at Nasik in 1923. Ivan Boyd was the principal of the school and Kamte thought of him as a considerate gentleman and a good teacher. He felt that Indians were still "on trial" though and suffered discrimination at the daily physical training; he was not granted an exemption despite his military training and time in the Indian Territorial Army whereas the British ex-army trainees were. In addition, when he came to the Police Training School he was a teetotaller, something which made him the subject of jokes; both Indian and British policemen enjoyed their evening drinks and dismissed him as a 'prig' who was practising temperance which he must have picked up at college. However, Kamte did start to drink after a Guest Night where the inspector general of police and the collector of Nasik were present. In his retelling his colleague Dick Gearing suggested that he throw a glassful of whiskey at the senior officials who were standing apart in a corner. Kamte did so, which led the inspector general to give him a dressing down for disrespecting the collector who was a guest. But the inspector general seemed to approve of him taking to the drink, and Kamte tendered a gentlemanly apology and the matter was settled.

At Nasik Tuesdays were Guest Nights when all shared the cost of drinks equally and the proceedings were made more exciting by boxing contests. Kamte's colleagues suggested that as he had no experience in the "manly art" they would teach him how to defend himself in the ring. This meant that on Wednesday mornings he would inevitably appear with a swollen nose and black eye before the civil surgeon. To turn the tables Kamte started to teach his British colleagues Indian wrestling, something which put an end to the boxing lessons. Amidst the boxing, wrestling, black eyes and swollen noses the tension was diffused by sharing drinks.

The trainees would begin their day at 6:30 am with a three mile run followed by hurdles and more strenuous physical training. Some of Kamte's colleagues could not keep step while marching whereas he wanted to reach the end without any complaint. Daily activity at Nasik would also include riding practice. One day when Kamte was taking the jumping course he noticed a ditch filled with water and lost his nerve and began to pull at the reigns. Ivan Boyd was watching and gave him an earful of, what seemed to Kamte like abuse. Kamte slacked the reigns and made the jump but felt humiliated. He wanted to get even so the following Guest Night he invited the principal for a beer, poured the beer over his head and challenged him to a fight. Again the principal called him the next day. Boyd explained to Kamte that he had shouted at him to save him from a dangerous fall and 'bloody fool' was not a deadly insult in English. Kamte learnt that he had to be less sensitive, and later when he became inspector general of police he would yell out similar insults just to toughen up his men.

One night Kamte's colleagues came in and stole his bicycle. He reported the incident the next day to the principal, who explained that this was 'ragging' and he should play his own prank on his fellow trainees. Kamte then reported the incident to the local superintendent of police who came to look into the matter. His colleagues denounced him for not being a 'sport' and not being able to handle a bit of harmless fun. But Kamte insisted that his report to the superintendent was in fact a joke, and so he was ragging them.

Kamte was a devotee of Shri Gurudev Dattatreya. For his first three weeks at the Training School he was not provided with permissible foods for his Thursday fast and so would end up starving. On the fourth Thursday he dined with Inspector Rao Saheb Akut, the instructor in the police manual, who had access to the permissible food. However, the principal reported this to the inspector general who deemed it improper for an officer of the Indian Police to dine with an inspector in spite of any personal relationship. Kamte had to give up his Thursday fasts and would have to get his wife to observe them for him. She did so for the next 49 years.

Kamte passed his drill examination in his first term with the benefit of his military experience, the horse riding test posed no problems, and he passed his first and second law examinations in the first nine months. However, he failed his Gujarati language examinations and would later have to catch up on Gujarati in Ahmadabad with some assistance from Dhirubhai Desai, Deputy Superintendent of Police. Dhirubhai would take Kamte to Gujarati dramas in the evenings and teach him any vocabulary he was not sure of. He later went back to Bombay, failed the test again, but eventually passed with a little help from his old college acquaintance, Miss Divatia, who was the daughter of his examiner, Professor Divatia.

***

Just as in the Indian Civil Service, the Indian officers entering the Indian Police in the early 1920s would be instructed by old British officers in both the technical processes and culture of their service. And as happened in the Indian Civil Service, the

Indianisation process quickened and by the 1930s it was increasingly likely that young Indian officers of the Indian Police would be trained by senior Indian officers of the service. Given that the Indian Police was more inherently provincial in its structure than the Indian Civil Service, in some instances the junior and senior Indian Police officers even belonged to the same local caste or community.

Narayanrao Kamte spent five months in Ahmadabad on probation before taking up his allotted post at Kaira in November 1924.[ccxxiv] His district superintendent was William Herapath, a bachelor whose sister kept house for him. Herapath took Kamte to the Ahmadabad Gymkhana and proposed him as a member and Miss Herapath introduced Mrs. Kamte to the vagaries of British etiquette, teaching her "all that a service wife was supposed to know." In keeping with custom Kamte and his wife would receive calls from those resident in station and then pay them return visits.

Kamte received his first homicide case from a village in the Dholka taluka on a Saturday evening. He did not go to the scene of the crime as he thought he needed permission to move outside of Ahmadabad. When Herapath saw him at Parade on Monday morning with his sword drawn, he thought Kamte must have returned from the crime scene. When he learnt that Kamte had not even been to the village he directed him to return his sword and proceed to the scene of the crime immediately. There had been no need to get permission.

Troubles continued for Kamte when he wrote a letter to the Inspector General of Police, Sir Francis Griffith. Kamte received a reply, but Sir Francis also wrote to the district superintendent. Herapath sent for Kamte and asked him how he had begun and ended the letter. Kamte replied that he had begun with "Dear Sir" and ended with "Yours Obediently". Kamte then received a lecture. Sir Francis had written to Herapath to enquire if he was training his underling properly. Herapath explained to Kamte that he belonged to a great service and there was no need to be so sycophantic. He simply had to start his letters with "Dear Mr." or "Dear Sir" if the recipient was a knight and end with "Yours sincerely", or, at the most, "Yours Faithfully". Herapath stressed that it did not matter if Kamte was writing to the home member in Delhi, he still had to maintain his dignity.

The learning continued a little while later, when Sir Francis was going on leave and some officers proceeded to the railway station to see him off. Like the other officers, Kamte offered Sir Francis a flower garland to bid him farewell. But by the time Kamte returned to Ahmadabad, Sir Francis had written another "stinker" to Herapath claiming that he was not training Kamte properly. Once again Herapath made it clear to Kamte that he belonged to a great service and was not to go garlanding Sir Francis, or anyone else for that matter. A bit more trouble ensued when Kamte went to use the practise firing range in Ahmadabad the day after his transfer orders for his posting to Kaira had been received. Herapath pulled him up for practising in Ahmadabad even after he had handed over charge. Initially he was going to back date Kamte's entry in the register, but then decided not to, and told Kamte "I mustn't teach bad habits to youngsters like you. I'll put today's date."

Durgagati Bhattacharyya hailed from a Bengali family which had once been zamindars but had more recently been reduced to government service.[ccxxv] He had tried for the Indian Army but performed poorly in the interview, and considered an attempt at the Indian Civil Service examination but thought that he was not well versed enough in English literature and the classics to succeed. He completed a B.Sc. and was studying for an M.Sc. in physics when he received news that he had cleared the examination for the Indian Police. He entered the Police Training College at Sardah in east Bengal in 1936 and was posted to Behrempore in Murshidabad for district training. When he arrived he found that the officials of the British Raj were fellow Indians. Indian Civil Service officers Motiram Kripalani, Karuna Hajara and Aga Hilaly were the district magistrate, district judge, and assistant magistrate respectively. Raghabendra Banerjee was the district superintendent of police, and Girija Dutta was the superintendent of the Behrampore district jail.

Bhattacharyya thought he was lucky to be trained by Raghabendra Banerjee. Banerjee knew his job and besides official work he was able to train Bhattacharyya in social manners and etiquette. Bhattacharyya would go to Banerjee's house on most days and came to be treated as Banerjee's younger brother. Banerjee's wife would treat him as her 'devar' and the children of the family called him 'kakababu'. Bhattacharyya thought that he came closer to Banerjee's family than Banerjee's own brothers and "in the course of time we developed genuine mutual love, respect and affection for each other."

The first part of Bhattacharyya's training was a two month stint at the Belganda police station where he quickly had to learn about registers and the documents which they contained and spent some days writing them all up. He also had to record First Information Reports of a few cognisable offences. All the paperwork was maintained according to the *Police Regulations, Bengal*, "which was like a Bible of the police in Bengal." According to Bhattacharyya, "It was a masterpiece prepared in the earlier days of the British Raj and consisted of 3 volumes." The first volume contained rules and regulations, the second was made up of model reports and documents which needed to be maintained in police stations and the third volume contained an elaborate index. Bhattacharyya then had to undertake the complete investigation of two criminal cases which had been reported and so he chose one case of burglary and another case of rioting. He completed the investigation, writing up the Case Diaries with some help from the officer in-charge and made the relevant entries in the Village Crime Note Book, an important record maintained in five main volumes. Besides making his own entries he enjoyed reading the previous entries and treated it as training for when he would rise to become superintendent of a district and have to make his own inspections of police stations.

Bhattacharyya was then sent for a month to the circle inspector's office at Jangipur. The circle inspector would train him in his duties and teach him to maintain registers and documents according to the Bengal Police Regulations. He would also take Bhattacharyya along on his inspection tours and supervision of important cases. Under the inspector's guidance Bhattacharyya would have to undertake thorough inspections of the circle's police stations in the same way that the circle inspector did. The circle inspector would hover over him as he recorded notes in the Inspection Book of the police station he was inspecting.

The third part of Bhattacharyya's training took place at the Reserve Office at the District Headquarters at Behrampore. The Reserve Office maintained an account of the Reserve Police Force and their armoury and ammunition depot. Bhattacharyya would attend and supervise firing practice, and take the opportunity to use his personal revolver, a Webley & Scott .38 bore. He would also have to learn the work of the Intelligence Branch office. He was trained under the inspector and became familiar with the documents and registers which had to be maintained and how each officer went about collecting political, terrorist and labour intelligence.

Bhattacharyya then proceeded for training in the

superintendent's daily routine work. He had to learn the general outline of the superintendent's work, including the registers, documents, returns and files which had to be maintained or sent up to higher officers. Bhattacharyya remembered that an important part of the superintendent's work was the preparation and maintenance of the budget in accordance with government manuals and guidelines. Raghabendra Banerjee would spend his afternoons in his office chamber and Bhattacharyya was ordered to attend to learn the intricacies of financial management. He remembered Banerjee being thorough in his checking and using coloured pencils to mark each item for different types of checks. Bhattacharyya just had to watch and pose the occasional question, which would allow Banerjee to explain the finer points. Bhattacharyya would sometimes fall asleep after lunch, but Banerjee was indulgent and would smile quietly. Banerjee would also take him out on tour in his Chevrolet for office inspections or supervision of cases of dacoity or murder or rioting. Bhattacharyya was always glad to be able to get out of town, and also collect his daily travel allowance which came to a princely sum of ₹6 a day.

***

Once a young Indian officer completed his training and passed the probationary period he would take up his first independent charge as an assistant superintendent of police. It was an opportunity to bring an Indian perspective to police work, establish his own relationships in his district, and work out his own means for projecting the authority of his rank. Indian officers would now have to manage the Case Diaries and First Information Reports themselves, and some would add their own innovations to the paper trail at the heart of the British system of policing India.

In January 1927 Narayanrao Kamte was transferred to Sholapur as Assistant Superintendent in charge of Sub Division

Pandharpur in Bombay.[ccxxvi] Pandharpur was a holy town, a place of pilgrimage for devotees from across the Deccan. During Ashadh, which fell in July, the number of warkaris, or pilgrims numbered over 100,000, an influx of people which posed endless challenges for the police. On his way to take charge of Pandharpur, Kamte had a discussion with his friend Madhusudan Bhat of the Indian Civil Service who was the Assistant Collector of Sholapur. Bhat suggested that Kamte look into the harassment and extortion of pilgrims who visited the temple of Vithoba. The Badves, who were the custodians of the temple, were entitled to a dakshina, whilst the pujaris would also demand a gift of equal value called 'ovalni'. The custom amounted to a form of double taxation for the hapless pilgrims.

Kamte decided to investigate the issue himself, and so entered the temple in plain clothes. He bowed before the idol and deposited his dakshina of one silver rupee. He was then picked up by one of the Badves, and then by a pujari who demanded his ovalni. Kamte pleaded that he had already deposited his dakshina which was all the money that he had, but the pujari ordered him to go home and fetch some more. Kamte asked the pujari to let go of his neck and to proceed outside. Once they were outside the temple Kamte let fly and slapped the pujari. This attracted the uniformed constables on duty, one of whom did not initially recognise the assistant superintendent of police and wanted to take him to the police station. The sub inspector however recognised Kamte, saluted and begged forgiveness for the erring constable. Kamte suspected the constables were receiving a share of the dakshina and ovalni money, and so decided to punish the constable, although lightly. The Badves and pujaris also asked that the pujari not be punished, but Kamte wanted to make an example of him. The case was eventually taken to court and Kamte recommended a token fine. Kamte thought his work at the Vithoba temple was a good example of what an Indian police officer could do; British officers had never entered the temple which meant that the extortion had been allowed to go on undisturbed for years.

On a visit to his Superintendent, Cyril Pegge's office, Kamte sat and observed his method of writing up Crime Registers. Pegge's reader would give him information on the daily progress of investigations from the Case Diaries and he would then note down the number of each diary and the date in the remarks column. Kamte then started following Pegge's method and introduced a few innovations of his own. Kamte added the name of the officer who had registered the offence, the officer who had visited the crime scene, along with their relevant dates, a note on the modus operandi, and the names of the accused. He also included the date of sending up the case, the date of the final judgement, the result of the judgement, and any delays by the magistrate which may have necessitated informing the district magistrate. He also entered the place of the offence, its distance from the nearest police station, and the dates of visits to the scene after the investigation was started. With these more detailed Crime Registers and a study of the Station Diaries Kamte could then detect which sub inspectors were just registering an offence and then sending their constables to the crime scene. He eventually found that this was happening about 80% of the time. He decided to punish the lazy inspectors, and as he moved up the police hierarchy to district superintendent and then inspector general he made his more detailed system of entries compulsory. These moves were so unpopular that after Kamte's retirement the sub divisional officers and superintendents joined forces to get his measures cancelled.

Eric Stracey had graduated in economics and politics from Loyola College, Madras in 1942.[ccxxvii] He had considered appearing for the Indian Civil Service examination but thought that he might struggle with the compulsory paper on an Indian language. He was an Anglo-Indian and had not studied one in school, having spent ten years on French instead. However, Stracey scored well in the interview for the Indian Police, topped the country in the written examination, and managed to clear the medical tests. He entered the Police Training College, Vellore in 1943 before being sent to Erode to take charge of his first subdivision.

Once at work in Erode Stracey would clear his mail before bed each night, which would leave the day for whatever matters might arise. One of his principal duties was to receive callers, and despite the best efforts of local police to deter them, many members of the public still had the courage and persistence to approach a higher officer. Some would come accompanied by their lawyer, who would address Stracey as "your good self", make a representation, and then leave a copy of it on the table. Stracey recalled paying closer attention to those callers who came alone, for whom he would make his own note on the grievance and follow it up. Many of the callers however would be Stracey's own subordinates who would come to discuss some problem, or just pay their respects and sometimes address him as "Your Honour".

Much of Stracey's office time was taken up reading Case Diaries sent up by investigating officers through their inspectors. He would have to give instructions, ask for clarifications, and wait for replies. He also had to take note of any delay, which in the instance of a Case Diary would be a departmental offence. Delays tended to lead to false "development" and "padding" and more generally just spoke of laziness which needed to be pulled up. The Daily Station House Reports, which were copies of the hour to hour occurrences at the police station also needed to be read, but Stracey thought that receiving them regularly was not as important as just making sure that they were being written up "contemporaneously". It was assumed that if the officer in charge of the Daily Station House Report kept it open then it was for an ulterior motive, like recording an arrest which had already been made or a duty which had not yet been performed. An open Daily Report along with the delayed Case Diary were perennial problems and Stracey thought that the solution was constant surprise visits to police stations to check the documents on the spot.

Another large part of Stracey's time was taken by petitions and written representations from the public. He would receive the reports of his subordinates who had looked into the petitions and would also receive other petitions which were serious enough that he would have to look into them himself and write his own report. They came in all forms, from hand written to typed or printed, signed, with false names or by Anonymous. Some were for Stracey's eyes only, others were sent to every official from the governor downward. A customary form of salutation was "Maharaja Rajasri, Great Sir, the Assistant Superintendent". Petitions covered a wide range of matters from domestic violence to secret murders, harassment by constables and torture, corruption, as well as land disputes over cattle grazing, crop seizure and water distribution. They were a mix of "devilish untruths" as well as valuable information which could save days of work. Standard forms of disposal included- "You are advised to settle matters in a panchayat", "You are advised to complain to a court of law", and instructions to the inspector would include "Inspector for Disposal", "Inspector, warn the parties", "Inspector for report" and "Inspector for personal enquiry and urgent report".

Stracey recalled the public being dissatisfied with the law on non-cognisable offences. The Criminal Procedure Code outlined a list of offences which the police could not investigate without direction from a court. Aggrieved villagers would walk for miles to a police station only to be told that by law the police could not interfere in their matter and they would have to approach a court. Stracey would at least get his staff to act as conciliators and warn the opposite party if the complaint was true and such action would be likely to do any good. But he remembered that such warnings could give rise to corruption, as the warning might be used to extort money to prevent any further criminal action.

***

It was the Congress's non-cooperation and civil disobedience campaigns which would challenge law and order around the country at regular intervals, break the comfortable routines of police work, and remind Indian officers that they were serving a foreign power. When faced with crowds practising varying degrees of peaceful protest Indian officers would have to conjure unconventional ways to minimise the use of force and avoid the need for mass arrests. Fortunately for them, in most cases they could draw on gentlemanly relationships with the local Congress leaders, who shared a similar education and culture.

Bishwa Nath Lahiri recalled the station superintendent of Mirzapur railway station calling him for help during the civil disobedience movement of 1930-31.[ccxxviii] The station superintendent reported that a group of youths had come in from Chunar without a ticket and were not willing to pay the fare and he needed some help from the police. Lahiri rushed to the station to find the platform teeming with hundreds of spectators, with a few perched on the boundary walls keen to witness the action. Some were carrying Congress flags and filling the air with slogans imploring victory for the Congress leadership. Lahiri found it difficult to get out of his car and tried to keep things calm by passing a few witty comments. When he did make his way past the crowd and came to inspect the offenders he found that they were all children, besides their leader who was holding a Congress flag.

Lahiri was in a quandary as to what to do with the children. He thought that to simply let them off would send the wrong message. He wanted some time to think, so whisked them all off to the district jail. He thought a solution might be to only arrest those who were 16 or older. But on learning of Lahiri's plan, all the kids declared themselves to be 16; they were keen for some jail time. Instead Lahiri decided to detain their leaders and release the youngsters some way out of town. He thought he had solved the problem, but then another group of satyagrahis arrived the next day on the station platform, and then another the following day. Lahiri was at his wit's end and sought some assistance from the Railway divisional superintendent at Allahabad. In the end, he was relieved of his daily trip to the railway station when the Congress leadership in Allahabad made it clear that ticketless travel was not an approved form of satyagraha.

Narayanrao Kamte recounted the civil disobedience movement, and the predicament it put Indian police officers in.[ccxxix] They were naturally sympathetic to their countrymen, patriotic Indians who would feel aggrieved by racial slights by the British rulers, yet would also maintain their "age old traditions" of loyalty to their paymaster. They did admire "British efficiency" and realised that India had benefited from many aspects of British rule, and so they remained "true to their salt" and "exercised more gentleness, patience, tact and understanding" than all except a few British officers would have done in their place. Kamte's challenge would prove much more serious than Lahiri's however. Lahiri's account of dealing with ticketless travellers in Mirzapur had a touch of farce about it. But when law and order broke down in Sholapur, something like an inversion of an old Kipling story played out; Kamte, the dashing, energetic young Indian police officer would have to come in and save the day as exhausted and petrified British officers gathered at a designated safe place ready to flee.

In March 1930 Kamte found himself back in his old subdivision of Pandharpur with the civil disobedience movement in full swing. By May of 1930 Gandhi had been arrested once again, and within 48 hours trouble broke out across India. Kamte had gone from Sholapur to Pandharpur to deal with the case of an old lady who had her shop near a temple and had refused to observe the Congress call for a hartal. A crowd had then proceeded to loot her shop and run away. Kamte visited the old lady's ransacked shop and called for the local Congress leaders. He asked them whether this was what Gandhi had taught them- to steal from little old ladies? Kamte asked the lady how much she had lost. He then asked the Congress workers, led by Balkrishna Phansalkar, whom Kamte described as "a Pleader and a most reasonable gentleman", to pay her the amount of ₹35 and the matter was thus resolved.

Kamte then received news of riots in Sholapur and read a telegram summoning him to the town. When he reached the Sholapur city limits he saw that the Navi Peth Police Chowky was being staffed by a white capped Congress worker who was busy directing traffic. When asked what he was doing, the Congress worker replied that the policemen had run away so he had stepped in to do their duty. Kamte then drove to his office to find another white capped Congress worker sitting in his chair. He manhandled the Congress worker and threw him out of his office, but found similar scenes at the district superintendent's office, and even at the Treasury where the Congress workers were standing guard.

Kamte then went to the Collector Henry Knight's bungalow to be told by his butler that the sahibs had all gone to the railway station to board a special train to take them to safety in Poona. His superior Harold Playfair, a demobilised army captain who carried a war wound, had also left for the railway station, and so he decided to drive there himself. He found the British men of Sholapur inside first class carriages on the north side of the station. British women and children had already been evacuated to Poona. Kamte saw Playfair "lying on his berth in a state of collapse". He found Knight in the next compartment "exhausted but still in command of himself". Knight briefed Kamte on the situation, including the murder of two policemen and the arson of the Sessions Court. He explained that the British were camping at the railway station under an armed guard and urged Kamte to join them. Kamte told Knight that he had just come from the city, and besides the small matter of Congressmen having taken over governmental duties, the place was relatively calm. Knight warned Kamte that if he returned to the city he would do so at his own risk. Kamte then returned to his office and rounded up his men. Most responded to his call, but some did not and he later brought charges of desertion against them.

In the days that followed Kamte assumed Playfair's charge and answered correspondence on his behalf. The cavalry soon arrived, as Cecil Reynolds came to replace the "very sick" Playfair, and Tehmus Kothavala of the Bombay Civil Service came to assist the "exhausted and over burdened" Knight. A company of the 4th Bombay Grenadiers and another company of the Ulster Rifles also came in from Poona. A week later the British returned from their carriages at the railway station to their bungalows to find that nothing had been looted in their absence. Eventually the British authorities declared Martial Law and appointed Colonel Cyril Paige as administrator. On the verge of a breakdown Knight proceeded on two months sick leave, handing over his charge to Kothavala.

With Martial Law in place, Kamte received orders to proceed to Pandharpur to arrest Balkrishna Phansalkar and bring him back to Sholapur. Paige told him that he would probably be murdered if he went to Pandharpur without an armed guard. Kamte replied that he knew the people of Pandharpur quite well and that there was no need for an escort. Paige insisted however, and so Kamte proceeded with one platoon of riflemen under the command of a subaltern.

On reaching the river before the town of Pandharpur Kamte requested that the platoon commander halt and wait there whilst he proceeded to the town. He was worried about the havoc that the British soldiers may create in the town, and was particularly concerned about preserving the modesty of Pandharpur's women. In addition, he did not want the soldiers to ruin the good reputation that he had built up for himself over the years. In the event of any trouble Kamte would fire a shot in the air which would be the signal for the platoon to cross the river and come to his rescue.

It was the day of Naraka Chaturdashi when Hindus take a ceremonial bath and eat sweets made for the occasion. When Kamte arrived at Phansalkar's house he was still bathing, but offered to come out at once. Kamte told him to finish his bath, eat his sweets and they would then leave together. Mrs. Phansalkar put the plate of sweets before her husband, but Kamte objected. He too was a Hindu, was he not to share the sweets on the auspicious day? Mrs. Phansalkar, of course, then served Kamte and they ate the sweets together.

On leaving the house Kamte encountered a crowd jeering and hurling abuse at him. But Phansalkar rebuked the crowd, telling them: "Mr. Kamte is a good man. I request you all to go away quietly without creating any trouble." The crowd obeyed their leader and so Phansalkar and Kamte crossed the river. As they left for Sholapur Kamte felt relieved that nothing untoward had happened to damage the cordial relations he had built up with the residents of Pandharpur throughout his career. Kamte spoke with a little snobbery of his young British army subaltern however, who had asked whether the "badmaash" had been rounded up. He thought the young soldier's "ignorance and inexperience were no more than was normal for his age and class". Mr. Phansalkar after all, was an educated and cultured gentleman.

***

Whilst Indian officers worked as assistant superintendents and eventually took charge of their districts, some were also brought into more sensitive roles in the elite Criminal Investigation Departments of their respective provinces. The General Branch of the Criminal Investigation Department dealt with crime and the Special Branch dealt with political intelligence. Alakh Sinha, who had joined the service as a deputy superintendent before World War I had multiple stints in the Criminal Investigation Department throughout his career.[ccxxx] As a relatively young officer he had to recommend prosecutions against fellow Indians for seditious speeches during the first non-cooperation movement of the early 1920s, and then many years later on the eve of World War II he headed the Criminal Investigation Department in Bihar and was joined for a time by his son Mithilesh, who had entered the Indian Police in 1928.

Alakh Sinha had been on leave when Mohandas Gandhi started the non-cooperation movement after World War I. Satyendra Sinha, the Baron Sinha, had been appointed Governor of Bihar and Alakh was posted to the Criminal Investigation Department to head the newly formed Prosecution Section. He had to examine reports from local police across the province on speeches which were being delivered by the non-cooperators, and table the evidence which could be gathered to prove sedition under section 124A of the Indian Penal Code. He would also have to forward his own comments on the applications of superintendents for prosecution of the offenders higher up the chain to the deputy inspector general, legal remembrancer, chief secretary, the member in charge of police and the governor.

Alakh worked with a staff headed by Jagatbandhu Bhaumick. Together they would have to study volumes of manuscripts which had been sent up by the district superintendents. If the speeches had been correctly reported they would come within the purview of Section 124A, but in many cases Alakh found the evidence insufficient, refused to sanction prosecution for sedition, and in these cases Governor Sinha would concur. He found that a solitary submission by a single policeman could not be used as first class evidence in a prosecution case and so he recommended deputing three officers who would each take their own record of the potentially seditious phrases, after which each would have to get their notes attested by a magistrate deputed to the meeting. He found support for his suggestion both from Robert McRae, the Deputy Inspector General as well as Governor Sinha. He recalled that in his 14 months in the position only 14 cases were sent up for trial.

Alakh remembered having to examine thousands of pamphlets and leaflets which were circulating at the time. He felt lucky that he could read them in a closed room as he was prone to getting emotional when he read harrowing accounts of Indians getting gunned down at Jallianwala Bagh. Many poems were written on the theme of a 12 year old boy opening his chest before General Dyer shouting "kill me first" and Alakh "felt miserable at having to do the work that I was doing". But he could not resolve to make the ultimate sacrifice and quit his job, and so continued to do what he thought was his duty as long as he was in the service. Later he would avoid getting anywhere near Gandhi or Rajendra Prasad, fearful that if he came too close he may just resign and join Gandhi's "non violent army". He did not think he could afford to resign, nor did he have "strength of character", and so he kept his distance despite many opportunities to meet the Congress leaders.

Over a decade later Alakh was sent back to the Criminal Investigation Department as Deputy Inspector General in charge of the Secret (Special) Branch. He had two assistants, John Johnston and Albert Blewitt. Alakh thought that they worked hard for him, but he never felt at home heading the Special Branch as he did not feel he commanded the confidence of all concerned. Nonetheless, Alakh did his job and in his role as head of the Special Branch he would submit Weekly Reports to the Government of India giving a sense of the prevailing political climate. Before the Congress Ministry came to power in Bihar in 1937 he had reported on the secret instructions which the acting governor of a neighbouring province had given to some politicians. The governor took exception to being featured in Alakh's report, which sparked off a correspondence between the governments of the two provinces. Alakh produced the evidence to support his contention, but the Governor of Bihar, Sir Maurice Hallett closed the matter with the gentle suggestion that Alakh not include the activities of governors in his reports in the future.

Not all the work at the Criminal Investigation Department revolved around political surveillance however. Alakh recalled some sensational embezzlement cases involving the misappropriation of money from the Government Treasury. The treasurer was a popular local figure who maintained three motor cars which would be available to those whom he had to oblige. When the irregularities came to light local officialdom, including the deputy commissioner, refused to believe the allegations. Alakh explained the modus operandi: when carrying forward the day's balance from the bottom of one page to the top of the next the treasurer would just drop a digit or a 2 would become a 1, and so lakhs of rupees would mysteriously vanish. If detected he would put it down to a slip of the pen and correct the "obviously unconscious slip". Eventually, the Central Accounts officer detected a discrepancy of over ₹11 lakh. The investigation was conducted by Alakh's assistant Blewitt and Superintendent Bimalendu Roy.

Alakh portrayed the treasurer at Chaibas as a hardened criminal who took advantage of the Treasury officer's indifference and lack of training in accounts and employed a youngster to forge his signature. In some cases he would not even need to resort to forgery as he could get the deputy commissioner's signature who trusted him implicitly. The deputy commissioner had just returned to India from leave in England and Alakh was told that he might deny even his genuine signatures if pressed. Alakh then took his concerns to the governor and stated that he would expose the deputy commissioner if he did not stick to the truth. The governor seemed shocked at the implication that a member of the heaven born Indian Civil Service could possibly speak an untruth. In the end the deputy commissioner co-operated and the case succeeded, but the treasurer died, and only part of his property could be seized to make up for the stolen money.

Alakh had been sent from the Criminal Investigation Department to the Central Range, in which time his son Mithilesh had replaced Blewitt. He then returned to the Criminal Investigation Department, which meant that his son was now his assistant, heading the Crime Branch. Father and son lived in their ancestral house, but for the sake of propriety they did not travel in the same car to work each day. Mithilesh would make sure to arrive before his father, and then later took the decision to move to an official residence.

Mithilesh had to investigate a railway disaster in August 1937 in which the Punjab Mail went down at Bihta just short of a masonry bridge.ccxxxi Carriages veered off the tracks into the river, 119 people lost their lives and many hundreds more were injured. Mithilesh consulted with his father who recalled from his time as Superintendent of Railways Police just the year before that there had been a patch of soft bank where floods had washed the track away and that it was possible that the track had not been properly replaced before the line was re-opened to traffic. Alakh then instructed Mithilesh to take over the investigation from the Railways Police.

Mithilesh and the Railways Police both arrived at the scene of the disaster and the Railways officers were quick to construct a theory of sabotage. A similar disaster had recently occurred only 30 miles away and it had been found that some miscreants had tampered with the railway line causing a derailment. Alakh's team had themselves recovered parts of the railway line at the time and a successful prosecution had ensued. Mithilesh thought the Railways officers were too keen to prove a case of sabotage rather than an accident. If they could prove that sabotage had occurred they would not have to pay compensation to the victims. Upon investigation Mithilesh found that the railway components had been scattered about with not one of the parts intact, unlike the earlier case in which plates and bolts were found lying intact pointing to the work of human hands. The track could then be reconstructed using the materials found around the site of the accident. Furthermore, there was a small snaking of the track leading up to the accident scene, the train engine had a history of mechanical defects, and the train was speeding at the time.

Mithilesh then put his theory of an accident caused by the negligence of the Railways forward to the senior Government Inspector, Harold Joscelyne. Joscelyne readily accepted Mithilesh's findings, but Sir John Bell, Agent of the East Indian Railways put forward his own theory of sabotage and requested the Railways Board to get the Government of India to set up a Commission of Enquiry headed by a High Court judge. The Government Advocate of Patna had been on the ill-fated train and the case was stirring passions across Bihar. The enquiry was shifted out of the province to neighbouring Allahabad where Sir John Thom, Chief Justice of the Allahabad High Court was appointed sole member of the Commission of Enquiry. The commission was held in Sir John's rooms at the Allahabad High Court and Mithilesh spent three months in Allahabad taking care of the Government of Bihar's case. The Police Final Report which had already been accepted by the magistrate was also accepted by Sir John. He criticised the Railways and recommended the payment of compensation in the case and in all future cases irrespective of the cause of the derailment.

***

Indian officers of the Indian Police were put through a system of technical training like that of their colleagues in the Indian Civil Service, and culture shock similar to that of their counterparts in the Indian Army. In their case though they did not travel to England, but attended Police Training Colleges all over India. New recruits in the early 1920s had the toughest time. Bishwa Nath Lahiri's account of his stint at the Police Training College at Moradabad is that of a spectator observing a strange new social world, whereas Narayanrao Kamte recounted his days at the Police Training College at Nasik as a struggle for survival and self-respect. Both would have to adapt to the hyper masculine culture of the Officers' Mess and the half century of service culture which it contained, and it was this cultural challenge more than any academic examination which gave Indian officers the most concern. They were being trained to replace British officers and would have to accept both their service culture, and the processes and procedures with which they ordered their task of policing India.

Out on the job Indian officers were initially taught by British officers like William Herapath, and later by Indian officers like Raghabendra Banerjee. When they got their first independent charge they showed that they were just as capable as their British predecessors in going out and investigating crime, supervising and pulling up erring subordinates, and receiving visitors and petitions on tour. Much of the work was routine, the police station was a government office like any other with its own elaborate paper trail documenting police actions and interactions with the public. In fact, it was paper, in the form of Case Diaries, First Information Reports and Station Diaries that came to power the British system of policing India. Indian officers would master the paperwork well enough to be able to make the system run smoothly and enforce law and order out in the districts all across the land. The British Raj would finally get a better class of police officers, from an unexpected source. Young Indians who entered the Indian Police in the 1920s and 1930s were highly educated, physically fit, devoted to their work and capable leaders of local constabularies.

But the challenges which the Indian officers of the Indian Police faced were unique. They were servants of a foreign power and would be put to the test when Congress agitations broke out and the administration threatened to break down. Alakh Sinha's memory of recommending prosecutions for sedition against Congress activists in the wake of Gandhi's first non-cooperation movement was typical of the dilemmas that all Indian officers of the services faced at that time. His solution to the dilemma was also typical. He knew that he could not, or would not leave the service, and so he did his work with a heavy heart. He tried to stay away from the charismatic Indian politicians of the day for fear of coming under their spell, and did his job according to the book, recommending the minimum number of prosecutions possible and trying to establish a less arbitrary standard of evidence. Narayanrao Kamte would mention another old idea which Indian policemen honoured; that of being true to their salt giver. They would be 'namak halals' rather than 'namak harams' and stay loyal to the power which paid their salaries.

Whilst Alakh Sinha faced a crisis of conscience alone in an office in Bihar, Narayanrao Kamte had to face potentially dangerous crowds in the small towns of the old Bombay Presidency. He knew how bad things could get if the nationalist movement turned violent, and so he relied on the reasonableness of the Congress leader Balkrishna Phansalkar, whom he took to be an educated gentleman like himself. Both were doing their job, their duty, their dharma, and so they would try to resolve potentially dangerous confrontations before they descended into violence. The gentlemen spoke the common language of educated middle class Indians, and accounts like these of interactions between Indian officers of the imperial services and Congress lawyers provide a clue as to just how orderly the transfer of power would be when Independence came in 1947.

Seven
High Traditions

The High Courts of India were initially quite small institutions. Each court in Calcutta, Bombay and Madras was made up of a Bench of a dozen judges and a Bar of around 50 barristers. All the judges and barristers were British. The solicitors were also British, as were many of the litigants. Indians would only enter the picture as vakils, and as litigants who would bring their suits over land and property. Thus, during the late 19th century, India's High Courts were very British institutions on Indian soil. Yet unlike the physical work of the Indian Civil Service which collected the land revenue, or the Indian Police which enforced law and order, or the Indian Army which defended India's frontiers, the work of the High Courts was exclusively intellectual. The High Courts functioned according to a system of common law and were shaped by ideas about the standing of the Bar in relation to the judiciary, and the judiciary's proper relationship with the government. Their development would thus rely on just how conscientious the first generation of British judges and barristers would be in practising the system of law which they brought with them to India.

A transparent system was created for the appointment of judges to each of the High Courts. Indians were technically eligible for consideration, however the way the system was designed made it seem that such appointments would be rare. The thinking of British policy makers was along the old East India Company lines; that it might be a good idea to have some Indian judges whose familiarity with local customs and languages would allow them to get through the routine work quickly and reduce the case arrears. It was not thought that many cases would concern high affairs of state, and initially Indian judges were appointed as an experiment, usually just one sitting with a full bench of British judges. Unlike the civil service or police or army, there was no highly developed racial theory based on climate or physique or morality or character put forward to prevent the elevation of Indian judges to the High Courts. British High Court judges did not have a professional racial hierarchy to maintain, and so the judiciary was, from the start, the most collegial of the elite institutions of the British Raj.

The judiciary was not exactly a service of the state, it was an organ of the state in its own right. There was never any explicit policy for 'Indianisation' of the judiciary, it was a process which took place without the need for government intervention. After the first and second generation of British barristers who worked at the Bars of the High Courts around India ended their careers, very few travelled to India to take their place. Much like in the case of the civil service, career opportunities for lawyers expanded in England, few were persuaded to travel to India to establish a practice, and by the start of World War I the British presence at the Bars across India had all but faded away. As the Bar came to be dominated by Indian lawyers, the judiciary gradually became more Indian as well. The initial practice of appointing one Indian judge to each Bench was gradually expanded to two or three, and then after World War I half of the High Court benches would be made up of Indian judges. By the 1940s Indian judges formed a majority in many of India's High Courts.

The period of the Indianisation of the Bar and the subsequent elevation of Indian judges to the Bench can be gleaned from the writings of a generation of Indian lawyers who started their careers around the time of World War I. The Englishmen at the Bar had become scarce, and so their teachers and mentors were fellow Indians who were amongst the first Indians to properly establish themselves as barristers at the start of the 20th century. In most cases their professional lives were a struggle at first; one of the reasons that many educated young Indians opted for the civil service was the inherent risk of a legal career. Yet after their initial days of struggle many experienced a period of prominence and prosperity during the 1920s and 1930s; they acted as counsel in sensational cases, read their names in the newspaper headlines, and commanded large fees for their services. Yet by the time of the 1940s they would have to give up their careers as high-flying barristers, and in the best traditions of their profession, heed the call and sit as judges in the courts which they had once dominated with their advocacy.

***

The amalgamation of the Supreme Courts and the Sadar Courts took place in the aftermath of the transfer from Company to Crown Rule and the codification of civil and criminal laws. Sir Charles Wood, the Secretary of State for India addressed the House of Commons on 6 June 1861 stating that the amalgamation of the courts would bring together "the legal knowledge of the English lawyers with the intimate knowledge of the customs, habits and laws of the Natives possessed by the Judges in the country." He later advocated that courts dealing in cases "exclusively between natives" be made up of judges "trained in the country whose knowledge of the native language will obviate the expense and delay of translating the proceedings."[ccxxxii]

The Indian High Courts Act of 1861 created High Courts at Calcutta, Bombay and Madras, and another was established at Allahabad in 1866. A subsequent Act of 1911 facilitated the creation of more High Courts, in Patna in 1916, Lahore in 1919 and Nagpur in 1936. The 1861 Act stipulated that a High Court bench was to consist of a chief justice and a maximum of 15 puisne judges, and the viceroy could appoint additional judges for two year terms. The expansion of litigation in the late 19th century led to the expansion of the Bench, and the

Act of 1911 raised the limit to 19 puisne judges.

Under the 1861 Act four categories of legal professionals were eligible to become judges of the High Courts; barristers with at least five years of practice, members of the Indian Civil Service with ten years' experience who had served as a magistrate for three years, judges from the lower judiciary with at least five years' experience, and pleaders of the High Court with ten years' experience. At least one-third of the judges, including the chief justice, had to be barristers, and at least one-third had to come from the Indian Civil Service. The remaining one-third would be appointed from the lower judiciary. Given that at the time of the drafting of the Act all barristers, officers of the Indian Civil Service and a large section of the lower judiciary were British, the prospect of Indians being appointed to High Court benches seemed quite remote.

Judges held their office at the pleasure of the British monarch and their salaries and allowances were under the purview of the Secretary of State for India in London. The chief justice determined which judge sat in which case and also constituted the division courts. It was the viceroy who proposed names for the Calcutta High Court and the governors of Bombay and Madras would propose names for their respective High Court benches. The Calcutta High Court was considered a notch above the other High Courts; the chief justice at Calcutta received a higher salary than his counterparts in Bombay and Madras and the advocate general for Bengal was an officer of the Government of India whereas his counterparts in Bombay and Madras were officers of their provincial governments.

***

Competition in the legal profession in England was just as tough as it would later become in India, and British barristers had been encouraged since the early years of the 19th century to travel to India to establish their practices before the courts of the East India Company. Later in the century when they gathered at the Bombay Bar Association after the establishment of the Bombay High Court, they would come to defend their professional rights and status as barristers with the same energy and perseverance as they would have before any court in England. They were members of a learned profession, and their turf battles were not usually with any Indians, but with their own countrymen on the bench of the Bombay High Court.

One of the early clashes between the barristers and judges of the Bombay High Court came when the Chief Justice Michael Westropp accused the Acting Advocate General Charles Mayhew of taking a professional shortcut. In December 1876 Mayhew went to Westropp's house during the Christmas holiday and applied for a rule nisi on behalf of his client. Chief Justice Westropp refused to grant the rule until Mayhew brought a more explicit affidavit before him. When a fresh affidavit was prepared Mayhew renewed his application the following day before Justice Robert Pinhey, under the impression that Westropp had left for Matheran. But in fact Westropp had not yet left Bombay and demanded an explanation as to why Mayhew had not brought the application before him. He accused Mayhew of "sharp practice" and suppressing the truth.[ccxxxiii] In January Mayhew appeared before both Westropp and Pinhey and offered an explanation; he honestly believed that Westropp had left for Matheran when he brought his application before Pinhey. Westropp did not accept Mayhew's explanation, labelling it a pure fabrication and accused him of doing things unworthy of his profession. Mayhew shot back, stating that the insinuations "were not honourable and becoming his high position."[ccxxxiv] The Bombay Bar then decided to support their man at a special meeting and condemned the remarks of the chief justice and formed a committee to look into the matter led by John Marriott, the advocate general and other senior barristers. The committee's report exonerated Mayhew of 'sharp practice' and stated that he did not deserve the censure of the chief justice. The advocate general and John Inverarity, a leading barrister, handed the report to the chief justice who nonetheless maintained his position and thought that his censure of Mayhew was well founded.

In 1880 at a meeting of the Bombay Bar Charles Farran moved a resolution that an acting advocate general "in the opinion of the Bar is entitled to the same precedence as the permanent Advocate- General, and that it is competent to any member of the Bar to hold a junior brief to the Acting Advocate-General."[ccxxxv] Farran wanted the contrary rule to be rescinded and the resolution was communicated to the Bench. The judges replied that the issue had already been decided by a Division Bench in 1865, which had ruled that an acting advocate general was entitled only to precedence in government business, but not in other business. The judges had no objection to a waiver of precedence from any senior barrister in favour of the acting advocate general as a matter of courtesy, but according to the 1865 decision the judges could not hold that he was entitled to any right of precedence. The resolution of the Bar could not, according to the response from the Bench, bind future barristers in the matter of their privileges.

The following year, a barrister from Karachi sought the opinion of the Bar on the matter of a barrister working with a pleader and the division of their fees.[ccxxxvi] At a meeting of the Bar Inverarity moved a motion that in the opinion of the Bar it was undesirable and contrary to etiquette that a barrister would partner with a pleader and agree to a division of fees. However, Henry Kirkpatrick moved an amendment that the Bar should decline to give an opinion as it would amount to providing a ruling on outside places with which the Bombay Bar had no concern. He thought that the Bombay Bar did not have the right to place restrictions on barristers who chose to practice outside Bombay. Kirkpatrick's amendment was seconded by Reginald Branson, but it was defeated and Inverarity's motion was carried.

In 1886 the Bombay Bar received a letter from the Bombay European Chamber of Commerce complaining of the Bar's rules which stipulated minimum fees for short causes, ex-parte and undefended long causes, and the rule requiring two counsel on long causes irrespective of the financial stake.[ccxxxvii] The Chamber also complained of frequent adjournments, insinuating that they were for the convenience of the lawyers involved. The Government of Bombay also received a memorial on the subject and then wrote a letter to the Bar suggesting it remove these rules. The Bar resented the tone of the government's letter and protested against the insinuations made about its senior members. The government replied, denying its intention to make any insinuation against members of the Bar and expressed surprise that the Bar should have read it that way. The Bar then refused to remove the rules and only modified the rule about the need for two counsel, taking the suggestion of the judges that two counsel only be required for suits higher than ₹5,000 in value.

By the 1890s the Bombay Bar had an awareness of its own identity, as well as the uniqueness of the Bombay High Court and its status in the Indian legal system. Outsiders came to be looked upon with suspicion, and the barristers of Bombay made their displeasure known when Charles Farran was elevated to the position of Chief Justice of the Bombay High Court and the Government of Bombay appointed Arthur Strachey, a barrister from Allahabad to the Bombay bench superseding Matthew Starling who had been an acting judge. In November 1895 at a meeting of the Bombay Bar John Macpherson moved a resolution recording the Bar's appreciation of Starling's excellent services and protesting against his supersession by Strachey.[ccxxxviii] A memorial was prepared in which the qualifications and service of Starling were highlighted, as was the special character of legal work in Bombay city, which was an important port and commercial hub with a cosmopolitan population quite unlike the remote inland city of Allahabad. In addition, Mr. Strachey, no matter how qualified, would be without the experience necessary in the kind of litigation which came before the Original Side bench in Bombay, for the Allahabad High Court had only appellate rather than original jurisdiction: "It is because we believe that the recent appointment and the circumstances in which it was made, will seriously impair that confidence and respect that we venture to make this protest."[ccxxxix] The memorial was signed by Macpherson as senior member of the Bar and by Lindesay Robertson as the Secretary of the Bar Association on behalf of the entire Bar and was forwarded to the Secretary of State for India in London. The Government of Bombay was unamused by the Bombay Bar's memorial and when Chief Justice Farran died three years later they brought another Allahabad man, Louis Kershaw in as Chief Justice of the Bombay High Court.

Besides asserting its rights and privileges before the Bench and the government, the Bar also had occasion to remind its own members of their professional obligations. In 1897 a report had been circulating in the local press which claimed that British barristers had refused to hold a brief for Bal Gangadhar Tilak who was facing a sedition trial before the Bombay High Court. The Advocate General, Basil Lang brought the report to the attention of the Bar and directed the Bar Association to write a letter to the press to contradict the report and emphasise that every member of the Bar was bound to accept a brief offered as long as it did not interfere with his professional arrangements and the fee was sufficient.[ccxl] Any refusal for political or other reasons would amount to a breach of professional etiquette and make the barrister liable to censure.

***

Just as British barristers would be ever vigilant in maintaining their rights and privileges before the judiciary, when they ascended to the bench and became judges of the Bombay High Court they would show equal tenacity in asserting the authority of the court before the Government of Bombay. These assertions could seem quite trivial, and even petty at times. Judges of the Bombay High Court would insist on setting the time zone according to which the court would run and would refuse to attend government functions unless accorded special standing positions during the governor's presentations. Attention to the smallest of details could take truly amazing proportions however, when a running battle continued between the Bombay High Court and the Government of Bombay for almost 40 years over the interpretation of a clause of a rule which regulated the appointment of officers to the court. More serious cases of conflict between the judiciary and the executive would also arise, and British justices of the Bombay High Court would challenge the Government of Bombay when they felt it had overstepped its authority and interfered with the administration of justice.

When Sir James Fergasson became Governor of Bombay in 1880 he ordered all government departments and the High Court to adopt Madras time as directed by the Government of India. However, he did not consult the judges of the Bombay High Court. Both Sir Michael Westropp and Sir Charles Sargent protested and refused to comply with the order, which meant that the High Court of Bombay continued using Bombay time for many years, whilst Bombay's government departments used Madras time. The stand-off was eventually resolved by the adoption of Indian Standard Time all across the country.

Sir James offended the Bombay bench once again by

ignoring the traditional practice of having High Court judges stand alongside the governor during presentations and instead ordered that they should stand before the governor like others who were eligible for a private meeting. The judges insisted on their special status, but the governor refused to budge. The Acting Chief Justice Lyttleton Bayley then wrote to Sir James, informing him that unless their special privileges were restored High Court judges would refuse to attend functions at Government House.[ccxli] After his return from England, Chief Justice Sargent took the matter up in an interview with the governor and succeeded in having the judges' standing position restored.

In 1903 the Chief Justice, Sir Lawrence Jenkins went so far as to submit a petition to the King protesting the Bombay Government's actions in a seemingly obscure matter in the Princely State of Kolhapur. A suit had been filed in the Bombay High Court by D.C. Fernandes, an Indian pleader from Kolhapur who claimed damages for malicious prosecution and wrongful imprisonment by Colonel John Wray, the British Political Agent in Kolhapur. Fernandes and Wray had a long standing enmity. Wray was not satisfied with some of the practices of the local Catholic clergy and wanted Fernandes to join in a protest movement which he was instigating. Fernandes refused and further annoyed Wray by appearing for an accused in a criminal case and later filing a petition against him to the Bombay Government. Fernandes alleged that Wray abused him and later tried to have him implicated in a criminal case by the Durbar of the Princely State of Kolhapur; Wray had accused Fernandes of being part of a conspiracy to poison his food and drinks at a banquet of the Kolhapur Durbar. The local police advised Wray not to press the matter for want of evidence, yet Fernandes was arrested and kept in custody for two months only to be released due to the anticipated lack of evidence. Fernandes then filed his suit against Wray for ₹10,000 in damages. Wray pleaded that Fernandes's arrest was the responsibility of the Kolhapur Durbar. Fernandes's case rested mainly on evidence which could only be obtained from the Princely State of Kolhapur.

In October 1902 Fernandes applied for a commission to issue to the Political Agent of Kolhapur for permission to examine witnesses in Kolhapur State. The commission was issued and Wray joined it. Three days after the issue of the commission the Political Secretary to the Government of Bombay wrote to the Political Agent in Kolhapur suggesting that the Governor of Bombay decline to further a suit in the High Court against their own political agent "on the grounds of general policy".[ccxlii] He argued that the internal affairs of an Indian prince should not be brought under examination in a court of British India. The political secretary instructed the political agent to return the commission, citing government orders that he was unable to execute it. Shahu, the Maharaja of Kolhapur was also advised not to co-operate with the case. In November 1902 Fernandes was advised that the Government of Bombay had undertaken the defence of his case against Wray.

When the commission was returned unexecuted, Fernandes issued a fresh application for its reissue and also applied for the Political Secretary to the Government of Bombay to be produced before the court to explain why his actions did not amount to contempt of court. The government solicitor then sought to settle the matter with the formulation that the Kolhapur Durbar had arrested Fernandes under the influence of Wray. A correspondence ensued between the High Court and the Government of Bombay regarding the issue of the return of the commission.

The chief justice and the judges of the Bombay High Court were not satisfied with the government's response, which led them to petition the King. The petition stated that the Government of Bombay's actions in not allowing the execution of the commission and advising its agent to have Maharaja Shahu withhold cooperation with the trial amounted to obstruction and interference with justice.[ccxliii] It was argued that the Court of the Political Agent was established and continued by the viceroy, that the Code of Civil Procedure extended to the Political Agent's Court which compelled it to examine persons in a commission received, and that "general considerations of policy" could not justify the complete exclusion of all evidence in the case. The Bombay judges pleaded with the King to protect the dignity and authority of his Bombay High Court and if necessary refer the matter to the Privy Council.

The Secretary of State William Brodrick, the Earl of Midleton considered the petition. The secretary of state did not agree with the High Court judges' argument that section 388 of the Criminal Procedure Code imposed a legal obligation to execute the commission.[ccxliv] If the case was still pending he thought it would be fit for consideration by the Privy Council, but also felt that given that the matter had been settled it should be dealt with by legislation. He requested the Government of India to take the matter into consideration when revising the Criminal Procedure Code. Midleton also argued that in cases of great political sensitivity in princely states when it was felt that the execution of a commission would not be proper, the political agent should explain the reasons respectfully to the court issuing the commission. He also thought that the Government of Bombay's reference to "grounds of general policy" went further than was necessary according to the needs of the princely state and was indefensible on a point of principle. The secretary of state however accepted the Government of Bombay's contention that the last thing it intended was to disrespect the Bombay High Court.

The energy to pursue a point of law never seemed to wane, and an even more protracted battle between the Bombay bench and the Government of Bombay ensued over Clause 8 of the amended Letters Patent of 1865. It was a seemingly obscure clause of a minor rule which provided a framework for the appointment of officers to the court. The clause read:

> "And we do hereby authorise and empower the Chief Justice of the said High Court of Judicature at Bombay, from time to time as occasion may require, and subject to any rules and restrictions which may be prescribed by the Governor in Council, to appoint...such clerks and ministerial officers as shall be necessary...and we do hereby ordain that every such appointment shall be forthwith submitted to the Governor in Council."

Successive chief justices of the Bombay High Court thought that the clause gave them the right, subject to rules and regulations framed by the governor, to appoint officers of the court. No rules were framed by the Government of Bombay however, until 1895 when the Government of India wrote to the Government of Bombay at the time of the appointment of Rustumji Sethna as pro tem registrar of the court. The Government of India wrote that it envisaged filling the post of registrar with men from the Indian Civil Service or Bombay Civil Service, and suggested to the Governor of Bombay that in making rules the Government of Bombay should restrict the office to these two classes.[ccxlv] The Chief Justice, Sir Charles Sargent however, argued that Clause 8 intended that the government would decide on the number and description of the officers of the court, but not restrict it to particular classes. The Government of Bombay then sent a draft of the rules to the High Court and the new Chief Justice, Charles Farran continued his predecessor's argument, protesting the wide interpretation of Clause 8, which if pursued to an extreme would interfere with the ability of the chief justice to appoint officers of the court. The Government of Bombay confirmed the rules nonetheless.

In 1911 the Government of India announced that the registrar's post at the High Court would no longer be opened to members of the Bombay Civil Service. This time the Chief Justice, Sir Basil Scott petitioned the King over the question of whether the Government of Bombay had the authority to limit the chief justice in the appointment of officers of the court.[ccxlvi] Sir Basil wanted the matter of Clause 8 sent up to the Privy Council for adjudication. The Government of Bombay however was keen that the matter not go to the Privy Council, viewing it as a matter of internal administration.

The chief justice's petition was considered by the Privy Council in November 1912. The Privy Council did not provide a judgement, but it did express the view that the intent and purpose of the clause was quite clear; that the words "rules and restrictions" governed the word "appoint", and that the Chief Justice of Bombay's position was not established. By 1919 the appointment of registrars had been extended to Bombay Civil Service officers and barristers, and Clause 8 had been amended by the omission of the sentence which stipulated that all such appointments be submitted to the governor.

Then, in 1922 when the Deputy Registrar Nasarwanji Gharda was to be appointed registrar of the court the issue of the government's rule making authority arose once again. The High Court wrote to the Government of Bombay arguing that the removal of the sentence requiring the governor's approval for appointments gave freedom of selection back to the chief justice.[ccxlvii] The Government of Bombay relied on the legal remembrancer's opinion that Gharda did not belong to any of the three eligible classes for the post and the appointments still had to be made in conformity with the rules and regulations of the government. The Bombay High Court contended that there had been no clear decision on the amended Clause 8 and asked for a decision from the Government of India. The Government of Bombay similarly requested a notification from the Government of India. The Government of India then wrote to the secretary of state to move the Privy Council for a ruling. The petition of the secretary of state was made for a declaration that the Order in Council of 1912 be amended by declaring that the Government of Bombay, rather than the Government of India, have authority to make the rules for the appointment of officers of the court. The hearing was held in camera and the Privy Council agreed that the Government of Bombay rather than the Government of India should be the authority to make the rules. The Government of Bombay then proposed fresh rules and sent them to the High Court, but turned down Gharda's nomination.

***

Given that the Indian High Courts were in their early years largely British institutions, their development into more truly Indian courts would depend on the manner in which Indian judges were elevated to the Bench. The issue of whether all judges would be equal in administering the law caused great controversy in the 1880s in the form of the Ilbert Bill, when the British community in India took offence to the idea that an Indian could sit in judgement over English men and women in the remote districts of the Raj. But more than a decade before that controversy erupted Indian judges were already being appointed to the Calcutta High Court, and in a series of contempt of court cases the matter was settled, at the level of the elite judiciary at least; both Indians and the British would have to respect the institution of the court, irrespective of the race of the judge.

The appointment of the first Indian High Court judge came about because one of the British judges of Calcutta's old Sadar Dewani Adalat, Justice George Loch had gone on leave and would not immediately be able to join the new Calcutta High Court. His position was to be filled by Justice Edward De Latour, but he died before he could take up his position. In July 1862 the Chief Justice, Sir Barnes Peacock realised that being one judge short, arrears from the appellate side were likely to accumulate, and in August he wrote to the government requesting the appointment of a judge to take De Latour's place.[ccxlviii] The full bench of British judges was not able to attend court every day, as one or two would be down with illness, and Sir Barnes argued that the appointment of another judge would actually save money as the arrears would be quickly cleared.

Sir Barnes's request was heard and the government decided to appoint a judge from among the ranks of Indian vakils. Initially Ram Mohun Roy's son Ramprasad Roy was to be elevated to the Bench. However, he died in August 1862 and it was Sambhu Nath Pandit who eventually took a seat on the bench of the Calcutta High Court in February 1863. Pandit only lived until June 1867, yet he did distinguish himself during his time as a judge. Condoling his death, Richard Doyne of the Calcutta Bar said:

> *"I have never heard the faintest expression of doubt that his appointment at the time was the best possible one...A great experiment was initiated in his person, namely whether the natives of this country were fit to be entrusted with one of the highest and most responsible offices under the crown...And so here it was in no small degree attributable to the personal worth of*

Sambhu Nath Pandit that an experiment the result of which no one doubts has established a system."[ccxlix]

Dwarkanath Mitter replaced Sambhu Nath Pandit on the Bench and it was William Tayler, a former member of the Bengal Civil Service, and Commissioner of Patna who crossed the line in his criticism of the new judge. Tayler was a legal man himself having enrolled as a vakil of the Calcutta High Court and also worked as a mukhtar, or law agent in Patna. At one time he received a lucrative retainer from the Rani of Ticari but was later dismissed from her employment. Tayler filed a suit against the Rani for recovery of a sum of money and the Rani filed a cross suit for the recovery of money received from her account. Tayler's suit was dismissed with costs awarded to the Rani. In execution of the decree one of Tayler's Bihar properties was attached, but he then sold it to Musammat Zuhoorun, concealing the attachment. Zuhoorun was then compelled to pay the claim of the Rani in order to save the property. She then filed a suit against Tayler for recovery of the sum of money which she had to pay to the Rani on account of the attachment of the property. Girish Ghose, the Principal Sadder Amin of Patna ordered in favour of Tayler, dismissing the suit with costs.

The case came on appeal to the Calcutta High Court and Chief Justice Peacock and Justice Mitter delivered their judgement on 19 November 1869. Both judges concluded that Zuhoorun was entitled to recover the funds, with Mitter adding: "a fraud has been perpetrated against her by Mr. Tayler in concealing from her the fact that the estate sold by him to her was under attachment in execution of a decree of court. I should have been extremely sorry if the state of the law were otherwise." Tayler placed an application for review before the Bench including new facts, but the review was rejected.

Tayler then appealed to the press, rather than the Privy Council. He wrote three letters to *The Englishman* on 7, 12 and 13 April 1869. A passage from his first letter from 7 April read:

> "I now purpose to show, and that by clear and unanswerable evidence, that this dishonoring and unmeasured imputation judicially cast upon me by Mr. Justice Dwarkanath Mitter has been recorded by him without one tittle of evidence to support it; that it is wholly untrue and manifedly absurd; and I beg you to observe that the learned Judge who placed it on record has not condescended to give one single reason, ground, or argument in support of his denunciation."

Shortly after the publication of the letters Tayler was charged with contempt of court and arrested whilst trying to leave for England. On 24 April 1869 he was sentenced to one month imprisonment and a fine of ₹500. In his judgement in *William Tayler vs Unknown* Chief Justice Peacock rebutted Tayler's narrative of victimhood with the facts of the case and observed:

> "I have now shown beyond all doubt that there was not a shadow of justification for Mr. Tayler's charges against Mr. Justice Dwarkanath Mitter, and that the public could not have been misled by any criticisms if they had been based upon the truth, the whole truth, and nothing but the

> *truth I have also criticised what Mr. Tayler has been pleased to style his intellectual and searching criticism, and I have no hesitation in declaring that his letters do not contain fair criticisms, but slanderous assertions and false statements."*

Tayler's initial apology was found to be insufficient, and he was given the opportunity to publish another one. He did so, retracting his opinions on Justice Mitter, and after two weeks in jail and in failing health he was released by the court on 27 April 1869. Justice Mitter stated: "Now I wish to declare publicly and emphatically that the judges are not and cannot be, influenced in the discharge of their duty by any attack made upon them by the press."[ccl]

More than a decade after Tayler's case the roles were reversed when an Indian editor went too far in his criticism of an English judge. Surendranath Banerjea was the editor of *The Bengalee* when a case came before the Calcutta High Court over whether a Hindu idol which was in the possession of Bhuttock Pandit in Burra Bazaar was the family idol of parties to the suit. Counsel for both parties suggested that the idol be brought to the court for examination. Justice John Norris was hesitant, but it was eventually agreed by all parties that the idol would be examined in the corridor outside the courtroom. An article then appeared in *The Bengalee* on April 28 1883 stating that Justice Norris had "certainly done enough within the short time that he has filled the High Court Bench to show how unworthy he is of his high office and how by nature he is unfitted to maintain those traditions of dignity which are inseparable from the office of the judge of the High Court in the Land." Banerjea went on to accuse Justice Norris of setting "the Hugli on fire" by dragging the idol into court and so diminishing its dignity and the family to which it belonged.

Banerjea was then found guilty of contempt of court. When he was better acquainted with the facts of the case he tendered an unqualified apology, but the majority of the judges sentenced him to two months imprisonment in the Presidency Jail. The only Indian judge on the Bench, Justice Ramesh Mitter agreed with the majority verdict, but disagreed with the punishment. He thought that the level of contempt shown by Tayler was not less than Banerjea, whereas the Englishman had only been awarded one month in prison.

***

By the start of the 20th century a generation of Indian barristers had established themselves at the Bar, largely taking the place of those English barristers who had dominated the High Courts since their inception. The Indian barristers who followed them after World War I would eventually rise to the Bench as Independence approached during the 1940s. Relatively few judges of the era left behind written records of their lives and times, but those that did chronicled an Indianisation of the judiciary which occurred in much the same way, and at much the same time as that which took place in the civil service, army and police.

Mehr Mahajan was the eldest of this group, starting his career as a mukhtar shortly before World War I.[ccli] He hailed from Kangra in the Himalayas and was the son of a prominent lawyer who was among the first generation to practice British law in the remote district. He would start his practice in Dharmshala before moving to Gurdaspur and then take up practice at the Lahore High Court after 1919. In Bombay two young men from very different backgrounds would come to make their names at the Bombay High Court after World War I. Mahomedali Chagla was the son of a family of wealthy Muslim merchants, and attended St Xavier's, Bombay and Lincoln College, Oxford before being called to the Bar from

Inner Temple in London.[cclii] Pralhad Gajendragadkar was from the small town of Satara, the son of a Brahmin family of teachers and pandits. He studied at Deccan College and Poona Law College and when he arrived in Bombay after taking his law degree he was overawed by life in the big city.[ccliii] W.S. Krishnaswamy Nayudu came from a landowning family of Chingleput District in the northern part of the Madras Presidency.[ccliv] He grew up in Madras city and studied at the Madras Law College before becoming an apprentice to some of the leading lawyers at the Madras Bar and eventually establishing a thriving practice of his own. Mohammad Hidayatullah belonged to an old Muslim family of Beneras which had more recently settled in central India.[cclv] Like Chagla, he travelled to England to study at Trinity College, Cambridge before taking the Bar examination in London. He would return to Nagpur rather than Bombay however, which when he started his practice did not yet have a High Court. Bhuvaneshwar Sinha's grandfather was both a landowner and a money lender, which meant that he should have grown up in material comfort. However, his father died whilst trying to treat plague victims and he was left to support his family from a young age.[cclvi] Battling his reduced circumstances, he studied at school in Arrah in Bhojpur district in Bihar before reading history at Patna College. Sinha attended Government Law College, Patna and then passed his law examinations before enrolling at the Patna Bar. Despite their diverse backgrounds, when Sinha and his peers arrived at the Bar they shared a common experience; they were all taught and assisted by the elder generation of Indian barristers in the workings of their courts, and the traditions of the legal profession.

Mahomedali Chagla had the most famous legal mentor of all. Chagla had known Mohammad Ali Jinnah during his days as a student at St Xavier's, Bombay. Chagla was the President of the Muslim Students' Union and Jinnah would often come to address the students to urge them to work for communal harmony, without which they would not be able to throw off British rule. Jinnah was President of the Home Rule League and would often speak at Shantaram Chawl, which was the city's venue for public meetings before the rise of mass politics. Chagla thought Jinnah's finest hour was when he led a demonstration against Lord Willingdon and broke up a meeting at the Town Hall at which loyalists wanted to present an address to the governor upon his retirement. Jinnah was at the height of his powers in the early 1920s; Chagla recalled that he was the "idol of the youth" and the "uncrowned king of Bombay".

Chagla would often go to Jinnah's chambers to meet him, sending his card, but Jinnah insisted that there was no need for such formalities and the young man could walk in whenever he wanted. He would go to court to watch Jinnah plead and thought of him as a master of advocacy. Naturally, he approached Jinnah before leaving for Oxford to ask if he could work for him upon his return when he had qualified as a barrister. Jinnah told him to first qualify, and then come and see him.

What had attracted Chagla was Jinnah's force of personality, but more importantly his patriotism and nationalism. Young Chagla joined his chambers after returning from Oxford in 1923 and remained there for six years. He would read Jinnah's briefs, accompany him to court and listen to his arguments. He was impressed by his lucid thought and expression and his straight and forthright manner would always leave a strong impression irrespective of the intrinsic merits of his case. Jinnah drilled home the message that the advocate had to do his best for his client no matter how bad the case was.

Chagla struggled early on for his first eight years at the Bar and had hardly any work. He recalled that Jinnah never enquired about his circumstances and thought he never came across a person with less humanity. Besides being cold and unemotional, Jinnah had no interests besides law and politics. Chagla did not remember him reading a serious book. He would occupy himself with law books, briefs and newspapers. Chagla thought that Jinnah was "a poor lawyer, but a superb advocate"; he was a first rate cross examiner with a striking personality and his presentation of cases was a work of art. He would not take long cases but was first rate at miscellaneous matters and was a master with a pile of summonses and motions. But Chagla felt he owed Jinnah a great deal, as he learnt the art of advocacy and "how to maintain the highest traditions of the legal profession."

Jinnah would maintain impeccable professional etiquette and believed that a senior lawyer should never recommend a junior to a solicitor. He knew how Chagla felt about not getting any help, but he told him that he would thank him later when he would be able to say that he achieved success at the Bar on his own merits. Chagla recalled that Jinnah was handling the defence in the Bawla murder case when the local advocate from Gwalior came to his chambers and asked him to recommend a junior. Jinnah replied that there were 200 juniors at the Bar and that the advocate should just choose one. Young Chagla was crushed, but in the end he thought his days of starvation did him good; it instilled an intense desire for success and capacity for hard work. Chagla would not leave chambers at the end of each day until Jinnah had finished his conferences and would head home. Jinnah would take Chagla and drop him off at the Bar Gymkhana.

John Inverarity was still practising when Chagla arrived and Chagla thought of him as one of the most eminent lawyers to ever practice at the Bombay High Court or at any High Court in India. He had been practising in Bombay since 1870 and by the early 1920s he was in decline and approaching retirement, but still gave glimpses of his greatness. Chagla recalled that he was nothing much to look at and was neither a great personality nor an impressive speaker. He had little talent for histrionics. But he did know all the tricks of the trade and was a forceful advocate and an astute lawyer.

Chagla would watch Inverarity sit in court and draft his pleadings whilst waiting for his case to be called. He recalled Inverarity's colossal memory; he would read the brief, tie it up with red tape and then start writing on a new foolscap paper recalling all the facts, dates and names. Bhulabhai Desai told Chagla that when he was a junior sitting in the library making copious notes for a brief he had been studying, Inverarity, who was passing by took the papers, tore them up and told him: "Young man, learn to trust your memory." Bhulabhai took the instruction literally and never made a single note for the rest of his career.

Inverarity would stay at the Byculla Club, which was a Whites only club, and would hold his conferences there. Indian lawyers would have to enter by the back door to get to his room. Jamshedji Kanga would have to go in by the back door to see Inverarity, something which stirred Chagla up but hardly bothered Kanga; Inverarity was a great lawyer and he would see him in whatever circumstances he had to. Inverarity's hearing deteriorated towards the end of his career and Chagla thought he was poorly treated by Justice Amberson Marten, who made no special allowance for the old man and would not speak loudly or repeat himself. Inverarity eventually stopped appearing in Marten's court.

After W.S. Krishnaswamy Nayudu completed his B.L. degree, he was taken on as an apprentice by a leading Original Side lawyer, T. Ethiraja Mudaliar in Madras. Nayudu resided at the Poonamallee High Road and would attend Mudaliar's chambers in the morning. He thought Mudaliar possessed a very reserved temperament, and would follow discussions between him and his other juniors and read the cause papers posted in the cases for the day. After a month or two Mudaliar found his young apprentice to be attentive and asked him to draft the concise statement of claim to be incorporated in the summons in original suits. He would then give him the pleadings of these cases and ask him to draft the issues. At 9:30 each morning Nayudu would collect the decisions which were gathered in the back sheet of the cause papers of the cases posted for the day and then bundle them up and give them to the Attender for delivery to court. Nayudu learnt a lot about Original Side work, how pleadings were prepared, how issues were drafted and followed the manner in which Mudaliar worked up cases by referring to previous decisions. He would attend court and follow Mudaliar's cases for three or four days a week. By early 1921 Nayudu completed the apprentice course and passed the apprentice examination in April 1921.

When Nayudu went to the Madras High Court Bar in 1924 he wanted to get himself attached to a senior lawyer's office and most often went to the Small Cause Court with the one or two briefs that came his way. The Small Cause Court schedule of fees was low, and he could never get much above it and would have to attend court on several days whenever his cases were posted. He could not miss any adjournment as he did not have a clerk of his own. Neither did he have any chambers of his own and so he used the chambers of T. Nallasivan Pillai. Sir Pitty Theagaraja Chetty, who had recommended his name to Mudaliar then suggested that Nayudu join the chambers of O. Thanikachallam Chettiar, a leading solicitor and partner in Messers Short Bewes & Company, a firm of European solicitors of long standing.

Nayudu joined Chettiar's office at the end of 1924. Chettiar would hold his office at Linghi Chetty Street between 7:30 and 9 am and would study some of the briefs entrusted to him by Bewes. Nayudu would arrive at 7:30 before Chettiar would take his seat and then be back at home at 9:30, get dressed, and be in the High Court or whichever court in which Chettiar was working by 10:45. Nayudu kept this routine up for a year. Chettiar would not even turn around when Nayudu was in the chambers, but Nayudu would intervene and pick up the case law and give him a case or two when he was working up a case and Chettiar would ask Nayudu to work some points of law. Chettiar would take Nayudu to court in his car, pick him up for drives along Marina Beach, take him to the Club, and eventually gave him a conveyance allowance of ₹35. Most of Chettiar's clients came to Nayudu when Chettiar became chief judge of the Small Cause Court in 1928, something which helped him to set up a lucrative practice of his own.

Having passed the law examination and the chamber examination, Bhuvaneshwar Sinha enrolled as a vakil of the Patna High Court without having seen any practice in December 1922. Nirsu Sinha complained that Bhuvaneshwar had not informed him that he was going to join the Bar that day. His master Parmeshwar Dayal also made a similar complaint and said that the young man should have arranged to get some briefs and some payments of fees besides consulting astrologers for an auspicious day on which to begin practice. Nonetheless, Bhuvaneshwar attended court for a week and made ₹27 with some help from both his seniors. Parmeshwar Dayal already had a number of juniors in his office as did Bhuvaneshwar's teacher Shiveshwar Dayal, so he decided to approach Nirsu Sinha and Shambhu Saran. Nirsu Sinha did not have any juniors attached to his office and began to use Bhuvaneshwar's services regularly. This came in handy when he was busy with his own public engagements as the unofficial 'Leader of the Opposition' in the Bihar legislature.

When Nirsu Sinha was absent from court the younger Sinha would be entrusted with all his briefs. Nirsu gave standing orders to his clerk to approach Bhuvaneshwar for any action in connection with the briefs, including presenting arguments if the case could not be passed over. And even when Nirsu was present in court he would ask Bhuvaneshwar to argue cases before the registrar for admission. Bhuvaneshwar got most of his cases admitted, which won him the confidence of the elder Sinha. Whilst Nirsu was away during the budget session of the Bihar legislature, Bhuvaneshwar would work into the night studying case law. If, having prepared his notes he was still unsure of any matter, he would run over to Nirsu's house and ask for his help in solving the difficulty. The elder Sinha never expressed exasperation and treated the younger Sinha with patronage and kindness.

When Mohammad Hidayatullah returned to Nagpur from Cambridge in 1930 his first sponsor was Yashwant Jakatdar. The practice at the Nagpur Bar at the time was that the young lawyer would be invited to appear in a case to prove himself. The case which was selected for Hidayatullah involved a question of professional ethics in which a lawyer had at first accepted a brief from one side, only to return it and accept a brief from the other side. Hidayatullah's motion was to stop him from accepting the second brief and Jakatdar asked him to supplement his argument which was based on Indian precedents with English rulings. The case was heard by Robert Jackson who was the Additional Judicial Commissioner. After Jakatdar had argued his part of the case he introduced Hidayatullah and requested that he supplement the case with English citations and added that it was the young lawyer's first case. Hidayatullah went on to cite the appropriate English cases only to be told by Jackson that he was "using a hammer to crush a butterfly!" Hidayatullah thought he was still at the Cambridge Majlis and needed to provide a fitting rebuttal. He replied that he did not care what he used as long as the butterfly was crushed. He saw a vein pop out of Jackson's head. Jackson then called him into the judicial commissioner's chambers. Hidayatullah was expecting a dressing down but instead received words of encouragement. Jackson then followed Hidayatullah's progress at the court and left a kind note before he retired.

***

After an initial period of uncertainty and apprenticeships in the offices of senior Indian lawyers, young Indian barristers would eventually get their first big break. In a profession in which name and reputation were so important, that first big case would launch their careers and bring a welcome end to days of struggle. For some it happened by accident, a messenger would seemingly appear out of nowhere with a first brief, for others however, it was the result of much hard work in self-promotion, and many cases done for free.

Mahomedali Chagla's first big break came in the form of the 'Trunk murder' case.[cclvii] A Gujarati pearl merchant invited another Gujarati pearl merchant to his house to show him a pearl necklace. When the visiting merchant arrived at the host merchant's house he stole the necklace, strangled his host, put him in a trunk of a taxi, drove all over Bombay, and dropped the trunk off at a well in Andheri. The taxi driver became suspicious and instead of taking the merchant home he drove him to a police station. The trunk and the dead body were subsequently discovered. The strangled merchant's younger brother was in the room whilst the act was being committed. Motilal Setalvad appeared for the main accused, whilst Chagla appeared for the brother. The case appeared in Justice Harilal Kania's court, and whilst Setalvad's client was convicted and awarded the death sentence, Chagla managed to get his client off. Later, Setalvad's client's advocate approached Chagla to draw up a mercy petition for the condemned man. Chagla told him that it would be a waste of money as there was no chance that the sentence would be commuted, but the advocate replied "drily" that Chagla should do his best, charge whatever fee he liked and "leave the rest to him". Chagla was later "shocked" to find that the petition had been successful and the sentence had been commuted.

On taking his LLB degree Pralhad Gajendragadkar moved with his wife to Bombay in June 1926 and stayed with his elder brother who was living in Girgaum.cclviii Gajendragadkar and his brother took the Number 8 tram from the Opera House via the Maharaja Building to Flora Fountain one morning. Gajendragadkar's brother had to go to Elphinstone College but dropped him off at the High Court, and before he left the elder Gajendragadkar told his brother: "Here is the building, magnificent in appearance and rich in tradition. This is your karmabhoomi. Go ahead. The blessings of father and mother are with you and my best wishes will accompany you throughout."

Gajendragadkar was lost at first, not knowing where the Appellate Side Bar room was. He had to make it clear that he was a lawyer joining the Bar rather than a client from the mofussil before he was directed to the Bar room. There he met Jahagirdar, Gumaste and Kane whom he already knew through family connections. They then took him around the building introducing him to other members of the Bar. Gajendragadkar thought that no one had ever joined the Bar so ignorant of court procedures, etiquette, formal requirements, or how to gain appellate side work than his young self. It was only his third visit to the big city and the crowds and the traffic almost frightened him. He was apprehensive as to how he would progress in his new career.

Gajendragadkar put his name board up near the entrance of the Maharaja Building. However, days passed without a brief, and once three months went by he began to wonder if he had chosen the right career. He had received an offer to take up a post as Professor of English at Karnataka College and thought it might be better to return to the family tradition of teaching. He had even started to prepare to switch careers, and spent his days in his law office reading college

English textbooks, when someone finally walked in and handed him his first brief.

A man appeared and handed Gajendragadkar a notice which had been served on his boss as a respondent in a first appeal and a notice of the stay petition which had been filed by the appellant. But more importantly, the emissary handed him a ₹100 note and advised him that the client, Mr. Rajguru of Poona would settle the balance at a later date. Gajendragadkar was somewhat unsure of what needed to be done and rushed down to ask Gumaste how to proceed. Gumaste gave him a copy of his vakalat form with his own name scribbled out. He put Ganjendragadkar's name in its place and instructed him to get his client's signature on the form and instruct his clerk to file it in the office. Gajendragadkar put his plans of a professorship at Karnataka College on hold. He felt it was his destiny to pursue his legal career.

The stay petition had been filed by the appellant's senior lawyer, but Gajendragadkar did not realise that the petition, which was supported by an affidavit, had to be contested with an affidavit in reply. Instead he spent his time preparing a long speech showing that the application was not justified. Many turned out to see how the young academic star would fare against the giant of the Bar Thakore. Thakore only uttered two sentences: "My Lord, we have filed the affidavit in support of our petition. But no counter affidavit has been filed and the rule should therefore be made absolute." Gajendragadkar wasn't sure what an affidavit was, and therefore what a counter affidavit was, and why a rule should be made absolute. His dreams of making a fine speech before the court in his first case "evaporated into thin air" and he "felt like going down to the bowels of the earth". The gallery pitied the young man.

The judge was Sir Lallubhai Shah, who was sympathetic to the young lawyer, and stated that Gajendragadkar obviously did not know that a counter affidavit was required and asked how long he wanted to file one. Gajendragadkar asked for two days. Shah gave him two weeks. When the case next came up for hearing Thakore made an elaborate argument only for Shah to discharge the matter. Gajendragadkar did not get a chance to speak and would have to wait for another day to dazzle the court with his oratory. He then resolved that Sir Lallubhai would be his role model should he ever make it to the Bench.

Mohammad Hidayatullah would help his brother, who had started as a barrister six months ahead of him, in cases which would require two lawyers.[cclix] His first paid brief was a case under Section 145 of the Code of Criminal Procedure which involved the reclamation of immovable property. Hidayatullah did not know Marathi and his opposing counsel instructed all the witnesses to only speak the language. Hidayatullah was unable to get an effective translator, the cross examination was ineffective and they lost the case. He later filed a civil suit to get the order overturned.

Hidayatullah's fees for his first year in practice came to ₹50. Even after a year on the job he felt he only had a patchy knowledge of the law and began to study in earnest. He started with criminal law, reading through the Indian Penal Code, the Code of Criminal Procedure and the Evidence Act. He read every Privy Council case on these three subjects and read every full bench case of the Nagpur Judicial Commissioner's Court. For every one paying case he would do three free cases. He chose the free cases carefully to make a name for himself.

Hidayatullah got his first break when he received a brief in the Dhantoli Abduction case. The case involved two prominent families. The boy had been with Hidayatullah at Morris College, Nagpur and was charged with abducting a school girl. However, the defence argued that it was a case of elopement. The boy had taken the girl in a taxi from her school and they managed to get through a police road block, but the train for their eventual destination was delayed. They then both proceeded to the police station where the girl claimed she was abducted. Hidayatullah successfully defended the taxi driver. But more important for Hidayatullah's career was the confrontation which ensued after he noticed the magistrate examining a witness using notes in the handwriting of the prosecuting counsel. Hidayatullah raised the issue and the magistrate hurriedly adjourned the case. But Hidayatullah stopped him and had the notes sealed and the case transferred to another Magistrate's Court. The accused was convicted but later acquitted in the High Court. The incident created newspaper headlines and Hidayatullah thought it was a great advertisement for himself and he came to get the briefs in most of the sensational criminal cases coming before the court.

***

Mehr Mahajan had not experienced the early struggles of Chagla, Nayudu, Hidayatullah or Sinha.[cclx] He was a legal princeling; his father was an eminent lawyer in Dharamsala who handed him both his first case and a fully trained clerk. His workload in Dharamsala and Gurdaspur and then Lahore initially featured the type of work which had kept lawyers busy throughout the 19th century- land and property disputes. However, as the years went on Mahajan would increasingly come to deal with commercial cases relating to taxes and trademarks and government attempts to forcibly acquire private companies. At the other end of India in Madras, Krishnaswamy Nayudu initially plied his trade in the Small Cause Court before his practice grew and he gained greater stature at the Bar.[cclxi] As Nayudu made his name at the Madras Bar he became increasingly immersed in cases which were influencing Hindu spiritual life in the province. During the 1930s he was called on to act on behalf of the Tirupati Devasthanam in its commercial dealings and litigation over land, and even became involved in an intricate and long running litigation when competing factions came to fight for control of the ashram of one of Madras's most revered Maharishis.

The civil cases which Mahajan initially dealt with in Dharamsala were, unsurprisingly, related to land and inheritance. In *Baisakhi Mal v Kaju Mal* the Gopalpur Tea Estate was sold by its European owners to Lala Kaju Mal. Sir Daya Kaul became interested in the estate and consulted Mahajan's father, who suggested that the only way to gain control over it was to get some villagers to pre-empt the sale, and if successful, to purchase the estate. Kaju Mal did not want to part with the estate as he belonged to a non-agricultural caste which could not buy agricultural land in the open market under the Alienation of Land Act. However, the Act did not apply to tea estates. Kaul agreed to the plan, entrusted the brief to Mahajan's father, and Mahajan did the 'devilling work'. A village Brahmin, Basakhi was persuaded to file the pre-emption suit. Lawyers opposing the suit pleaded that the tea garden was not agricultural land and no pre-emption suit could be filed against it and that the suit was benami. Eventually the suit was partially decreed and the decision was upheld by the Privy Council. It was decided that a tea garden was agricultural land, but that neither the machinery nor forestland were pre-emptable.

Another of Mahajan's early cases involved Inder Singh, a large landholder in the United Provinces, Mandi and Kangra. Inder Singh was born of his father Uttam Singh and his lawfully wedded Rajput wife, whilst Thakar Singh was born of Uttam Singh's union with a lower caste woman from U.P. Uttam Singh died and Thakar Singh claimed half of his property. Naturally, Inder Singh opposed the claim on the basis that Thakar Singh was Uttam Singh's illegitimate son. Mahajan recalled that hundreds of witnesses appeared in the case- "most of them who had been handsomely paid to tell lies." The district judge declared Thakar Singh legitimate on the basis of documentary evidence, however an appeal was filed in the High Court which overturned the District Court's verdict. The case went all the way to the Privy Council which confirmed the High Court's judgement. Mahajan appeared in the case for Thakar Singh and thought that the High Court and Privy Council reversed the judgement of the lower court on the basis of the testimony of liars. He learnt that "it was not very difficult to procure a large number of people to tell lies if they were handsomely paid."

Mahajan continued his practice at Gurdaspur during World War I, and before leaving to work at the Lahore High Court he appeared in a case involving the partition of the property of a leading Sehgal family of Lahore. Rai Bahadur Buta Mal had four sons; Mul Chand, Lala Kanshi Ram, Rai Sahib Shankar Das, and Lala Behari Lal. The case had been transferred from Lahore to Gurdaspur and Mahajan remembered that "The brothers fought like enraged bulls in Court." Mahajan represented Lala Behari Lal who managed the family's land and a cotton ginning factory at Kot Radhakishen. As the case proceeded Shankar Das claimed that Lala Kanshi Ram, a lawyer, had acquired property through his legal practice which amounted to joint family property, whilst Behari Lal claimed the factory for himself. The litigation dragged on for several years and Mahajan recalled "Most of the claimants died during the course of the litigation." The case was transferred back to Lahore and a senior judge decided against Behari Lal's contention as well as those of the other brothers and some aspects of the case were still undecided when Mahajan became a judge in the 1940s.

In 1935 Mahajan took on an income tax case on behalf of the trustees of *The Tribune*. The case revolved around the interpretation of the term 'charitable purpose' in the Indian Income Tax Act. The trustees claimed that the profits earned from the sale of the paper should not be subjected to income tax as the paper had been started by its founder as a charitable concern. The income tax officers however, claimed that the proceeds were business profits and needed to be taxed accordingly. A full bench of the High Court decided the case against the trustees of the paper stating that the founder had started the paper for the political advancement of India, which could not be considered a "charitable" purpose. The trustees then appealed to the Privy Council, for which Mahajan prepared a note briefing the lawyers in London. The trustees won on appeal, and the case made law, establishing that political education could qualify as a charitable purpose.

Mahajan also started doing trade mark work and was approached by clients in the vegetable oil business. They were marketing a brand of vegetable oil called 'Kottogem'. The Tatas took exception to the brand name as they had been marketing their own coconut product called 'Cocogem' and claimed an infringement on their trademark. The test of an infringement would rest on whether the use of one brand name would mislead consumers into buying what they thought was a different brand. Mahajan spent ten days arguing the matter in the High Court and managed to win the case for his clients.

A much bigger commercial matter arose when the Punjab Government of Sir Sikandar Hyat Khan used its Emergency War Powers during World War II to acquire the Lahore Electricity Company. Mahajan brought a suit on behalf of the company's Board of Directors challenging the acquisition. He argued that the government's actions were male fide, had no connection to the war effort, and were instead motivated by a desire to give jobs in the company to Muslims. The company was Hindu owned and most of its directors were

Hindus and Mahajan claimed a mandatory injunction against the government's acquisition to return the company to its owners. The matter went to a High Court bench presided over by the Chief Justice, Sir Douglas Young who ordered an injunction, accepting Mahajan's contention that a government abuse of power had occurred. The case created a sensation across the country and Mahajan thought it was the only time a government in India had been found to be abusing its war time powers.

During the late 1930s Krishnaswmy Nayudu became Standing Legal Adviser to the Tirumalai Tirupati Devasthanam. The legal work of the Devasthanam was mainly on the Appellate Side of the High Court as appeals and revisions for and against the temple trust came through from suits which had started in the mofussil courts. Nayudu would also give his legal opinion in the more important cases which the Devasthanam had to deal with.

In one such case the Devasthanam decided to make a head ornament, or Vajra Kreetam, set with precious gems for the Mulavigraham of Lord Venkateshwara. The gems came from the temple's already vast collection of emeralds and rubies and were supplemented by some new purchases. The Devasthanam contracted Messrs Surajmal Lallubhai for ₹10 lakh for the making of the head ornament. The two parties then got into a dispute over the settling of accounts, and it seemed like the case was headed for litigation. However, Nannusanker Tawker, the manager of the firm approached Nayudu and they agreed on a settlement and the ornament was delivered to the temple. On one of his later visits to the temple to worship Srivaru the temple authorities brought the Vajra Kreetam to Nayudu and expressed their gratefulness. Nayudu felt pleased at his little contribution in avoiding a protracted litigation.

A more socially contentious case involved a suit which had

come up from the Chittor Subordinate Judge's Court in which some worshippers had filed an injunction preventing the entry of Harijans to the temple. It was the time of the Congress Ministry in Madras in the late 1930s and the temples had been opened up to the Harijans by legislation. Nayudu appeared for the Devasthanam before the High Court and was asked to see the Chief Minister O.P. Ramaswami Reddiar, who suggested that he engage Sir Alladi Krishnaswamy Aiyar as Senior Counsel. The lawyers then took to quoting from the Vedas and Shastras before the court in support of their respective contentions that Harijans were, or were not allowed in temples. Eventually the judge sided with Nayudu and Sir Alladi and held in favour of permitting the Harijans to enter the temples of Madras.

The Tirupati Devasthanam got into another web of litigation in the 1940s over its possession of extensive forest lands in Kalahasti in Chitoor District. The Devasthanam took many of its tenants who had refused to hand over possession of lands on the expiry of their lease to court. Nayudu inherited the cases from his predecessors and the junior in the case would come to his house on the weekends to keep him updated. Nayudu was kept on his legs in court for ten days as he went through the documents which related to the demarcation of the encroachments on the forest lands and the precise location of the properties. The effort was worth it however, as the judge decided entirely in favour of the Devasthanam which managed to reclaim 3000-4000 acres of forest property.

Besides Nayudu's work for the Devasthanam he was also engaged by a devotee named Perumalswamy in a case against his guru, Sri Ramana Maharishi of Tiruvannamalai. Nayudu and Perumalswamy had met at the house of the sculptor M.S. Nagappa with whom Perumalswamy had placed an order for a bronze sculpture of the Maharishi. The sculpture was close to completion, but some differences had arisen between Perumalswamy and his Guru which led him to request Nayudu's legal services.

Perumalswamy narrated his account to Nayudu. Initially when Sri Ramana Maharishi had come to Tiruvannamalai and settled on the hill with his elderly mother Perumalswamy and other disciples attended on them. However, as word of the Maharishi's spiritual powers spread and his following grew, the Maharishi's relatives arrived to take control of the ashram and sidelined his original disciples. There were undercurrents of caste tension as the disciples were of a different caste to the Guru and his relations. The Guru remained aloof from the factionalism in his ashram, but as time passed Perumalswamy assumed the leadership of the original disciples and their quest for justice. By the time the bronze statue was complete the conflict between the two factions had become acute and Perumalswamy wanted Nayudu to appear in a Second Appeal which had been filed against a decision from the District Judge of North Arcot.

The Tiruvannamalai ashram had been built on land which belonged to a religious trust whose head was in Kancheepuram. The property had been built without the permission of the trust, and so Perumalswamy and his followers approached the Kancheepuram Trust to grant them the lease of the land on which the ashram had been built. The head of the trust was willing to grant them a lease for seven years, however the lease had to be registered at Kancheepuram rather than Tiruvannamalai. Perumalswamy then tried to get ten cents of the land at Kancheepuram included in the lease deed for the Tiruvannamalai property so that the sub registrar of Kancheepuram would have jurisdiction to register the lease deed which would include both the token amount of land at Kancheepuram, and the larger more important land at Tiruvannamali. The object of this legal creativity was, of course, for Perumalswamy and his group to evict the Guru's relatives from the Tiruvannamalai property and take control of it themselves.

Having secured his lease, Perumalswamy then instituted a suit against his Guru for evicting him from the ashram property as a trespasser and sought to recover the land. It was a gambit played in the hope that the Maharishi's relatives would recognise the due claims of Perumalswamy and his group and accommodate them in the management of the ashram. The District Munsiff at Tiruvannamalai held Perumalswamy's lease to be fraudulent, after which he appealed and the District Judge of North Arcot agreed with the lower court.

It was at this point that Nayudu was called on to file a second appeal. Nayudu remembered being in a difficult situation. The Maharishi was a saintly man with a large following of devotees, and Nayudu also had great regard for him. If Nayudu were to be seen litigating against the respected Maharishi he may be misunderstood by elite society, the general public of Madras, as well as his fellow lawyers at the Bar. But Nagappa the sculptor counselled him that it was a purely professional matter. In addition, in Nayudu's meetings with Perumalswamy he had been impressed with his sincerity and devotion to the Maharishi and felt that he only wanted to remove the group controlling the ashram rather than instigate action against the Guru personally.

The appeal was admitted by Justice James Stodart, an Indian Civil Service judge. He heard Nayudu's arguments and thought that a point of law arose, but later called Nayudu aside. He said that he had heard "whispers" about the case and advised Nayudu to get his client to "adjust the matter smoothly". Nayudu inferred that Stodart had been approached by some of the Maharishi's followers. Being an Indian Civil Service judge Stodart followed the law and had to admit the appeal, but at the same time he did not think it advisable to keep the litigation going, and so had his quiet word to Nayudu.

The Second Appeal came up before Justice Abdul Rahman. The court was packed with members of the Bar, whose sympathies were with the Maharishi, and Nayudu had to battle the impression that he was party to an unholy action against the saintly figure. He felt he was doing his duty as a lawyer however, besides which he was not working for free; Perumalswamy and his followers had raised a large amount and paid Nayudu a decent fee.

The question of fraud came up again in court and Nayudu argued that there was no intention to commit fraud against the law of registration, and both the leasor and leasee had intended that both the Kancheepuram and Tiruvannamalai properties be the subject of the lease. He further argued that the ten cents of Kancheepuram land had not been nominally included and that Perumalswamy had an intention to use the land for a specific purpose. Nayudu held forth on the general principles of the law of fraud, and referred to Section 28 of the Indian Registration Act. The judgement came down in favour of Nayudu's client, allowing the appeal and remanding it to the district judge on the remaining points of law which had not been decided. The lawyer opposing Nayudu later embraced him in the court's quadrangle in the midst of a crowd of barristers and told him that he had argued the case ably.

The District Court at North Arcot then found in favour of Perumalswamy and the case was then sent back to the High Court before Justice Abdul Rahman. By that stage World War II had broken out and Madras city had begun an evacuation under the threat of a Japanese invasion. The High Court buildings were on the sea shore, and so the court needed to be shifted to the buildings of a Convent School at Theagarayanagar. Nayudu's opposing counsel Krishnaswamy argued that it was futile to consider the matter any further as the original duration of the lease, seven years had passed. Nayudu did not object and so the matter ended there.

Some of Perumalswamy's followers told Nayudu that they thought the main reason that they were able to get a fair hearing and at least succeed on a technical point of law was that the three High Court judges were all from out of the province; they would be less influenced by the spiritual stature of the Maharishi. Justice Stodart was a British officer of the Indian Civil Service, whilst Justice Abdul Rahman was from north India, and Justice Ponnambalam Ramalingam was from Ceylon. But Nayudu did not accept their argument; "I have always faith in our own judges who come from our own state that they would do justice between man and man as the facts and the law of the case demands and could never be influenced by extraneous circumstances." Nayudu thought that besides creating some sensation and increasing the ill feeling between the two groups of devotees, no great benefit was gained by either party. Later Perumalswamy told Nayudu that his followers had started another ashram down the hill from Tiruvannamalai. They had installed their bronze statue and took to worshipping it, rather than their living Guru up on the hill.

***

Whilst most of the leaders of the Indian nationalist movement had qualified as barristers, very few members of the Indian Bar ever devoted themselves to politics full time. Mehr Mahajan dabbled in Congress politics in Punjab before the coming of Gandhi, Krishnaswamy Nayudu had an indirect involvement with the Justice Party in Madras, and Mahomedali Chagla was a political disciple of Jinnah during his early nationalist days but later split from his mentor and the Muslim League as they moved closer to a demand for Pakistan. In some cases lawyers actively sought out politics, but in others it was politics which came to the lawyer. When Mohammad Hidayatullah became Advocate General of the Central Provinces and

Berar, the government's top lawyer, he would find himself in the difficult situation of having to prosecute a heavy load of cases arising out of the Quit India movement of August 1942.[cclxii]

Hidayatullah recounted the violence which ensued as police chowkies, station houses and treasuries were stormed and police lost their lives defending them or defending themselves. The Viceroy Victor Hope, the Marquess of Linlithgow promulgated the Special Criminal Courts Ordinance which set up Special Courts to try these cases outside the Sessions Courts which normally functioned under the Code of Criminal Procedure. The Federal Court then declared that these Special Courts were not duly invested with jurisdiction. However, some trials had already been decided and the accused sentenced to punishments including death. So the next day the viceroy promulgated the Special Criminal Courts Repeal Ordinance which repealed the earlier ordinance and divided the cases into two classes; those which were pending were transferred to the regular courts and the previous proceedings were declared void, whilst those which had resulted in a conviction were confirmed and held to have been tried in conformity with the Code of Criminal Procedure. A right of appeal and powers of revision were also provided for.

The subsequent ordinance was also challenged and Hidayatullah's first task was to defend it. He had the entire Bar ranged against him and only the assistance of his two government pleaders. Appeals from other High Courts ended up in the Federal Court but Hidayatullah was not called to help. Whilst the hearing in the Nagpur High Court was going on, Patrick Spens, the Chief Justice of the Federal Court visited. Hidayatullah knew when Spens would land up in his court and timed it such that the chief justice would be able to hear his self-contained argument. He then proceeded to draw out the meaning of the phrase "in accordance with the

Code of Criminal Procedure" from the ordinance, arguing that "in accordance with" gave the phrase greater weight than the words "under the Code of Criminal Procedure" would have given it. Hidayatullah argued that the original phrase ruled out questions over whether the procedure laid down by the code had been complied with. Spens heard him for five minutes before suggesting that he bring his argument to the Federal Court. The Registrar of the Nagpur High Court then conveyed an invitation for him to visit New Delhi.

The Nagpur High Court decided in the government's favour and appeals were filed in the Federal Court. Almost all the advocate generals of India were present and the gathering of legal luminaries included such names as Sir Alladi Krishnaswamy Aiyer, Sir Noshirwan Engineer, Narain Aasthana, Mahabir Prasad and Sir Brojendra Mitter. The hearing was before Justices Spens, Varadachariar and Khan. Hidayatullah drew on cases from the South African courts and felt that his arguments were well received. He had the most difficult time convincing Justice Sir Zafarullah Khan however. Sir Zafarullah posed the hypothetical scenario of some Indian villagers trying an offender and sentencing him to punishment and wanted to know if the viceroy could then pass an ordinance validating the sentence. Hidayatullah wanted to address the point at a later time but Sir Zafarullah wanted his answer. Hidayatullah then quoted from Cooley's *Constitutional Limitations* which stated that the Legislature "cannot make good retrospectively acts which it had previously no power to permit." He also added "The last sentence, I presume, applies to one of your Lordship's villagers." Sir Zafarullah replied: "Or your Special Courts."

Hidayatullah won his case in New Delhi, but he thought that the '1942 disturbances' made his tenure as advocate general a particularly difficult one. A large number of appeals were taken to the High Court as a result of the ordinance, the most important of which was the Chimur and Ashti riots case. The

Sant Tukdoji had his ashram there and his followers had beaten Inspector Jarasandh and his constables to death. Hidayatullah thought that Jarasandh was foolish to fire on the mob in the first place, and then at such long range that it had barely any effect. But he did think Jarasandh was a brave man; whilst the constables ran away and were chased and cut down, Jarasandh stood his ground on a narrow iron bridge and faced a crowd of hundreds with an empty gun. Hidayatullah recalled that although the policeman was defending the British Raj, he stood fast to his duty and nothing detracted from his valour, even the fact that he was opposing fellow Indians who wanted Independence.

When the case came before the court Hidayatullah wanted to set some standard for correct identification of the culprits. There were scores of accused and each would have a number. The defence managed to cast some doubt on the reliability of eye witnesses who were inconsistent in their identification of the culprits. Even in cases in which only the sentence was questioned, the conviction itself would also be examined. The prosecutors prepared a chart showing the nature of the evidence, as did the defence, and Hidayatullah requested that they cross check their charts and reduce them to those they could agree on and leave the sentencing to the courts. The case lasted for many days and there were arguments about the nature of vicarious liability under sections of the Indian Penal Code. With the help of the charts and the defence's decision not to contest the fact that offences were committed, but only the identities of those involved, each applicant took only a few minutes. In one case Chief Justice Sir Frederick Grille snapped at Hidayatullah, saying: "You are not trying these cases. I am." To which Hidayatullah replied: "I am quite aware of this. If I were trying the case I would know what to do since I would not hang a dog on such evidence."

Hidayatullah's second important case was from Yaoli.

Kanaiyalal Munshi from Bombay appeared for the defence. During riots at Ramtek the Government Treasury had been broken into and looted. The police force of six constables did not offer any resistance and watched the mob burn the Civil Court building and break open the strong room. The mob carried away the cash in handfuls and head loads and made a hole in the back wall of the room. The Reserve Bank of India would maintain currency chests at outlying treasuries which were in the custody of the local Treasury officer and the bank claimed that the provincial governments should pay for the loss. The other provinces conceded the bank's claim, however Hidayatullah did not, and the case went to the arbitration of Sir Benegal Rao in the Secretariat in New Delhi.

Hidayatullah and his team wanted to bring the case within the ordinary law of bailment and prove that the provincial government had taken good care. The case came to revolve around the question of whether the currency was goods or chattels and the distinction between bailment and agency. They looked into the Treasury Rules, the resource manual and audit rules, and came to rely upon *Giblin v McMullen* from 1869. *Storey on Bailments* Article 27 seemed to work against them and so they found a copy of *Jones on Bailment* which supported their case. Upon being asked for a narration of the facts Hidayatullah suggested that he file the inspector's affidavit and the case was adjourned before lunch on the first day. Back in Nagpur Hidayatullah called a meeting and the inspector began his narration of events. Hidayatullah and his team gathered enough material for the affidavit, ended up winning the case, and he was sanctioned special fees by the Governor, Sir Henry Twynam.

Cases of detention under the Defence of India Act would result in writs of habeas corpus in the High Court. Cases could be appealed before the High Court and heard by a bench of three judges, however the government had made a rule that detainees could not be interviewed by counsel. Matters came to a head in the case of the detention of the Leftist Congress activist Purshottom Deshpande. Deshpande's advocate complained that he could not receive instructions because he could not interview his client. Hidayatullah applied to the chief secretary to grant the interview but was declined. He then went straight to the governor who allowed the interview, but stipulated that a grille had to be placed between the lawyer and the client when they met in jail. The press had some fun, turning out headlines playing on the name of the Chief Justice, Sir Frederick Grille.

The case of Vimalabai Deshpande reached the Privy Council and he was ordered to be released. It was a case before Justices Bose and Sen and things got heated. The detention had originally been ordered by the deputy inspector general of police and was continued by the Government of the Central Provinces and Berar. Hidayatullah argued that the governor had seen the order, however Justice Sen insisted that the secretary to the governor had not filed an affidavit confirming this. The judges took the view that what was relevant was that the detention was started by a subordinate officer and went into detail on the law of malice, castigating the Central Provinces and Berar Government, the chief secretary and Hidayatullah as advocate general. The court and later the Privy Council held that the police officer who ordered the detention at the start of the process had to satisfy the court that his order was reasonable and that this had not been done in the case. It was the first case of intervention by a High Court in India, and Hidayatullah thought that the judges laid down the true foundations of a writ of habeas corpus. Hidayatullah recommended an appeal to the Privy Council and was supposed to travel to London to argue the case, but World War II was raging and he decided against the journey in order to avoid the danger of German U boats.

In another case a detainee made an application for his release but the jail authorities had made a rule that the application had to be made in triplicate. All three copies were handed over to the Jail Superintendent, Masoom Ali who sent them to the Inspector General of Prisons, Colonel Nilkanth Jatar. A complaint was then filed in the High Court that the copies were not being forwarded. One copy was then sent to the High Court and another to the advocate general. Contempt of court proceedings were then initiated against Ali and Jatar for delaying proceedings. The original had not been sent and Justice Sen wanted to know who held it. The original was with Hidayatullah and Jatar held the third copy. Apologies to the court were filed, the case proceeded, and Hidayatullah also filed an apology on behalf of Masoom Ali. The judges recalled Jatar's war service and let him off with a warning. Masoom Ali received a fine, but the sum was paid by the Government of the Central Provinces and Berar.

***

The leading Indian barristers of the 1920s and 1930s became the natural candidates for elevation to the Bench in the 1940s. Those who were appointed as judges of the High Courts in the early 1940s would be the last to have to pass the British rulers' tests of political loyalty and suitability. Judges who were considered for appointment in the late 1940s would have to be cleared by Indian nationalist leaders in New Delhi, who had their own ideas about the ideal High Court judge. Yet whether it was a British chief justice trying to persuade an Indian barrister to give up his lucrative practice, or the Indian home minister trying to transfer an Indian judge from one High Court to another, gentlemanly agreements prevailed and Indian barristers and judges would be persuaded to make career adjustments in both the 'best traditions of the Bar', and later, the 'interest of the nation'.

Mahomedali Chagla was sitting in the Bar Gymkhana in Bombay on a Sunday in February 1941 when he received a message that the Chief Justice of the Bombay High Court, Sir

John Beaumont wanted to see him.[cclxiii] Sir John offered him a place on the bench of the High Court and told him: "Chagla, you are doing very well at the Bar, and I am sure you will do much better. There are always glittering prizes to look forward to at the Bar. But a time comes when one feels that it is better to decide cases, lay down the law, help the development of the law, rather than spend all your time arguing other people's cases. You will get a salary of ₹4000, which, in my view, is reasonable. You will have plenty of leisure. You will have security. You will have status. Considering everything I would press you to accept my offer." Chagla asked for some time to consider the offer before he eventually accepted it. Sir John would tell him that he had to "put up a fight" with the Government of India for his nomination. The government thought that Chagla's political career "was pretty lurid" and that there were many "black marks" against him. But Sir John had countered these arguments, telling the government that he was not concerned with the politics of the man to whom the judicial post was offered but only his potential qualities as a judge. He further assured the government that Chagla could be "trusted not to bring politics to the Bench."

Pralhad Gajendragadkar followed Mahomedali Chagla onto the bench of the Bombay High Court. His offer came from the Chief Justice, Sir Leonard Stone, who insisted that he would not take 'no' for an answer.[cclxiv] There was some delay in Gajendragadkar's appointment though; the problem was not politics or questions of trust, but a stand-off between the chief justice and the Government of India over the merits of the candidates sent up to fill the vacancies on the Bench. The senior District Judge, Pestonji Moos had protested to the highest authorities that Sir Leonard had overlooked him for a position on the bench of the Bombay High Court and that justice should be done to his candidacy. The government referred the matter back to Sir Leonard, who made it clear that he had already considered Moos's claim, and if the government forced the district judge on him he would give

Moos a chamber in the court but not assign him any work. Both Gajendragadkar and Rajaram Bavdekar took their seats on the Bench in March 1945.

Mehr Mahajan had been sounded out by Sir Douglas Young in November 1942 for an appointment as a justice of the Lahore High Court.[cclxv] Mahajan excused himself, but the following month when Sir Douglas repeated his offer Mahajan tried to wriggle out of the situation by saying that he did not want to be appointed as a temporary additional judge. Sir Douglas retired in January 1943 and was replaced by Sir Trevor Harries. Sir Trevor had been a justice of the Allahabad High Court and then chief justice at Patna, and in his capacity as President of the Bar Association Mahajan offered Sir Trevor felicitations on assuming the chief justiceship at Lahore.

Sir Trevor soon began trying to persuade Mahajan to come to the Bench. Mahajan realised that it would mean a 40% paycut, and he would have to refund over a lakh of rupees to clients whose cases he would have to give up. But over tea at Sir Trevor's residence Mahajan accepted the chief justice's arguments that making such a sacrifice was in keeping with the highest traditions of the Bar, that when offered a judgeship one could not refuse, and that to administer justice was the highest form of service to the country, the crowning glory in a legal career. Mahajan also liked the idea that he would be superseding four additional judges, one of whom was British. Sir Trevor then sounded out the Governor, Sir Bertrand Glancy, and by April 1943 wanted to know if he could tell Sir Bertrand that Mahajan would accept the offer should it be made. Mahajan accepted the offer "in the best traditions of the Bar", although he had some moments of regret later on when he began to feel the full extent of his financial loss. In May 1943 Mahajan accepted a gentleman's agreement not to return to practice after retirement from the Bench, and the official communication appointing him as a judge of the High Court of Lahore came through in July 1943.

Mahajan recalled the deluge of letters and messages which poured in from both British and Indian judges and felt that "the stream of parties did not dry up for about a year."

Bhuvaneshwar Sinha was appointed as an additional judge on the Patna High Court in January 1943, and was made a permanent judge of the court at the end of that year.[cclxvi] By late 1949 he was the third most senior judge on the Bench with Sir Clifford Agarwala about to retire, but he thought that the Congress Government in the state did not want him to be chief justice; "Unfortunately Bihar is notorious for its indulgence of caste distinctions which even prevail over public welfare." A British judge of the Indian Civil Service was appointed chief justice for only three months, the next in line in seniority was no longer eligible because he was not an Indian citizen, and Sinha was passed over for the position. Sinha thought that the Bihar Government prevailed on the Centre to appoint the Advocate General, Lakshmi Kant Jha to the chief justiceship though he would have only two years on the Bench before he reached the age for retirement.

Sinha sensed "animosity" against him, and as judges were being asked to take pay cuts under the new Constitution he decided to write a hand written letter to the Home Minister in New Delhi, Vallabhbhai Patel in December 1949. Sinha explained that he had gone to the Bench at a relatively young age before he had a chance to earn and he still had a large family to raise and educate. He was not in a position to take the suggested salary reduction, and so he sought the home minister's blessings to return to the Bar. He made the point that he was not legally bound to not practice at the Patna Bar, but still felt morally bound not to do so. He thought Patel's reply was quite "laconic". Patel suggested he stay on the Bench without taking a pay cut.

A couple of months later Bhuvaneshwar received an offer through Shri Krishna Sinha, the Chief Minister of Bihar to go to the Assam High Court as chief justice, but he replied to the home minister, through the chief minister, that he was not keen to take up the offer given that he suffered from asthma and he did not think that Gauhati's damp climate would be congenial. Bhuvaneshwar thought the matter rested there, but then in September he received another offer from Patel, this time for the chief justice's post at Nagpur. He made it clear to "Shri Babu" that he and his government, particularly the revenue minister, did not want him to become chief justice at Patna, and that he had remained quiet on the issue and just wanted to be left alone for the next four years so that he could retire and collect his pension. The chief minister persisted, but a few weeks later Bhuvaneshwar refused to go to Nagpur once again, explaining that he could not run another house at Nagpur whilst his children and grandchildren were studying in Patna. Furthermore, he thought that the Nagpur High Court "being the last to come into existence, was not rated very highly as a High Court." Nagpur was not held in much respect and the chief justice received less pay than his peers on the other High Courts of India. But Shri Babu did not give up, and in November 1950 he visited Bhuvaneshwar at his residence with a message from Patel in New Delhi. Patel wanted Bhuvaneshwar to accept the Nagpur post "in the interest of nation". Now that it was a matter of the "interest of the nation" he could not refuse. Bhuvaneshwar advised Shri Babu to inform the home minister that he would go to Nagpur at short notice, even if it meant leaving his family behind in Patna.

Mohammad Hidayatullah was not sounded out by the Chief Justice of the Nagpur High Court, Sir Frederick Grille during 1945 for a position on the Nagpur bench.[cclxvii] Sir Frederick just called him into his office and informed him that with the imminent retirements of Justices Niyogi and Puranik, he had taken the liberty of recommending Hidayatullah's name for an appointment to the Bench. His Majesty had accepted the nomination, and Sir Frederick had not informed Hidayatullah in advance as he thought he would refuse. Now that the work had been done, he did not want Hidayatullah to embarrass him by refusing. Hidayatullah would have liked to have been informed in advance, but of course could not say no. Sir Frederick later welcomed him to the Bench and informed him that he would sit with Sir Bhiwani Niyogi who would be acting chief justice after the court vacation.

It was probably good timing for Hidayatullah as a new Congress Ministry had taken office after World War II and he was not sure if the new political bosses, despite their protestations, would really have wanted him to continue as Advocate General of the Central Provinces and Berar. When it was later announced that Bhuvaneshwar Sinha would be the new Chief Justice of the Nagpur High Court the outgoing Chief Justice, Vivian Bose expressed some apprehension that an outsider should be appointed, but advised the judges to give the new chief justice their co-operation. Hidayatullah remembered going to the railway station to receive Sinha. The new chief justice said: "I am keeping my eyes and ears open." To which Hidayatullah replied: "You may be sure sir, that we too are doing the same."

Krishnaswamy Nayudu had been making unsuccessful attempts to gain a place in the lower judiciary for many years, but it was in 1947 that his name started circulating as a possible justice of the Madras High Court.[cclxviii] In fact, it was on Independence Day, 15 August 1947 that the Mayor of Madras invited Nayudu to a function of the Madras Corporation which was presided over by the Chief Minister, O.P. Ramaswami Reddiar. Some of his advocate friends approached him and told him that he was about to be elevated to the Bench.

Dr. B.V. Narayanaswami Nayudu, the Principal of Pachaiyappa's College took an interest in Krishnaswamy Nayudu's career. He was a good friend of Chief Minister

Reddiar as well as P.S. Kumaraswamy Raja who subsequently became chief minister. He had written to Nayudu in October 1948 that he had been in touch with the chief minister and Nayudu's name was definitely up for selection and that he was a certainty to be elevated to the Bench. But a month later he wrote that he had once again been in touch with the chief minister who had been given the impression that Nayudu was not keeping good health. Nayudu took objection to the scheming of "interested persons"; he was in good health but had not met the chief minister recently who had not been able to see the fact for himself.

Vacancies on the Bench kept arising, and Nayudu's colleagues kept being appointed. In 1949 P.S. Kumaraswamy Raja became chief minister, and Dr. Narayanswami Nayudu lobbied him on Krishnaswamy Nayudu's behalf. Eventually the chief minister asked the recommending authority "What about Krishnaswami Naidu?", after which Nayudu made his way on to the list. Nayudu received the call and was informed that he was being appointed to the Bench as an additional judge for one year. He was a little concerned at the temporary appointment but the next morning he called on the chief minister and the chief justice and started receiving visitors and messages of congratulations.

There was some delay, but Nayudu was appointed as a justice of the Madras High Court two days before India became a Republic on 26 January 1950. A few months after Nayudu took his place on the Bench an old time Congressman, Dr. P. Varadarajulu Naidu from Salem told him of a conversation he had with the invisible hand of judicial appointments of the day, Vallabhbhai Patel in New Delhi. Patel had asked Dr. Naidu about Krishnaswamy Nayudu, and after being given a glowing account of his background and his hard luck story of being overlooked for the Bench, Patel then asked whether it was true that Nayudu had been a member of the Justice Party, the Congress's traditional opponent in Madras politics. Dr. Naidu replied that it was true, but it could not be a disqualification for the Bench as many of the Congressmen of Madras had at one time or the other journeyed through the Justice Party.

***

Whilst British barristers had largely disappeared from India's High Courts by the 1940s, British judges remained until Independence. The Indian judges who joined them on the Bench would thus work with the last generation of British judges to sit in courts in India and took the opportunity to assess their British colleagues, both as men and as legal professionals. Their opinions were not always flattering, and it was evident that the future of the High Courts, once very British institutions on Indian soil, would depend on Indian judges and lawyers' professional competence, and their fidelity to the traditions of their courts in the years after Independence.

Mahomedali Chagla began work on the bench of the Bombay High Court as a chamber judge dealing with chamber notices, summonses and notices of motion.[cclxix] His associate brought him a pile of papers concerning the cases he would have to hear the following day. Chagla was not impressed; if he had to do so much reading it would have been better to stay a barrister and get paid for it. He said that it was the counsel's job to tell him what the contents of the cases were and then he as the judge would decide. He followed this practice of not reading papers beforehand throughout his career. He thought that a judge would at least tentatively have his mind made up if he read the papers beforehand. Chagla claimed that he only once reserved judgement. He thought it was better for a judge to get the matter off his chest immediately; the mind was still full of the case and the arguments and facts which had been presented. Reserving judgements often led to forgetting facts and arguments and immediate delivery in court meant that any mistake which the judge might make could be immediately corrected by the lawyers.

As a judge on the Bombay High Court in the 1940s Chagla worked under Chief Justices Sir John Beaumont and Sir Leonard Stone. He thought highly of Sir John, both as a man and as a judge. He was quick in his judgements and decisions. He remembered that when Sir John first sat on the appellate side as a new chief justice he had to decide on a case with some obscure local laws and the Bar was unsure whether he would be able to handle the intricacies of the cases, but he acquitted himself well. Sir John would take short notes when the appeal was opened and once he had heard enough he would take a short nap.

Chagla thought that the Bar did not do Sir John justice when it denied him a reference when he did not recommend Harilal Kania for the chief justiceship. Chagla did not think Sir John was given to racial prejudice and remembered an instance when he fought hard for the appointment of Ganpat Rajadhyaksha over the government's preference for Eric Weston, given that he knew of Rajadhyaksha's work as a district judge but was not familiar with Weston's. He thought it was ironic that Sir Chimanlal Setalvad moved the motion that the Bar Association withhold its customary reference to the outgoing chief justice when he knew that Sir John had offered the chief justiceship to his son Motilal. Sir John later asked Chagla to sit with him and Kania on income tax cases to break up the tension. Chagla was not familiar with income tax work, but thought he was safe as Sir John would deliver the verdicts. But then Sir John once lost his voice and put Chagla in a tight spot by asking him to deliver the verdict instead.

Chagla thought Sir Leonard Stone was charming, but did not have Sir John's knowledge of Indian law. He showed confidence in Chagla and it was rare that he did not accept

Chagla's advice, particularly on the appointment of judges. Chagla sat on the appellate side when Sir Leonard was chief justice, was impressed by both Pralhad Gajendragadkar and Yadnayeshwar Dixit, and then recommended both their names for elevation to the Bench. Sir Leonard was worried about the arrears of criminal cases and so whenever appeals would come up for admission he would admit them and then enhance the sentence. The number of appeals declined, however Chagla recalled that he and Gajendragadkar did not approve of Sir Leonard's method and so spent a whole session trying to bring down criminal arrears. A lot of these cases were dacoity cases which were quite lengthy because of the identification of articles and the subject matter of the dacoity.

Sir Leonard asked Gajendragadkar to sit with him in the very first week after his elevation to the Bench.[cclxx] Like Chagla, Gajendragadkar did not think that Sir Leonard was a particularly brilliant lawyer but that he was a good administrator who wanted to introduce some method into the preparation of the boards for hearing cases. Under his new system lawyers knew when their cases were listed on the daily board. A monthly list would be displayed from which a weekly list would be produced and from the weekly lists the daily boards would be prepared according to the serial order. In one instance Sir Leonard passed a case off to Gajendragadkar, but continued taking notes. Gajendragadkar thought it odd that he would keep taking notes given that he was not hearing the case, and peeped over to find that he was preparing notes for his official visit to Ratnagiri the next day. When Gajendragadkar would whisper to him about points raised by the counsel he would say "Yes you are right", "I agree with you", and when he told him he was going to dismiss the appeal he said "Of course there is no substance in the appeal at all."

Gajendragadkar thought the members of the Bench

constituted a "happy family". The only note of discord he recalled was when at lunch Sir Leonard asked which of the judges was hearing a particular case. An Indian prince had met him at a club and asked that the case be disposed of early as it had already dragged on too long. The case was on Justice John Blagden's board, and Blagden asked the chief justice not to mention the matter again or he would treat it as interference with the administration of justice. The judges were all taken by surprise and then had to persuade him to not take such a "pedantic" view of the matter. Chagla also remembered the incident; both he and Justice Kania counselled Blagden against taking the matter further and they then proceeded together to the chief justice's office. Sir Leonard assured them that he had no such intention but was only concerned about growing arrears and wanted to bring Blagden's attention to this particular case.

On the opening day after the Nagpur High Court's vacation Mohammad Hidayatullah sat on the Bench with Sir Bhiwani Niyogi.[cclxxi] After the political drama of his days as advocate general, Hidayatullah's first case was much more subdued; it revolved around the applicability of different schools of Hindu Law. The case concerned the partition of the property between sons and whether their mother was entitled to a share. Hindus of the Chanda district had been governed by the mitakshara, and the Komtis of the district were also governed by it, unless it could be shown that they had migrated into the district from the other side of the river, in which case they would be governed by the smriti chandrika. If they had in fact crossed the river at some point, they would be deemed to have brought the Madras School of Hindu Law with them.

The lawyers for the prosperous Komti community enjoyed the case, citing every conceivable book on Hindu Law, original texts, histories, anthropological surveys, gazetteers and authoritative books on castes and tribes. Hidayatullah remembered having a tough time of the case and he had a few sleepless nights. Acting Chief Justice Niyogi gave him valuable assistance however, providing him with books from his private library and checking the translations from the original texts. In his judgement Hidayatullah had to delineate the outer boundaries of Telangana and in the end found no evidence of Komti migration from across the river, which meant that they were to be governed by the law of the Chanda district. Hidayatullah received his reward when Sir Bhiwani concurred with his judgement: "I concur. I have nothing useful to add to the elaborate, well considered and scholarly judgement proposed to be pronounced by my learned brother."

Hidayatullah felt his time on the Bench with Sir Bhiwani was too short. He wished it could have been longer, for he remembered his senior judge's fatherly interest and the soft corner he held for him. Hidayatullah recalled that Sir Bhiwani was a "tower of strength" during his early days on the Bench. He thought Sir Bhiwani and Sir Frederick were a contrast in styles. Whilst Sir Bhiwani would always want to get to the bottom of every case, Sir Frederick would want to see the end of it as quickly as possible. He recalled Sir Frederick's practice of taking three cases a day; two simple ones, one each at the start and finish of the day which he would take for himself, and a more complicated one which he would pass off to Hidayatullah. In this system it seemed as though Sir Frederick was getting through his cases quickly, but Hidayatullah insisted he was doing ten times the work. He even felt that the burden of doing justice would fall to him given that lawyers were afraid to develop their points in front of Sir Frederick.

Hidayatullah recounted an instance in which the first case of the day could not be taken up due to the death of one of the parties. This meant that Sir Frederick was presented with the second, more complicated case of the day. The counsel, Mangalmurti was running late, coughing and huffing and puffing outside the courtroom, and as expected Sir Frederick was anxious to dismiss the case. He pushed the file over to Hidayatullah for his signature, by which time Mangalmurti entered the courtroom. Sir Frederick told him the case had been dismissed. Hidayatullah then interrupted, telling counsel that he was lucky that he had not signed the order. A little confrontation ensued in which Sir Frederick asked Hidayatullah if that meant he was not signing the order for dismissal. Hidayatullah told him that was so and Sir Frederick stormed off. Hidayatullah then went to his chamber. Ten minutes later Sir Frederick came to thank him for saving him from embarrassment. He told Hidayatullah: "I admire your firmness." Hidayatullah suggested that they go back and hear the case, but Sir Frederick thought better of it. He suggested they adjourn the case until Friday (when he did not hear cases). Later that evening Bodbe, the lawyer opposing Mangalmurti came to thank Hidayatullah with some other members of the Bar, for "Such were the traditions of the Bench and Bar."

***

Mohammad Hidayatullah's picture of the Nagpur High Court at Independence was quite revealing. He looked to his fellow Indian judge, Sir Bhiwani Niyogi as a father figure and role model for his dedication to the work of a judge and felt pleased when he received his praise. He could even engage in some gentle ridicule of his senior British judge, pull him up for his allergy to hard work, and inform his readers that it was he who had to step in to ensure that justice was done when lawyers would not be able to develop their arguments before Sir Frederick Grille. Sir Frederick, who had spent decades in the Nagpur judiciary was increasingly the odd man out. The court was largely Indian; Hidayatullah sat as an Indian judge with fellow Indian judges and Indian lawyers who appeared in the court represented Indian clients. By the 1940s they all worked to uphold the traditions of the Bar and Bench at a High Court which only a decade earlier had been an obscure Commissioner's Court in the centre of India.

The Indian judges who rose to the Bench in the 1940s did not preside over the type of sensational sedition trials which created headlines in the early 20th century. Yet politics could never be kept completely away from the law, particularly when the state was challenged. After all, the High Courts were dependent on the power of the state to act as a guarantor of their ability to enforce the law. When the 'Quit India' cases came to court in Nagpur, Mohammad Hidayatullah just followed his brief as a lawyer, as he would have in any other case. He had to prosecute Congress activists who had challenged the state during August 1942, but he tried, like other Indians in similar situations to work according to the law and discard those prosecutions for which there was insufficient evidence.

Yet Hidayatullah's memories of his work as Advocate General of the Central Provinces and Berar are perhaps even more valuable for their illustration of the depths to which constitutionalism had taken root in colonial India. He first had to travel to New Delhi to defend the government from challenges to its ordinances, which had suspended the normal processes and procedures of the criminal law, before a bench of the Federal Court of India. Besides defending the Government of India's ordinances, he spent a much larger amount of time in a protracted litigation between his provincial government and the Reserve Bank of India over who should pay the bill for the looting of a treasury. When Hidayatullah returned to Nagpur he had to face the ire of the justices of the Nagpur High Court in cases in which Congress activists had been detained by the local police. Legal arguments would ensue over which grade of government officer had the authority to initiate such detentions and the procedure through which they should communicate with the court. Cases would even travel as far as the Privy Council, and

Hidayatullah would suffer some embarrassment when one of the triplicate forms required to release a prisoner was not forthcoming from his office.

By the time Indian barristers had come to senior standing at the Bar and were called up to the Bench by British judges they did so as colleagues, men of equal professional and financial standing, carrying on the traditions of almost century old institutions which had their own aura and dignity. This collegial relationship was reflected in the gentlemanly conversations about appointments to the Bench which drew on old ideas of honour. The judiciary was thus the least racially ordered institution of the state, and when British judges started quarrelling amongst themselves on the bench of the Bombay High Court it was the Indian judges who stepped in and tried to cool tempers. When Justice Blagden thought that Chief Justice Stone may have been interfering in the administration of justice in order to do a favour to an Indian prince he had met at his club it was Justices Chagla and Gajendragadkar and Kania who attempted to mediate. It was 1946, and the British judges were on their way out anyway, but the political upheavals taking place across India did not make their way inside the walls of the Bombay High Court. The court's judges viewed the matter as a potential threat to the integrity of the Bench and were most concerned about the damage that the incident may cause to the reputation of their institution, irrespective of the nationality of the judges at war with one another.

When Mahomedali Chagla became the first Indian Chief Justice of the Bombay High Court after Independence he assumed responsibility for a court which, like the other High Courts of India, had been transformed from British to Indian institutions in a matter of three decades. Independence might have seemed like a time for a new beginning, the creation of a new order and the discarding of the old British ways, yet when he recalled his promotion to the chief justiceship, Chagla saw himself as continuing a tradition, rather than disrupting it;

> "I was the first Chief Justice to be Indian and I fully realised the weight of my responsibilities. The Bombay High Court had a long line of distinguished Chief Justices, and had very high traditions as one of the premier High Courts of India. When I took office, I offered a prayer that I would have the capacity to maintain those traditions and that when I retired it should not be said of me that I had in any way lowered them or had not proved worthy of them. Whether my prayer was answered or not, it is for others to judge."[cclxxii]

Eight
An Immovable Bloc

The Montagu-Chelmsford reforms had launched an Indianisation of the Indian Civil Service, Indian Police and Indian Army, and a similar process had been at work in the judiciary for decades. Yet the centrepiece of the reforms was an overhaul of the central and provincial legislatures; the franchise was expanded, elected members formed majorities on the floors of the councils and assemblies, and Indian politicians were given responsibility for government departments in the provinces. This overhaul of Indian electoral politics amounted to an 'Indianisation' of the legislature and it was a process which divided the Indian National Congress from the start.

The period between Edwin Montagu's August Declaration in 1917 and the passage of the Government of India Act at the end of 1919 was one of momentous political activity in India and one which led to sudden political transformations and realignments. As Mohandas Gandhi began to develop his programme for non-cooperation with the government throughout 1920, the issue of 'Council Entry' came to be bundled into the protest agenda. Yet the issue was so large and profound that it could not simply sit unnoticed in a long list of points for non-cooperation such as a boycott of foreign cloth, British titles and government ceremonies. At issue was the Congress attitude towards the legislature, the organ of the state which as politicians and democrats was a natural home, a forum in which they could potentially develop constituencies, represent interests, influence government policy and take the nationalist cause closer to the corridors of power.

By 1923 the Congress had fractured over the issue of Council Entry, and a section of the Party which refused to maintain Gandhi's boycott of the councils and instead wanted to take non-cooperation inside the legislatures and 'wreck them from within' formed their own Swaraj Party. The Swarajists contested elections in 1923 and 1926, but by the time that another civil disobedience movement was launched in the early 1930s the old Council Entry issue took on a new ideological colour. Since its inception in 1885, the principle divisions within the Congress had taken place over the ways to best represent the Indian nationalist cause before the British Raj, but after almost five decades new political ideologies concerned more with reshaping India's economic structure began to attract young Congressmen. Marxists and socialists within the Congress gathered to form their own Congress Socialist Party, and it was the new Left Wing within the Congress fold which continued the opposition to Council Entry, whilst many of Gandhi's followers from the 1920s who had initially opposed entering the councils began to form a Right Wing and assume control of a new Congress Parliamentary Party.

Despite the ideological excitement of the 1930s, when another round of constitutional reform came in the form of the Government of India Act 1935, the Left Wing of the Congress, Mohandas Gandhi, Jawaharlal Nehru and Subhas Chandra Bose were all sidelined by the more conservative members of the Party who wanted to contest elections and potentially form ministries, or Congress governments in the provinces. When the Congress did form ministries after the elections of 1937 an old issue was settled, and a glimpse of the future appeared. Gandhi's almost two decade old call for a boycott of the councils had faded away and the Congress Ministries would be the means by which Congressmen would come more fully into the legislatures across India and begin to work with the executive in providing day to day administration in the provinces. Congress was now the government, rather than a party of protest and had to reconcile some of the inherent contradictions within its support base, besides repairing its adversarial relationship with the bureaucracy and police. The ministries would also be a chance for the Congress to project its electoral power and validate its claim to speaking for all of India. It was an opportunity for the Party to show what it was capable of, and the benefits which a Congress government would bring to the people in an independent India.

Two of the tallest leaders of the Congress were, if not politically, then ideologically relegated by the formation of the Congress Ministries in 1937. Mohandas Gandhi had dominated Congress politics throughout the 1920s and 1930s and his most persistent critic and challenger on the national stage had been Subhas Chandra Bose. Despite their vastly different political and ideological outlooks, they both shared a scepticism, and even a hostility to the structures and institutions of the British Raj, and both advocated revolutionary changes to Indian society and the state in a new political order. Gandhi was attracted to a vision of internal spiritual and material regeneration which started with the Indian villager and his or her village, whereas Bose was drawn to the contemporary political ideologies of the strong state which were dominating Europe during the 1930s. Yet despite the fact that Gandhi continued to play king maker during the late 1930s and Bose was elected Congress President in 1938 and 1939, neither of the leaders were able to take the Congress along with them and convince the majority of Congressmen of their ideological visions to remake Indian society and create a new Indian state.

***

At the time that the Montagu-Chelmsford reforms were

unveiled Mohandas Gandhi was still a figure at the margins of elite Indian politics. His political and social work in South Africa had made headlines in India, yet he was still something of a curiosity, and an outsider to those who had spent decades at the centre of Indian nationalist politics. Gandhi did not support the idea of dyarchy, or the transfer of responsibility for selected government departments to Indian ministers in the provinces as it was a constitutional structure in which British interests were put ahead of Indian ones.[cclxxiii] Like most other politicians within the moderate strand of Indian nationalism he wanted the number of British officers in the Indian Civil Service reduced, and hence the number of Indian officers increased, a cut in expenditure on defence, tariff protection for local industries and a reduction in taxes. Although not entirely satisfied with the Montagu-Chelmsford reforms he had decades of experience in dealing with the British political system in South Africa and thought it best to accept the reforms and then continue to press for further concessions in the years ahead. Amongst the major figures in nationalist politics at the time he received support from Mohammad Ali Jinnah, Pattabhi Sitaramayya and Madan Mohan Malaviya, whilst Chittaranjan Das, Bal Gangadhar Tilak, and Hasrat Mohani opposed his position and demanded full self-government.

After the massacre at Jallianwala Bagh in April 1919, the Congress held its annual session in Amritsar at the end of that year. Chittaranjan Das was leading the opposition to the Montagu-Chelmsford reforms as they had been put into legislation in the form of the Government of India Act 1919, and suggested that the Congress pass a resolution which expressed disappointment at the nature of the reforms. However, Gandhi intervened, insisting that the Congress co-operate with the reforms and offer its thanks to Edwin Montagu for his efforts. Eventually a compromise was reached in which the resolution referred to the reforms as 'disappointing' but thanked the British Government nonetheless for its efforts.

As 1920 progressed Gandhi's discussions on non-cooperation took place largely in the context of the Khilafat movement which had gained the support of Indian Muslims who sought to have the Caliph, or head of world Islam restored to his position in Turkey. In fact, an agenda for a non-cooperation scheme was worked out at a Khilafat Conference and in May 1920 the Khilafat Committee adopted the technique of non-cooperation as a means to further its cause. Gandhi then included the Jallianwala Bagh massacre in a list of political grievances in order to gain Congress support for the developing programme of non-cooperation. Yet he had thought of the Jallianwala Bagh massacre as a domestic issue, whereas the Caliphate was an international one and so better suited to a boycott of the Peace Celebrations which were being organised by the British Government after the end of World War I. In July 1920 a boycott of the councils was also included in the list of institutions which would be boycotted by the Khilafat movement under a programme of non-cooperation.

Gandhi took his plans for non-cooperation to the Special Session of the Congress at Calcutta in September 1920. Initially he just sought a resolution on the Khilafat issue and the Punjab wrongs, however Motilal Nehru wanted to broaden the resolution's appeal. The site of the political contest was the Subjects Committee. Motilal supported the resolution for non-cooperation, as did the Muslim attendees and it marginally won the day over opposition to it led by Chittaranjan Das. Council Entry had been put in the whole non-cooperation bundle and so Gandhi's position on the Montagu-Chelmsford reforms turned from one of urging thanks and co-operation, to protest and non-cooperation within a year. For the moderates within the Congress the

Montagu-Chelmsford reforms were a hard won constitutional concession and they were eager to take their places in the reformed legislatures in Delhi and the provincial capitals, yet in Calcutta most Congressmen were asked to vote for the entirety of the non-cooperation programme rather than its individual items, which meant that a large minority left the session feeling that it had not been heard.

Despite the Congress vote in favour of non-cooperation in Calcutta in September 1920, Motilal remained hesitant about a boycott of the new councils, whilst Das and Tilak had come to oppose it. Elections were due in November 1920 and the electoral prospects of the Congress in each of the provinces influenced the positions of the national leaders. The Congress did not yet have a strong base of support in Punjab and was likely to struggle at election time which meant that Lala Lajpat Rai opposed Council Entry. However, it was felt that the Congress had a reasonable chance of victory in Bengal and Maharashtra so Gandhi's boycott of the councils was opposed by Das and Tilak. Motilal eventually came to support their position in favour of entering the councils, despite the fact that the Congress was not fully prepared to contest an election in the United Provinces.

The Congress did boycott the council elections which took place in November 1920, and the issue of Council Entry was relegated at the Congress Session in Nagpur in December 1920. Das still held reservations over Gandhi's programme of non-cooperation which had been adopted by the Congress in September however. He financed a delegation to Nagpur and sought the co-operation of moderates and provincial leaders in tempering some of the more extreme calls to action in Gandhi's programme. Specifically, he wanted the boycott of schools by students and the boycott of law courts by lawyers amended. Those clauses were moderated somewhat; parents would play a role in the decision of students under 16, students over 16 would consult their conscience, and lawyers would only have to make "greater efforts" to suspend their practice in the courts. Despite these amendments to the non-cooperation programme the Congress largely supported Gandhi's programme as it had in Calcutta. In addition, Gandhi was instrumental in getting the Congress to adopt a new creed of 'swaraj', and it was at this time that Gandhi promised that swaraj would be established within a year. At the time many within the Congress just interpreted this to mean that the Party would remain committed to Gandhi's non-cooperation programme for one year however, rather than the actual achievement of swaraj within the year.

The non-cooperation movement had been gaining momentum through 1921 and the All India Congress Committee approved the start of civil disobedience in November 1921. However, there were instances of violence in Bombay and Madras, and when a mob burned down a police station, killing the local policemen in Chauri Chaura in Gorakhpur in the United Provinces in February 1922, Gandhi called off non-cooperation and the civil disobedience which had been planned for Bardoli in Gujarat. It was at this time that tensions in the Congress came to the fore once again; Gandhi's decision to call off non-cooperation had been met with disappointment by the senior leadership of the Party, including those leaders who had not supported the idea to start with. He had inspired the Congress and the Indian public to political action, and then told them to stop just as they were getting into stride. Das wanted to continue with non-cooperation, but when that did not happen he then wanted Gandhi to accept Viceroy Reading's offer of a Round Table meeting to achieve something specific before the year which was supposed to bring swaraj ended. However, Gandhi insisted that the Ali brothers, his colleagues from the Khilafat movement, be released from jail, a position which ended the negotiations with the viceroy and prevented a Round Table Conference taking place.

Both Chittaranjan Das and Madan Mohan Malaviya represented significant sections of the Congress which were becoming frustrated with Gandhi's leadership and wanted to contest elections to the councils. Das raised the issue in April 1922, and then in October 1922 the Civil Disobedience Committee advised against a revival of civil disobedience on a national scale. Motilal Nehru had also come out to openly support Council Entry. He and Das argued that the most effective means of non-cooperation with the councils was to enter them. Das had put together a plan of action; enter the councils with a majority, demand swaraj, and if it was not received, wreck the councils. In Das's scheme the Congress would not give up the political space created in the reformed councils to its rivals, and it would be able to take non-cooperation inside the councils and bring them to a halt. Yet other more moderate Congressmen who had remained with the Party like Madan Mohan Malaviya, Mukund Jayakar, and Narasimha Kelkar were not interested in wrecking the councils, but working within them and bringing a nationalist perspective to governance. Aligned against the forces within the Congress who, for a variety of reasons, wanted to enter the councils was a group of young followers of Gandhi which came to be known as the 'No Changers', that is, they wanted 'no change' to the Congress policy of boycotting the councils.

Chittaranjan Das took up the Congress Presidency in August 1922 and continued to argue for Council Entry at Gaya in December 1922. Motilal moved a motion in favour of Council Entry at Gaya whilst Chakravarti Rajagopalachari, a leading 'No Changer' appealed in Gandhi's name to defeat it. The motion in favour of Council Entry was defeated by a proportion of 2 to 1. Das took it as a personal defeat, resigned and formed the Swaraj Party with Motilal Nehru on 31 December 1922. A Special Session of the Congress later met at Delhi in September 1923 which agreed to allow Congressmen in the Swaraj Party to enter the councils. Swaraj Party candidates contested elections in November 1923 and fared well across the country. In Bengal the Swaraj Party members became ministers, refused their salaries and resigned, effectively taking non-cooperation inside the legislature, and in the Indian Legislative Assembly in Delhi they demanded a Round Table Conference to initiate a new round of constitutional advance.

Gandhi had been in jail since March 1922 and was released in February 1924. During his time in jail the ruler of Turkey, Kemal Attaturk had effectively ended the Khilfat movement by abolishing the Caliph and establishing a Turkish Republic. Gandhi returned to daily Congress politics, and in June 1924 he sought to have those who had entered the councils the previous year removed from Congress office bearer rank, impose a requirement that Congressmen spin a prescribed amount of khadi in order maintain their membership of the Party, and condemn the political violence which had been spreading through Bengal. The first two of Gandhi's proposals were defeated, and the third was only carried by a slim margin. In November 1924 Gandhi then came to an agreement with Motilal and Das to allow Swaraj Party members to sit in the councils as an integral part of the Congress, as long as khadi spinning was made mandatory for Congress membership. In 1925 Gandhi effectively stepped away from his leadership of the Congress, handed control of the Party to the Swarajists and established his own All India Spinners Association.

During 1926 the Swarajists and Gandhi went their separate ways, following their own political programmes with varied results. Under the system of dyarchy the Indian ministers in the provinces had limited powers, but they could exercise patronage, and so rather than continuing the Swaraj Party aim of 'wrecking the councils from within', a section of the Party began to advocate the acceptance of offices, a position which came to be known as 'responsive co-operation'. Motilal opposed responsive co-operation, but the idea had the support of moderates like Kelkar and Jayakar. Shortly before the elections of 1926 Malaviya formed an Independent Congress Party in alliance with Lajpat Rai and the Responsive Co-operators. The result was that the Swaraj Party vote fractured and its candidates returned to the legislatures in significantly smaller numbers. Gandhi on the other hand, had announced that he would remain silent throughout 1926. His followers, the No Changers began to focus on work in the villages, putting their efforts into flood relief, national schools, the promotion of khadi and village handicrafts, anti-liquor campaigns and the upliftment of Harijans. Their work had only limited success in regenerating the villages in which they worked, but it did expand the Congress base and took Gandhi's name deeper into rural India.

Young leaders in the Congress had begun to demand complete Independence, rather than Dominion status or self-government within the British Empire. However, through 1926 Gandhi warned them not to take on a bigger political responsibility than they were capable of handling. During this time he had been leading an agrarian movement at Bardoli in Gujarat and campaigning against untouchability, but then experienced health problems during 1927. This was also around the time that he had left one of the causes most dear to his heart, Hindu-Muslim unity, to the will of God. Motilal needed Gandhi's support to resist the growing pressure for the Congress to adopt a goal of complete Independence and invited him to attend the Congress Session in Calcutta in December 1928. Gandhi was hesitant to attend, because cloth woven at mills might be displayed, however Motilal assured Gandhi that any cloth displayed would be hand-spun. Gandhi attended the Calcutta Session and as a compromise between the old moderates and the young radicals he effectively gave the British a new deadline of 31 December 1929 for the achievement of Dominion status.

Elections due for the end of 1929 had been postponed until after the publication of the Simon Commission Report. Motilal's position was that Congressmen in the Swaraj Party should not attend the legislatures for the remainder of the term, yet his appeal to Congressmen in June 1929 to withdraw from the legislatures received stiff resistance from the provincial units of the Party. Congressmen in Assam, Madras, Bombay and Punjab were all involved in legislative business which their constituents expected them to complete. The division in the Party was so marked that the matter was referred to the Working Committee in July 1929 and then to the All Indian Congress Committee later that month. Delhi, Bombay, Andhra and Karnatak all supported Motilal's call for a boycott, whilst Bengal, the United Provinces, Maharashtra and Madras were in favour of continuing to work within the legislatures. Gandhi stepped in to mediate the growing dispute and managed to defer a decision on withdrawal from the legislatures until the Congress Session which was to take place in Lahore at the end of the year.

The Congress declared its goal of purna Swaraj at Lahore in December 1929. It was at the Lahore session that the Party also resolved to boycott the councils, and efforts to enforce the boycott began a few days later in January 1930. Jawaharlal Nehru was Congress President and he directed the provincial units of the Party to get their legislators to resign from their posts. The following month the All India Congress Committee called for the resignation from Congress elective bodies of all those who had not followed the instruction to resign or those who were seeking re-election in the forthcoming elections. The diktats coming from both Nehru and the All India Congress Committee prompted resistance from Congress moderates. Whilst a majority of Swaraj Party members of the Indian Legislative Assembly in Delhi resigned, only a minority of members of the Bombay Legislature did so. In Punjab only one Congressman resigned, whilst in Madras a significant number resigned only to be re-elected in the following election. The call was heeded however, in the United Provinces, Bengal, Bihar, Orissa and Assam where almost all Swaraj Party members resigned their seats in the provincial legislatures.

At the end of January 1930, Gandhi made Viceroy Edward Wood, the Earl of Halifax, better known as Lord Irwin an offer. If the viceroy could meet 11 demands then the Congress would not embark on another round of civil disobedience and would participate in a Round Table Conference. Amongst the 11 points were a total prohibition on alcohol, the imposition of a tariff on foreign cloth, the abolition of the salt tax, and the release of political prisoners who had not been charged with murder. When the viceroy failed to satisfy the 11 points, Gandhi and his followers set out from the Sabarmati Ashram on 12 March 1930 to march to Dandi to defy the British authorities and produce their own tax-free salt. He was then arrested and the Congress launched civil disobedience across India. Political protests were more decentralised than a decade earlier; neither Gandhi nor the Congress central leadership were able to exercise tight control on the forms which civil disobedience took in the provinces. A Round Table Conference was held in London towards the end of 1930, yet it made little progress without the involvement of the Congress leadership, most of which was in jail.

Gandhi was released from jail at the start of 1931 and negotiations began with the viceroy for a settlement. Gandhi and Irwin reached a pact in which the Congress would put an end to civil disobedience in exchange for a range of government concessions, including the release of civil disobedience prisoners and the right to make salt for domestic consumption in salt producing areas of the country. Gandhi travelled to London for the Second Round Table Conference but was unable to resolve disagreements over communal representation in a new constitutional structure and differences over the federal nature of such a structure persisted. He returned to India to revive civil disobedience; another round of flag raisings, boycotts, picketing and processions started once more across the country. Gandhi was jailed again, yet the enthusiasm was not the same as in 1930. The absorbing political issue of 1932 was the Communal Award, and Gandhi's fast against the Award from jail in Yeravada captured most of the political headlines. By the middle of 1933 the Congress took the decision to end civil disobedience and left it to individual Congressmen to continue resistance. Unlike in 1931 it was essentially a voluntary end to civil disobedience, the British Government was not forced to make any concessions. With another round of civil disobedience at an end and public enthusiasm at a low ebb, the perennial demand within the Congress for Council Entry arose once again.

Mukhtar Ansari and Bidhan Roy started a push for Council Entry in December 1933. Sundara Satyamurti was in favour of a revival of the Swaraj Party, yet Chakravarti Rajagopalachari who, like Vallabhbhai Patel and Rajendra Prasad had been a staunch 'No Changer' during the 1920s, had come around to argue for direct Congress control of parliamentary activity. By this stage Gandhi had resigned himself to the fact that a large section of the Congress would always be in favour of Council Entry and thought it better to allow Congressmen to contest elections rather than have them sit idle. With Gandhi's blessings those Congressmen in favour of returning to the councils held a conference in May 1934 to discuss their way forward. Young Congress socialists like Ashok Mehta, Minoo Masani, Yusuf Mehrally, and Achyut Patwardhan came together under the leadership of Jayaprakash Narayan and held their own conference at Patna prior to the All India Congress Committee meeting, seeking to prevent a "drift to constitutionalism and to put a more dynamic programme before the country...".[cclxxiv]

A Congress Parliamentary Board was then set up, and a tussle for control ensued. Gandhi wanted the Parliamentary Board to be controlled by the central leadership through the All India Congress Committee whereas the provincial parties wanted to maintain autonomy in managing their affairs in the councils. Vallabhbhai Patel and Rajendra Prasad quickly took up the leadership of the new Congress Parliamentary Party. The Congress did contest the elections of 1934 and put up a strong showing in the Indian Legislative Assembly in New Delhi and in most of the provinces barring Punjab and Bengal. There was also an attempt to reconcile Gandhi and his followers with a parliamentary programme; it was argued that once elected to the councils the Congress legislators could help with Gandhian rural development work. Yet it was at this time that Gandhi grew even more disillusioned with the direction which the Congress was taking. He threatened to quit the Party and many of his supporters who had stayed true to his vision also began to think of forming a new party.

The young Socialists formed their own Congress Socialist Party in October 1934 in order to maintain a distinct socialist grouping within the Congress and push the Party's ideology leftward. During the mid 1930s they, along with Nehru maintained the opposition to Council Entry within the Congress, yet they recognised that it would be "suicidal" to cut themselves off from the nationalist movement, even if it was only a "bourgeoisie democratic revolution".[cclxxv] The

Socialists thought that the barristers of the Congress were under the happy delusion that they represented Indian society as a whole. What they as Socialists could do was link them to the working class and the peasantry who would then radicalise the Congress agenda. The Congress Socialist Party also sought an alliance with the Communists and the two groups began to work together in the union movement.

The challenge from a more organised and focused Left within the Congress brought the forces on the Right together. Vallabhbhai Patel thought the Socialists' ideology was "nonsense" and Pattabhi Sitaramayya called their leaders "scum".cclxxvi Gandhi thought their programme was "intoxicating and dangerous".cclxxvii Nehru occupied the middle ground, calling the Congress Socialist Party a "curious and mixed assemblage".cclxxviii He felt inclined towards their ideology but didn't think he would join them, even if he had the freedom to do so. Subhas Chandra Bose however cheered on their attempt to generate a "radical tendency" within the Congress.cclxxix

Jawaharlal Nehru had been in Europe whilst the debate over Council Entry had been going on, and his position came to be similar to that of his father in the 1920s. He would not oppose Council Entry if the intention was to wreck the councils from the inside, but he would remain opposed to the acceptance of ministerial offices. He had little enthusiasm for Council Entry in principle however, and thought that if the Congress went back to the councils it would get absorbed in petty issues rather than major social transformations.cclxxx Assuming the Congress Presidency in 1936 he, along with the leaders of the Congress Socialist Party, continued to argue that should Congress enter the councils anger against the British Government would be diluted as it would not have to take sole responsibility for the failures of the administration and the Party would end up doling out patronage to the middle class and become part of the government machinery.ᶜᶜˡˣˣˣⁱ Pattabhi Sitaramayya was also concerned that the Government of India Act 1935 was so restrictive that it would not allow the Congress to implement much of its agenda, whilst Congressmen from Punjab and Bengal also opposed Council Entry as they had little hope of forming a ministry in their Muslim majority provinces.ᶜᶜˡˣˣˣⁱⁱ

But it was the Bombay barrister Kanaiyalal Munshi made the most detailed survey of the question. He argued that the Government of India Act 1935 had encouraged communal divisions and if the Congress remained outside the arena of electoral politics reactionary communal forces would step in to take its place. The Congress workers were already prone to demoralisation in the absence of either civil disobedience or participation in electoral politics, and the sight of communal forces forming ministries with the support of the government would only intensify this feeling. Munshi suggested that the Congress contest elections and form ministries, understanding the limitations imposed by the 1935 Act- "to build power as well as stability, to master the day to day details of the administration and by slow degrees overhaul the departments; and to control the civil service and render the Governor a mute spectator."ᶜᶜˡˣˣˣⁱⁱⁱ He received support from Rajendra Prasad who was also concerned that rival parties not be allowed to exercise power. Prasad wanted to show the Indian people that the Congress could do constructive work, something which would only enhance its power.ᶜᶜˡˣˣˣⁱᵛ Munshi and Prasad's arguments won the day and both Nehru and Gandhi had to relent once again on the issue of Council Entry. The Congress contested elections in 1937, winning absolute majorities in five out of the eleven provinces: Madras, Bihar, Orissa, the Central Provinces and Berar and the United Provinces, and came close to a majority in Bombay. Congressmen entered the legislatures, and they eventually accepted ministerial offices on the condition of non-interference by the provincial governors. Having been defeated by the Right over the decision to contest elections, the Congress Socialists turned to act as an internal opposition to the Congress Ministries and went out and worked in the field to bring about their vision of the empowerment of the working class and peasantry.

Whilst the Right Wing was comfortable with Nehru as president and did not see him as too much of a threat, they were less content with Gandhi's choice of Subhas Chandra Bose as president in 1938. Bose formed a Left Consolidation Committee of the Communists and the Congress Socialists and in his presidential address at Haripura in 1938 he urged the Left to "democratise" and "reorganise" the Congress on a broad anti-imperialist basis. The members of the Congress Working Committee were wary of Bose's talk of the election for the presidency of the Congress being about "ideologies, policies and programmes" and felt that it was the Working Committee which was supposed to decide policies and programmes, whilst the president was supposed to be more of a chairman who represented the unity of the Party, which in turn represented the Nation. Yet despite opposition from the Congress establishment, Bose won a narrow victory for re-election at Tripuri with support from the Left Wing and defeated Gandhi's candidate, Pattabhi Sitaramayya.

Congress Working Committee members then resigned and Govind Pant had a resolution passed calling on Gandhi to compose the Working Committee. Bose tried to find a formula to work the resolution, but having failed he too resigned. Yet when given the choice between Gandhi and Bose even the Congress Socialists fell in behind Gandhi, whom they saw as the best bet to launch an effective struggle against the Raj. Bose, having resigned from the Presidency of the Congress, formed the Forward Bloc in May 1939. The Forward Bloc had a similar objective to the Congress Socialist Party; its aim was to bring on a Left consolidation within the Congress and oppose both the British Raj and Indian counter revolutionaries. It was itself opposed by both the Right and Left Wings of the Congress however. Elsewhere, the Congress Socialists and Gandhi fell out with one another. The Socialists opposed the Gandhian constructive programme as a means to achieve Independence and Gandhi opposed the Socialists' call for students to leave their schools and colleges and for workers to go on strike. Gandhi demanded their full commitment to his programme if they wanted him as their leader. Bose then fell out with Gandhi over launching another round of civil disobedience and left India in 1941.

***

Upon Gandhi's return to India in 1914 he established an ashram and conducted his first satyagraha campaign amongst the peasants of the indigo plantations of Bihar. The great prize in popular politics at the time was 'self-government' and so wherever he went he presented his views on the subject. Speaking at Benaras Hindu University in February 1916 he said "No amount of speeches will ever make us fit for self-government...it is only our conduct that will fit us for it" and asked rhetorically that if India's temples were not clean then what would Indian self-government look like?[cclxxxv] Gandhi maintained this basic position for the rest of his political career. Yet despite his ability to galvanise the country with his techniques of non-cooperation and civil disobedience and his attempts to communicate his political vision with both Congress elites and the Indian masses, a fundamental misunderstanding over political means and ends persisted through the 1920s and 1930s.

Throughout 1917 and 1918 Gandhi continued to use satyagraha in mill strikes in Ahmadabad and land revenue revolts in rural Gujarat. In November 1917 he spoke to a

Gujarat Political Conference and declared that "Swaraj is not to be attained through an appeal to British democracy."[cclxxxvi] The main impediment to swaraj was the internal divisions of Indian society and so "Government of self" was the first step towards attaining it. He asked: "If we cannot regulate the affairs of our cities, if our streets are not kept clean, if our homes are dilapidated and if our roads are crooked, if we cannot command the services of selfless citizens for civic government and those who are in charge of affairs are neglectful or selfish, how shall we claim larger powers?"[cclxxxvii] He declared that political activity "should be two fold. We may petition the Government, we may agitate in the Imperial Council for our rights; but for a real awakening of the people, the more important thing is activities directed inwards."[cclxxxviii] In July 1919 he spoke to satyagrahis in Gujarat and made it clear that satyagraha was only the negative element of a greater project and the positive element was "constructive work".[cclxxxix]

It was in the context of the planned civil disobedience movement in Bardoli in Gujarat that Gandhi began to advocate a series of measures which would come to be known as the 'Constructive Programme' in *Young India* on 2 February 1922. He was pleased to report that villagers had accepted the need for National Schools, the admission of untouchables to these schools, the provision of healthcare to untouchables and allowing them the right to draw water from village wells. In addition, the villagers were to spin yarn and weave their own khadi. In the wake of the violence at Chauri Chaura and the suspension of civil disobedience, in the 16 February edition of *Young India*, Gandhi offered the constructive programme of daily spinning, visiting untouchable homes, the establishment of National Schools, bringing untouchable children into National Schools, organising social service, combating alcoholism, and establishing real panchayats in the villages across the country. He then began to make the work of the constructive programme a precondition for any further civil disobedience; it was the skills and discipline inculcated through constructive work that would allow for a successful civil disobedience movement. Gandhi tried to position the constructive programme as the source of energy which would sustain the Congress and even went so far as to say that his leadership would be "perfectly useless" if he could not convince Congress members of its necessity.[ccxc] It was also to be a source of Congress unity and he continued to exhort Congress workers to take up at least one element in the constructive programme as part of their daily routine.

After a section of Congressmen formed the Swaraj Party and contested the elections of 1923 Gandhi increasingly began to hold up the legislative councils as mere debating chambers in contrast to the real action of the constructive programme. In January 1925 he had to once again explain his concept of swaraj: "real swaraj will not come by the acquisition of authority by a few but by the acquisition of the capacity by all to resist authority when it is abused" and so "swaraj is to be attained by educating the masses to a sense of their ability to regulate and control authority."[ccxci] He wrote, "Ample work awaits those patriotic young men who do not mind the village life and who can derive pleasure from silent and sustained labour, not too taxing and yet taxing enough for its monotony."[ccxcii] It was also in the mid 1920s that he became particularly committed to spinning as a means to regenerate rural India. He wanted Congress workers to "Spin, spin, spin until stagnation vanishes."[ccxciii] He claimed that the handloom would both provide a new industry for the entire country and keep the impulses of violence and division under control.

Gandhi reiterated that swaraj was not so much about an end goal but the means adopted to achieve it. Even after the success of the peasants' satyagraha at Bardoli in 1928 he encouraged them not to bask in their victory and urged them to greater commitment to the constructive programme. He made his point clear when he told them: "Driving out the English will not by itself establish swaraj in India...Do we want the swaraj of barbarism, freedom to live like pigs in a pigsty without let or hindrance by anybody."[ccxciv] He was starting to grow weary after almost a decade of saying the same thing and getting relatively little response. He had become critical of the Congress and remained aloof from its agitations in the late 1920s, but wanted to give some encouragement to his constructive workers and told them to "plod on for some time, hold themselves in peace and be satisfied with apparently small results."[ccxcv]

In 1929 as the pressure from the younger generation within the Congress for a commitment to the goal of complete Independence became irresistible, Gandhi only intensified his plea to Congressmen that their real work lay in the constructive programme rather than talk of Independence. In June of 1929 he wrote that the "army for swaraj" should measure its success by "how many lavatories they cleaned, and how many wells in how many villages, how many bunds they built, how many patients they attended upon, how much khadi they wove, how many wells or tanks they dug, how many night schools they conducted and so on."[ccxcvi] And even as the Lahore Congress passed its resolution for complete Independence, he urged that Congress workers "should work in the villages- should educate the villagers."[ccxcvii]

Tired of trying to convince the Congress rank and file to embrace his constructive programme Gandhi set up something of a splinter party of his own, the All India Village Industries Association. The AIVIA would still remain under the Congress, but through it Gandhi could more fully concentrate on his constructive programme and work with those Congress supporters who embraced his ideas rather than have to persuade those who were sceptical; the only condition for membership of AIVIA was a commitment to the constructive programme. In August 1935 Gandhi lamented that the constructive programme was only propped up by "a handful of earnest reformers scattered all over the country. Not all of them are able to raise funds locally nor are they all sure of the policy to be followed."[ccxcviii] Eventually, in 1937 the event which Gandhi had been trying to prevent for almost 20 years happened and the Congress contested elections and formed ministries across India. He simply noted that the legislatures were for the few, whereas constructive work was for all.[ccxcix] But he did hope that the legislators would use some of their new found powers to put the constructive programme into effect.

Subhas Chandra Bose was more than a generation younger than Mohandas Gandhi and he carried with him many of the frustrations which the young members of the Congress felt with their old leader. Bose had studied at Fitzwilliam Hall, Cambridge after World War I and was successful at the Indian Civil Service examination in July 1920. Yet he was one of the few who resigned his post on a point of principle; he felt that "it would be impossible to serve both masters at the same time- namely the British Government and my country…"[ccc] Instead he returned to India to join the nationalist movement and upon reaching Bombay on 16 July 1921 he immediately proceeded to Mani Bhavan for an interview with Gandhi in order to seek a "clear conception of his plan of action".

Bose wanted to understand the successive stages of Gandhi's plan and how they would lead to "the ultimate seizure of power from the foreign bureaucracy". Specifically, he wanted to know how Congress activities were going to culminate in the non-payment of taxes, how the non-payment of taxes could force the British Government to leave India, and how Gandhi could promise 'swaraj within one year' as he had been doing since the Nagpur Congress in December 1920. Bose was satisfied with Gandhi's response on the first of these issues; he would attract 10 million members to the Congress and raise ₹10 million, focus on his khadi campaign in order to provoke a government crackdown which would start a round of civil disobedience, and with Congress workers filling the jails the people would then withhold the payment of taxes. Bose was unconvinced on the other two points however. He asked Gandhi whether he thought that boycotting foreign cloth would force the British Government to come to terms with the nationalist movement. But he understood from Gandhi's response that he did not think the boycott of foreign cloth would be the means to bring about such a settlement- "What his real expectation was I was unable to understand." Bose thought that either Gandhi did not want to reveal all the secrets of his plan, or he did not have any clear conception of the tactics which would force a concession from the British Government. Further, it seemed that the achievement of swaraj within one year was "a matter of faith" for Gandhi but "by no means clear" to Bose. He left the meeting trying to convince himself that "there must have been a lack of understanding on my part". Yet he later came to the conclusion that there was "a deplorable lack of clarity" in Gandhi's plan and Gandhi himself did not know how the stages of his plan would win freedom for India. Bose later expressed frustration with Gandhi's call to end non-cooperation in February 1922. He called it a "national calamity".

After the meeting at Mani Bhavan Bose proceeded to Calcutta and quickly became immersed in Bengal politics. He met with Chittaranjan Das and immediately found a political mentor whose outlook was much closer to his own. Amongst his first political assignments Bose was given the charge of the

Bengal Provincial Congress Committee's Publicity Board. He had taken part in the non-cooperation movement and been jailed, but after his release he followed Das into the Swaraj Party and became the Chief Executive Officer of the Calcutta Corporation in April 1923. Later in 1923 he also became General Secretary of the Bengal Provincial Congress Committee. Yet in October 1924 he was arrested again, and after a brief detention in Alipore and Brahmapore jails he was deported to Mandalay in Burma in January 1925. His time in jail in Burma was long and hard, and after a hunger strike his health began to deteriorate throughout 1926. He was first offered a release on the condition that he not return to India and proceed to Switzerland, but he refused. A plan for his transfer to Almora was also floated, but given further deterioration of his health he was released unconditionally in May 1927.

After his release from Mandalay and return to India, Bose began to play a larger role in national politics. It was at the Madras Session in December 1927 that he was appointed General Secretary of the Congress along with Jawaharlal Nehru. He also became President of the All India Trade Union Congress in 1928 and remained in the post until 1931. Bose thought the issue of the Simon Commission was a good one to launch another civil disobedience movement to drive the British out of India and in May 1928 he proceeded to Gandhi's Sabarmati Ashram but was unsuccessful in urging him to come out of retirement. Bose then spoke before the All India Youth Congress in Calcutta on 25 December 1928, expressing his growing frustration with Gandhi's leadership:

> *"The actual effect of the propaganda carried on by the Sabarmati school of thought is to create a feeling and impression that modernism is bad, large-scale production is an evil, that wants should not be*

> *increased and the standard of living should not be raised, that we must endeavour to the best of our ability, to go back to the days of the bullock cart and that the soul is so important that physical culture and training can well be ignored."*

At the Calcutta Congress of December 1928 Bose, with the support of Nehru proposed a resolution for the adoption of complete Independence as the goal of the Congress. Whilst moving the amendment he stated: "The fact that I rise today to move the amendment indicates a fundamental cleavage between the elder school and the new school of thought in the Congress." In a glimpse of the future, he attended the Calcutta Congress as the General Officer Commanding of the Bengal Volunteer Corps, a group which he had trained as a military unit complete with martial uniforms. Gandhi defeated Bose's Independence resolution and both Bose and Nehru offered to resign from their general secretary posts. Later, at a meeting of the Congress Left Wing at Lucknow both decided that rather than dividing the Congress on the issue they would form Independence Leagues to continue their campaign across the country.

By the time that the Congress did adopt complete Independence as its goal in Lahore, Bose was arguing for mobilisation of the peasantry, workers and youth to launch a complete boycott of the British Government and the formation of a parallel government. Upon returning to Calcutta from the Lahore Congress however, he was once again arrested and sentenced to one year in prison. He was elected mayor of Calcutta whilst behind bars, and briefly took up his post upon being released from jail, only to be taken back into custody in January 1931, and then released once again in March 1931. Amidst the civil disobedience campaign Bose was arrested once more in January 1932, spending a year in detention without trial during which time his health deteriorated again. In this instance the British Government allowed him to travel to Europe for treatment and he reached Vienna in March 1933.

It was after Gandhi once again suspended civil disobedience that Bose issued a call for a change of Congress leadership from Vienna. He sent a proposal for the establishment of a new party, a Samyavadi Sangha to an All Parties Indian Conference held in London in 1933. He outlined ten principles for the Sangha, including commitments to the peasants and workers rather than the landlords and capitalists, the establishment of a system of economic planning, breaking down the caste system and the abolition of landlordism. Bose also stood committed to a federal structure with a "Central Government with dictatorial powers for some years to come."[ccci] Bose reiterated his concern about the potentially anarchic nature of democracy in India when he wrote: "It [the Samyavadi Sangha] will not stand for democracy in the Mid-Victorian sense of the term, but will believe in government by a strong party bound together by military discipline, as the only means of holding India together and preventing a chaos, when Indians are free and are thrown entirely on their own resources."[cccii]

During the early 1930s Russian communism and Italian fascism were thought to be the political ideologies of the future. Most saw them as opposing ideologies, yet Bose wanted to bring their best qualities together and create a new ideology for India; "Both Communism and Fascism believe in the supremacy of the State over the individual. Both denounce Parliamentarian democracy. Both believe in party rule. Both believe in dictatorship of the party and in the ruthless suppression of all dissenting minorities. Both believe in a planned industrial reorganisation of the country. These will form the basis of the new synthesis."[ccciii] It was during this period that Bose wrote an account of his involvement with the Congress during the 1920s, *The Indian Struggle*. The work was an elaborate critique of Gandhi's leadership of the Party but interestingly, at a time when Bose was considering the political ideologies of Europe and India, there was only one mention of Gandhi's constructive programme. For Bose and many other Congressmen it barely registered as an alternative political ideology. In fact, it was explicitly dismissed as "non-political" and "social work".

Whilst *Hind Swaraj* of 1909 has often been read as Gandhi's enduring political manifesto, it was in *Constructive Programme* of 1941 that he provided an explanation of the ideology which motivated him during the height of his political career in the 1920s and 1930s. Congressmen, and particularly Subhas Chandra Bose, had always been excited by Gandhi's civil disobedience campaigns, but assumed that they had been started to bring the British Government down and achieve Independence. In *Constructive Programme*, Gandhi made it clear; "Civil Disobedience can never be directed for a general cause, such as Independence. The issue must be definite, capable of being clearly understood, and within the power of the opponent to yield." Thus, civil disobedience was just one tool to be used when the occasion arose to right a particular wrong. It was also just one part of Gandhi's broader constructive programme; "For my handling of Civil Disobedience without the constructive programme will be like a paralysed hand attempting to lift a spoon."

Likewise, most Congressmen had initially taken the word 'swaraj' quite literally and translated it into English as 'self-government' in the formal political sense. Self-government was most often equated with Dominion status which was why the claim for Dominion status was so dearly held for so long by the more moderate Congressmen. By the late 1920s swaraj had morphed into complete Independence or purna Swaraj for the younger generation in the Congress, which meant evicting the British rulers and India's emergence as an independent nation. Yet Gandhi's concept of swaraj was, from the start, radically different. He aimed for the complete material and spiritual renewal of India which would be brought about by remaking Indian villagers and their villages. This was a much bigger task than the Independence which the younger Congressmen wanted and something which explained Gandhi's lack of concern for Congress manifestos demanding formal political independence. Even in 1941 the difference between the two conceptions of swaraj remained, and Gandhi reiterated that "Therefore, complete Independence will be complete only to the extent of our approach in practice to truth and nonviolence", and "Let the reader mentally plan out the whole of the constructive programme, and he will agree with me that, if it could be successfully worked out, the end of it would be the Independence we want." To the last, the Independence which Gandhi wanted and the Independence that most Congressmen wanted remained vastly different things.

The disagreement between Bose and Gandhi continued even after Bose left India. Bose had travelled from Peshawar to Kabul in January 1941 disguised as an elderly deaf and mute Pathan, Mohammad Ziauddin. Upon reaching Afghanistan he wrote his *Forward Bloc- It's Justification*, which also became known as *The Kabul Thesis*. Bose largely took up the critique of Gandhi's leadership of the Congress which he had left off in *The Indian Struggle* a decade earlier. He spent a significant portion of *The Kabul Thesis* attacking the "Gandhism" and the "Gandhi movement" which had dominated the Congress over the previous 20 years. In attacking "Gandhism" he seemed to be attacking both Gandhi's tactical leadership of the Party as well as the body of ideas which he represented. Yet Gandhi would himself lament that "Gandhism", which was actually the constructive programme, had few takers. The misunderstandings continued as Bose dismissed Gandhi's "non-political" work such as the All India Spinners Association and the All India Village Industries Association, arguing that they would undermine the political dynamism of the "Gandhi movement". These organisations were, of course, at the heart of Gandhi's politics. The two different conceptions of formal political independence, and the spiritual and material renewal of India remained to the end, as Bose further stressed that he wanted "undiluted Independence" and not Gandhi's "substance of Independence".

***

When the Congress went to the polls during the winter of 1936 and 1937 it did so as a relatively united parliamentary party eager to show its electoral strength and implement many of the measures which it had been promising to the Indian people over the previous years. The Congress put in a strong showing in northern, central and western India, providing a preview of the type of governments which it would run in these regions in the decades after Independence. Candidates had to be selected by the new Congress Parliamentary Board, caste issues reared their head, but once the campaign started new political stars were born. Across the country the Congress tried to tap into anti-landlord sentiment amongst a section of the peasantry which had been given the vote as a result of the new Government of India Act and promised better days ahead under Congress Ministries.

The Congress campaign in the United Provinces sought to capitalise on both anti-landlord sentiment in the province, as well as the larger national issue of bringing the British Raj to an end. The two themes came together as Congress campaigners highlighted the support which the landlords had given to the British Raj in the recent past. The farmers of U.P. were asked to show their defiance against the landlords by voting for the Congress and refusing to pay illegal dues or comply with illegal demands for unpaid labour. The British Raj was held responsible for widespread poverty, the plight of the farmers, and urban unemployment, whilst the public was reminded of the lavish salaries and benefits of government officials. Political meetings would be held as close to government offices as possible to demonstrate growing Congress might and the increasing weakness of the authorities. Although he may not have been enthusiastic about the elections, the people of U.P. were drawn to the figure of Jawaharlal Nehru. He travelled the entire province, addressing large crowds in towns and villages, and even those who could not hear his speeches first hand would be inspired in the retelling. The Congress went on to achieve a clear majority in the Assembly and proceeded to form a ministry of its own in U.P.

In Bombay, Gujarat remained a Congress bastion and much of that strength was attributed to another emerging leader, Vallabhbhai Patel. He did not quite have the film star quality that Jawaharlal Nehru had in U.P., but his last minute visits to electorates and his ability to galvanise local Congress propaganda machines saved the day for many a Congress candidate. And unlike the situation in U.P., the larger landholders of Gujarat were actually supporters of the Congress and rallied to their flag at election time. The Congress swept the polls in Gujarat, but the scene in the south of the old Bombay province, in modern day Maharashtra was quite different. There the larger landholders had turned against the Party after its earlier commitment to abolish the khoti system of land tenure. The Congress did reasonably in Poona and Bombay, and although it did not gain a clear majority in the Assembly it emerged as the single largest party and was able to assume power with the support of

Independents.

Rajendra Prasad had been elected President of the Bihar Provincial Congress Committee in 1936, and although candidate selection was subject to final approval by the Central Parliamentary Board, which he also sat on, most nominations were unanimous and even when he had reservations he would bow to the majority opinion. Prasad lamented however, that "It is a matter of shame that in Bihar the P.C.C. had to take caste labels into account in certain constituencies because the success of candidates there depended on such considerations."[cccliv] The campaign in Bihar shared similar themes to neighbouring U.P., with an emphasis on getting as many voters to the polling booth as possible and drawing on the help of local men of influence. Aeroplanes were even chartered on election days, with Congress workers dropping leaflets urging a vote for the local Congress candidates. Wealthier candidates hired their own cars to take their voters to the polling booths. Congress campaigners also stirred up feeling against the landlords, and reminded the voters of the pain of the agricultural slump of the early 1930s and of their part in anti-landlord campaigns of the recent past. Extravagant promises were made and the rural voter was told to come to their local Congress candidate who would hear their grievances rather than the local landlord. The Congress went on to win two-thirds of the seats in the Bihar Assembly.

In the Central Provinces and Berar it was the President of the Provincial Congress Committee Ravi Shukla who went out into the villages to garner support from the newly enfranchised peasantry. He formed gram sabhas and krishak sabhas to put pressure on the administration to reduce the revenue demand and galvanise support on the land. He also tried to reach out to another new group of voters, the Harijans, who had 20 reserved seats in the Assembly. Shukla's great rival within the provincial Party was Dwarka Mishra, who also went out to gather support for the Congress from both landowners and peasants. He organised kisan sabhas to demand the grant of farm loans from the government, and like Shukla's gram sabhas he formed malguzar sabhas to have the revenue demand lowered.

The most fierce political tussle in the Central Provinces and Berar turned out to be between the Congress and the Hindu Mahasabha. Tempers boiled over on occasion and one of Balakrishna Moonje's meetings in Kamptee was disrupted when some Congress toughs in the audience started to misbehave. In Bilaspur, Raghuvendra Rao had to be given over to police protection when some Congress volunteers allegedly tried to assault him. But when election time came, the Congress swept to a two thirds majority in the Assembly on an appeal to a higher power. In the rural areas local Congress activists would send out word that Gandhi wanted their vote. Villagers would then stream into the polling booths, place their votes in the green Congress box, and bow in front of it before returning to their villages.

***

When provincial Congress units could not resolve their leadership disputes amongst themselves the High Command, which in many instances amounted to one man, Vallabhbhai Patel, would be called in to broker a settlement between rival factions and then enforce the writ of the Party leadership. This need for the enforcement of party discipline was inevitable in such a large national party operating in a federal structure, and some of the techniques of conflict resolution used in 1937 would become staples of state politics as the Congress settled down to governance in the decades after 1947.

Kanaiyalal Munshi had been a strong contender for the

leadership of the Bombay Congress but he, like Vallabhbhai Patel was a Gujarati, and so his elevation may have seemed like favouritism on Patel's part, something which would have generated opposition from the Maharashtiran bloc of legislators. When Patel asked for Munshi's opinion, he recommended Balasaheb Kher for the leadership. Khurshed Nariman was the President of the Bombay Provincial Congress Committee and had a natural claim to the prime minister's post when the Congress formed a ministry. Yet Patel was wary of Nariman for his ability to garner the support of most factions within the local Party and his good relationship with British officialdom, the combination of which might have loosened the grip of the High Command in New Delhi. As if to confirm Patel's fears, the Maharashtrian bloc had defied the High Command by passing resolutions both in favour of accepting ministerial offices, and electing Nariman as the Party leader. Nariman only realised what was happening however a few hours before Vallabhbhai Patel convened a conference to decide on the leadership issue. At Patel's conference on 12 March 1938, he formed a 'subcommittee' consisting of himself and Gangadharrao Deshpande. Patel would speak for Gujarat and Bombay City and Deshpande spoke for Maharashtra and Karnataka.[cccv] After two hours of discussions, Patel emerged to announce their agreement of Balasaheb Kher as leader of the legislative Party and presumptive Prime Minister of Bombay. The motion was then carried by acclamation.

The Central Provinces and Berar encompassed a large section of central India which included both Hindi and Marathi speaking districts. The Hindi speaking region had elected a larger number of Congress legislators than the Marathi speaking region and so it seemed natural that the leader should come from the Hindi region. However, the strongest contender, Ravi Shukla was pulled down by his rival Dwarka Mishra, and so Narayan Khare from the Marathi speaking region was elected as a compromise candidate. Khare selected his own Cabinet which was evenly split with three Marathi ministers and three Hindi ministers, whilst he kept the important Home portfolio for himself.

The Governor, Sir Francis Wylie was the President of the Cabinet and he would often meet with ministers informally to try to gather consensus before Cabinet meetings. Cabinet seemed to become a rubber stamp for the governor and Shukla, who held the Education portfolio, and Mishra, who held Local Self-Government objected to Khare's style of functioning; they wanted Cabinet to provide a united front before the governor. Khare agreed in principle, but sensed that the two Hindi ministers might try to unseat him and so started inquiries through the Home Department against them and began to invite Congress legislators to his home to gather support. Khare became even more suspicious when Shukla and Mishra went to meet Vallabhbhai Patel in Bombay and returned demanding that he give up his Home portfolio to a Hindi minister. Khare refused and Mishra and two of his colleagues resigned.

Khare did not forward the resignations to the governor, and the rebel ministers placed the matter before Patel in Bombay, who placed the matter before the Congress Working Committee which called a meeting of the Congress Assembly Party in Pachmarhi. Hindi and Marathi ministers remained divided on the issue of Khare's Home portfolio and he refused to give it up. Forty four Congress legislators put forward two options; either the existing Cabinet continue, or all Cabinet ministers resign in favour of a new set of ministers. The first option was chosen and the Cabinet continued.

The Congress Working Committee then met in Bombay and Khare forwarded the resignations of the three ministers to the committee. The Working Committee then called a meeting of the Congress Legislative Party and sent Vallabhbhai Patel, Abul Kalam Azad and Jamnalal Bajaj who facilitated an agreement whereby Khare would give up his Home portfolio, the ministers would withdraw their resignations, a Cabinet reshuffle would take place, and both sides would call off their media war. In the event of a disagreement over the new Cabinet, the presidents of the three sub regions would be mediators and Khare would withdraw his Home Department inquiries against his Cabinet colleagues. Another condition stipulated that Khare's son would have to resign from his post of Honorary Surgeon at Mayo Hospital and Shukla's son would also have to resign his recently obtained position of Lecturer at the Law College. Shukla's son complied and resigned, however Khare's son not only did not resign, but applied for another term. The application was rejected by Mishra who was in charge of Public Health.

The agreement remained fragile however. The Hindi ministers claimed that Khare was continuing his investigations against them, whilst Khare thought that the Hindi ministers continued to conspire against him. In addition, there was no agreement on who should get the prized Home portfolio. Khare then gave his own resignation and that of his Marathi ministers to the governor without informing the Congress Working Committee. Sir Francis then asked the Hindi ministers to resign but they refused to do so unless instructed by the Congress Working Committee. He used his Special Powers for the first time and accepted the resignations of the Marathi ministers and dismissed the Hindi ministers. Sir Francis invited Khare to form a new ministry, which he did without consulting the Congress Working Committee. Khare was then summoned by the Congress High Command. Congress President Subhas Chandra Bose advised him to resign from the premiership of the ministry and as Leader of the Central Provinces and Berar Congress Party. He agreed to resign but asked that he be allowed to re-contest, something which the Congress

Working Committee would not agree to. Bose even chaired a meeting of the Central Provinces and Berar Parliamentary Committee with Patel in attendance. Shukla was elected and he eventually formed his own Cabinet in which he took the Home portfolio and combined other portfolios to have a smaller Cabinet, with two other Hindi ministers and two Marathi ministers.

***

When the Congress formed its ministries and began the work of putting its anti-landlord, pro-peasant campaign agenda into practice, it had to do so through the legislative and administrative structures which it had taken responsibility for. The new Premier of the United Provinces, Govind Pant announced his ministry's intention to reform the tenancy laws in August 1937 and quickly established the Tenancy and Land Revenue Committee. The committee had a majority of Congressmen but also included representatives from the landed interests, the National Agriculturalists, the Muslim League and Independents. The deliberations of the committee stretched from November 1937 to April 1938. In April 1938 a draft bill was placed before the Legislative Assembly, however there were still some contentious aspects of the bill which the Tenancy and Land Revenue Committee could not agree on which prompted the revenue minister to send the bill to a Select Committee.

The Select Committee then took five months over the bill before presenting a new version to the Assembly in October 1938. The landlords of U.P. had felt that they had been marginalised in the Select Committee's deliberations and so decided to appeal to both the Governor, Sir Maurice Hallett and the Congress Parliamentary Subcommittee. The governor refused to intervene in the matter, however the Congress Parliamentary Subcommittee was willing to hear the landlords' grievances. Yet when the time came they could not decide amongst themselves on exactly what those grievances were.

The bill then began to make its way through the Legislative Assembly in November 1938 and continued to be debated on the floor until April 1939 when, after three readings it was finally passed. However, the bill still had to make its way through the upper house, or Legislative Council in which landlord interests were well represented. During June and July 1939 Pant conducted hectic negotiations with the landlords of the Council to ensure passage of the bill but eventually had to concede to their demand for another Select Committee. The Legislative Council's Select Committee examined the bill and the Council then passed it in August 1938. The bill still awaited the governor's signature in November 1939, but eventually became law in the form of Act 17 1939.

The result of this legislative effort was an Act which harmonised the differences in tenancy laws between Agra and Oudh, granted hereditary rights to statutory tenants, made their ejectment less arbitrary, reduced the amount of sir lands owned by the zamindars (which in itself provided more land for tenants to claim hereditary rights), made landlord demands on tenants other than rent illegal, and made the procedure for payment of rent easier for tenants. Landlord involvement in the law making process was not without its results though; smaller landholders were exempt from the new law on sir lands.

***

Friction between the Congress ministers and the services began within the first weeks of the Congress Ministry in Bombay. Ministers took exception to their departmental secretaries exercising their routine functions, and did not see why they could not issue orders directly, rather than having to work through the bureaucracy. Ministers even objected to secretaries writing minutes in files, which prompted the Governor, Roger Lumley, the Earl of Scarborough to intervene and explain that these were the normal duties of civil servants in government offices.[cccvi]

The Revenue Minister, Morarji Desai developed a reputation for bypassing his secretary, giving direct orders, and interfering in the postings of deputy collectors. In some cases he would cut the collector out of the grievance redressal process and go straight to the commissioner. In others he would go straight to the collector without referring the matter to his secretary. In one instance he called directly on his collector for a report on a Public Works Department matter when the government had already officially called for such a report. On another occasion a deputy collector had passed an order which had been appealed and it would normally make its way up the hierarchy to the collector, commissioner and then Revenue Tribunal but Desai, who had no standing in the matter, acted on a letter from an MLA and asked the collector directly for a report. He was pulled up by his Prime Minister Balasaheb Kher on the matter and claimed that they were partly done "through oversight", and that he had subsequently instructed his personal assistant that all papers endorsed by him should be sent through the secretary of the department.[cccvii] Desai did however insist that there was no harm in the minister requesting a report on the facts of a case even though it may be pending before a tribunal. Later, with more and more citizens emboldened to take their grievances directly to the minister, the director of information had to issue a press note in which it was stated- "The Public should realise that the Congress Ministry has not replaced the ordinary administrative machinery through which it must function to remedy grievances or attend to requests from the public."[cccviii]

Congress activists in the districts wanted to continue their adversarial relationship with the police and kept making speeches against the administration. Kher was asked to reign them in and the Inspector General of Police, George Shillidy told his force to ignore Congress triumphalism during its first days in power.cccix Morarji Desai became involved once again. The issue of a police Patel in Surat who had been a strong supporter of the British administration during the days of the civil disobedience movement came to light. He had subsequently been accused of corruption, but local officials had found the allegations to be untrue. Desai thought that whilst the allegations may not stand up in court, he was sure that the Patel was corrupt and so he should be dismissed. The governor was forced to speak to the prime minister to try to prevent any victimisation of the police. Subsequently the government decided that a police Patel was not in service of the Crown and so it did not have standing under the Government of India Act 1935 to act, but the legal remembrancer disagreed and thought Patels were civil servants. Kher agreed to look into the matter. Whilst police were concerned about victimisation from the Congress, Congress workers saw the police as village tyrants and wanted their powers curbed. They even put forward a proposal that police Patels be elected. The proposal was opposed by the administration with elaborate arguments about the executive nature of the police Patel's role. Morarji Desai was unconvinced by the bureaucracy's arguments and the matter dragged on until the end of the Congress Ministry when it was put to rest with a note from Kher- "This can now wait."cccx

Matters took an ironic turn however, when the unions launched a strike to protest against the Industrial Disputes Bill of 1938 and the Congress Ministry had to rely on the Bombay Police to enforce law and order. The unions had objected to the compulsory submission of industrial disputes to arbitration, something which would impinge on their right to strike. A strike had been called and the government had made thorough preparations, giving police protection to mills, workshops and factories, and placed reserved forces of armed police on standby. On 7 November 1938 at the Elphinstone Mills strikers tried to take workers out of the mill by force and were only pushed back by mill staff using fire hoses.[cccxi] Police came to the scene and stone pelting ensued. A sub inspector and some constables were hit and the police then opened 16 rounds of fire. Two workers were hit in police firing and 17 more were hit in the stone pelting. At the Spring Mills at Naigaum workers were also hit by stone pelting strikers as they came out from work in the evening. Police chased the stone pelters, who had gone to the rear of the mill to continue their attack, and another order for firing was given in which 28 rounds were released. Twelve police officers were injured and one mill worker died. In total there were 72 injured during the day's violence in addition to the 1 death.

Criticism poured in for the Congress Ministry's tough handling of the dispute, but it did not worry Vallabhbhai Patel. He pointed out that the strikers had openly stated that their success would depend on their ability to provoke the police into firing at them, which meant that they had no reason to complain. When the government submitted its response to a specially convened Disturbances Enquiry Committee it did so on Home Minister Kanaiyalal Munshi's instructions.[cccxii] It made the case that the unions were being used by the Communists as part of a broader conspiracy to destabilise an inexperienced Congress Ministry in order to capture political power in the province for themselves.

***

The Gandhian influence on the Congress Ministries was most

felt in attempts to impose prohibition on the sale and consumption of alcohol. It was an issue dear to Gandhi and one which also received the support of many Congress leaders in the provinces; with the presentation of the first budget of the Congress Ministry in Bombay the Finance Minister, Anna Latthe made it clear that drinking was an "evil" and the Congress was "irrevocably committed to a policy of prohibition".[cccxiii] Propaganda was distributed throughout the province in cinema halls and in the villages through magic lantern slides, leaflets, and posters, and Congress committees were formed to prevent illicit distillation and smuggling of liquor. There were plans to more stringently enforce prohibition in mill areas and make sure that liquor shops were shut on mill pay days. Meetings of panchayats even passed resolutions welcoming prohibition. Mill owners also lent their support, with notices placed in the mills stating that those who did not comply with prohibition would not be recruited and anyone caught bringing liquor into the compound would be severely punished. Kanaiyalal Munshi even offered to have the police enforce the law rather than excise officers.

The problems started when the government devised a way to make up the revenue shortfall from the loss of the liquor excise. The Kher government proposed a 10% property tax, thinking that it would target the rich residents on Malabar Hill. But there were fewer of them than expected. The tax hit small property owners particularly hard, and so after some representations they came to be taxed at a reduced rate of 5%. What surprised the government was the opposition from the Muslim community. It thought that a law enforcing prohibition would be in complete accordance with the tenets of Islam. However, the Muslims of Bombay city made the case that as Islam prohibited investments in interest charging financial instruments they had put their money into property and so were disproportionately affected by the property tax.

Opposition from the Parsi community was expected however, given that the Parsis were large property holders who also controlled large segments of the alcohol industry in the province. They decided to form an Anti-Prohibition Committee and took on the services of a British barrister to explore a possible legal challenge to the property tax. Sir Byramjee Jeejeebhoy even planned to throw a cocktail party the day after prohibition was to be imposed. He took another route though, and started his own suit in the Bombay High Court contesting the legal basis of the property tax. Muslims took to the streets however, and the police responded to stone throwing with firing but there were no fatalities in this instance. Prohibition was enforced but came under increasing legal challenge after the end of the Congress Ministry. The Bombay High Court even ruled large sections of the Prohibition Rules ultra vires, necessitating a Governor's Act to keep the prohibition regime going during World War II.

***

The Congress Ministries also began to honour Gandhi's commitment to overhauling Indian education. The Bihar Ministry was amongst the most active in reforming and expanding education, and it quickly appointed an Education Reorganisation Committee under the chairmanship of Professor Khushal Shah. The committee submitted its report and among its most important recommendations was the implementation of free and compulsory primary education within municipal areas for boys. The municipalities of Bihar were not in a position to finance the implementation of such a recommendation, and so the expenditure was taken up by the Government of Bihar. Another committee was formed to look into the promotion of Hindustani in the educational system. The Hindusthani Committee was chaired by Rajendra Prasad, and its members included Sachchidananda Sinha, Abul Kalam Azad and Tara Chand. The committee members argued that only the mother tongue should be taught at the primary stage, but that English should be the medium of instruction in secondary schools, and the Government of Bihar accepted their recommendations. Furthermore, Gandhi's Wardha scheme of education was implemented on an experimental basis in selected districts throughout Bihar. The idea behind the scheme was that education should become less theoretical and more practical. Students would be trained in the production of handicrafts, which would be sold, and the proceeds would continue to fund the new education system.

It was the mass literacy drives which took place during the Bihar Congress Ministry however which received nationwide attention. The Minister for Education, Syed Mahmud launched a campaign to eradicate adult illiteracy in April 1938. Teachers and students were asked to spend their vacation wiping out illiteracy across the province. Many came forward to answer the call and spent the summer establishing literacy centres and night schools across Bihar. By the end of the summer of 1938 the government claimed that 300,000 adults had been educated to literacy over the previous four months.[cccxiv] At this stage the campaign had been run by volunteers and had not yet received any financial assistance from the government. The campaign entered its second phase in November 1938 when the government began to get more involved and formed a Provincial Mass Literacy Committee and allocated ₹80,000 for the cause. The committee then recruited and trained thousands of workers, printed primers and charts and opened literacy centres across Bihar. The workers were still volunteers drawn from teachers and students and inspectors of the Education Department, but the drive had been scaled up and more than 12,000 literacy centres were opened, reaching approximately 150,000 students for each six week course of instruction.[cccxv] The literacy drive branched out to focus on women, the police constabulary, village chaukidars, industrial workers, and the second phase brought close to 500,000 adults to literacy.[cccxvi] The programme even caught the attention of world authorities in the field of adult education. Frank Laubach, a missionary involved in efforts to raise literacy around the world wrote: "The significance of the Bihar campaign is hardly to be exaggerated. If it turns out to be a signal success as it promises to do, all India will be encouraged."[cccxvii]

According to the 1931 Census female literacy in Bihar stood at 2.5%. Rather than attacking the problem by focussing on adult female literacy in the districts, the Government of Bihar decided to establish primary schools for girls in every thana headquarters, a girls middle school in each sub-divisional headquarters, and a girls high school in each district headquarters. Female primary school teachers were also trained in centres in Muzzafarpur and Gaya. Girls were exempted from fees in primary school, and those studying in middle English schools had to pay a reduced fee. Government scholarships and stipends assisted girls in studying up to the graduate level. Similarly, the number of Harijan students also began to rise at all levels of the education system with the award of scholarships and the exemption of fees. In addition, free boarding and lodging was provided to Harijan and Tribal students in Monghyr, Ranchi and Muzzaffarpur, private hostels were supported by the award of government grants, and throughout the ministry the Government of Bihar worked closely with the Harijan Sevak Sangha in the disbursement of scholarships to deserving students.

***

The Congress Ministries of 1937 bore all the hallmarks of the type of governance which the Congress would provide in the years after 1947. There were issues of state leadership which would have to be sorted out by the High Command in New Delhi, there were some frustrated efforts to impose the Congress way of doing things on the bureaucracy, there were attempts at prohibition, and some success in education. The Congress Ministries maintained a strained relationship with the labour movement; it needed the electoral support which the working class could provide but it was, in the end, the government and had to maintain law and order when strikes threatened to spiral out of control. The Congress also made an early start in implementing land reform in key provinces such as U.P. In rural India it could afford to align itself more openly with the peasants and project the landlords as an exploitative class which would be tamed under a Congress government. Yet the Congress attempts at land reform in the United Provinces worked through the established institutions of the state, particularly the provincial legislature with its intricate rules for the drafting and passage of legislation, the frequent resort to committees, the need to appease the landlords whom the Congress had little electoral use for, and the requirement of support in both the upper and lower houses of the legislature before a bill could receive the governor's signature and become the law of the province.

The Congress came into the state structure in 1937 and began to implement its agenda for governance after the alternatives advocated by both Mohandas Gandhi and Subhas Chandra Bose were unable to garner the allegiance of the majority of Congressmen. The anti-statist ideology inherent in Gandhi's constructive programme never found a following amongst Congress elites, Congress workers, or even the villagers of India. He had spent the best years of his political life during the 1920s and 1930s tirelessly repeating his message for the implementation of his constructive programme. But it was hard work, and also rejected as anti-modern, social rather than political work, and generally treated dismissively by the decision makers within the Party. It was also quite a challenging idea; rather than asking Congressmen to either work with or against the Indian state, Gandhi was asking them to think of it as largely irrelevant to a more profound renewal of India. If his ideal of swaraj was attained the state, and even government, would hardly be required. Yet by the 1930s Gandhi's initially enthusiastic followers had tired of constructive work and even civil disobedience and quickly switched to the formation of a parliamentary party, to which he had to reluctantly give his blessings.

If Gandhi's anti-statism had few takers within the Congress, Party members never really embraced Subhas Chandra Bose's hyper-statist vision either. Whilst Gandhi's constructive programme could be worked on in the villages of India by anyone who was willing, Bose's ideal of a mega-state could only remain a vision of the future. Although Bose had a clear idea of a new Indian state which would be a synthesis bringing together the best features of the communist and fascist states of Europe, his ideal would have to wait for Independence, it was not something which Congressmen could engage with or contribute to in the present. Despite Bose's youth and dynamism and his natural affinity with the rising Left Wing of the Party, when the time came he could not rely on their support for his plans to take the Congress in a new direction. Even the young Socialists of the Congress, despite their dismissal of Gandhi's political and economic ideology decided to keep faith with his leadership of the Party; they knew that he alone remained the best man to maintain Congress unity, engage with the largest section of Indian society, and guide the country to Independence. Whilst Bose could not win the political allegiance of the Congress Left, his ideology was met with scepticism on the Right. The 'Mid-Victorian' democracy which he poked fun at when he floated the idea of a new party had actually been a cherished ideal amongst most Congressmen since the inception of the Party in 1885. Even by the 1930s most of the senior men within the Congress units across the country were lawyers reared in British law and political philosophy, natural liberals and democrats, and keen guardians of individual civil liberties.

The Congress was ultimately an immovable bloc of lawyers, and it stayed true to the political philosophy of Edmund Burke which had influenced its outlook from the start. They had all along been excited by Gandhi's novel means of political agitation, but never accepted his ends of a spiritual and material swaraj. They translated swaraj into English quite literally as 'self-government', something which would result in Indians taking over the services and legislatures, governors' mansions and eventually the viceroy's residence. They had control of the provincial units of the Party and could exercise their votes on major motions and resolutions, shaping and deciding Party policies and tactics at its annual sessions. They were a much larger and more enduring force than the Congress Socialists who only came to organise themselves and attempt to influence Party policy in the mid 1930s. When the Congress had to decide on whether to co-operate with a new round of constitutional reforms in 1935 and 1936 it was not the arguments of Mohandas Gandhi, or Jawaharlal Nehru or Subhas Chandra Bose which won the day. It was Kanaiyalal Munshi, one of the stalwarts of the Bombay Bar who suggested that the Congress contest elections, form ministries and start the 'slow overhaul' of the government machinery. He was, in many ways, the enduring Congressman, speaking for the wishes of the majority within the Party throughout the country.

Nine
A Little Parliament

The councils, which became such contentious arenas in Indian politics during the 1920s, dividing nationalist politicians over the varying degrees of co-operation they should offer, had a history dating back almost a century to the days of Company rule. A Governor General's Council was established under the Charter Act of 1833, and another Charter Act was passed in 1853 which gave the Council a more fully legislative character increasingly distinct from the executive government. Like most of the elite institutions of the state at the time, the Governor General's Council was an exclusively British institution, and when, during the 1850s the Council began to take on the character of a local Indian Parliament, a dispute arose at the highest levels of government over the ideal function of the institution.

Sir Charles Wood, the President of the Board of Control did not want the Council to do anything other than pass laws, but the Governor General James Broun-Ramsay, the Marquess of Dalhousie thought it natural that "an independent body of ten or twelve British gentlemen" would "assert their legislative independence".[cccxviii] One of those British gentlemen, Sir Barnes Peacock, the Chief Justice of the Supreme Court and later Chief Justice of the Calcutta High Court sat on the Council as an ex-officio member and became a crusader against the government, embarrassing it in full public view by raising issues which were thought to be beyond the Council's jurisdiction. Roles seemed to be blurred, with a member of the judiciary using his seat in the legislature, to go to war with the executive. The issue even came to the attention of Parliament in 1861 as Henry Grey, the Earl Grey told the House of Commons: "That a judge should be the leader of the opposition is intolerable."cccxix

The concerns raised in London over the crusading judge, and the events of 1857 led to another reform of the councils. The Crown had taken over from the Company and it decided to clip the Council's wings, make it something closer to a committee rather than a budding parliament, and also bring Indians onto India's highest law making body for the first time. The decision to appoint Indian members to the Council was made not to provide representation to the Indian people, but to provide the British rulers with some sense of Indian opinion, something which they might otherwise be quite deaf to. It was thought that this ignorance of Indian feelings and aspirations may have brought on the Mutiny, and greater Indian participation in the Council would prevent such events from happening again. It was a durbar approach, and during the late 19th century, when most of the Indian appointees were princes and landlords, the councils could easily pass for historical durbars at which local Indian rulers would come to pay their respects to the central ruler, make a show of supporting his decisions and decrees, and then return to rule over their distant little kingdoms. Yet the councils were not durbars, they were not feudal institutions, but modern ones and it was only in the 1890s when a new generation of Indian lawyers took the place of princes and landlords in reformed and expanded councils that their true character started to become evident.

Before co-operation or non-cooperation had become an issue in Congress politics and the Party was still resolutely moderate, its leaders would enter the councils, try to make their voices heard, influence legislation and have to be content with moral victories and small concessions. It was only with the Montagu-Chelmsford reforms that the scope of the councils changed significantly. For the first time a system of direct elections was created; the franchise was expanded to include the middle class, and those elected represented territorial constituencies rather than 'groups and interests'. Despite a slow start in 1920, the elections of 1923 and 1926 were spirited contests in which middle class lawyers, both within and outside the Congress, took their rival visions of political progress to middle class constituencies and sought a mandate to sit in the Indian Legislative Assembly in Delhi. Election fever would fade in 1930 with the onset of civil disobedience, but return in 1934 as the Congress sought to project its strength at the polls. Throughout the period elections reflected the pressing issues and changing divisions and alignments within the mainstream of Indian politics. In 1923 voters were asked to choose between a gradual journey towards Dominion status and immediate self-government. In 1945 they were asked to choose between a united India or the partition of the country.

The Indian Legislative Assembly in Delhi did not feature a system of dyarchy like the legislatures in the provinces. There were no Indian ministers at the Centre, and so the Assembly largely remained a debating chamber in which the elected majority of members had little responsibility for the workings of the government, but came to master the rules and regulations of the house to articulate the nationalist cause. The proceedings of the Assembly would retain a sense of a theatre rather than a legislature, as no matter what procedural tricks and techniques the Indian members used to advance their position, the viceroy would always be able to 'certify' legislation and essentially have laws passed by decree. Indian members would thus have to remain content to play the part of legislators, immersing themselves in the details of legislative procedure, knowing that when the debates ended, the government would always have its way.

***

Under the Act of 1853 the Legislative Council had six members, all of whom were British. Given that the Legislative Council did not have an Indian member, Council members and the British establishment could only learn of Indian opinion indirectly. In 1860 Sir Henry Frere, Member of the Viceroy's Executive Council pointed to the "futility of trying to govern India with the aid of the official opinion alone".[cccxx] He thought it was necessary to bring Indians into the Legislative Council as "unless you have some barometer and safety valve combined in the shape of a deliberative council I believe you will always be liable to very unlooked for and dangerous explosions".[cccxxi] Sir Henry felt that no one could be opposed to the move "unless he is prepared for the perilous experiment of continuing to legislate for millions of people, with few means of knowing, except by rebellion, whether the laws suit them or not."[cccxxii]

Whilst a new Act for reform of the Council was making its way through Parliament in 1861, Sir Charles Wood assured the House of Commons that the purpose of the Act was to prevent the Council from becoming a "debating society".[cccxxiii] The House of Lords was also assured that the bill would "prevent its assuming again the functions of a little Parliament."[cccxxiv] This stated aim of not allowing the Council to become a 'little Parliament' did seem to be fulfilled given how restricted the powers of the new Council were; the Council could not frame its own rules, questions could not be asked, it could not look into any subject apart from the immediate legislation before it, the budget could not be discussed, resolutions could not be moved, grievances could not be enquired into, information could not be requested and the conduct of the government could not be examined. However, the 1861 Indian Councils Act did give the viceroy the power to appoint between six and twelve additional members to the Legislative Council for two year terms, at least half of whom were to come from outside the government.

Annual financial statements were tabled but discussion was not allowed except in the case of the imposition of a new tax, and most bills were passed by the Council in a single sitting with minimal discussion. The viceroy would preside over the Council proceedings and held veto power and the ability to promulgate ordinances for six months.

In 1862 the Viceroy Charles Canning, the Earl of Canning appointed three Indian princes- Raja Sir Dinkar Rao Raghunath of Gwalior, Raja Deo Narain Singh of Benares, and Maharaja Sir Narendra Singh of Patiala to the new Legislative Council. The practice of appointing Indian rajas and nawabs along with Indian landlords would continue for the next 30 years; of the 45 Indians appointed during this period 7 were Indian princes or chiefs and 25 were large landholders. Indian princes and landlords did not prove to be the window into Indian opinion that the British authorities had hoped for however. In 1868 Sir Henry Maine wrote that the early Indian appointees showed "the utmost reluctance to come and the utmost hurry to depart".[cccxxv] Furthermore, Indian princes, merchants and landlords did not form a bloc which represented broader Indian interests as might have been expected, and even supported the hated salt tax. When in 1878 the Vernacular Press Bill roused Indian opposition outside the Council and was being condemned as a "Black Act" by Indian journalists, Indian members on the floor of the Council failed to put up any opposition to the measure. Viceroy Lytton had introduced the bill in order to combat what he saw as growing sedition and calls to rebellion in the Indian language press. The Indian member of the Council present for the discussion on the bill, Maharaja Sir Jatindramohan Tagore stated that whilst he supported freedom of the press, he had to express his regret at some of the writings of the lower class of Indian newspapers which had forced the government to take the drastic measures featured in the bill. He would support the bill however, as he did not think that it would affect the higher class of Indian papers.

During the 1870s and 1880s the Indian members of the Council showed little interest in proceedings and when they did speak they read from prepared manuscripts. Despite the general lack of engagement, the interest of Indian landowners and princes would be stirred when bills relating to taxation, inheritance and property were brought before the Council. The early Congress leader Womesh Bonnerjee related an anecdote to an audience in Croydon on 14 October 1888 in which he lamented the fact that the proceedings of the Council were in English and many of the Indian zamindars and rajas were not familiar with the language and could not participate actively in the debates. When one such Council member was asked how he decided to vote he replied: "When the Viceroy lifts up his hand one way I know he wants me to say yes and when he lifts up his hand in a different way I know he wants me to say No and I say No."[cccxxvi]

***

Soon after its formation in 1885 the Congress began to urge an expansion of the Legislative Council. Viceroy Dufferin had sensed the need to accommodate the Congress and in keeping with his 'loaves and fishes' policy he made several recommendations for expanding the Legislative Council, some of which made their way into the Indian Councils Act of 1892. The provincial Legislative Councils were expanded and the Central Council was also enlarged to have between 10 and 16 additional members. Not more than ten members were to be from outside the government so that it could maintain its majority. Four members were to be sent up by the non-government members in the provincial councils and the fifth was to be nominated by the Calcutta Chamber of Commerce. Five more were to be nominated by the viceroy on the recommendation of university senates, municipalities and other chambers of commerce. By 1892 the principle of election had made its way in, albeit indirectly. Dufferin made the standard reassurance to the British political establishment that the small reforms were not intended to create a parliament in India; "There should be no mistake about our aims; the Act was not to be regarded as an approach to English Parliamentary Government."cccxxvii

It was in 1892 that Legislative Council members also won the right to ask questions. The first question was asked the following year by Raja Uday Pratap Singh, the Maharaja of Bhinga on 16 February 1893. His question concerned the hardships caused by the system of collecting supplies for the convenience of government officers whilst they were on tour in the districts. Legislative Council members could not ask supplementary questions, but there was no restriction on the topics which they could cover in their original questions. Yet as late as 1905 and 1906 this right was not fully used; only 13 questions were asked during these years. Some Indian members raised questions on political issues, particularly the Partition of Bengal, whilst most concerned themselves with the railways, telegraphs, taxes and exchange rates. In some cases questions were not answered simply because collating the required information would be too much of a burden for the bureaucracy.

The Indian Councils Act of 1892 also allowed discussion of the budget for the first time. A financial statement was placed before the Council each year and members were able to offer their suggestions. The finance member would reply to any points raised and the viceroy would then close the debate with his remarks. However, the budget was to be discussed as a whole rather than item by item and was still not open to a vote. In addition, Legislative Council members could still not submit or propose a resolution or initiate a division on financial matters. Between 1892 and 1909 non-government members would rarely move amendments to bills and divisions were seldom initiated. Even when Indian members were united in their opposition, the government would push bills through the Council using its permanent majority.

The Act of 1892 also opened the way for a new type of Indian public figure to enter the councils. The maharajas and nawabs and zamindars gradually came to be overshadowed by Indian lawyers. The lawyers took greater interest in proceedings; their legal training meant that they were able to follow them much more closely, give longer and more informed speeches, engage in English debate and hold forth on issues of public policy. Rash Bihari Ghose and Gopal Krishna Gokhale emerged as two of the leading lights of the newly expanded councils. Ghose took great interest in bills relating to the budget, tariffs, education, civil and criminal law, and sedition. He spoke on the Indian Tariff Amendment Bill of 1894, pointing out that duty had not been placed on British cotton products simply to please Lancashire and Manchester. A decade later he opposed the Prevention of Seditious Meetings Bill which had been brought before the Council in the wake of the protests against the Partition of Bengal. He argued that there was no urgent need for the bill, and if there was then it was a sad commentary on the nature of the British administration. Gokhale was an authority on economic policy and would come to be known in the Indian press as the 'Leader of the Opposition'. He used economic data to demonstrate India's 'deep and deepening' poverty which had been caused by huge defence expenditures, excise duties on Indian textiles, heavy taxes and a lack of irrigation. At a discussion on the budget on 25 March 1903 he held that Indian finances were "virtually at the mercy of military considerations". He wanted to reduce and eventually abolish the excise on Indian cotton goods, lower the land revenue, provide free primary education, and make factory owners responsible for the education of their workers' children. In December 1903 Gokhale opposed the Official Secrets (Amendment) Bill. He understood that the Indian press was the only effective check on the conduct of the government and criticised it for its confidential circulars with which it sought to evade the political concessions provided by the British Parliament and the liberal commitments of the Queen's Proclamation. Gokhale came to lead the new generation of lawyers in Indian politics who could bring their rhetorical skills to the floor of the Legislative Council and work through its procedures to make small alterations to legislation and win moral victories during debates and discussions.

***

Gilbert Elliot-Murray-Kynynmound, the Earl of Minto became viceroy in November 1905 and had to take some action to address the growing Indian political discontent which resulted from Curzon's decision to partition Bengal earlier that year. He, like Dufferin almost 20 years earlier wanted to keep the moderates in the Congress on the side of the British administration. He realised that another round of constitutional concessions would be necessary and that there was a need to increase Indian participation in the administration. The viceroy recognised that "politically India is in a transitional state, that new and just aspirations are springing up amongst its people, which the ruling power must be prepared not only to meet but assist."[cccxxviii] Minto appointed the Arundal Committee to look into increasing Indian participation in the councils. John Morley, the Viscount of Blackburn had been in correspondence with Gokhale, and whilst Gokhale wanted to see India develop into a self-governing dominion within the British Empire, Morley maintained that India would remain the "theatre of absolute and personal government".[cccxxix] Viceroy Minto and the Secretary of State Morley created a scheme for constitutional reform which then lay dormant for the next three years. A new Indian Councils Act was passed however in November 1909 and the new constitutional concessions came to be known as the Minto-Morley reforms. At the inauguration of the new Council the viceroy made it clear once again that "We have aimed at the reform and enlargement of our Councils, but not at the creation of Parliament."[cccxxx] For Morley, the adoption of English political institutions in India was inconceivable, but "the spirit of English institutions" would have to be introduced as the bureaucracy and executive could not remain autocratic for ever.[cccxxxi] Speaking to the House of Lords on December 17 1908 Morley said: "If I were attempting to set up a Parliamentary system in India, or if it could be said that this chapter of reforms led directly or necessarily up to the establishment of a parliamentary system in India I, for one, would have nothing at all to do with it."

The number of members of the Council was raised from 16 to 60. Seven ex-officio members took the total strength of the Council to 67 members, of whom 27 were elected. Members were still to be elected by classes and communities and 'interests' rather than territorial constituencies however. Five were elected by Muslims, six by landlords, one by Muslim landlords, one by the Bengal Chamber of Commerce, and the remainder would be sent up by the non-government members of the provincial councils. The largest such 'constituency' which a Legislative Council member could represent was thus made up of 650 people.

The Indian Councils Act of 1909 gave Council members the right to move resolutions on any matter of public interest and prompt a division in the Council. The resolutions were to take the form of recommendations to the government, which the government was under no obligation to accept. Foreign policy was still beyond the scope of the resolutions and the viceroy could disallow a resolution on the grounds that it was inconsistent with the public interest and held veto power over any of the Council's decisions. The first resolution under the new rules was passed by Gopal Krishna Gokhale on 25 February 1910 recommending an end to indentured labour of Indians sent to work in Natal in South Africa. The new rules also enlarged discussions on the budget. The financial statement would be presented prior to the budget which would be followed by a general discussion. Members could now move resolutions recommending alterations to the budget, and heads of revenue and expenditure could be voted on. Defence expenditure was still beyond the purview of discussions and could still not be put to a vote however. The final budget would then be presented, with explanations of any recommendations of the Council which had not been accepted. This would be followed by a general discussion and the debate would then be closed by the viceroy. The viceroy as President of the Council used his power to suspend the rules and procedures of the Council to ensure the passage of a bill much less frequently after 1909. And whilst the majority of bills were still passed without debate, much discussion took place on the Select Committees. In addition, it was only with the passage of the 1909 Act that Council members won the right to stand whilst speaking. Previously Legislative Council members would give their speeches sitting; the rule had been implemented to give the Council proceedings the feel of a committee, rather than a budding parliament.

During the Minto-Morley era Indian members of the Legislative Council had to make full use of the two main tools available to them; questions and resolutions. During 1911 only 151 questions were asked, but by 1919 the number had risen to 397. In 1920 Vithalbhai Patel alone asked 116 questions. One question by Kamini Chanda had 15 sub sections. Whilst supplementaries were allowed they were not common as the supplementary could only be asked by the member who asked the original question. Questions were the way that Council members would seek information from the government, however it was when members moved resolutions on matters of public interest that the government would have to defend and explain its policies on the floor of the Council. Dadabhai Naoroji moved a resolution urging the abolition of excise duty on Indian cotton products. Madan Mohan Malaviya moved a resolution that the duty on the import of sugar products be raised to protect the domestic sugar industry. Gopal Krishna Gokhale moved resolutions for budget surpluses to be used on education, sanitation and healthcare, and cost cutting in government departments. It was at this time that Indian members also began to regularly move resolutions in favour of Indianisation of the Indian Civil Service and Indian Army. There were resolutions on a wide range of topics; the separation of the executive and the judiciary, reform of the criminal justice system, the abolition of indentured labour, the establishment of a Public Services Commission, and a High Court in Punjab. By the end of 1917, 168 resolutions were passed of which 24 were accepted by the government.

The Imperial Legislative Council retained an official majority which meant that non-government members could never impose their will and the government would always be able to pass its legislation. Yet there was much more criticism of the government and more resistance put up to controversial bills. During the middle of 1910 the Council witnessed concerted criticism from non-government members over a bill to renew the Prevention of Seditious Meetings Act 1907. Gopal Krishna Gokhale led a group of Indian members including Madan Mohan Malaviya, Sachidananda Sinha, Mazharul Haq, Bhupendranath Basu and Raghunath Mudholkar in opposing the bill. On 6 August 1910 Gokhale observed that the country was relatively peaceful and passing such a "draconian" bill would only embitter relations between the Indian people and the government; the proposed bill gave dangerously wide powers to the government which were likely to be abused. Sinha criticised the bill for curbing freedom of speech and giving excessive powers to the police. Similarly, when the Press Bill, which sought to curb the spreading of seditious ideas in the media was brought to the Council and passed in February 1910, Indian members urged 55 amendments, of which 2 were accepted. They argued that the bill was reminiscent of the Vernacular Press Act of 1878 and compared it to a tax on knowledge which would prevent the development of journalism in India. In March 1915 the Defence of India Bill was introduced to give the government wide powers in ensuring public order in defence of the country. Thirty three amendments were moved of which two minor ones moved by Dadabhai Naoroji were accepted. Indian members did try to discuss certain bills in great detail and managed to amend the Indian Court Fees Bill 1910, the Indian Factories Bill 1911, the Indian Patent and Design Bill 1911, the Criminal Tribes Bill 1912 and the Indian Companies Bill 1912. In the case of the Indian Factories Bill 1911, 30 amendments were moved by Indian members of which 7 were accepted. Indian members did play a greater role in shaping the White Phosphoros Matches Bill and the Patna University Bill, whilst the Musalman Waqf Validating Bill 1913 and the Hindu and Musalman Disposition of Property Bill 1916 were amongst the few bills sponsored by Indian members which were passed by the Council. There was some effort of members to introduce their own bills but Gokhale's Elementary Education Bill and Basu's Special Marriage Bill were both rejected by the government on technical and financial grounds.

Indian Council members would use the limited tools available to them to extract information from the government and bring minor amendments to legislation, but their patience and faith in British good intentions were tested in December 1917 with the appointment of a Sedition Committee under

Justice Sidney Rowlatt. The Rowlatt Committee recommended that the ordinary law was not sufficient to deal with a more confrontational nationalist movement outside the councils and so the powers in the Defence of India Act should be continued even after the end of the war. The government then decided to implement the committee's recommendations, introducing the Indian Criminal Law Amendment Bill and the Indian Criminal Law Emergency Powers Bill into the Council in February 1919.

When a motion was moved to refer the Indian Criminal Law Emergency Powers Bill to a Select Committee on 6 February 1919, Vithalbhai Patel moved an amendment seeking a deferral of consideration of the bill until the term of the Council had expired. Debate on the motion went on for eight hours over two days and twenty Indian members took the opportunity to speak. Patel argued that the government should work to remove the grievances which were stoking "revolutionary crime" rather than pass such oppressive legislation. Surendranath Banerjea called it "a peril to the sacred rights of personal liberty", Mohammad Ali Jinnah argued that the law was against the basic norms of "law and justice". Srinivasa Sastri labelled the law "a callous disregard for liberty". Tej Bahadur Sapru, K.V. Rangaswami Ayyangar and Madan Mohan Malaviya all supported Patel's amendment. Indian members moved 150 amendments and divided the house 16 times but the government retained its official majority and so any serious challenge to the law was impossible and the Indian Criminal Law Emergency Powers Bill was passed on 18 March 1919. The patience of Indian moderates in the Council had been pushed too far, and Jinnah and Malaviya even resigned from their Council seats in protest.

***

The Montagu-Chelmsford reforms and the passage of the Government of India Act 1919 sought to bring moderate Indian politicians back on side by creating a new and enlarged legislature in Delhi. The first Indian Legislative Assembly of 1920 had 145 members of whom 104 were elected. Fifty two were elected by general constituencies, thirty from Muslim constituencies, nine from European constituencies, seven by landowners, four by chambers of commerce and two from Sikh constituencies. There were 41 nominated members of whom 26 were government officials and 15 were from outside the government. Nominated members from outside the government usually included Anglo-Indians, European merchants, Indian Christians, labour leaders, representatives of the Depressed Classes and tribal leaders from the North West Frontier Province. Some among these nominated members virtually became permanent nominees; Lieutenant Colonel Sir Henry Gidney represented Anglo-Indians for almost 20 years, whilst Mylai Chinna Rajah represented the Depressed Classes for 25 years and Narayan Joshi represented labour for an equally long period.

But despite the presence of nominated members it was always the lawyers and landholders who dominated the Assembly. Among the elected 104 members around 40 would be landowners and another 40 lawyers, with a smaller number of merchants. Whilst the landowners were difficult to beat in their own constituencies, when they came to the Assembly their political skills reached a limit. They did not represent any section of society outside of their own properties, and although they could have held the balance of power in the Assembly, they lacked the political skill to unite and instead joined the various political groups formed by the lawyers who had popular followings in the middle class, could speak on national political issues and had the professional debating skills and mastery of legislative procedure to advance Indian interests on the floor of the Assembly. The franchise for the

Council of State was even more restricted than for the Assembly; in 1921 its electorate across India totalled only 17,644 eligible voters. The first Council of State had 60 members of whom 33 were elected, 17 were nominated government officials and 10 were nominated from outside the government. The 'upper house' in Delhi would thus remain the preserve of landlords and merchants.

The term of the Indian Legislative Assembly was three years. Two sessions were held each year; the Delhi session was held from January to March and the Simla session was held from August to October. From 1921 to 1926 the Assembly met in the old Imperial Legislative Council building and in January 1927 it was moved to a new Council House which went on to house India's Parliament after Independence. The attendance of at least 25 members was necessary to constitute a sitting of the House. Members of the government would sit on the right and the Opposition on the left of the Chair. However, with political groups in the First Assembly still weak, seating arrangements did not pose a problem. From the Second Assembly the front seats were distributed according to the proportional strength of the political grouping. In the new chamber after 1927 there were fewer front seats and so an accommodation had to be reached; half the front seats would be allotted to official members who represented the government view and once allotted a seat a member had to remain in it.

The President of the Assembly would direct the days of sitting, which would be influenced by the amount of business to be transacted, and the viceroy addressed a joint session of both houses during the first week of each session. The home member would lead the government bloc, express the government's view and act as a de facto prime minister on the floor of the Assembly. The first half an hour of each session was generally given to answering questions put by the non-government members. New members would be sworn in, and the deaths of former members of the House would be condoled. After question hour, motions of adjournment moved by the non-government members would be brought to the notice of the House. The president would then announce a time, usually 4 pm, for the discussion of the adjournment motion. Elections of committees would sometimes be held after question time, which would be followed by discussions of resolutions and bills for the rest of the day. During the Delhi session certain days would be allotted solely for the discussion of the budget. Meetings of the Assembly would begin at 11 am and whilst there was no set time for their conclusion, proceedings usually finished by 5 pm. At the beginning of the week the Leader of the House would list the business for the week ahead. A copy would be placed on each member's table and the Leader would make a short speech on it but no further discussion would ensue. The Leader of the House would then notify members of any changes to the agenda by the government after consultations with leaders of political groups. Controversial bills were generally discussed early in the session as non-government members could not always attend the later part of the session and such arrangements helped to facilitate detailed discussion of bills and minimise wastage of time in criticism. Official days were exclusively for the processing of government business.

A major advance in the new Assembly was the power to vote on supplies, or funding to government departments. Members could assent or refuse assent to a demand for a grant or reduce the amount of any demand, however defence and political expenditures could still not be discussed. Given that the budget was subject to a vote, the government would feel some pressure when supplies and services were withheld or the entire budget was thrown out of the House. However, if the Assembly voted against a demand the viceroy could simply 'restore' it by declaring that it was essential to the discharge of his duties. In addition, the viceroy could authorise any expenditure he felt necessary in an emergency, certify that a bill disposed of by the Assembly was in the public interest, place it on the statute book himself, and promulgate ordinances in the event of an emergency.

Unlike the provinces where dyarchy had been introduced, there were no Indian ministers at the Centre and the Assembly remained an 'advisory body'. However, the Viceroy's Council began to function as something closer to a Cabinet and submitted its financial and legislative proposals to an Assembly presided over by an elected president rather than the viceroy himself. The old insistence by British officials that they were not creating a little Indian Parliament also began to grow more faint and Indian members certainly saw the institution as a parliament in the making. When doubts about correct procedures arose they would look to the practices of the House of Commons for clarity, language which was deemed 'unparliamentary' was published in *Decisions of the Chair*, and elected members would most often quote from May's *Parliamentary Procedure* when arguing for the provision of parliamentary privileges for themselves as members of the Assembly.

***

The first election after the passage of the Montagu-Chelmsford reforms generated little excitement among Indian voters and the candidates who stood for election were largely those who had sat in the councils of the Minto-Morley era. A boycott of the councils had been incorporated into the Congress programme of non-cooperation in September 1920, and in the following weeks Congress workers took the call for a boycott to all parts of the country, trying to persuade both potential candidates and the electorate that the Montagu-Chelmsford reforms had fallen short of swaraj. They further argued that swaraj would not be obtained on the floor of the councils, and their campaign achieved success when only 25% of the electorate voted at the end of November 1920.

Elections to the Indian Legislative Assembly in Bombay were largely formalities, as candidates were declared elected without a contest. For the two non-Muslim seats in Bombay city, both Jamnadas Dwarkadas and Sir Chimanlal Setalvad were elected without opposition. Salehbhoy Barodawalla was similarly elected unopposed in the city's Muslim seat. Given the lack of any substantial contest for the Indian Legislative Assembly most attention focussed on the contest for the Bombay Legislative Assembly and Council. Elections were orderly; candidates addressed their electors with an outline of their positions on the economic issues of the day, and highlighted their records of service in the municipal and educational bodies of Bombay. Hormasji Modi was not standing for the Indian Legislative Assembly, but sought election to the Bombay Legislative Council. His electors were drawn from an even smaller elite than the one which elected the Bombay Legislative Assembly, and he added a sharp attack on Gandhi's new programme of non-cooperation. He outlined a staunchly moderate vision of gradual political progress to his electors, and spoke for the older generation of public men which rejected Gandhi's boycott call when he explained: "Self government is not to be achieved by subverting the foundations of our society, by teaching the rising generations irreverence and indiscipline and by cutting them off from all those avenues of knowledge which have made possible our political awakening."[cccxxxii]

The only major party at the polls in 1920 was the National Liberal Federation which had been formed by some disgruntled Congress moderates. In 1922 Liberal members of the Assembly formed a Democratic Party under the leadership of Hari Singh Gour. One of its stated aims was to develop a party organisation, something which would be essential for parliamentary government. The Democrats claimed 48 members and played the role of a moderate opposition working for political concessions and reforms of the administration. After the formation of the Democratic Party there were 145 divisions in the First Assembly, of which 57 went against the government. To carry any of their motions the Democrats needed the support of other non-government members which they usually lacked, but they did manage to get some support on the motion to reduce the salt duty in 1923. Besides the Democrats there were also two other nominal parties in the first Assembly, the Nationalists and the Unionists. The Nationalists were even more moderate than the Democrats, whilst the Unionists made an early attempt to represent Muslim interests in the Assembly. None of the three parties were able to enforce party discipline, and on most occasions sectional interests prevailed. When Hari Singh Gour introduced a bill to define the legal limitation for Hindu money lenders, he was unable to rely on the support of all his fellow Democrats and the bill was defeated by 34 votes to 27. Gour was more successful in bringing a bill for the amendment of the Special Marriage Act of 1872 in order to allow Hindus to marry according to the Act without renouncing their faith, yet the bill only passed narrowly without the support of many Democrats.

It was towards the end of the first Assembly that the Liberals began to put up more concerted opposition to the government. A confrontation arose in 1923 between the Assembly and the government over the Princes Protection Bill, which had been introduced by the government to prevent the circulation of literature "calculated to excite disaffection against the Rulers of Indian States." The Assembly refused to allow the introduction of the bill which forced Viceroy Reading to use his special powers to secure the legislation for the first time. He 'certified' the bill which was then sent to the Council of State and subsequently gave the bill his assent. Yet it was on the issue of the government's proposal to double the salt tax in the budget of 1923-1924 that the most important division of the first Assembly took place. The tax increase was defeated 59 to 44, which prompted the viceroy to use his emergency powers for the second time by certifying it. The bill even received some criticism within the Council before being passed. Indian members started to doubt the sincerity of the new system and on 10 July 1923 Nand Lal moved a resolution that the relevant section of the Government of India Act 1919 be amended so that the viceroy would not have the powers to overrule the Legislative Assembly. He added, "We have been given all the paraphernalia of a Parliament, but at the same time we have not got any real power."

***

In the elections which took place in November 1923 for the second Assembly the voters were in most cases presented with a clear choice between the new Swaraj Party of Motilal Nehru and Chittaranjan Das, and the Liberal Party which represented the moderates who had served in the first Assembly. The Swaraj Party's campaign was quite straightforward. Its candidates portrayed the Montagu-Chelmsford reforms as a sham which were designed to keep India in a permanently subservient state to Britain and vowed to continue non-violent non-cooperation until the system was radically changed. Further, the Swarajists claimed that they would not concern themselves with trivial reforms of government departments but would work to bring about the transfer of power from the bureaucracy to the people themselves. If elected, the Swarajist members of the Assembly would put together a demand for such a transfer of power and place it before the government prior to the start of the

Assembly session. If the government rejected the demand they would proceed with their tactic of obstruction, whereas if the demand was accepted they would come to the negotiating table. This aggressive posture of the Swaraj Party put the Liberals on the defensive however. In a political arena in which 'non-cooperation' had become associated with commitment to the nationalist cause, the Liberals had to struggle to not be labelled 'co-operators'. Liberal candidates insisted that they did not indiscriminately support the government, and that they were 'critics' of the government rather than 'co-operators'. They wanted to maintain their efforts to advance the Montagu-Chelmsford reforms and continue on the path to Dominion status, or self-government within the British Empire. Further, Liberal candidates pointed to their own record of achievements in the first Assembly and contrasted it with the 'failure' of the non-cooperation movement.

The Bombay seats for the Indian Legislative Assembly which had gone uncontested in 1920 saw a more spirited contest in 1923. The two non-Muslim seats featured a total of five candidates; Vithalbhai Patel of the Swaraj Party, Sir Chimanlal Setalvad and Jamnadas Dwarkadas of the Liberal Party and two Independent Parsi candidates, Naoroji Dumasia and Jehangir Petit. Vithalbhai Patel got straight to the point: "You know me, my views and my methods of work. I seek no office under government, and shall endeavour, if elected to the Assembly, by all legitimate means to obstruct and embarrass the Bureaucracy at every stage and at every step and allow them no peace of mind unless and until the national demands are conceded to the satisfaction of the Indian National Congress."[cccxxxiii] Sir Chimanlal emphasised his 30 years of public service, assured his electors that he too wanted "stable swaraj", and spent some time speaking on the status of Indians in Kenya.[cccxxxiv] Yet his election was doomed as the Liberal vote was split with Jamnalal

Dwarkadas, and the Independent Naoroji Dumasia managed to corner the significant Parsi vote. Mohammad Ali Jinnah had an easier time in the Bombay Muslim seat. He stood unopposed, yet he did make his thoughts on the political situation of the time known to his electors. His position was somewhere between the aggressive posturing of the Swarajists and the moderation of the Liberals; he reserved obstruction of the legislatures as a last resort if the government did not listen to the will of the majority on the floor of the House.[cccxxxv] He also made a plea for Hindu-Muslim unity, pointing to previous pacts between the two communities and suggested that the way to ensure further agreements was to send the best men to the Councils.[cccxxxvi]

The Swaraj Party won 48 seats and became the largest party in the Assembly. There were 24 Independents who coalesced under the leadership of Jinnah and together with the Swarajists they formed a Nationalist Party under the leadership of Motilal Nehru. The Nationalist Party thus commanded an absolute majority in the Assembly and was able to regularly defeat the government on motions of national importance, obstruct the budget and stage walkouts. *The Times of India,* generally considered a pro-British paper at the time, lamented the poor showing of the Liberals who lost many of their seats and the success of the Swarajists, yet it did think that the elections were at least in one way a great success; they had captured everyone's attention.[cccxxxvii] Polling had risen to 41.9% and the paper noted that "The candidates have been really keen on getting in, polling has been fairly brisk, and there have been signs on all sides that the people are settling down to democracy." The "general excitement" and "heightened reality of proceedings" had been evident and the editorial concluded that "Democracy has come to stay; in fact it is now positively popular."

On 5 February 1924 T. Rangachariar moved a resolution in the

Assembly suggesting a revision of the Government of India Act 1919 to secure provincial autonomy and Dominion status within the British Empire. When the resolution was taken up for discussion three days later, Motilal Nehru moved a substitute motion as an amendment to recommend to the viceroy that a Round Table Conference be called to discuss a new constitution for India, the Assembly then be dissolved, and the new constitution be placed before a newly elected Indian legislature before being embodied in a statute of the British Parliament. The debate continued for three days, gaining the support of Malaviya and Jinnah and was adopted despite government opposition on 18 February 1924 by 76 votes to 48. Nehru's motion came to be known as the 'National Demand'.

But rather than a Round Table Conference, the government formed a committee under Sir Alexander Muddiman to explore possibilities for advance within the boundaries of the Government of India Act 1919. Motilal Nehru refused to serve on the committee. The Muddiman Committee thought that the existing constitutional system was working well, and when its report came up for discussion in the Assembly in 1925, Nehru moved an amendment to the home member's recommendation that the Assembly accept the principles of the report and reiterated his National Demand of the previous year. The amendment was also carried 72 to 45 but was rejected by the government which hardened the Swarajist position to one of 'no redress of grievances, no supplies'. The Assembly then rejected four of the government's financial demands for grants, not on the merits of each demand, but as a political protest. The Finance Bill of 1924-25 was also rejected, to much acclaim in the Indian press, but the viceroy eventually restored the grants and certified the bill.

By March 1926 the Swarajists decided to ask the government to provide its position on the National Demand which had been passed two years earlier. They would stage a walkout from the Assembly if the government's response was not satisfactory. On 8 March 1926 Motilal Nehru gave a speech on the floor of the Assembly criticising the government for refusing to provide political concessions and warned that the whole country would soon be 'honeycombed' by secret societies. He told the members that the Swaraj Party would go back to its electorate and return to the next Assembly in increased numbers to push for further political reforms. The government did not seem to respond to the National Demand and so Motilal led a walk out of the Swaraj Party; "There is no more use for us here. We go out into the country to seek the suffrage of the electorates once more. We do not give up the fight." With the absence of Swarajists however, Jinnah was left without the numbers to be able to censure the government.

Divisions within the Nationalist Party came to the fore when Jinnah did not support Nehru's position of rejecting the budget and then also withheld his support for the Swaraj Party's candidate for President of the Assembly, Vithalbhai Patel. Within the Swaraj Party Malaviya, Kelkar, Jayakar and Lajpat Rai were also unhappy with the Party's obstructionist policies and wanted instead to pursue a policy of 'responsive co-operation'. Those who believed in responsive co-operation united under Jayakar's Responsive Co-operation Party and together with Independents and Nationalists they formed an Indian National Party in Bombay in April 1926. Lala Lajpat Rai resigned from the Swaraj Party in August 1926 and along with Malaviya formed the Independent Congress Party under which Liberals, Independents, Responsivists and Hindu Sabhaites gathered. Whether they gathered under Jayakar's banner or that of Lajpat Rai and Malaviya, Responsive Co-operators all wanted a return to the older style of moderate politics which sought Dominion status through work in the legislatures.

***

The election of 1926 was largely fought between the Swaraj Party and its splinter parties, the Indian National Party and the Independent Congress Party. The Indian National Party had been formed in Bombay and it was there that Jayakar and Jinnah came together to put up a united opposition to the Swaraj Party. The debate had once again been reduced to the merits of co-operation and non-cooperation with the government. The terms of the argument were remarkably similar to the 1923 contest between the Swaraj Party and the Liberal Party, with the new Indian National Party filling the void left by the Liberals. The contest became more heated however, as Swarajists accused the Responsivists of being 'political wobblers', whilst the Responsivists went so far as to say that the Swarajists had 'prostituted' the Congress. Responsivists made the further charge that the Swarajist position of withholding co-operation in the Assembly unless the National Demand was met was an unrealistic one, in addition to being damaging to the nationalist cause given that so much important legislation was due before the Assembly in the new term. The Swarajists responded by claiming that the Responsivists had tired of the nationalist struggle and wanted to offer co-operation with the government and the bureaucracy when such a course was futile without the concession of full self-government.

Whilst the debates between the Swarajists and the Responsivists in Bombay were quite sharp, they were largely confined to a disagreement over political tactics in the forthcoming Assembly. In the United Provinces and Punjab however, the campaign took a communal turn. In addition to dissatisfaction over the Swarajist policy of obstruction in the previous Assembly, Lala Lajpat Rai and Madan Mohan Malaviya were concerned that Hindu interests were being relegated as they were being constrained in taking up Hindu causes in the Assembly so as to not alienate the nationalist Muslim supporters of the Party. Their Independent Congress

Party thus went to the voters of U.P. and Punjab on this issue, aiming to establish a new political bloc which could champion Hindu interests in the next Assembly without constraint. Lala Lajpat Rai made the point that the Swaraj Party's practice of walking out of the Assembly took a disproportionate number of Hindus out of the chamber when crucial legislation was coming up for a vote, leaving it to the minority communities to exercise influence much beyond their numbers. He further complained that the Swaraj Party leadership was not sensitive to Hindu concerns and urged electors to vote for candidates who would "fight for the Hindu cause".[cccxxxviii] Motilal Nehru's rebuttal did not address the specific sense of Hindu grievance but instead chided Lajpat Rai for indiscipline in breaking away from the Swaraj Party and highlighted his inconsistency on key issues in the preceding Assembly. When the results came in and the Swaraj Party suffered heavy defeats in U.P. he complained- "It was a fight between the forces of nationalism and those of the low order of communalism reinforced by wealth, wholesale corruption, and falsehood."[cccxxxix] Despite participation touching almost 50%, the Swaraj Party could only manage to win 38 seats compared to the previous 48. The Responsivist group returned with 18 members, electing Malaviya as its leader and Jayakar as deputy leader and came to be known as the National Party within the Assembly. Putting aside their competition at election time, the Swarajists and the Nationalists came together to censure the government during the third Assembly. A Central Muslim Party took shape under the leadership of Sir Zulfiqar Ali Khan, whilst independent minded Hindu and Muslim members formed an Independent Party under Jinnah.

During the third Assembly Swarajists, Responsive Co-operators and Independents all began to use budget proceedings as their preferred means of expressing opposition to the government. The budget would be presented on the last day of February each year, and March would be a month of legislative obstruction. During the first stage of the budget the finance member would make a long speech outlining the government's economic policy, its expenditure, sources of revenue and proposals for new taxes. During the finance member's presentation members were not yet allowed to speak; general discussion took place in the second stage. The non-government members would then speak and the government members would address their criticisms. During the general discussion the representatives of economic interest groups could discuss pressing issues such as the cotton excise duty, salt duty, exchange rates, the agricultural and industrial sectors, the state of the railways, funding for education, and the development of economic infrastructure. The general discussion would also inevitably feature criticism of the non-votable part of the budget, particularly the defence budget which had, since the earliest days of Indian nationalism been thought to be a drain on the country's resources.

The third and most important stage of the budget proceedings was the voting on demand for grants, or funding for government departments. Non-government members would move their motions for reduction of funding as each demand for grants was presented. There were time limits on discussion and eventually the 'guillotine' would drop, bringing discussion to a close. Although defence funding could not be voted on, Indian members found an indirect way to attack it; they would reduce the votable 'supply ancillery'. For example, expenditure on the Secretariat Department of the army could be voted on and used to indirectly attack defence expenditure. By the third Assembly a distinction developed between substantial cuts for the purposes of economy and 'token cuts' which were usually proposed to express a political grievance, obtain information from the government or stimulate a public debate. The procedure stipulated that the larger proposals for budget reductions were taken first, but in the case of token cuts they were presented in the order in which they were received. General motions for reductions could not be moved nor could reduction motions be moved by proxy.

In the budget debate of 1927 Jayakar's reduction of the Demand under "Executive Council" to a token ₹1 was adopted 65 to 56. He declared: "The one method allowed in this House in which our sense of great dissatisfaction and resentment could be brought to the notice of the House and the Government is by moving this cut as a vote of censure on the Government." Chaman Lal repeated the practice in the budget discussions of 1928, winning a vote to reduce the Demand for the "Executive Council" to ₹1 by 58 to 53. He said that the cut was moved because the executive councillors did not command the confidence of the House and the purpose was "to censure the Executive Council for continuing a system of government which has been condemned by the people's representatives." The same thing was done in the budget session of 1929 by Motilal Nehru who won the vote 63 to 52. Jinnah supported the token cut- "I say that there is only one course open to us, now on this motion, and that is to pass this vote of censure against the government, for failing to make an adequate response to our demands repeatedly."

There was opposition to the Simon Commission in the Assembly, and Lala Lajpat Rai's resolution informing the government that the members of the Assembly would boycott the commission was adopted on 16 February 1928. The debate lasted two full days, but there were still some Indian members who were in favour of co-operating with the Simon Commission. It was also a demonstration of how Indian politicians viewed their roles in the Assembly. The scene was described by *The Times* on 17 February 1928:

> *"The public galleries of the Central Assembly were crowded for watching the debate on the Simon Commission and 134 out of 145 members were present. One incident shows how seriously non-official leaders took this occasion for demonstration of political grievance. Mr Harchandri Vishindas, a non-official member from Sindh died when he was being brought to the House in an ambulance car. The member was very ill in Karachi and only came to Delhi in an urgent response to a call by the Nationalist Party whip so that he could vote against the Commission."*

***

For the first four years of the Assembly Sir Frederick Whyte, a former member of the House of Commons performed the president's role. On 24 August 1925 Vithalbhai Patel was elected President of the Assembly. During the 1920s mention of "Mr. Patel" in the Indian press referred to Vithalbhai rather than his younger brother Vallabhbhai. The brothers hailed from Nadiad in Gujarat and the story goes that Vithalbhai took Vallabhbhai's passage to study law in England when the postman delivered the envelope to "Mr. V.J. Patel, Pleader". Both brothers ended up studying in London at different times and both returned to India to practice law and take up politics. When Vithalbhai became President of the Indian Legislative Assembly, he took his job seriously. On his election he stated: "In the discharge of my duties I shall, I assure you, observe strict impartiality in dealing with all sections of the House irrespective of party considerations. (Cheers). From this moment on I cease to be a party man. I belong to no party. I belong to all parties. (Hear, hear)." When Patel said that he would belong to no party he was speaking quite literally. When he sought re-election to the Assembly at the end of 1926 he did so as an Independent from Ahmadabad rather than as a Swarajist from Bombay. When he was elected president for the second time he stated:

> *"For the brief experience that I had as the occupant of this chair I have found, as I stated when addressing you last, that anyone who aspires to fill this great office with any hope of success must lay aside all that is personal, all that is of party, all that savours of political predilection, and learn to subordinate everything to the great interests of the House as a whole. He may have his political opinions, he may retain them, he may have his prejudices, but in his general decisions and in his treatment of individual members no trace of them should find any place. All I can promise is that I shall ever endeavour to the best of my capacity to regulate my conduct in the Chair on the lines which I have just indicated."*[cccxl]

During his time in the Chair Patel would assert the authority of the president's position before members of the Assembly, the viceroy and the Government of India, as well as the Indian and international media. When the Swarajists staged their walk out on 8 March 1926, Patel did not join them. He explained; "the President of the Assembly, like the Speaker of the House of Commons is above all party politics and therefore not bound to accept the mandate of the party to which he belonged before he was elevated to the Chair." He did however, assert that the Assembly was no longer a representative legislature and advised the government not to bring any controversial bills into the Assembly or he may have to adjourn the House sin die. Patel was equally strict in keeping members to the rule book when they returned to the Assembly. On 26 February 1927, when a member of the Assembly tried to discuss general railway policy during a motion for the specific reduction of supplies for administrative working expenses for the Railways Patel intervened, stating: "I would be failing in my duty if I were not to point out to the Honourable Member that he ought to make a distinction between a general discussion of the Railways budget and the particular cut which we are now discussing. It is not right that the discussion on a particular cut should be turned into a general discussion of policy."

Patel's confrontation with the government started to intensify when a division on the second reading of the Public Safety Bill on 24 September 1928 resulted in a tie of 61 votes for and against, and he gave the deciding vote against motion. His reasoning was largely legalistic rather than political, explaining to the Assembly; "If any party or any individual member seeks to put such an extraordinary measure on the statute book, he must persuade the House and get a majority in his favour. The Honourable the Home Member has failed to secure a clear majority in his favour and cannot expect the Chair to give his casting vote in favour of the motion." Patel got into a more personal clash with the viceroy over the Public Safety Bill the following year when he ruled it out of order on the basis that it was an abuse of the forms and procedures of the House. The point at issue was that the Meerut Conspiracy Case was pending before the courts, and given that the subject matter of the bill was similar to that of the court case, it could be considered sub judice which would make a free discussion of the bill on the floor of the Assembly difficult. Patel held that the court case and the bill were identical in subject matter and used his power as president to rule the motion out as a violation of the forms and procedures of the House which led the viceroy to criticise his action in an address to the Assembly on 12 April 1929. Patel then wrote a letter to the viceroy protesting his criticism as a violation of the independence of the Chair. At his address to the Assembly at the next session the viceroy assured the members that he would maintain the dignity of the House and the Chair, but he eventually restrained the president's powers, amending Rule 17 which allowed the president to prevent the discussion of a motion.

Whilst there was no statutory privilege protecting members from offensive comments in the press, the Assembly did have other ways of making its displeasure known. On 14 September 1928 Motilal Nehru brought to the attention of the president articles published in the *Times of India* and London's *Daily Telegraph* which included comments thought to be derogatory to the honour of the Assembly. The articles had implied that Patel had colluded with Nehru and been partial in his actions in the passage of the Public Safety Bill and showed bias against the government in treating the proposals to establish a separate Secretariat for the Assembly. Patel then took the only action within his power and cancelled the press pass of A.H. Byrt of the *Times of India*, a veteran of the paper. C.M. Rice was a young freelance journalist with the *Daily Telegraph* who only had a single entry press ticket which made action against him more difficult. Patel made it clear that neither journalist would be allowed to re-enter the press gallery until their newspaper owners offered the Assembly an apology for their conduct. The proprietors of the *Times of India* duly apologised and Byrt's press pass was restored four months later.

After the appointment of the Simon Commission, the Congress declaration of its goal of complete Independence in Lahore in December 1929 and the subsequent call from the Congress leadership to withdraw from the legislatures, Patel was increasingly torn between his constitutional role as President of the Assembly and his political role as a Congressman. As passions were being stirred in the Assembly over the Simon Commission Patel kept his cool, explaining; "My political opinions are well known, and they have not at all varied since I assumed the office of the President of the Assembly. There will, therefore, be no doubt whatever of the opinion which I would publicly desire to express upon the question of the forthcoming Statutory Commission if I were not debarred from speaking freely by the reserve imposed upon me by my office...".[cccxli] He had consulted his friends but thought that there would be "no useful purpose" in resigning. In response to calls to resign after the Lahore Resolution, Patel explained his position on the floor of the Assembly on 21 January 1930; "I feel I would be nullifying and indeed destroying all the work it is claimed I have done during the last four years and more, were I to tender my resignation in obedience to the mandate of the Congress." It was only later in May 1930, with the declaration of a new round of civil disobedience imminent that the call of his conscience became overwhelming and Patel eventually resigned his post as President of the Indian Legislative Assembly.

***

After the frustrations of the Simon Commission the Swarajists began to show less interest in the proceedings of the House. An election was due in 1929 but the term of the existing Assembly was extended to 1930. There was less discipline among the Swarajists and only Malaviya's group attended proceedings regularly. Jinnah's strength was also reduced by the emergence of the Central Muslim Party which usually supported the government. Easier legislative victories ensued for the government until the Assembly was eventually dissolved on 31 July 1930.

The Congress and the Responsivists boycotted the elections for the fourth Assembly in September 1930. Elections were held in the backdrop of the civil disobedience movement and voter turnout fell to 26.1%. With both the major legislative groupings within the Indian nationalist movement staying away from the polls, the keen ideological and personal contests of 1926 were absent and the field was left to the very most moderate Independent politicians. In this sense the elections of 1930 had come full circle and resembled the elections of 1920. Forty Independents formed a Nationalist Party under Sir Hari Singh Gour, and with Jinnah having left for London some other Independents organised themselves under Sir Abdur Rahim. It was Rahim's group which held the balance of power and was key to the defeat of any government legislative initiatives. Even the landholders organised themselves as a group of eight under Raja Sir Vasudev. Attendance became poor and party discipline eroded which meant that the government won most of the divisions in the Assembly. On the Criminal Law Amendment Bill some Nationalists voted with the government and they were also divided over the Ottawa Trade Agreement. Despite the efforts of Sir Abdur and Sir Hari, the restrictive Indian Press Bill passed with a large majority. Towards the end of the Assembly the government was able to push through controversial bills such as the Indian Army (Amendment) Bill and the Bengal Criminal Law Amendment Supplementary (Extending) Bill which would have received stiff opposition in previous assemblies. The fourth Assembly was extended for one year beyond its stipulated three year term and was finally dissolved in December 1934.

Elections to the fifth Assembly were due in November 1934.

The civil disobedience movement ended in May 1934, and the Congress had decided to contest elections. The main political debate was no longer between the old Congress Swarajists and the Responsivists over co-operation or non-cooperation in the Assembly, or between the Congress and the Liberals over swaraj or Dominion status. The British Government had published a White Paper after the London Round Table Conferences outlining a new round of constitutional reforms and part of the paper dealt with what came to be known as the 'Communal Award'. Whilst separate electorates had been in existence since the days of the Minto-Morley reforms before World War I, the principle was greatly expanded to potentially include 18 different types of separate electorates. The Congress came to occupy a neutral position on the Award; although it rejected the principle of separate electorates, it did not reject the Award in order to maintain the support of nationalist Muslims who were largely in favour of it. Madan Mohan Malaviya and Madhav Aney rejected the Award however and formed their own Congress Nationalist Party to contest the 1934 elections. It was acknowledged from the start that the only point of disagreement with the Congress was on its position on the Communal Award and that an accommodation would be reached between the two parties to avoid putting up candidates against each other wherever one candidate had an overwhelming chance of success.

Madan Mohan Malaviya went out on the campaign trail denouncing the Congress position of neutrality on the Award. He appealed to the voters to launch an agitation to "kill" the Award, arguing that India could not achieve self-government on the basis of so many separate electorates.[cccxlii] The general argument against the Award was that it was another British attempt to 'divide and rule' by giving disproportionate representation to Muslims and the Scheduled Castes at the cost of the majority of Hindus. Given the Congress position of neutrality on the Award it tried to play the matter down on the campaign trail; ideally the Congress wanted to put the issue of the Communal Award into the background until some future time when the Party could reach a better accommodation with the minority communities. Instead Congress leaders like Vallabhbhai Patel framed the election as an opportunity for voters to help the Congress project its electoral strength across the country, and as a positive alternative to the White Paper the Congress began to advocate the formation of an Indian Constituent Assembly to frame a new constitution for the country.

The plans envisaged by the Government of India Act 1935 for a federal structure and vastly expanded houses of a Federal Assembly and a Council of Ministers at the Centre never actually came into being, and so the Assembly and Council in New Delhi carried on under the framework of the Government of India Act 1919 until 1947. The fifth Assembly featured 44 Congress members and 11 Nationalists who usually voted with the Congress. Bhulabhai Desai emerged as the new leader of the Congress on the floor of the Assembly at the head of a new generation of Congress legislators including Sundara Satyamurti, Govind Pant, Asaf Ali, Narhar Gadgil, V.V Giri and N.G. Ranga. Jinnah led a group of 22 Independents which held the balance of power however, and Jinnah's group which was mainly Muslim squared off against the Congress Nationalists who were mainly Hindus on communal issues. He also clashed with the Congress on the Communal Award as well as the Congress's complete rejection of the Government of India Act 1935. He won the day on 7 February 1935 when Bhulabhai Desai's motion to reject the report of the Joint Parliamentary Committee was defeated and his own proposal to accept autonomy for the provinces was accepted.

Adjournment motions came to be more frequently used by

Indian members during the 1930s. An adjournment motion was used to either obtain information from the government or express a serious view of a government action which might have impacted or be about to impact the Indian public. The adjournment motion was started with an assault by the mover followed by speeches by the government and non-government members. The mover would make a reply before it was put to a vote. If the adjournment motion was carried it would mean that the Assembly took a serious view on the matter and it could be interpreted as a vote of censure against the government. The first attempt to censure the government in the new Assembly came with an adjournment motion to discuss the prevention of one of the Assembly members, Sarat Chandra Bose from attending proceedings. When the motion was put to a vote on 22 January 1935, the government was defeated by 58 votes to 54. During the fourth and fifth Assemblies adjournment motions were added to budgetary obstruction as the preferred means of legislative opposition, with 30-40 being moved during each session. The viceroy would even have to step in and disallow about one-third of adjournment motions annually.[cccxliii]

Indian members of the Assembly could also use the option of sending a bill to a Select Committee at the second reading to stop the government rushing it through. Another method was the motion to circulate a bill for opinion. Non-government members would usually want law and order and special powers bills circulated. By reference to a Select Committee the Assembly was, in principle committed to the bill and so the committee could not alter its fundamentals, whereas circulating a bill meant that the Assembly had not yet committed to its provisions. If a bill had not been suitably altered by a Select Committee, members could move motions for amendments on the second reading of the bill. Each clause of the bill would be examined individually. Amendments would be proposed to either modify a clause or remove it from the bill entirely. If previous motions for amendments were lost, members could move amendments to save them in a modified form. The Chair would sometimes disallow these amendments to amendments however. The most amended bills of the fifth Assembly were the Indian Companies Bill 1936, the Indian Insurance Bill 1937, the Motor Vehicles Bill 1938, the Indian Income Tax Bill 1938, the Excess Profits Bill 1940, and the Drugs Bill 1940. If a bill could not be amended then the final opportunity for obstruction was the third reading or the motion to pass. However, members rarely pressed for a division on the third reading as the government position was generally secure if it had won the division during the second reading. Yet Congressmen did try for a division on the third reading of the Indian Army Bill 1937 and Criminal Law Amendment Bill 1938, but were predictably unsuccessful in both cases. The fifth Assembly was thus kept busy with these adjournment motions, select committees, amendments, amendments to amendments and the circulation of bills. The Assembly also rejected all five of the government's budgets after 1935, and the viceroy was forced to certify the Finance Bill each year to secure its passage. World War II broke out in 1939, new elections were postponed, and the Congress decided to withdraw its members from the Assembly.

The fifth Assembly carried on for ten years, and after the passage of the Government of India Act 1935 the Indian Legislative Assembly became known as the Central Legislative Assembly. By the time that elections were held after the end of World War II the terms of the political debate had changed radically. The contest was now between the Congress, running as the sole voice of Indian nationalism, and the Muslim League championing the establishment of Pakistan. The Congress also had to turn to argue with the emerging force of Hindu nationalism in the form of the Hindu Mahasabha which put up candidates out of concern that the Congress might reach a settlement with the Muslim

League and concede a Pakistan. In addition, the Congress had to deal with the growing assertion from the Harijans, or Scheduled Castes who had found a leader in Bhimrao Ambedkar. He appealed to the community to unite behind candidates of the All India Scheduled Castes Federation to take on a Brahmin dominated Congress and secure their representation in any new constitution making body.

Initially the Congress attempted to frame the 1945 elections as a chance for the people to exercise a positive vote for Independence and a new federal constitution in which citizens' liberties would be guaranteed. The Congress invoked its 60 years of service to the struggle of Indian nationalism and further pitched for the support of labour, peasants, and the backward sections of society claiming that an independent state would protect their interests and initiate a programme of rapid economic modernisation. Yet as the campaign gathered momentum the principal election issue quickly became Pakistan. When Mohammad Ali Jinnah addressed his electors in Bombay city, the people who had regularly elected him to the Assembly for over 25 years, he asked them to vote for Muslim League candidates for in their success or failure lay "the fate of the community-whether they should live or perish."[cccxliv] Given that the League's goal was Pakistan, if sufficient numbers of League candidates were not returned all its efforts since the Lahore Resolution would be wasted. Jinnah argued that despite being educationally backward, Muslims were more politically conscious than Hindus. Days later, he expanded on his idea of Pakistan which would be a federal state with eastern and western zones. He had claimed all of Bengal and Assam besides all of Punjab and Delhi in his Pakistan, and so he reassured the Hindu minority which would find itself in the new Muslim state that its rights would be protected. Jawaharlal Nehru then went on to accuse Jinnah of "lowering the political standard of the country", and argued that World War II had shown that small states like

Pakistan had little chance of survival.cccxlv Vallabhbhai Patel joined in denouncing the Pakistan idea, arguing that India's Muslims had not changed nationality when they changed religion, besides which it was unrealistic to ask Hindus in the proposed Pakistan to accept assurances of their safety when the League would not accept assurances of the safety of Muslims in a united India.cccxlvi Patel invited Jinnah and the League back to the negotiating table for a settlement with the Congress.

The Congress secured 56 seats in the new Assembly and elected Sarat Chandra Bose Leader and Asaf Ali Deputy Leader. The Muslim League won all 30 Muslim seats and elected Mohammad Ali Jinnah Leader and Liaqat Ali Khan Deputy Leader. Unlike the previous Assembly which ran for more than ten years, the sixth Assembly had a short life of 16 months; it met between January 1946 and April 1947. In keeping with the practice of earlier Assemblies Indian members passed many adjournment motions and resolutions censuring the government. The most lively debates occurred over the release of Indian National Army soldiers who were being held by the British and the issues arising out of a mutiny in the Indian Navy in Bombay in February 1946. In September 1946 the Congress formed an Interim Government and was later joined by the Muslim League. The old posture of opposition and protest became a thing of the past, and both Congress and League members started to exercise greater party discipline now that they were in government.

***

Despite the protestations of successive generations of British rulers, they had in fact created a little Indian Parliament in Delhi. The institution which dated back to the 1830s in Calcutta had, over the course of a century witnessed the changing structures of British rule, the decline of the Indian feudal class, the emergence of the Indian middle class, the creation of a national politics and the eventual division of the country. After 1919 the Assembly in Delhi seemed to have all the forms, processes, procedures and even the layout of a parliament, lacking only the power of a sovereign legislature. The concern had been expressed during the drafting of the Montagu-Chelmsford reforms that power needed to be devolved to Indian members who would be elected by larger electorates in order to prevent the Assemblies from becoming debating chambers, platforms for political rhetoric rather than day-to-day governance. Whilst that argument was accepted at the provincial level and a system of dyarchy was established in the provincial legislatures, the idea of Indian ministers sitting in a de facto Cabinet in Delhi proved too large a concession in both 1919 and 1935. The Indian Legislative Assembly thus did become a debating chamber and a platform for political rhetoric, with its character on full display in the divisions and walkouts of the 1920s and the adjournment motions and rejections of the budget in the 1930s. Yet despite its limitations, the lasting value of the institution lay in the way in which Indian politicians came to express their political agendas, whether of support or opposition to the government through the established procedures of an Assembly which operated in all but name and power as the Indian Parliament in waiting.

Between the passage of the Indian Councils Act of 1892 and Indian Independence in 1947 three generations of Congressmen passed through the central legislatures in Calcutta and Delhi. Gopal Krishna Gokhale led the Congress contingent from its initial entry in the 1890s until the time of World War I. Although frustrated by the constraints placed on its activities in the councils this early generation of Congress moderates, which included names like Dadabhai Naoroji, Surendranath Banerjea and Rash Behari Ghose saw their inclusion as the fulfilment, albeit slow and partial and halting, of the noble promise of British rule. The next generation of Congressmen to come into the councils was led by Motilal Nehru after World War I, and whilst less grateful to the British rulers and more combative on the floor of the Assembly, they too were trained lawyers committed to mastering the procedures of the Assembly and turning it into as much of an Indian Parliament as possible. By the mid 1930s Motilal and his generation had passed away and so a younger group came forward to contest elections and take their place. Men like Govind Pant, Sarat Chandra Bose and Bhulabhai Desai all took their place in the Assembly, and although proceedings became more marginal to the major political mobilisations happening outside the chamber, the Congress and its leaders remained engaged and committed to the institution all the way up to the transfer of power in 1947.

The Congressmen who came into the central legislature over a 50 year period were overwhelmingly lawyers, many of whom had been educated in England. Thus, even when a section of the Party wanted to enter the Councils as an extension of the non-cooperation movement in the early 1920s only to 'wreck them from the inside', such an aggressive and disruptive attitude seemed suspiciously out of character. Vithalbhai Patel straddled two generations; he served in the Bombay Legislative Council after the Minto-Morley reforms, entered the Council in Delhi in 1918, observed the Congress boycott call in 1920, and then joined Chittaranjan Das and Motilal Nehru's Swaraj Party to contest elections in 1923. He went to his electors claiming that the course ahead for the Swaraj Party was clear; it would take non-cooperation to the Assembly, put a demand before the British for full self-government and if it was not accepted proceed to disrupt the chamber. However, something quite different actually happened. Patel was successful at the elections of 1923 and towards the end of the second Assembly he was nominated and elected as its president. In this role he would not be able to disrupt the chamber, but would actually be responsible for maintaining order and seeing that business was transacted according to its rules and regulations. Patel then transformed, or reverted, to become the most scrupulous and faithful defender of the forms and procedures and dignity of the institution in its history. He not only exerted the authority of his own position as president before the viceroy and the executive, but defended the honour of the house when it was brought into disrepute in the press. He had become such a stickler for the rules and the realisation of the full authority of the president's post that when Bhagat Singh disrupted proceedings by throwing a bomb into the chamber on 8 April 1929 and the home member, supported by the Government of India and the Chief Commissioner of Delhi claimed full control over the Assembly and the surrounding areas, Patel insisted on his ability to control security for the Assembly and closed its galleries. It took one month, but the matter was resolved when the viceroy intervened and an agreement was reached in which Patel would control security for the Assembly's inner precincts, whilst the police would control its outer precincts.

Although the Indian Legislative Assembly remained a debating chamber in the years after World War I, it did nonetheless pass a huge body of legislation which came to shape much of Indian life and economy. The six Assemblies which sat between 1920 and 1947 passed 729 laws, of which 686 were initiated by government members and 43 by members from outside the government. Much of the legislative business of the Assembly was routine and non-controversial and as many as 284 of the bills passed during this time went through without discussion. The largest number of laws, 158 in total, related to finance, insurance, currency and banking, whilst the next largest body of laws, 133, related to power, industry, commerce and trade. Such laws were required to regulate a developing economy and Indian members generally allowed subject experts from among their ranks to speak on these bills and rarely opposed economic legislation unless there were obvious advantages being extended to British businesses. Legislation regulating workplace relations such as the Workmen's Compensation Act 1923 and the Trade Union Act of 1926 sought to define the liabilities of employers and began to provide some degree of welfare to workers. Naturally, it was legislation which aimed to give the government special powers in addressing law and order issues which raised objections from Indian members always anxious to defend civil liberties and due process of law. But among the small number of bills which were sponsored by members from outside the government it was the relatively unheralded Indian members, Sir Hari Singh Gour and Har Bilas Sarda who were most prolific. They came from a staunchly moderate strain of Indian politics and saw their work in the Assembly as less that of disruption, and instead focussed on initiating and shaping legislation. During their legislative careers they introduced 20 bills each, and Sarda achieved some success when he had the Child Marriage Bill, which increased the legal age of marriage for girls passed with the support of members from the Swaraj Party and Nationalist Party. He had made his own contribution to the huge corpus of laws dating back to the 19th century, some of which is still on the books in the 21st century.

Ten
An Idea of India

The Congress's tilt at radicalism from the 1930s had largely fallen away by the 1940s. The Gandhians, the followers of Bose and the Congress Socialists had all been marginalised by a more conservative section of leaders which started to take control of the organisation and transform it from a protest movement into a parliamentary party. Whilst all the major leaders had tried to resist it, the 'drift to constitutionalism' became irresistible, and radical talk turned to more sober demands for 'national control' of the state and its services. Particularly national control of the army. The days of non-cooperation were long gone and the Congress was eager to demonstrate its strength at the polls by forming governments in the provinces; the results of the 1945 polls affected each party's representation in the transitional government.

During 1945 and 1946 the Congress was in talks with the British Government for an imminent transfer of power when Party leaders were put in the tricky position of having to deal with Indians in the armed forces who had revolted against their British masters in the name of Indian nationalism. The British had decided to put a section of the defeated Indian National Army on trial and their story had the potential to ignite political action which the Congress might not have been able to control. Similarly, a year later a large mutiny in the Indian Navy started off the coast of Bombay. The navy ratings saw themselves as incipient revolutionaries and participants in the Indian nationalist struggle. Jawaharlal Nehru largely handled the politics emerging out of the famous INA trials, whilst Vallabhbhai Patel dealt with the mutiny of ratings in the Indian Navy. Yet despite their differing political ideologies, both came to the same conclusion on the issue of what to do with the rebellious soldiers of Indian nationalism.

Amidst the INA trial, the Naval Mutiny and the hectic parleys over the transfer of power, the issue remained of what to do with the elite services of the state. The British had wanted the position of the services to be guaranteed in a treaty, and opinion in the Congress was divided. Amidst the uncertainty, Vallabhbhai Patel emerged as a staunch defender of the continuity of the services, securing their position in a Premiers' Conference before taking the matter to the Interim Government. Moreover, during 1946 and 1947 he seemed to be everywhere; directing affairs of state, having a hand in judicial appointments, military campaigns, official appointments in the princely states, keeping the peace in Delhi, and negotiating formalities in Cabinet. There did not seem to be any major issue which he was not called upon to handle. In all this work he had to liaise with the senior Indian officers of the services and rely on their goodwill and competence if he was to keep the state running at a time of instability.

The results of the Indianisation of the services became evident across the country during 1947. Senior army officers were called on to fight in Kashmir and an Indian judge was sent to Srinagar as prime minister. A middle ranking police officer in Bengal fought a losing battle to contain riots in Dacca, and then took over a police office and kept the paperwork flowing smoothly in Calcutta. An Indian Civil Service officer ascended to the post of cabinet secretary, but spent September 1947 trying to contain violence on the streets of Delhi. An Indian general created a plan to annex the Princely State of Hyderabad, and took the administrative system of British India with him. Despite the uncertainty surrounding their future, all the officers of the services stayed at their posts and did their jobs much beyond what was strictly required of them. Yet two years later, in 1949, the issue of the terms under which they would continue to serve was still formally unresolved. Not all Congressmen had worked with them as closely as Vallabhbhai Patel had. In fact, when the question of a constitutional guarantee for the services came before the Constituent Assembly, those Congressmen who rose to speak expressed something ranging from tepid support for the guarantee, to outright hostility.

***

The Indian National Army did not turn out to be the liberation army that its Indian soldiers or commanders thought that it would be. Mohan Singh had expected that the Indian National Army would be a force put onto the battlefield to fight for India's freedom. When it became clear that the Japanese only intended to use it to maintain law and order in its territories in South East Asia he disbanded the Indian National Army at the end of 1942, only to be placed under arrest. The Japanese would need a new Indian leader and after more than a year they found their man, Subhas Chandra Bose. Bose had been in Europe during the early years of World War II, but had not received any firm commitment of support from the Germans or the Italians, so when he was called to Japan for a meeting with the Japanese leadership he took Japanese Premier Tojo Hideki's statement of support for Indian Independence and pledge that Japan had no territorial ambitions in India at face value. Shortly afterwards he arrived in Singapore and another Indian National Army was born.

The Japanese took Bose into confidence; they planned a surprise attack on north-east India in 1944. Fierce fighting did occur, and climaxed with the Allied victory at Imphal in India's north-east after the British and Indian forces chased the Japanese back into, and eventually out of Burma. It was a particularly bloody period of the war; 30,000 Japanese soldiers died in the fighting and close to 18,000 Indian and British soldiers lost their lives. The Indian National Army did not play a large role in the fighting however; only 8,000 Indian National Army soldiers were sent to the front with the 230,000 Japanese soldiers. Indian National Army soldiers were attached to the three main Japanese divisions, serving as guides and interpreters and spies, but the three small Indian National Army units were mainly kept in the rear. The Regimental Commander Shah Nawaz Khan even wrote to Bose of his disappointment in April 1944; he had thought that the Indian National Army would be "the spearhead of an advance into India...When we actually arrived at the front line, the type of duty that was given to us was (a) road making or preparing (b) repairing bridges (c) extinguishing jungle fires (d) driving bullock carts carrying rations for Japanese troops."[cccxlvii] Later Khan marched through the jungle for days, reached Kohima, held a symbolic flag raising on Indian soil, and then found that the battle had already been lost.

Bose had thought that the sight of the Indian National Army men marching onto Indian soil and the propaganda they would project would prompt the surrender of Indian Army units. The Indian National Army did have some success in the case of three or four of its smaller units and gave the Japanese a momentary advantage in battle, but it was the Indian Army men who were particularly hard on their former colleagues. When the time came they did not want to let the Indian National Army men surrender and it was General Slim who instructed his troops "to give them a kinder welcome".[cccxlviii] As the Allied forces drove back into Burma the Indian National Army men surrendered and deserted in large numbers. Bose did not have much information about the details of the battles until late in the campaign, but he led his troops in retreat through Burma, and insisted that the men and women of his army cross rivers before he did.

At the end of the war the British rounded up 23,000 Indian National Army soldiers. Four thousand were categorised as "whites"; their plea that they were intending to escape from the Japanese was accepted and they were released. An additional 13,000 were considered "greys"; they were judged to have been misled and were similarly released. That left 6,000 soldiers who were dubbed "blacks"; they were the ringleaders, some of whom may have committed war crimes, and all were held for trial. Gurbakhsh Dhillon, Shah Nawaz Khan and Prem Sahgal's crimes seemed most clearly established and so they were the first to be chosen to stand trial at the Red Fort in Delhi. The Congress seized the moment to intensify the pressure on the Raj. Whilst news of the Indian National Army had largely been blocked out from India during the war, news of the trials and the Indian National Army fight for Indian freedom spread quickly. The idea of an army raised for the liberation of India from British rule stirred the imagination of the Indian people, drawing on a millennia old tradition of armed resistance to foreign rule. Jawaharlal Nehru later wrote, "I had judged rightly for immediately there was an amazing reaction in the whole of India and even the remote villages suddenly knew of the INA."[cccxlix]

In August 1945 Nehru expressed his concern for the Indian National Army men and whilst acknowledging Bose's "passion for freedom", he called the men of his army "foolish" and "misguided" for having aligned with the Japanese and Germans.[cccl] Patel added his voice to the growing call for the release of the Indian National Army men and called on the government to offer "clemency".[cccli] Nehru understood the passions which the soldiers of the Indian National Army had stirred and the need for the Congress to take a position on their fate. The 1945 elections were a test of strength for the Congress and the Muslim League, and Congress leaders felt the need to inject some fresh energy into popular nationalism after the memory of the Quit India movement had started to fade. Amidst a campaign dominated by arguments over Pakistan, the Congress merged the legend of the Indian National Army with the "struggle of 1942" in order to maintain public enthusiasm for the Party and its candidates as elections drew near.

Nehru began to use the spectre of nation-wide violence should anything happen to the Indian National Army men to both threaten the British in the ongoing talks over the transfer of power, and convince the Congress of the necessity of taking a position on the issue. He was the Congress leader who had elevated the Indian National Army issue in national political discourse and led efforts to have the Indian National Army men released. He even went so far as to describe the Red Fort Trial as "the symbol of India's struggle for freedom."[ccclii] The Congress Working Committee had formed an Indian National Army Defence Committee, and the All India Congress Committee declared: "It would be a tragedy if these officers, men and women were punished for the offence of having laboured however mistakenly for the freedom of India."[cccliii]

When the trial came in November 1945, it had an element of show, both for the British and Indians. The British Government wanted to make an example of the three Indian officers in order to reassure its own British military leadership and rank and file that the law would be followed and disloyalty would not go unpunished, however it had no intention of putting thousands of other Indian National Army soldiers on trial. The Congress on the other hand took the opportunity to produce its finest legal talent in front of the Indian and international media. Many of the Congress lawyers had not supported the Indian National Army and continued to be opposed to any armed insurrection against British rule, but they nonetheless argued that the soldiers of the Indian National Army had been waging a legitimate war for the liberation of their homeland. When arguments closed Khan, Sahgal, and Dhillon were all found guilty of waging war against the British Government. They were to be discharged from the army, sentenced to transportation for life and forfeited their back pay and allowances. The sentences were then reduced by the Commander in Chief Sir Claude Auchinleck and the three men were set free.

There had been some low level political intrigue on the HMIS Talwar off the coast of Bombay in late 1945. Balai Dutt had organised some fellow officers into a clique known as the Azad Hindis, or Free Indians. On 2 February 1946 Dutt was caught with glue on his hands whilst plastering anti-British slogans on the Talwar. He was sent for interrogation where he announced himself to be a political prisoner. On 8 February Commander Fred King, the Commanding Officer of Signals on the Talwar lost his temper when some ratings harassed some female members of the Royal Indian Navy who were passing by and called them 'Coolies', 'Junglies' and 'Black Bastards'. The ratings, or non-commissioned sailors, started a hunger strike ten days later. A Central Naval Strike Committee was formed and a list of demands was made; they wanted political prisoners of the Indian National Army released, action against Commander King, demobilisation of the Royal Indian Navy personnel with provision for peacetime employment, scales of pay equivalent to the Royal Navy, quicker promotions, an end to recruitment of British officers, gratuity pay, retention of kit at the time of release, and better food. The ratings broadcast their demands and the strike spread through the establishment and then onshore. The strike broke out on 18 February 1946, spread to Karachi, and ratings and civilians ran riot in both cities.

The ratings called upon the Left Wing Congress leader Aruna Asaf Ali to be their spokesperson and intervene on their behalf in their negotiations with Naval authorities on the day that the strike broke out. She was not keen to be associated with the trouble and so told them to remain calm, take up the service grievances with the naval authorities, and political grievances with the political leadership. If they wanted the support of the nationalist movement then she directed them to Vallabhbhai Patel, the highest authority in the Bombay Congress. Aruna Asaf Ali then contacted Patel on the ratings' behalf. He told her that "the ratings did not resort to the strike under his advice" and so "it was no business of his or hers to interfere".[ccclix] He insisted that the ratings had to maintain discipline, something which Asaf Ali then relayed to them. She later tried to play peace maker and even sent a telegram to Jawaharlal Nehru to rush to Bombay to try to control the situation.

Meanwhile, Vallabhbhai Patel kept advising the ratings to maintain non-violence and opposed their call for a strike. He told them that he was in touch with the authorities in New Delhi and he was trying to bring an end to the strike. Leading Signalman Mohammad Khan eventually took Vallabhbhai Patel's advice to surrender, but he insisted on a written assurance that the ratings would not be victimised. He remembered, "the worthy Sardar flew into a rage and thumping the table said 'when you don't trust my words, how can you trust my writing? I assure you on behalf of Congress that not a single one of you will be victimised.'"[ccclv] Khan then read out a message from Patel to his men:

> *"In the present unfortunate circumstances which have developed, the advice of the Congress to the RIN ratings is to lay down arms and go through the formality of surrender which has been asked for. The Congress will do its level best to see that there is no victimisation and the legitimate*

demands of the naval ratings are accepted as soon as possible."[ccclvi]

Khan reminded his men that they had vowed that they would be guided by the national leaders at the start of their revolt and so they would have to follow their direction to surrender.

The navy ratings who mutinied in Bombay were never held up as heroes of Indian nationalism as the men of the Indian National Army were after the end of the war. There was a certain romance in the Indian National Army story; the raising of an Indian force in South-East Asia which fought its way back to India under the leadership of Subhas Chandra Bose to liberate the motherland from British rule. The navy ratings rebelled much closer to home, off the shores of Bombay, objecting to bad food and insults from their British superiors. Theirs were service grievances, considered relatively petty and less useful in political campaigning. However, the fates of the Indian National Army soldiers and Indian Navy mutineers remained much the same after Independence.

Initially Jawaharlal Nehru did express some concern over what would happen to the Indian National Army men who had been rendered penniless and stripped of any pensions or benefits which may ordinarily have been due to them. An Indian National Army Enquiry and Relief Committee was formed to help Indian National Army men find work and some assistance was given for a time, but many thousands of Indian National Army men were left to fend for themselves after India's Independence. As the Congress came to be a part of the Interim Government in the lead up to the transfer of power Vallabhbhai Patel viewed the public fervour for the Indian National Army as "natural but temporary" and something which the Congress had to be "tolerant" of.[ccclvii] By the end of 1946 Nehru began to worry about the effect that any agitation in the name of the Indian National Army might have on the morale of the Indian Army, noting that "Army discipline has to be maintained."[ccclviii] In his letters he pointed out the negative effects any reintegration of Indian National Army men would have on the Indian Army; he wanted to ensure its efficiency and avoid any political agitation or unrest.[ccclix] Publicly Nehru denied that the Indian National Army men were kept out of the Indian Army for political reasons and cited their long period of demobilisation and low recruitment quotas as reasons for their lack of reintegration. He described the initial attempts to assist the Indian National Army men with employment as providing "psychological satisfaction to the INA and to the public generally".[ccclx]

Joyanto Chaudhuri gave the Nehru Memorial Lecture at Cambridge in May 1973 and mentioned a meeting which Nehru called in early 1948 to seek advice on the issue of the reintegration of the Indian National Army men into the Indian Army. Nehru called Chaudhuri along with P.V.R. Rao from the Defence Ministry and General Shrinagesh who each expressed their views, giving different reasons but coming to the same conclusion that the reinstatement of the Indian National Army men would be "incorrect, probably unwise and certainly disruptive". Nehru heard the trio out and at the end of the meeting said: "I disagree with your reasons but I agree with your conclusions."

But whilst there were at least some attempts to rehabilitate Indian National Army men, the navy ratings received little sympathy from the civilian powers in New Delhi. Navy Headquarters shared this position, and despite shortages of skilled manpower at the time of Independence it still refused to take the ratings back in, arguing that such a decision would only be an encouragement to others to mutiny and "a potential source of indiscipline" in the service.[ccclxi] Some of the ratings sent petitions to the Congress leadership as well as the

Ministry of Defence insisting on their contribution to the attainment of Independence and requesting reinstatement, but neither the political nor bureaucratic authorities paid them much attention. Those who were dismissed with disgrace were barred from any further military employment, were not paid any benefits and adverse remarks remained on their records.

***

Indians in the Indian Civil Service had come a long way since the days when British authorities would try their best to concoct schemes to stop their progress and Behari Lal Gupta had to fight for the right to try British settlers in the districts of Bengal. The results of the Indianisation of the service which had started after World War I became apparent during the transfer of power in 1946 and 1947. Hiralal Patel, who had studied at Oxford in the mid 1920s, learnt at the foot of Astad Gorwala in the districts of Sind and then held a range of key economic portfolios in India and Europe became India's top civil servant, ascending to the post of cabinet secretary. Initially Patel had to make his claim for the post before the last Englishmen to rule India. However, as Independence drew closer and he looked for guidance from India's new political leadership he was directed, like many other officers of the state, to India's first home minister for an answer to his questions.

Patel recalled that by 1945 the Government of India was looking ahead to ensure the smooth management of the transfer of power when it would eventually occur and began to take steps to establish a Cabinet Secretariat in New Delhi on the model of the Cabinet Secretariat at Westminster.[ccclxii] At the time in India the Viceroy's Executive Council was served by the Law Department. The Secretary of the Law Department was the Secretary to the Executive Council, who acted as a de facto cabinet secretary. But as power was being transferred to Indian hands using the British template of governance, it was thought that a Cabinet Secretariat modelled on the British one would be necessary.

Sir Eric Coates, the Head of Military Finance was appointed cabinet secretary and was placed in charge of organising an efficient secretariat. The basic task of the new secretariat was to make sure that the decisions taken by the Cabinet were implemented, and that the various government departments did not deviate too much from Cabinet priorities. Patel was informed in early 1946 that as soon as he could be relieved of his post as Officiating Secretary to the Department of Industry and Civil Supplies he would take over as joint secretary in the newly formed Cabinet Secretariat. Along with his role at the Cabinet Secretariat, Patel took up the role of Establishment Officer during 1946 and 1947, keeping track of Indian Civil Service officers and marking the more capable ones for senior appointments.

A Military Wing was incorporated in the Cabinet Secretariat, which initiated the more functional merger of the civilian and defence establishments in New Delhi. Patel recalled that until the transfer of power there was a large divide between the civil and military sides of government. The military side was known as the War Department, headed by the commander in chief and it seemed to act independently of the civilian government. It was only the officers of the Accounts and Audit Department who had a channel of communication with the War Department and a good working knowledge of its functioning. As in the British model it was considered necessary for senior officials from the Cabinet Secretariat to have a good understanding of the workings of the defence establishment. Sir Claude Auchinleck, the Commander in Chief drew up a plan for Patel to go around the military installations of the country to get a better idea of their working. Patel spent a couple of months visiting army, air force and navy installations during 1946. His guide was Major Gopal Bewoor who became Chief of Army Staff after Independence.

Patel recalled that the British wanted to be as correct as possible in matters of protocol and ensure that Congress ministers were seated correctly at the Cabinet table according to "inter-se seniority". He was asked to see Jawaharlal Nehru to get the requisite information. Patel fixed an appointment with Nehru for the day before the swearing in of the Interim Government. He posed his question to Nehru, who just burst into laughter and suggested that he go and see Vallabhbhai Patel. Vallabhbhai was also amused but gave Hiralal the required order of seniority. As he was about to leave, Vallabhbhai asked him to stay on for a briefing on the likely events of the following day. Hiralal gave him some information which he thought may prove useful and then told Vallabhbhai that he would always be available to provide further information or assistance as the need may arise.

At the end of 1946 and beginning of 1947 Sir Eric Coates went on short leave. Normally Patel as the next senior officer would take his place but instead the home secretary was invited to officiate. Patel mentioned his feelings to the viceroy's Secretary George Abell, who then communicated the conversation to the Viceroy Archibald Wavell, the Earl of Wavell who was in Simla. Wavell then called Patel to Simla and explained that the cabinet secretary had to deal with other government secretaries who were much senior to Patel and so it would be best to let a senior secretary officiate. Patel argued that this line of reasoning had never been used in the past and the viceroy's own secretary was a case in point. In addition, he had been brought into the Cabinet Secretariat on the tacit understanding that he would replace Sir Eric so long as there were no problems with his work. Wavell insisted that he had not found fault with Patel's work, but just wanted to explain his reasons for the decision. Sir Eric retired shortly after and the viceroy appointed Patel to the post of cabinet secretary himself. In his new role Patel soon found himself writing the minutes at the Viceroy's Executive Council meetings. He remembered it as a difficult task given how "long and lively" the meetings were. The chairman would rarely try to sum up the discussions or declare a decision which had been arrived at. Patel thought he had to use his own judgement to deduce the decision arrived at the end of a "rambling discussion".

Louis Mountbatten was named as Wavell's successor and was sworn in as the last Viceroy of India in March 1947. He got down to business immediately and kept up a hectic daily schedule of meetings with all the important political leaders. Patel recalled that he had brought with him his own group of officers, personal private secretaries and typists. He wanted to ensure that there be no leaks from his political discussions and negotiations, and it was only towards the end of the process that a key figure like Vappala Pangunni Menon was included in his inner circle of advisors. Even Patel as cabinet secretary only met him at meetings of the Executive Council. Patel thought Mountbatten's approach was for the best as it minimised leaks and rumours and all the stakeholders felt that their rivals did not enjoy any special privileges in the ongoing political dialogue.

A Partition Council was set up and Patel was appointed partition secretary in the Partition Secretariat. As cabinet secretary Patel had to ensure the implementation of the directives of the Emergency Committee of the Cabinet which was chaired by Mountbatten. He was also the Indian representative on the two member Steering Committee. The Steering Committee was assisted by ten Expert Committees which themselves had subcommittees. During the summer of

1947 Hiralal would meet Vallabhbhai every evening and inform him of the progress made by the Expert Committees, indicate where agreement was likely to be difficult and brief him on the agenda for the upcoming Partition Council meetings. There was generally no consensus before these meetings and he would suggest ideas for possible settlements on issues which had not yet been resolved. Hiralal had to make sure that Vallabhbhai was properly briefed for any eventuality which may arise and not taken unawares during Council meetings. He thought his task was made easier by the fact that he enjoyed Vallabhbhai's complete confidence.

***

The formal transfer of power occurred and the British had begun their departure from India, however in the weeks and months leading up to and following Independence on 15 August 1947 the structure of the state was put under strain by violence arising from the partitions of Punjab and Bengal. It was the violence in Punjab which spilled over into Delhi and Patel recalled the Capital being on "the brink of disaster" during September 1947. The pervasive sense of chaos also caused the relationship between Indian Civil Service officers and their new political masters to take a new turn. Whilst officers like Hiralal Patel had earlier looked to Congress leaders as potential patrons in the new order, Cabinet ministers in New Delhi had little experience of government administration and would come to rely on officers like Patel to restore order in the Capital. Patel and his colleagues themselves had little experience of dealing with violence and anarchy on such a scale and would have to quickly improvise a system based on their years of training and experience to minimise communal clashes, ensure the movement of essential supplies and maintain sanitation to prevent the outbreak of an epidemic.

A hint of things to come in Delhi came a week after Independence Day when an explosion took place in the house of a Muslim science student who was thought to have been trying to make a bomb. A stabbing was reported a few days later near Diwan Hall and Wavell Canteen close to where a reception had been arranged for the refugees coming in from Pakistan. A Hindu worker and a Muslim worker then got into an altercation at Birla Mills which started a melee. The police were able to control the fight but reports of stray incidents of violence kept coming in. The local Delhi administration was simply not up to the task before it. Many Muslim officers in the administration had left for Pakistan as had more than half the city's police force. They could not be relied upon, nor could many of the city's Hindu policemen who had roots in Punjab and had heard of the horrors faced by their relatives in their villages. There was also a shortage of soldiers available to maintain order given that many of the army formations which had been allocated to India were still held up in Pakistan.

There was a brief lull in violence during the first week of September as the district magistrate imposed a curfew. However, Hindus and Sikhs and Muslims were using the quiet time to prepare for further hostilities, and when a bomb went off in the Hindu locality of Karol Bagh more looting and stabbing and arson ensued. In the violence which followed, old stores of arms and ammunition were put to use. The local police were helpless, and a police picket at Turkman Gate could only be rescued with difficulty. A sub inspector was shot dead and even with the deployment of troops restoring order posed a great challenge. What made the task so difficult was that both sides were well armed and prepared for the fight. Patel thought that "stabbing was developed into an art"; it seemed to satiate the need for vengeance, and it was mainly women, children and the elderly who were the victims. The frenzy was not confined to the streets, but bands of refugees coming into the city from Pakistan would rush into houses and drag residents out onto the street to be stabbed. Groups of Sikhs struck terror in the heart of government quarters in New Delhi, so much so that Muslim servants had to be evacuated into refugee camps for their own safety.

The Chief Commissioner of Delhi was a Muslim whilst his deputy was a Sikh. Patel thought that both were capable officers but Sikh refugees coming into the city saw the chief commissioner as partisan, and Muslims on their way out thought that his deputy was suspect. Muslim refugees had taken shelter in the old Muslim forts and tombs of Delhi and rationing had to be administered. Given the lack of basic sanitation in the refugee shelters the authorities had to try to prevent the outbreak of an epidemic. Patel decided to discuss the situation with V.P. Menon, the Secretary to the States Department in one of their daily meetings, and they decided that the home minister needed to be informed and some special arrangements be immediately put into place. Menon suggested that they put Astad Gorwala in charge of the city. He was in Delhi as Chairman of the Prices Commodities Board, but it was thought that such an appointment may involve the suppression of the local Delhi administration, besides which it was doubtful whether Gorwala, Patel's old mentor, would have the necessary weight and authority for the task. Instead the suggestion of a high level committee appointed by the Emergency Committee of the Cabinet was put to the home minister. It would have more credibility and avoid suppressing the local administration. Vallabhbhai approved and put the idea to the Emergency Committee of the Cabinet. The matter was decided on 9 September and the new committee was formed with Cooverji Bhabha, the Commerce Minister as chairman and Hiralal as vice chairman.

Delhi was divided into five zones. Each zone was to be

entrusted to a senior government official who was appointed as an administrator. Each administrator was given a quota of men and materials and was told to do what needed to be done and only keep Headquarters informed of their situation and requirements every four hours. A skeleton Headquarters was put together at the Delhi Town Hall with a wireless to maintain contact with the zones and a mobile reserve at its disposal. The committee wanted as much decentralisation as possible whilst maintaining co-ordination given the lack of available manpower. There was some debate over whether this was the best plan; it was argued that the creation of a new committee would destroy what little confidence people had in the local administration. However, as the debate was going on, news came through of some Muslims shooting down Hindus near Ajmeri Gate. Hiralal rushed to see Vallabhbhai, but as they were discussing the debate around the new committee, reports came in of Hindus being killed by Meos on Lodhi Road and another of a Muslim being hacked down not far from where they were speaking. Vallabhbhai was "visibly shaken" and then asked Hiralal what the point was of standing there and discussing the issue and to get to work with the new committee.

Patel remembered his first visit to the Delhi Town Hall along with the Chairman Cooverji Bhabha, Shyamaprasad Mukherjee, the Minister for Industry and Supply and Kshitish Neogy, the Minister for Relief and Rehabilitation. Parts of the city which were usually buzzing with activity such as Darya Ganj, Chandni Chowk and the Jama Masjid were deserted during the middle of the day. As the cabinet secretary and cabinet ministers approached the Town Hall they came upon a small crowd which had gathered around the corpse of a stabbing victim. The chief commissioner and deputy commissioner met Patel and the ministers and briefed them on the situation and the action they were taking to bring it under control. A pressing need was for a cleanup of the city;

the streets had not been swept and in some cases corpses had not been cleared. The ministers left, and Patel then got to work.

Delhi Town Hall soon became the 'Central Control Room' issuing instructions to the administrators and workers in the zones and receiving a constant flow of demands for information and assistance from the public and official organisations across the city. The system of decentralisation seemed to be working and so the committee decided to implement the maximum possible co-ordination between the police, the magistrate and the various organs of local government. The Emergency Committee devolved most responsibility onto Patel and within a couple of days the committee had ceased to function, though individual members continued to offer assistance through the Control Room. However, Patel was also cabinet secretary and still occupied with Partition issues and so he also had to devolve much work to his "Lieutenants" Krishen Lall and Lakshmi Jha, both officers of the Indian Civil Service who were appointed as secretaries to the committee.

Late each night Patel would chair a meeting at which the day's events and any unsolved problems would be reviewed and solutions would be found and instructions issued. After each late night meeting Patel would then brief the home minister and committee chairman. The next morning the committee chairman would then inform the Central Emergency Committee of the previous day's events. Patel and Bhabha would then make their requirements for manpower, material or equipment known before the Central Committee which would promptly issue the necessary orders. Importantly, Patel was given the power to requisition the services of any officer of the Government of India he required. In some cases Indian Administrative Service probationers still under training were called into service, one of whom was killed whilst doing his duty. Troops were in scarce supply, with only a few Gurkhas, Madras paratroopers and a contingent of armed police from the Central Provinces and Berar being readily available. The government had to call upon the services of army cadets still under training and used the Territorial Army for escort duties. Volunteers from the Congress, the Jamiat Ul Ulema and even the Scouts were also called upon to make their contribution. Each group had an accredited representative with access to the Control Room and would provide daily briefings on their activities and requirements and receive orders on deploying their men and materials.

Each government department including the Health and Food Departments, the Railways Board and the Delhi Municipal Committees were represented in the Control Room. They were given their own desk at which their representative would work as the liaison officer between their organisation and the Control Room. Each organisation was expected to use its own resources to fulfil the directions from the Control Room, but given that in most cases resources needed to be pooled it was the work of Lall and Jha to effectively plan the instructions and allocate resources. The zonal system was put into effect on 11 September and the administrators were soon able to bring large scale rioting under control. They were not able to prevent every incident and so could not restore the confidence of Muslims in the administration and persuade them to return to their homes. Instead they managed to arrange for secure escorts to the refugee camps.

Communications were hampered by the fact that the normal means of transportation had dried up. The public transport system had broken down, and tonga drivers stayed off the roads. Only a few would go out on the streets on foot or cycle, and even the workers of the Control Room had to be picked up for work from their residence. Each operation that the

Control Room commanded required reliable transportation. Requisitioning squads were formed under magistrates, however they had little success. They had trouble finding car owners, and when they did the drivers would be missing, and when both could be found simultaneously an essential part would be discreetly removed preventing the Requisitioning officer driving the vehicle away. So the Control Room quickly started collecting and hoarding all types of spare parts, taking disused vehicles from the roads, and collecting batteries lying around at railway stations. They even managed to collar some Muslim mechanics and put them to work in improvised workshops as long as they could convince them of their security. Volunteer drivers were called up and car owners were given coupons for petrol if they offered their cars for Control Room operations. The Defence Department was called in and offered as many jeeps as possible. However, even when sufficient numbers of vehicles were available the reliability and willingness of the drivers proved a problem. Many drivers were themselves refugees from Pakistan and were not keen to deliver relief supplies to Muslim neighbourhoods; they would lose their way or develop engine troubles to avoid delivering the goods. Their reluctance was not only based on malice, but also the personal safety of the driver. In one case Patel recalled a Sikh driver who had been cajoled into making a delivery of food supplies to the Muslim camp at the Purana Qila, however upon entering the camp he was surrounded by a mob and only just rescued. The success rate of the operations only improved when cadets from the Officer Training College were drafted in as drivers.

Sanitation proved another major challenge. The municipal sanitation workers had stayed off the job for over a week. The filth had piled up and when combined with looting and arson, dead bodies were rotting on the street. Neighbourhood residents were called on to form volunteer squads to clean the streets and pile up the filth at places where it could be disposed of or destroyed. It took some time for the effort to gather momentum and even when the sweepers returned they were slow in their work, eager to scavenge for valuables where possible. Volunteers from the Congress, Jamiat Ul Ulema and the Scouts all helped, special vehicles were assigned for the task of waste removal, and sweepers were brought in from the United Provinces. Later the army came in with a hygiene squad which made it possible for the filthiest parts of the city to be disinfected. It took a week for the spectre of an epidemic to subside.

The distribution of food was also in disarray. Ration shops remained closed, distributors did not want to venture out, and those that did could not get money out of their bank accounts or arrange transport to move supplies. The Control Room organised a system for the delivery of supplies to ration shop owners, but there was the initial problem of a lack of fuel for cooking. There were sufficient stocks of food but it was salt and fuel which were scarce and needed to be brought in from outside the city. Even when fresh supplies did begin to arrive there was an additional shortage of labour to unload and transport the supplies to the shops. The Control Room re-allocated transport from less pressing operations and ordered a local cloth mill to provide the required labour.

The Control Room also had to meet the basic requirements of the increasing numbers in the Muslim refugee camps. Arrangements were made for the supply of food and clean water and medical and sanitation services. Officers of the Indian Civil Service acted as camp commandants and they were assisted by Indian Administrative Service probationers. There was an attempt to set up an office at the camps, but the camp commandants could not communicate effectively with the huge numbers who had gathered under the makeshift tents until the navy lent them some loudspeakers.

They were also under darkness for the first couple of nights until the army lent them powerful searchlights. Military engineers and officers from the Public Works Department also helped to erect a system for the supply of clean water and installed a telephone connection. The camp commandants would go around the camp themselves and make a show of filling up drains and digging ditches. The fountains of Humayun's Tomb had filled up with stinking water and volunteers covered them with sand as they did with slit trench latrines. Supplies had to be ensured, the sick needed to be cared for, and inoculations had to be administered to prevent an epidemic. Like other parts of the city the camps would keep in constant touch with the Control Room which would most often have to improvise a solution for problems as they arose. Supplies would come from donations, stocks from shops and warehouses were requisitioned, Public Works Department storerooms were raided for their picks and shovels, loans were made from the New Delhi Municipal Corporation, and in some cases the camp commandants would load up empty tar barrels left lying about and take them for use at the camp.

***

Far from the corridors of power in New Delhi, Durgagati Bhattacharyya was still a middle ranking police officer in Bengal as Independence approached.[ccclxiii] He was an officer in Dacca in the days leading up to the partition of the province and his recollections provide a picture of the challenges of dealing with both communal violence, and a new political leadership whose trust he did not enjoy. When he was eventually transferred out of Dacca and returned to Calcutta at the time of Independence he would be given charge of the Security Central Office and have the more mundane task of getting the routine daily processes of a city police office going once again.

Bhattacharyya had been transferred to serve as additional superintendent at Dacca in early 1946. He thought of it as perhaps a punishment posting for throwing too many cocktail parties in Calcutta with foreign liquor. He was about to take up his post in August of 1946 when the Calcutta riots broke out. He was not on duty at the time but witnessed the carnage which started as Muslims returned from a League meeting on the Calcutta maidan shouting the slogan "Larke lenge Pakistan", or "We'll take Pakistan fighting". Bhattacharyya left Calcutta whilst the city was still under curfew. He reached Dacca and took charge of one of the city's two police administrative zones. Rioting had not been as bloody in Dacca as in Calcutta but small incidents continued to occur and Dacca had its own history of communal tensions which could break out at any moment. A Control Room was established and each of the additional superintendents would man the room around the clock doing eight hour shifts each and there were two or three squads of armed policemen and vehicles on standby ready to go out in case of an incident. In serious cases Bhattacharyya would go out himself, whilst for smaller incidents he would send an inspector or sub inspector with some armed police who would try to stop the violence, make preliminary investigations, arrest the culprits and leave some police behind to bolster the local patrol.

All the mixed localities had a police patrol made up of four constables from the District Armed Police. Four constables of the same religion would be posted together, split into pairs, instructed to do their duty, and would try to surprise their neighbourhood by backtracking over their route. Despite this, Bhattacharyya found that whenever a Hindu would be killed in one neighbourhood a Muslim would be killed in another on the same day. Officers could never prove that the killings had happened in the presence of their constables who would invariably claim that they were at the other end of the street when the incident took place. Later the officers tried to pair off Hindu and Muslim constables but the plan met with resistance. The constables feared that they might be abandoned by their fellow constable and killed by members of his community. Instead pairs of Hindus and pairs of Muslims were then sent out in the hope of securing the lives and property of both communities.

Bhattacharyya would go out to try to prevent an apprehended attack. He would have to provide police protection to the Fire Brigade as members of one community would block their way in dousing fires in the properties of the other community. Bhattacharyya recounted four instances in which he had to open fire. In the first instance he had received information of a boatload of potential murderers and arsonists sailing up a river to attack a village. Bhattacharyya went out with his armed constables and stood on the high bank of the river. He gave the obligatory warnings to the approaching boatmen and threatened to open fire if they did not stop. He could not tell whether they were Hindus or Muslims and when they did not heed his warnings he ordered his men to open fire. One of the police guides was familiar with some of the figures on the boat and tried to stop the constables from further firing. However, the guide ended up getting shot through his cheeks, but miraculously the bullet did not damage his teeth or jaw structure. He was rushed to hospital and Bhattacharyya offered to donate blood to someone who was, after all, an innocent police informant. There was no need however, and the guide was stitched up and made a full recovery. But Bhattacharyya did not know whether his constables' bullets had hit any of their intended targets, for no one had made a report of injury or death. The police made subsequent enquiries at the village which they thought the would-be rioters belonged to, but the villagers claimed not to have known anyone who had gone out the previous night. According to the rules, the divisional commissioner had to hold a magisterial enquiry as to whether the firing ordered by a superintendent was justified, but Bhattacharyya was exonerated.

Later Bhattacharyya received information that a bus load of Muslims travelling through a Hindu neighbourhood was likely to be attacked. He went and boarded the bus with two armed constables and his orderly guard and instructed the driver to proceed. His information was good and the bus was met by a small group of Hindus with swords and daggers which started throwing stones. Bhattacharyya did not warn the hostile crowd, but opened fire with his Lugar pistol and told the driver not to stop. The bus was able to continue without further attacks, but when Bhattacharyya returned to the scene of the confrontation in his jeep with a small police party he found a young man dead on the road. He had earlier shot the youngster through the head and he had died on the spot. Bhattacharyya had not aimed at the young man, the road had been too bumpy for such a precise shot; he had just fired in the air as a warning shot. He arranged for the body to be removed from the site and taken for a post mortem.

In the third case, Bhattacharyya had received a telephone call from the Vice Principal of Jagganath College that two Muslims had been surrounded by a mob which was about to kill them. The pair had taken shelter under the vice principal's verandah and he was trying to persuade the mob not to kill them. Bhattacharyya was at his own residence, and so could not go out with an armed police party but instead went out with his Lugar pistol and his armed orderly. When he reached the vice principal's house Bhattacharyya learnt that the Muslims were not from Dacca and did not know they had strayed into a Hindu area. They fell at his feet and begged him to save them. Bhattacharyya then tried to persuade the mob, but when that did not work he warned that he would open fire. The mob did not seem worried by the threat; they saw only two policemen, neither of whom had a rifle and so they started to advance. Bhattacharyya opened a round of fire. The vice principal then came forward to try to avert a disaster. He enquired with the mob as to whether anyone was hurt, and then proceeded to vouch for Bhattacharyya's character, and argued that the killing of the two Muslims would not be an act of patriotism and would not solve the communal conflict or help stop the killings going on in Dacca. The vice-principal's intervention seemed to work, the mob dispersed and Bhattacharyya called for an armed police contingent to take him and his orderly and the two Muslims to safety. Bhattacharyya thought the main impediment to preventing the killings and arson and loot was the lack of reliable information. In cases in which the police received timely information they were able to reach the scene and prevent the violence, but most often there were no telephones in the poorer quarters of the city where much of the violence occurred.

Local Muslim leaders had been full of praise for Bhattacharyya until an incident in which he had been trying to save a Muslim locality from arson. His actions had led to the death of several Muslims and only one Hindu. The Muslim League leaders were informed and Bhattacharyya was transferred out of Dacca to Bakarganj for the second time. He was not sorry to leave the daily routine of witnessing bloodshed and damage to property in Dacca. Preventative patrols had helped control the violence somewhat, but he would not miss the need to take quick action, which in many cases would prove futile as the police would arrive on the scene too late.

***

More than half of the officers of the Indian Police in Bengal were Muslims and most had opted to go to Pakistan. This left a large number of senior posts vacant which needed to be filled up from the level of inspector and deputy superintendent. Bhattacharyya reported to the inspector general's office in Calcutta and the senior Assistant Inspector General Upananda Mukherjee told him to take up the post of Deputy Commissioner of Police, Security Central Office. Bhattacharyya then called on the Inspector General Sukumar Gupta and the newly appointed Police Commissioner Surendranath Chatterjee. He took up his new post on 14 August 1947. The following day he presided over a flag hoisting ceremony in full uniform on the lawns of his residence on Pretoria Street. A larger ceremony was held on the Brigade Parade Ground where the Indian Army, Indian Air Force, Indian Navy, Indian Police, Home Guards, Boys Scouts and Girl Guides took part in an Independence Day parade in which the Governor Chakravarti Rajagopalachari took the salute. Ministers of the West Bengal Government and high officialdom of the state and central governments were all in attendance. Bhattacharyya recalled the governor arriving in an open horse drawn carriage and taking his seat on a dais with the Prime Minister of West Bengal at his side. Bhattacharyya also attended the event in full uniform, and he remembered a garden party in the afternoon at which the governor played the attentive host, sitting at the tables and chatting with most of his guests.

Perhaps the first law and order challenge after Independence in Calcutta occurred when it was announced that Government House would be thrown open to the public. Thousands rushed in and moved all through the building save for a few bedrooms and the dining room. They thought of Government House as the nation's, and indirectly, the public's property and a few took to looting the silverware and paintings. The commissioner of police had to get his deputies to take a contingent of policemen to clear the public from the building. They did so with difficulty and then had to tell those waiting outside to leave.

On 16 August Bhattacharyya had to attend office and try to get the routine of departmental work moving again. It had broken down in the few weeks before Independence as most British and Muslim officers had left and Hindu officers had not yet taken up their new postings. Bhattacharyya took charge of the Security Central Office from a British officer and then got to work with the assistance of two British officers who had decided to stay on. The Security Central Office was a part of the Calcutta Police Department, however it also received orders from the Intelligence Bureau in New Delhi. The office was in charge of passports and had to verify the background and character of the applicant before recommending or declining the issue of a passport. The office was also responsible for the registration of foreigners in Calcutta, received reports on foreigners in the districts and sent an annual report to the Intelligence Bureau. The Security Central Office would liaise with foreign consulates in Calcutta and Bhattacharyya found himself in high demand on the diplomatic circuit as he had the power to allow a foreigner to stay in the city for three days without a visa. The office would also monitor the flow of international mail and kept an eye on persons of interest and even undertook some intelligence work on the Soviet Union and China. It inherited the "automatic telephone tapping wire recorder" from the days of the war, and Bhattacharyya and his officers were authorised to tap any telephone line they required. They would sit and rewind the wire and listen to the previous few days conversations with a stenographer present to record any important details. When Bhattacharyya took over he continued the tapping of an important political figure of Bengal but did not pick up much political intelligence, only getting to listen in on a few infidelities in Calcutta's high society.

Another legacy from the days of the Raj was the illegal occupation of Muslim houses by Hindu neighbours in cases when the Muslim residents had fled for safety during the violence of Partition. When they returned to reclaim their property they would be met with the argument that Hindus had lost their properties all over the east of Bengal and so the new residents would refuse to leave. The police would be given the task of forcing the Hindus out of Muslim properties, yet this was a tough task given the determined resistance put up by entire neighbourhoods. Force was often required and so the task was given over to assistant commissioners and deputy commissioners. Bhattacharyya and his colleague from the Special Branch, Prasad Bose sought advice from the commissioner of police who directed them to another senior officer of the Indian Police, Hari Ghosh Chaudhuri. However, Chaudhuri could not give them any clear advice and so joined them in seeking out the Chief Minister Dr. Bidhan Roy. They all went to seek his orders, but Roy simply told them that they had been in the service for long enough to find a solution for themselves and that they must have faced similar problems during British rule and to use their good sense, experience and tact to manage the situation. Bhattacharyya recalled, "Such advice I had received later many times in my service." The trio were not entirely satisfied with Dr. Roy's advice and so sought out a higher authority. Mohandas Gandhi was staying at a house on Beliaghata Road, attempting to bring peace to Bengal. They went to the house without an appointment, bowed before him, posed their dilemma and sought his advice. In the instances the trio outlined, Gandhi conceded that they had no alternative but to use minimum force or non-violent means to evict the Hindus from the Muslims homes. He told them to believe in truth and justice and act according to their conscience. Bhattacharyya was impressed with Gandhi's "simplicity of thought".

***

Mehr Mahajan is not a name commonly associated with the drama of Indian Independence, but between 1946 and 1949 he found himself in the thick of the action.^{ccclxiv} During this time he was a judge of the Lahore High Court, served on a commission which looked into the Indian Navy Mutiny in Bombay, and then sat on the Boundary Commission which was to decide on the partition of Punjab. He subsequently accepted an offer to become Prime Minister of Kashmir just prior to the state's accession to India, spent a brief period as a Constitutional Advisor to the Princely State of Bikaner, and then returned to a newly established East Punjab High Court before being promoted to the Federal Court of India. The country was in a state of political flux, but legal continuity, and British rulers, Congress politicians and Indian princes all thought that the advice and expertise of a man with Mahajan's legal experience would be useful as they made decisions about the future of the institutions they represented.

With the partition of the country decided and the city of Lahore going to Pakistan, the Indian Punjab required a new High Court. The East Punjab High Court was thus created at the stroke Viceroy Mountbatten's pen on 14 August 1947. Dewan Ram Lal was appointed chief justice and Teja Singh, Amar Bhandari, Acchru Ram, Gopal Khosla and Mehr Mahajan were appointed as justices of the court.

On 29 August 1947 Dewan Ram Lal wrote to Mahajan from Amritsar describing the events of the previous weeks and asked whether Mahajan could come to take his oath of office. Ram Lal had left Lahore on the night of the 12th of August in tense circumstances. The Frontier Mail which had left the station an hour earlier had been attacked at Harbanspura, and there had been a bomb explosion on the platform on which Ram Lal sat earlier in the afternoon. When he reached Simla he swore in Sir Chandu Trivedi as the governor of the new state of East Punjab, and Sir Chandu then swore him in as chief justice. The new High Court was scheduled to open on 20 August and as there were no trains running Ram Lal borrowed Bakshi Sir Teja Singh's car and Acchru Ram's driver and reached Amritsar by 10:30. He got to work completing two or three jail appeals and was surprised that there was no heavy load of habeas corpus applications. At the close of the court on the 21st Ram Lal went to Lahore to Chief Justice Sir Abdul Rashid's house to discuss the division of the Lahore High Court's library and furniture. They could not agree on a division and so referred the matter to the Partition Council. Ram Lal also went to Mahajan's house in Lahore only to find his servants in a frightened state. He managed to retrieve two of his cars, six of his servants, three truckloads of furniture and library books and brought them back to Amritsar under military escort.

Ram Lal wrote that the warrants of appointment of the judges of the new East Punjab High Court had arrived but the governor had not yet given him authorisation for swearing them in and he would call Mahajan to Amritsar once he received the authority. It was uncertain whether Justice Donald Falshaw would be appointed but they needed another judge, and Ram Lal doubted whether they could get Sir Muhammad Rahman. If he did come he would likely have been the only Muslim in the court from the chaprassis up to the judges. Ram Lal recounted that ministers had given him oral assurances that pending the establishment of a new capital for the Indian Punjab the High Court would be located at Simla and the Government of India would release houses for the judges. Jawaharlal Nehru and Vallabhbhai Patel had also given instructions that the Punjab Government and the High Court should be located together, however Ram Lal thought the provincial ministers were "weak and open to influence" and so the location of the new High Court remained unsettled. He was going to see the Governor Sir Chandu Trivedi about the matter but worried that if they did not know where the court would be located they could not assign work appropriately which would mean that lawyers would not be available and hearings would have to be cancelled. Ram Lal assured Mahajan however, that assuming the court was to be located in Simla he had allotted him a fine residence; Fazal Ali's old house called Fir Hall, second only to The Retreat.

Ram Lal thought of himself and his family as typical refugees with family members and luggage scattered, and most of their property and wealth back in Pakistan. He was not optimistic about things settling down and given the daily round of atrocities it seemed as though another war was about to break out. Doing a quick head count of the new Bench he mentioned that Acchru Ram and Teja Singh were in Simla, Khosla was in Mussoorie, but they did not even know where Bhandari was. Amritsar was not a pleasant place to be writing from. There were no eggs and not many potatoes. There was not much fruit besides the local pears. But from the night he spent in Lahore Ram Lal thought things were still more depressing there.

***

Ordinarily Mahajan would have proceeded to Amritsar to take his oath of office from Ram Lal and continue his work as a High Court judge. However, in May 1947 when he was sitting in the Lahore High Court he had received a message from the court registrar informing him that the Maharani of Kashmir, Tara Devi wanted to meet him at Faletti's Hotel. Mahajan met Tara Devi and the Yuvraj, Karan Singh for tea at the hotel in the evening. Bakshi Sir Tek Chand was also present at the meeting, and Tara Devi, who hailed from the same district as Mahajan suggested that he give up his place on the Lahore

High Court and take up the prime minister's post in Kashmir. Mahajan advised her that he could not resign without the permission of the British monarch. Karan Singh then asked Mahajan whether the prime ministership of Kashmir was such a small thing that it could be refused so easily. Mahajan said he would think it over and if in the future the Maharaja, Hari Singh invited him to Kashmir to discuss the matter he would accept the invitation. Tara Devi had not forgotten his commitment and on 25 August sent him a letter carried by Captain Harnam Singh asking him to come immediately to Srinagar. Mahajan was in Dharamshala and the rains meant that he could not move out of the district. However, Tara Devi was persistent and on 7 September sent Harnam Singh and a military escort to bring him to Srinagar. The military wagon that had been sent for Mahajan's journey got stuck in the mud however, forcing the group to journey from Dharamsala to Srinagar on foot, horseback and lorry.

Upon reaching Srinagar Mahajan was offered the prime ministership of Kashmir for a five year period, and then left for New Delhi to seek the necessary permission to take up the post. Along with the Defence Minister Baldev Singh he met Vallabhbhai Patel on 19 September. Patel practically ordered Mahajan to accept the offer and leave for Srinagar immediately. Mahajan was given eight months leave from the East Punjab High Court and permission to take up service in Kashmir which Patel thought "was in the interest of India in the circumstances that had arisen." Mahajan also met Nehru and communicated Hari Singh's position that he was willing to accede to India and would consider administrative reforms of the state at a later date. Nehru expressed some irritation at Hari Singh's views however, and insisted on immediate changes to the state's administration and wanted Sheikh Abdullah to be set free. Mahajan also went to see Gandhi. They talked for an hour and Gandhi told him that he did not want any harm to come to Hari Singh, and if possible the state should accede to India with a democratic administrative system. Mahajan then communicated the theme of his talks with the political leadership in New Delhi to Hari Singh before leaving for Amritsar to take up his duties as a High Court judge.

On arriving at Amritsar Mahajan filed the necessary papers to process his eight months leave. But the Governor, Sir Chandu Trivedi did not seem in any hurry and may not have known of New Delhi's interest in the matter. On the night of 10 October 1947 Mahajan was woken up by a call from Patel in New Delhi who wanted to know why he was not in Srinagar. Mahajan replied that he had not been granted leave or received permission to serve in Kashmir. Patel then called the governor to get the relevant permissions expedited and called Mahajan again at 1 am and told him to board Edwina Mountbatten's plane which was leaving from Amritsar the next day. Mahajan then received a call from the governor granting him his eight months leave and permission to serve in a princely state.

Mahajan flew with Lady Mountbatten to New Delhi and began his meetings with Patel, Nehru and Gandhi. He also spoke for an hour with Lord Mountbatten who was now governor general. Mountbatten thought Mahajan had an unenviable job and was not sure what advice he could give him. He had been rebuffed by Hari Singh when he had visited Kashmir earlier in the year to discuss the matter of accession. Mahajan thought Mountbatten's view was that Hari Singh would have no option but to opt for Pakistan, though Mountbatten stated that as Governor-General of India he would be happy if Mahajan advised Hari Singh to accede to India. Mountbatten told him to see V.P. Menon in whom he had great confidence. Mahajan went to find Menon in the company of Shyamaprasad Mukherjee. They both advised him to bring about the accession of Kashmir to India "anyhow".

Mahajan arrived in Srinagar on 12 October carrying a message for Hari Singh from Nehru. Mahajan conveyed Nehru's request that Sheikh Abdullah, who had recently been released from custody be allowed to visit New Delhi. Hari Singh was not keen, sensing that the move would mean trouble for both himself and Mahajan. He thought Abdullah wanted to be Prime Minister of Kashmir and would persuade Nehru to put him in the position after which he would revive his "Quit Kashmir" movement and take power. Hari Singh wanted to keep the Sheikh within Kashmir, but on Mahajan's advice he allowed him to go to New Delhi. Before Abdullah went however, he came to the Palace to seek an interview with Hari Singh. Abdullah wanted to see the Maharaja alone, and Mahajan agreed, but Hari Singh insisted on Mahajan's presence. Abdullah made his resentment known both in his discussion and his rude behaviour to Mahajan and the deputy prime minister. He made it clear that a prime minister from outside the state was unnecessary and that Hari Singh should repose his trust in him and handover the state administration. He would then behave as a dutiful son to the Maharaja and act as a loyal subject.

Some leaders of the Muslim Conference and influential Muslim religious figures in the state approached Mahajan. They told him that he should advise Hari Singh to accede to Pakistan in which case they would remain loyal to him and ensure that he remained an independent ruler within the Pakistani state. The National Conference leaders however, were leaning towards accession to India and Mahajan remembered the ill feeling between Sheikh Abdullah and Jinnah which made any rapprochement between the two difficult. Mahajan also learnt of Pakistani plans for an invasion of Kashmir from a friend in Srinagar. According to his source, a tribal raid was being organised with the approval of the

British Governor of the North West Frontier Province. The plan was being shaped by a retired member of the Indian Political Service and its aim was to take Srinagar by Id at the end of October. Mahajan passed his information onto Hari Singh who had heard similar stories from his Muslim friends who had been over to the Frontier but he came to rely on the word of another Pathan palace insider who advised him that these were all just stories being spread as part of the cold war to pressure him to accede to Pakistan. Hari Singh was confident that a battalion of his Dogra soldiers would be able to defend the state from any tribal raid from the west.

Hari Singh's estimation of his military strength was misplaced. Mahajan recounted the fact that before the British Chief of the State Forces had left he had dispersed small units of the army to far flung parts of the state which meant that they were not in any position to put up a combined defence. Attempts to blow up key bridges which would facilitate entry to the state had not been executed as the Chief Engineer did not have the requisite dynamite; he went to Delhi to get supplies but by the time he returned it was all too late. At Muzzafarabad and Dumel, the likely places through which the Pakistani raiders would enter the state, there was only one battalion, commanded by Narain Singh. Hari Singh had sent instructions to disarm the Muslim soldiers who made up 40% of the battalion, but Narain Singh refused, citing the fact that they were loyal soldiers who had served under him in Burma. Narain Singh was later killed by his Muslim troops who joined forces with the Pakistani raiders as they advanced on the road from Muzzafarabad to Srinagar.

Major Agha Shah of the Pakistan Army had been in Srinagar for a week or ten days before Mahajan had taken over as prime minister on 15 October. He sought an interview, and Mahajan requested a briefing from his deputy prime minister before denying Shah's request. He cited the fact that he was new in the job and had not had time to acquaint himself with the state's politics. Major Shah insisted he could not wait, and so Mahajan agreed to meet him. Mahajan knew the major from Lahore, he was the son of the Chief Justice of the Lahore High Court and so they met with customary courtesy and affection and sat down to talk. Major Shah had been doing the rounds of the state administration, trying to get some commitment on accession to Pakistan. He then told Mahajan that he should give his solemn word that he would advise Hari Singh to accede to Pakistan. Mahajan then told Shah: "I was prepared to seriously consider this question and that after due consideration give such advice as I thought proper, keeping an open mind on the question of whether accession to the State of Pakistan would be more beneficial than its accession to India." However, he first wanted the Pakistani blockade lifted. Shah then sent a telegram to Jinnah who was in Lahore, but Jinnah wanted the question of accession decided before the blockade would be lifted. Jinnah invited Mahajan to discuss the matter in Lahore, but Mahajan refused. Major Shah got aggressive towards the end of the meeting, threatening Mahajan with dire consequences. Mahajan replied that it were such threats which would throw Kashmir into India's hands.

Mahajan then relayed his conversation with the Pakistani major to Hari Singh. By this time Hari Singh's position had hardened and he had resolved not to accede to Pakistan; if he had to build roads to connect the state with India he would do so. Mahajan asked Hari Singh why he had not resolved the matter prior to 15 August, something which could have avoided the present troubles. Hari Singh replied that he had been advised differently by his previous prime minister and still harboured the hope of an independent Kashmir. Mahajan flew with Hari Singh from Jammu to Srinagar on 23 October. They had been in Jammu to see for themselves the communal violence enveloping the region and thought it safer to fly back to Srinagar rather than travel by road. The annual Dusshera Day parade was to be held on 24 October and there was some discussion over whether or not it should be held. Hari Singh thought it should be cancelled given that there were not enough State Forces to conduct the ceremonial parade. Mahajan advised him that cancellation would create panic in Srinagar and if the parade went ahead the confidence of the townspeople in the ability of the State Forces to put up resistance to any invaders would be bolstered.

Hari Singh took Mahajan's advice, the parade went ahead on the Parade Ground on Baramulla Road outside town, and later in the evening a durbar was held in the old Palace on the banks of the Jhelum. Mahajan recalled a good turnout of officials and leading public figures, plenty of pomp and show, the customary offering of nazars, and not much panic amongst the residents of Srinagar. He was still confident of the State Force's ability to ward off any invasion. But on the way from the Durbar Hall back to the Palace the lights went out. Srinagar had been plunged into darkness. Yet the Palace had its own electricity supply, and so the Dusshera Dinner proceeded. As the guests were in the drawing room, Mahajan called the power station at Mahoora. A chowkidar came on the line to inform him that a wounded army captain had come on horseback telling them that the raiders were coming and to run away. The staff of the power station had thus fled, the chowkidar was still there however, and could not see any raider. Mahajan then instructed the electrical engineer at Srinagar to leave with a team for Mahoora. After dinner, as Mahajan was about to leave for his residence the wounded captain road up and told him that the Dogra Forces had met the raiders at Garhi, but unlike the reports of the chowkidar he gave an "optimistic account" of the fighting and told Mahajan that they were being driven back. Later that night Mahajan received a call from the Dogra

Chief of Staff. He had to retreat to the Srinagar side of Uri town, as his forces had not been able to destroy a bridge on the Garhi side of Uri. Nonetheless, he was still confident of halting the raiders' advance. A call also came through from the electrical engineer who had reached Mahoora but found that raiders had entered the power station. Mahajan called him back to Srinagar. Amidst the ceremonial parade, durbar, power failures and wounded soldiers riding in on horseback, Kashmir's deputy prime minister had left for New Delhi carrying the Maharaja of Kashmir's letter of accession to India and his call for military assistance to defend the state.

***

The day after the Dusshera Parade officials and citizens started to come to see Mahajan in a "panicky condition". He assured them that they would be able to save the town, but those who wanted to leave Srinagar in their own cars would be provided with a military patrol. Mahajan wanted as much transport as possible and to evacuate those who wanted to get out; he was in favour of a wholesale evacuation as civilians were likely to hinder rather than help in any defence of the town. National Conference members on the other hand condemned those who wanted to leave as cowards and took to deflating car tyres and stopping tonga drivers transporting people out of the town. On the afternoon of 25 October after consultations with the commanding officer of the Srinagar Forces, the governor and the inspector general of police, a decision was taken to give the raiders a receding battle. The effort was to be focused on defending Srinagar from invasion. V.P. Menon arrived in Srinagar, went straight to Mahajan's residence and told him he had come to take him to New Delhi. Until he reached New Delhi a decision over military aid could not be taken.

Mahajan and Menon reached New Delhi and drove straight

to the prime minister's residence on York Road. Both Jawaharlal Nehru and Vallabhbhai Patel were apprised of the situation and Mahajan made his request for military aid on any terms. Nehru thought that even if Srinagar was taken by the raiders the Indian Army was strong enough to retake it, that any operation would take some time for planning and deployment, and one could not simply be provided on Mahajan's demand. Mahajan then issued an ultimatum to the Prime Minister of India: the Indian Army had to be sent to Srinagar that evening or he would fly to Lahore to negotiate terms with Jinnah. At this point Nehru got upset and said "Mahajan, go away." But before he could leave, Patel whispered in his ear "Of course, Mahajan, you are not going to Pakistan." Amidst the whispers Nehru had been passed a note. Sheikh Abdullah was in the next room listening to the conversation, and agreed with Mahajan- the Indian Army had to be sent in. Nehru told Mahajan to go and rest at Baldev Singh's house. He was calling a meeting of the Defence Council and he would convey its decision through the defence minister. After lunch Baldev Singh told Mahajan that two companies of Indian Army troops were being sent to Srinagar. Singh told Mahajan that the commander of the force would need as much information as possible and fortunately Mahajan had brought with him a plan which detailed where the clashes had taken place, the location of the raiders and the distribution of the State Forces.

On the morning of 27 October Mahajan and Menon flew to Jammu and Hari Singh signed some formal documents which Menon took back to New Delhi. Before leaving New Delhi Mahajan had requested that Nehru write out the conditions on which Hari Singh had been given military assistance. Nehru wrote out his conditions in his own handwriting. The first was that Kashmir accede to India in matters of defence, external affairs and transport. The second was that the state administration be democratised and a new constitution framed on the lines of the State of Mysore. The third was that Sheikh Abdullah be brought into the administration, along with the prime minister. The first condition had already been met, the second would take time, and the third meant Mahajan would most likely be forced out as Prime Minister of Kashmir.

Once the security situation improved Mahajan invited Sheikh Abdullah to Jammu to share in the management of the administration in what Mahajan described as "an experiment in Dyarchy". Mahajan asked Abdullah to draw up a document outlining the way he thought the administration should function and an opinion from Nehru of how his condition of bringing Abdullah into the administration along with the prime minister should actually work. They both proceeded to New Delhi and held a conference at the prime minister's residence at which Patel and Menon were also present. Abdullah wanted to be appointed prime minister of the state with Mahajan taking up a ceremonial dewan's post. After three hours of discussion it was decided that Abdullah would be the Head of the Emergency Administration, and Mahajan would remain prime minister.

Mahajan spent the last couple of months of his tenure in Kashmir on problems of infrastructure and requests for military aid from New Delhi. There was only one fair weather road connecting Jammu with India and the telephone and telegraph system worked through Lahore. Both the telephone and telegraph lines had to be reconstructed through Pathankot and a new radio station was built at Jammu. The Central Public Works Department and the Sappers and Miners of the army were brought in to build a bridge over the Ravi and lay a tarred road to Jammu. Mahajan would go out in his jeep to monitor the construction of the road. Later the Jammu airfield was covered with wire netting to turn it into an all-weather airstrip. The requests of the Indian Army Commander in Kashmir to Army Headquarters in New Delhi for more military aid generally elicited little response. Mahajan and Sheikh Abdullah would travel to New Delhi to see Nehru and request more men and ammunition. Nehru then sent for the commander in chief and the chief of general staff. The chiefs said that more arms could not be spared and the requested battalions were engaged elsewhere in evacuation work. But Mahajan continued to sit on a dharna at Nehru's residence and managed to get Gorkha battalions flown into Jammu and sent to Kashmir by road. They did not make it in time to save the town of Kotli however, which became part of Pakistan administered Kashmir.

Mahajan began to fall out with the political leadership in New Delhi over its decision to take the dispute to the United Nations. Neither he nor Hari Singh nor Sheikh Abdullah thought it was a good idea. But Hari Singh had signed away control of external affairs when he acceded to India, and Patel told Mahajan that he and Hari Singh had no choice but to agree to New Delhi's position. At this point Mahajan asked Patel to write to Hari Singh to relieve him of his position. Mahajan was eased out of Kashmir and by the first week of March 1948 Sheikh Abdullah took over as prime minister of the state.

**

Whilst the politicians engaged in efforts to persuade the Maharaja of Kashmir to accede to India and then sent the Indian Army to force Pakistani raiders out of the state, it was men like Harbakhsh Singh who were called on to do the fighting.[ccclxv] Mehr Mahajan's account of the efforts he had to make to get New Delhi to send adequate military reinforcements towards the end of 1947 and beginning of 1948 point to just how little planning or preparation had been done by the civilian authorities for a potential military operation in Kashmir. This would be born out in Harbakhsh's experiences on the battle front.

Harbakhsh had been down with the flu at Ambala Military Hospital during October 1947. He would listen to the news on the radio twice a day and on 29 October he heard that Lieutenant Colonel Ranjit Rai, Commanding Officer of the 1st Sikh Battalion had been killed in Kashmir. Harbakhsh had not yet fully recovered, but he was the next in command to Rai and so the following morning he was discharged from the hospital and rang his friend, Wing Commander Arjan Singh and asked him to fly him to Delhi. There Harbakhsh rang the military secretary's office to offer his services in command of the 1st Sikh Battalion. The Deputy Military Secretary Colonel Shiv Misra said that they had been looking for him and he was to report to the Delhi and East Punjab Command for instructions. He went to the Headquarters of the Delhi and East Punjab Command and met the General Officer Commanding, Lieutenant General Dudley Russell who told him that he would fly to Srinagar the next morning. Harbakhsh would not be the Commanding Officer of the 1st Sikh however, he would be Deputy Brigade Commander of the 161 Infantry Brigade.

Harbakhsh arrived at Safdarjung Aerodrome at 5 am the next morning to be told by the Despatching Officer Captain Dinesh Misra that the Brigade Commander Brigadier Janak Katoch had been wounded the night before and so he would now be going to Kashmir to take over Katoch's forces. Misra was not sure if Indian forces still held the airstrip at Srinagar, they would have to find out upon approach. As Harbakhsh and his pilot approached the Srinagar airstrip he noticed palls of smoke rising from the surrounding villages, a sign of arson and destruction at the hands of the Pakistani raiders. Harbakhsh was unsure if the airstrip was safe to land on and so instructed the pilot to make a trial run. If they did not receive any hostile fire they would land on the second attempt. They were able to land and were met by Lieutenant Colonel Pritam Singh who briefed Harbakhsh, telling him of the battle which was raging on the edge of the airfield where about 30 Indian riflemen were engaging about 200 raiders who had burnt and looted the village of Ilgam. There was only one company defending the airfield.

Harbakhsh noticed some Sikh troops unloading parts of a mountain gun from an aircraft. It turned out that the young Sikh officer supervising the unloading was Harbakhsh's nephew, Second Lieutenant Jabar Singh of the Patiala State Forces. The young second lieutenant explained that he had instructions to unload two mountain guns which had been loaned by the Indian Army to the Patiala State Forces during World War II and then return with the crew to Patiala. Speaking as his uncle, Harbakhsh asked Jabar to order his crew to assemble the mountain guns and put them behind their only jeep and place them on the perimeter of the airfield where the Indian troops were outnumbered by the Pakistani raiders. Jabar then pulled a piece of paper out his pocket. It was an instruction from the Maharaja of Patiala, Yadavindra Singh not to participate in the fighting under any circumstances. Harbakhsh pocketed the order and then tried a different tact. He pointed to the dire situation at the edge of the airfield and suggested that if the raiders captured a part of the airfield the departure of Jabar and his Patiala forces would be in doubt. Jabar went back to speak to his troops, but Harbakhsh could tell that they did not seem interested in fighting. So having spoken as an uncle, and then appealed to their sense of self preservation, Harbakhsh decided to get out the rule book. He walked up to the Patiala troops, called them to attention and shouted: "As Senior Commander in the field area I order you to assemble your guns and follow me." He then cited the field service regulation which stated that an order from a superior commander could be disobeyed or changed by a field commander provided that he was satisfied that it needed to be done and could later justify it. Harbakhsh pointed his finger at the young officer and said: "Should you disobey my order, I will have you summarily court-martialled and shot for showing cowardice in front of the enemy, under the powers I enjoy as a Force Commander in Battle." A Havildar responded to Harbakhsh's order saying that they were willing to fight but that the guns which they had brought from Patiala did not have sights. Harbakhsh responded that the distance between themselves and the raiders was so short that they could fire with open sights. The Patiala forces did join the battle, and when they saw how effective their fire was and the backs of the fleeing raiders Harbakhsh had a tough time stopping them from shooting.

On Harbakhsh's instructions Pritam Singh had moved the Brigade Headquarters from the airfield to a house half a mile along the road to Srinagar. Harbakhsh arrived at the new Headquarters, met the staff and was briefed by Brigade Major Dilbagh Singh. The 1st Sikh had been forced to pull back from Baramulla by the raiders, had firmed in on an elevated position outside of Pattan ten miles from Srinagar and were surrounded by about 2000 Pakistani raiders. More battalions had been arriving and were being deployed for securing the airstrip and blocking access to Srinagar. The only reserve the brigade commander had at his disposal was a platoon of the 2nd Punjab which was guarding the Headquarters. Major Sampuran Singh, the Officiating Commander of the 1st Sikh called in from Pattan pleading with Harbakhsh for ammunition and reinforcements. Harbakhsh did not have reinforcements but offered the mountain guns from the Patiala forces as long as Sampuran could open the road half way to Srinagar from his side and escort them to his location. Sampuran agreed and so Harbakhsh instructed Pritam to tie the mountain guns behind jeeps and take them to the meeting spot the next morning.

That night Harbakhsh was woken up by Dilbagh who told him that the Chief of Staff of the Kashmir State Forces Colonel Kashmir Katoch had come to see him along with civilian liaison officers Durga Dhar and Bakshi Mohammad. Katoch told Harbakhsh that his mounted cavalry had been fired upon as they approached Ganderbal from Srinagar and that when another patrol was sent it was engaged with small arms fire just 4 miles from Srinagar. Katoch thought that the Pakistani forces would enter Srinagar the next morning and wanted to know if Harbakhsh had any troops he could spare to stop their progress. Harbakhsh remained silent, and he thought Katoch would understand. He did not know either Bakshi or Dhar and so did not want to divulge the fact that he did not have a soldier to spare. Bakshi may have misinterpreted Harbakhsh's silence and said that if he were given just three battalions he could direct them to positions on the three roads leading into Srinagar from the north. At the time Harbakhsh did not think that they had even one whole battalion in the Kashmir Valley. He wished the visitors a good night and then instructed the brigade major to have the 2nd Punjab Platoon which had been guarding the Headquarters loaded onto civilian buses. In the morning they would go and inspect the scene of the shooting on the road to Ganderbal.

Harbakhsh travelled with the soldiers in the direction of Ganderbal where they were led to a house which was supposed to be occupied by Pakistani forces. Harbakhsh and his men approached the house in assault formation. Seeing that the house was defended by riflemen on the roof, he told his men to go to ground. As he was thinking of making an encircling move, he saw a man waving a white flag on the roof of the house. They were Gurkhas of the Kashmir State Forces. Harbakhsh then returned to Headquarters and began to make plans to clear the raiders from the villages to the south of the airfield. He decided to send the 2nd and 4th Kumaon out at dawn on the morning of 3 November. The 2nd

Kumaon patrol was to search villages on the way to milestone 8 on the Baramulla Road. The 4th Kumaon was to search the village of Ilgam where fighting had taken place a couple of days earlier and take up a position guarding access to Srinagar near village Badgaon. Major Somnath Sharma, Commander of the 4th Kumaon had reported seeing locals hiding in the surroundings.

As the morning progressed Harbakhsh began to plan the operational measures needed to be taken to secure Srinagar from the increasingly serious threat the raiders were posing. He decided to withdraw the 1st Sikh from Pattan to milestone 4 Shelatang on the Baramulla-Srinagar road the following day. Harbakhsh did not want to pass the message over the wireless, which was prone to interception, so he arranged for Wing Commander Meher Singh to fly him over the 1st Sikh position so that he could drop the message. Harbakhsh returned to Headquarters to enquire on the progress of 2nd and 4th Kumaon, only to find that the 'locals' whom Major Sharma had seen turned out to be raiders who were attacking his position above Badgaon with mortars and light machine guns. Sharma asked for air support and Meher Singh was ready to go but needed the exact position of the 4th Kumaon on a map. Harbakhsh then rushed to the operations room of the Brigade Headquarters and cut a small section of the map on the wall and brought it back for the pilots to use on their mission. The mission seemed to be successful and the raiders were dispersed but later Harbakhsh saw Brigadier Lionel Sen with his head in his hands. Sen told him that Major Sharma had been killed. The 4th Kumaon had suffered 14 other casualties and Harbakhsh instructed the 2nd Punjab to recapture their position and recover the fallen soldiers. Sharma's body was sent back to New Delhi the following day.

Sen assumed command of the Indian forces in the Valley and Harbakhsh became his Deputy. On the morning of 4

November Home Minister Vallabhbhai Patel and Defence Minister Baldev Singh arrived at Brigade Headquarters with their secretaries and Lieutenant Colonel Billy Short. Sen began his briefing to the civilian leadership but Harbakhsh thought that Sen was painting an overly gloomy picture of the Indian position in the Valley and that he had been affected by the death of Major Sharma. As his Deputy Harbakhsh could not contradict Sen publicly, but he did speak to Baldev Singh suggesting that the Indian position was not so bad and to convey his thoughts to Vallabhbhai Patel. On his way out Patel told Sen: "Brigadier, You hold on, we shall send you reinforcements!"

Harbakhsh had issued the order for the withdrawal of the 1st Sikh to Shelatang and thought it his duty to meet them during their withdrawal and show them their new position. After Patel had left, Harbakhsh went by jeep and saw the 1st Sikh coming through at mile 7 on the Baramulla-Srinagar road. He directed them to the high ground which would make for an ideal position for the deployment of their light machine guns. Harbakhsh did not think that Sen was very interested in the deployment of his troops and so he ended up conducting operations himself.

On the evening of 6 November General Kulwant Singh took over command of what was to become the Jammu and Kashmir Forces. Harbakhsh sought Sen's permission to proceed to Shelatang. He then arranged for armoured cars to be redeployed to the area and for the air force to step up their patrolling. When he arrived at the 4th Kumaon position he met Pritam Singh and later contacted Sampuran Singh and they made a plan for the 1st Sikh to engage the raiders head on whilst the 4th Kumaon would attack village Zainkut from the left of the 1st Sikh cutting the raiders off from their base and capturing it. The 1st Sikh was to have a company loaded onto buses and ready to rush along the Baramulla-Srinagar road to occupy some trenches which had been dug and left behind by the 2nd Kumaon a few days earlier. The operations went according to plan and Harbakhsh asked Kulwant's permission to chase the enemy. He was told that this was Sen's job as brigade commander. Sen had been instructed to proceed, whilst Harbakhsh was required back at the airstrip for another task. Harbakhsh held a dismal opinion of Sen and lamented the fact that he did not follow orders to chase the raiders back. He stopped at Uri rather than going on to Domel and destroying the bridge over the river Sindh. Yet Harbakhsh put the ultimate blame on Kulwant, who should have seen the advantage of pressing on to Domel, but was persuaded by Hari Singh to divert troops to Poonch where some Kashmir State Forces were holed up.

Harbakhsh then became Commander of the Sri Garrison which was given the task of maintaining law and order in Srinagar, mopping up the enemy still in the Valley and protecting the line of communication to the 161 Infantry up to Baramulla. A Srinagar Defence Scheme was put into effect and law and order was enforced in the town by the imposition of a curfew and flag marches by infantry and armoured cars. The Valley was eventually cleared of raiders by deep patrols of the infantry, supported by Hari Singh's cavalry and the air force.

The Jammu and Kashmir Forces Headquarters was set up in Jammu on 8 November 1947 under the command of Major General Kulwant Singh. That evening Harbakhsh received a call from Headquarters in Jammu that the Prime Minister of India would be arriving in Srinagar at 9 am the next morning; he would be received by Hari Singh and Shiekh Abdullah and as Commander of the Sri Garrison Harbakhsh should be there. Nehru's plane touched down on time and after being received by the appropriate dignitaries it was Harbakhsh who was to drive him to Lal Chowk in Srinagar where residents were to welcome the prime minister on his first visit after the town had been defended from a Pakistani invasion. Harbakhsh remembered "tremendous enthusiasm" amongst the gathered citizens at Lal Chowk with the red flags of the National Conference all around. Sheikh Abdullah spoke, followed by Nehru, and shouts of "Hindustan Zindabad" (Long Live India) and "Pakistan Murdabad" (Death to Pakistan) rang through the air. Nehru was then taken to a nearby National Conference office and later attended a luncheon at Hari Singh's Palace. Harbakhsh later took Nehru back to the airstrip where he and his party were seen off.

***

Positions were reversed in Hyderabad where a Muslim Ruler of a Hindu majority state in the middle of India did not want to accede and New Delhi had to send in the army. The military invasion of Hyderabad took place almost a year after troops had been sent into Kashmir, giving the military leadership ample time to prepare 'Operation Polo'. It was Joyanto Chaudhuri, the Sandhurst graduate who had served in the Middle East and Europe during World War II who was chief of general staff in the lead up to the operation.[ccclxvi]

Chaudhuri was promoted to major general and selected to command the 1st Armoured Division in the Indian action against the State of Hyderabad. He flew down to Ahmadnagar where parts of the 1st Armoured were stationed, however some parts had been left in Hyderabad which was its official station. Chaudhuri drew up a plan which was based on the plan of General Eric Goddard, Head of the Southern Command. He took his plan to the Commander in Chief General Roy Bucher who showed it to Mountbatten who approved. The necessary orders were issued and Chaudhuri thought it would be a good idea to do a rehearsal whilst in Ahmadnagar and Sholapur. He instructed the Armoured

Division to rehearse the plan but it turned out that the rehearsal was tougher than the actual operation; it rained, which made it possible for the tanks to get bogged down in the local black cotton soil.

A few days prior to Operation Polo Chaudhuri received a message from Vallabhbhai Patel to come and see him in Dehra Dun. Patel told Chaudhuri that if things went well he would take the credit, but if things went badly he would take the blame, in any case he would be supported. Patel asked him how long he expected the operation would take. Chaudhuri thought it would take seven days. Patel then cross examined him for half an hour before he was convinced. They continued their discussions over lunch and Chaudhuri returned to Army Headquarters where he reported his discussions with Patel to Bucher.

Chaudhuri was chief of general staff and had to hold discussions on the plan of attack with both Bucher and Goddard. Chaudhuri thought highly of Goddard's plan which emphasised the capture of Hyderabad city. The main force would move from a base in Sholapur to the west and another smaller force would move from Bezwada in the east. Bucher however, seemed to disagree with Goddard's plan on almost every point. He wanted to attack from the south where the terrain was more suitable for tank movements and the distance from the border to Hyderabad city was the shortest. Chaudhuri and his staff thought the only good feature of Bucher's plan was the minimisation of the distance from the border to the city, however the matter of preliminary advance, communications and administration all worked against it. Bucher stuck to his plan and Chaudhuri argued with him over the details. Goddard seemed reluctant to press his case for an attack from the west and in the end the commander in chief disagreed with most of the operational plan but relented on the advice provided by his staff. Bucher also held a high opinion of the Commander in Chief of the Hyderabad Forces, Major General Syed Ahmad El Edroos. Bucher thought that under El Edroos's leadership Hyderabad would put up stiff resistance, leading to a long drawn out and bloody battle. Chaudhuri and Goddard also disagreed with the commander in chief on this point. Chaudhuri had known El Edroos from his time in Secunderabad before World War II. He had seen him commanding the Hyderabad Cavalry in joint manoeuvres with the Indian Army and whilst admiring his personal charm, Chaudhuri had not been impressed with his military knowledge. He and Goddard noted that El Edroos had never commanded troops in operations or manoeuvred large formations and so the gap between theory and practice would become evident once the fighting started.

The operational plan of the Southern Command was accepted with a few minor modifications and Army Headquarters began to raise and equip the troops. Chaudhuri got stuck in the middle of a standoff between the civil and military establishments however when Bucher made it clear that whilst the re-equipping was going on there would be no other troop movements until the situation in Hyderabad started to deteriorate. Baldev Singh wanted to move the 1st Armoured Division to Poona and then on to the Hyderabad border as quickly as possible. The defence minister summoned Chaudhuri twice and asked him to give the orders for the move towards Hyderabad but he needed the permission of Bucher to do so, who would insist that the troops were not yet ready. In this case he agreed with Bucher as too early a move would alert the Hyderabad Forces to Indian plans, upset negotiations between Hyderabad and the Government of India, and give the civilian authorities in New Delhi the false impression that Indian troops were ready for the operation. The situation in Hyderabad started to deteriorate in March 1948 and the Government of India became adamant about mobilising the troops. Bucher agreed and at the end of April the 1st Armoured Division moved from Jhansi to Poona and Ahmadnagar. The moves were supposed to be a signal to Hyderabad that the Government of India was serious about preventing any spillover of law and order problems into India and was ready for any trouble ahead.

Chaudhuri had learnt from his service and training abroad of the need to send in a civilian administration behind any military action to take over the local government when it fell. He and the General Staff had difficulty convincing the civilian authorities of this need, but fortunately by this time the defence secretary was Hiralal Patel, "a far seeing and intelligent man". After Patel had been briefed he then spoke to V.P. Menon and an agreement was reached on the need for a ready civilian administration to move into Hyderabad when the time came. The Chief of the Southern Command was to have an advisor from the civil service, a police advisor, a railway advisor, a medical officer and a civil engineer all ready at Poona. However, this skeleton civil administration would operate under orders from the senior military officer. Hyderabad's 16 districts had been earmarked for the allocation of a district collector and district superintendent, five pairs would come in from Bombay, three from the Central Provinces and Berar and eight from Madras. The Ministry of Defence hosted conferences which were attended by representatives from the Home Ministry and the States Ministries as well as chief secretaries and inspector generals of police from the states involved. Representatives of the General Staff attended these conferences at the start to explain the necessities of a skeleton administration. At the time that Chaudhuri was chief of general staff he attended these meeting with the director of military operations, Brigadier Sam Manekshaw and found the contacts he made with the civilian officials useful for when he would later move into Hyderabad.

Chaudhuri thought that India's Agent-General in Hyderabad, Kanaiyalal Munshi wanted "strong intervention" and seemed to be working to bring it about. Bucher was not in favour of military intervention but thought that if it did come it would probably do so as a result of Munshi's instigation. In fact, Bucher thought that the road ahead would be smoother without Munshi and wanted someone more committed to a peaceful resolution of the stand-off. He suggested Satyavant Shrinagesh, Jayavant's elder brother who so liked a fight at West Buckland School 30 years earlier, and who was by now General Shrinagesh, as a possible replacement. Yet despite the Army Chief's concerns, Munshi kept his job. In May 1948 General Kulwant Singh returned from Kashmir to take over the role of chief of general staff. Chaudhuri was sent to command the 1st Armoured Division. He was pleased for he had been involved in planning the Hyderabad operation from the beginning and would now get to see it through to completion. Before sunrise on 13 September 1948 Indian troops entered Hyderabad. On the afternoon of 17 September Mir Osman Ali Khan, the Nizam of Hyderabad announced a ceasefire and allowed the entry of Indian troops to Secunderabad and a ban was placed on the Razakars, the private militia raised to defend the Nizam's rule. In the four days of fighting 1200 Razakars were killed. The Indian Army suffered ten casualties. Chaudhuri was met by El Edroos five miles from Secunderabad where he was formally offered the Nizam's surrender. El Edroos then took Chaudhuri to Munshi's residence.

Chaudhuri soon settled into his role as Military Governor of Hyderabad. He was advised by Zain Yar Jung, "a jewel of a man and pro Indian to the core" who had the ear of Vallabhbhai Patel in New Delhi. Patel also had his own eyes and ears in Hyderabad in the form of Aravamudu Ayanggar, a local lawyer who would send him reports on Chaudhuri's conduct and the general happenings in city. Chaudhuri would attend music and poetry recitals and whenever he had the urge to hear some light music he would invite the Nizam's string orchestra to his Guest House where they would perform a programme. He found Hyderabad's cultural life to be quite fascinating and was impressed by the Hyderabadis' impeccable manners. He noted that no matter which class his visitors came from they would always appear in clothes cleaned the day before so as not to show discourtesy. He could not say the same of the erstwhile Ruler however. Chaudhuri "could not believe that the great Nizam was such a shabby individual. With oil stains on his face and on his hat...". Whenever Chaudhuri would receive instructions from New Delhi which required the Nizam's co-operation, he would go and meet him and pose his request in courtly English which would then be translated into courtly Urdu and the Nizam would usually consent. Chaudhuri did not take a tape recorder with him "because it would have frightened the old man".

During his time as Military Governor of Hyderabad Chaudhuri variously attempted to break up a gun running syndicate, abolish zamindari, fund the Archaeological Department and provide a building for a women's college. He would go out in his jeep from village to village giving little talks assuring the population of the Government of India's friendship and the need to maintain religious harmony. When the time came for Nehru to visit Hyderabad Chaudhuri had a difficult time getting the Nizam to greet him at the airport. The Nizam objected that he had never even gone to receive a viceroy during the days of the British Raj. Chaudhuri replied that he was not referring to any viceroy but to independent India's first prime minister. On Zain Yar Jung's advice the Nizam agreed to go to the airport, but Chaudhuri still had to make sure that he was properly dressed. The Nizam wanted to wear his stained but comfortable 35 year old coat. Chaudhuri objected, but they reached a compromise and the Nizam agreed to cover the stain with a scarf.

Vallabhbhai Patel also visited Hyderabad along with V.P Menon. Chaudhuri was relieved when he learnt through Menon that Patel was pleased with his conduct as military governor. Patel had earlier told Chaudhuri that when he reached Hyderabad he would be in charge as military governor rather than the agent general. Later Chaudhuri would visit Munshi who would give him advice, to which he would say little. Munshi took the hint, excused himself with an illness and asked for a flight to Bombay. Chaudhuri also dissolved the Cabinet which the Nizam had created in the hope that it would advise him as military governor. His priority was to maintain law and order and prevent religious clashes and for this purpose he put El Edroos in charge of law and order for Hyderabad city. El Edroos had better local knowledge and appreciated the trust which had been placed in him. Chaudhuri enforced a curfew on the city and later demilitarised one brigade of the Hyderabad Army. With El Edroos's co-operation Indian forces were able to capture Qasim Razvi, the leader of the Razakars and kept him in a military cell. Chaudhuri then sent a telegram with the news to the home minister. In December 1949 Chaudhuri received a message from New Delhi. His time as Military Governor of Hyderabad had come to an end.

***

An Interim Government of India had been formed in September 1946, and prime ministers and premiers of the provincial governments were called to a conference in New Delhi on 21 and 22 October to discuss the maintenance of the administration after the British secretary of state ceased to be responsible for the services.[ccclxvii] Of the eleven provinces, eight were under Congress control and were represented by their prime ministers, whilst Sind, Bengal and

Punjab sent senior officials to state their positions. The Conference was presided over by Vallabhbhai Patel, the Home Member in the Interim Government and began discussions on the establishment of an All India Service to replace the Indian Civil Service. In his opening remarks Patel stated: "the main question was whether a Central or Provincial Service should replace the I.C.S."[ccclxviii] Patel realised the need for making "adequate allowance" for "provincial susceptibilities" in a large and diverse country but argued that it was for the protection of these "susceptibilities" that an All India Service was required. Only an All India Service modelled on the Indian Civil Service would be free from political and communal biases and remain impartial and efficient. A provincially controlled service would not be able to act independently or remain above local factionalism. Patel stressed the need for a politically non-committed All India Service and maintained that there would be advantages to the Centre and the provinces in such a system. The Centre would stay in touch with local realities, maintain contact with the provincial governments and maintain uniform standards for administration across the country. The provincial governments would receive the best of a national pool of talent for the higher posts in the administration. Patel argued that this could only come about through central recruitment and central control of the cadre which would provide the necessary security to allow officers to act independently.

None of the non-Congress provinces accepted Patel's argument for an All India Service. The Congress ruled provinces also had their reservations; Govind Pant from the United Provinces, Tanguturi Prakasam from Madras and Gopinath Bardoloi from Assam all accepted the need for central recruitment and training for an All India Service but argued in favour of provincial control over promotions and dismissals. Sri Krishna Sinha from Bihar agreed to central control reluctantly, which left only Bombay, Orissa and the Central Provinces and Berar in full support of Patel's proposal. Nonetheless, when the Conference continued the following day Patel stuck to his original argument, stating that it was "desirable that an officer should not be exposed to the serious penalty of removal or dismissal from service before his case is examined by an independent and impartial authority not under the control of the provincial government." Patel's position ended up being the position of the Conference. The Congress provinces all fell into line in the spirit of party discipline, and besides the issue of an All India Civil Service, the principle of central control for an All India Police Service was also settled. The Conference's Draft Scheme was circulated amongst the provinces in November and altered in some minor details before being approved by Patel and placed before the Cabinet. The Indian Administrative Service was then created by Executive Order.

During the Cabinet Mission to India earlier in 1946 the secretary of state tried to allay the fears of both the British and Indian officers of the services by expressing the hope that a treaty between Britain and India would include a clause making allowance for those officers who wished to continue serving in India whose services the Government of India wanted to retain. Assurances were given by the Congress leadership at that time, but the situation became more complicated by early 1947. Despite opposition from both Jawaharlal Nehru and Vallabhbhai Patel, generous compensation packages were offered to those British officers who did not want to continue in service after the transfer of power. A similar compensation package was initially going to be offered to the Indian officers, however it was agreed that given the ample opportunities opening up in the service with the departure of British officers and their natural patriotism and desire to continue serving their country, they would not receive the option of compensation but would continue in their posts. Even after receiving the offer of compensation some British officers still wanted to stay on as long as certain conditions could be met. However, the new nationalist leaders both at the Centre and in the provinces refused to entertain any requests for special conditions of service and most British officers eventually left in August 1947.

After the chaos of late 1947 had subsided, Patel took the matter of the services to the Cabinet once again on 30 April 1948. Up until this point the Draft Constitution did not make any reference to an All India Civil Service or Police Service. However, the issue of a special constitutional protection for the All India Services was on the Cabinet agenda, and it was Patel who saw the measure through Cabinet once again. He had written to Nehru days earlier arguing that to leave the services to the whims of the central or provincial legislatures would be "a grave mistake".[ccclxix] He also reminded Nehru of the assurances they had both given to the British Government during the Cabinet Mission, suggesting that there had been an "understanding" that they would see that the rights and conditions of the serving officers would be safeguarded. Given that they were "honour bound", the best way to fulfil their commitments was by the inclusion of a constitutional guarantee. Articles 308-313 of the Constitution were all discussed and adopted in the Constituent Assembly on 7 & 8 September 1949. They covered the officers' terms of service under the president, protections against arbitrary dismissal, and the formal creation of the new Indian Administrative Service and Indian Police Service.

On 10 October 1949 the Constituent Assembly debated an article of the Draft Constitution which would guarantee officers of the All India Services the same conditions of service which they enjoyed prior to Independence. The guarantee would become Article 314 of the Indian Constitution, and the precise wording which Assembly members gathered to discuss read:

> "Provision for protection of existing officers of certain services. Except as otherwise expressly provided by this Constitution, every person who, being a member of a service specified in clause (2) of article 282-B of this Constitution or a service which was known before the commencement of this Constitution as an AR India service continues on and after such commencement to serve under the Government of India or of a State shall be entitled to receive from the Government of India and the Government of the State, which he is from time to time serving, the same conditions of service as remuneration, leave and pension, and the same rights as respects disciplinary matters or rights as similar thereto as changed circumstances may permit as that person was entitled to immediately before such commencement."

Hundi Kamath, formerly of the Indian Civil Service, immediately took issue with the drafting of the article. He felt it must have been drafted in a hurry and thought its construction was "execreble" and "messed up". He insisted that any Assembly which passed such an article would be held up to ridicule. He thought the blame lay with having to draft the Constitution in English, which gave greater impetus to efforts to promote Hindi as the national language. The article had been drafted by a committee led by Kanaiyalal Munshi, of the Bombay Bar. Kamath then suggested a series of amendments which tidied up the article's language and construction.

Mahavir Tyagi, a former army man who had joined the Congress after the massacre at Jallianwala Bagh started the substantive discussion. He was not in favour of the article in principle and had questions about remuneration. Indians in the civil service had received promotions out of step with their years of service or seniority and given the exodus of British and Muslim officers there were many more secretaries all drawing high rates of pay. He wondered whether the guarantee envisaged in the article meant that future Parliaments would not be able to reduce the number of secretaries or their pay.

Rohini Chaudhuri, a veteran Congress member of the Assam Legislative Assembly welcomed the article as it maintained a standard of conduct which a government should maintain with its civil service. He put the matter in context; a transfer of power had occurred rather than a revolution which would upset the old order and so the old obligations of the previous government needed to be honoured. However, he wanted the officers of the civil service to take a pay cut as a gesture of reciprocity. He did not like the fact that civil servants were drawing higher salaries and living more lavish lives than ministers and suggested that ministers should be provided with government cars and better houses to allow them to meet civil servants at a level of equality. He thought it only right given that the Congress leaders had given up their prosperity and leisure and status and spent much time in jail whilst the civil service officers "remained quietly at their own desk, earning their own bread and doing their ordinary work." But he did go on to add- "If at that time all the members of the Civil Service had also resigned there might have been great difficulty for us to carry on the work in the period of transition."

Rustom Sidhwa, a long time Congressman and former Mayor of Karachi stated: "We are proud of the services." But he did not want to be dictated to by them and thought they should trust the political leadership to fulfil the commitments made rather than insist on a constitutional guarantee. Panjabrao Deshmukh, a farmers' leader from central India did not support the article either. Like Sidhwa he argued that the word of the political leadership should be enough, and if they were not trusted then a constitutional guarantee would be of little value anyway. But unlike Sidhwa he did not think that the services were particularly insistent on any such guarantee. In fact, he thought the guarantee was hardly a guarantee at all tempered as it was by the phrase "as changed circumstances may permit". Given the prevailing financial strain, the Parliament may have to cut civil servants' pay in a mere matter of months, reverting to the clause on "changed circumstances". It seemed odd to give such an extravagant promise tempered by an equally easy escape clause.

M. Ananthasayanam Ayyangar, a Congressman who had sat in the Central Legislative Assembly before the war did not think the article was necessary either. India had not even pledged to feed its population, and it was making a constitutional pledge to maintain the service conditions of the civil service. He saw that the heaven born service of the British Raj would continue to be the heaven born service of independent India. The 400 Indian members of the civil service "committed excesses thinking that this was not their country" and "They cared more for their money and the salaries they got." Ayyangar argued that the loyalty of Indian officers to the British monarch had been purchased at the price of such extravagant salaries. He continued his attack, ending with an allusion to Shakespeare's *The Merchant of Venice*; "Till now, they have not shown a gesture, they have not shown that they are members of the Independent Sovereign Republic. They must also contribute their mite to its growth. We assume they are still sticking to their pound of flesh." He said that the politicians should "take an axe in our hand" to cut off a bloated civil service, and further argued that the senior civil servants had to take responsibility for the growing talk of corruption in their departments. Ayyangar then closed with an appeal that the amendments be withdrawn and the article be passed "though not without hesitation." This confused Brajeshwar Prasad and likely all those who had listened to Ayyangar's speech. Ayyangar had started by opposing the article, launched into the strongest attack against the civil service of any member of the Constituent Assembly, and then closed with an appeal to pass the article in question.

Brajeshwar Prasad, a Congressman and former Municipal Commissioner of Gaya was in favour of the article. He thought it suspicious that so many members of the Assembly were opposed to its inclusion in the Constitution and thought it was important that the Assembly honour the commitments previously given. Politicians would come and go and it was not certain that the current political leadership would remain. Furthermore, Prasad had "no faith" in universal adult franchise and thought that with so many illiterates voting some party with a radical ideology could come to power and do away with the solemn commitments made to the services.

Shibban Saxena, a Congressman and professor of mathematics pointed out the irony of the Congress criticising Indian Civil Service conditions of service and its role in perpetuating British rule for decades and then suddenly enshrining its rights in the new Constitution. He was not happy with the work or record of the old civil servants and whilst he acknowledged there may be some capable officers among them, he thought that many of the country's current ills were down to their behaviour. Kuladhar Chaliha, a Congressman who had resigned from the Assam Civil Service as a young man invoked Greek mythology when he said that they were between Scylla and Charybdys; bound to honour the commitments made by the leaders of the Independence movement, but also answerable to their constituents to whom they had promised to reduce civil service salaries. He wanted the Drafting Committee to modify the article so that future generations were not tied down by it. Ramnarayan Singh, one of the longest serving Congress members of the Central Legislative Assembly, like his colleagues found it hard to support the article but could not bring himself to oppose it given that the great leaders had given their commitments in the past. He did however find it difficult to understand the need for such an article. It may have been necessary at the time of the transfer of power given the uncertainty that the civil servants felt about their future, but two and a half years later they knew that the machinery of government could not operate without them.

Vallabhbhai Patel rose to speak and immediately took issue with M. Ananthasayanam Ayyangar. He thought that if he was so dissatisfied with the service then he should have moved a resolution to dissolve it and run the system in a vacuum for he had not proposed any substitute. Ayyangar had stated that the guarantee should not have been given in the first place, and Patel questioned what he had been doing over the past three years whilst the discussions over the transfer of power were being held in public view. The British had made the transfer of power contingent on guarantees to the members of the services who reported to the secretary of state and held covenants with the British monarch. They had even suggested a treaty on the question. There was also the suggestion that Indian officers be given compensation should they want to leave the service and not serve the new dispensation and be paid a proportionate pension. These terms were put before the Cabinet and then before Parliament. The British were told that the issue of Indian members of the services had to be left to the political leadership on the basis of trust. Patel wondered where all the naysayers were when all of this was going on and dared them even now to provide a better substitute: "I must confess that in point of patriotism, in point of loyalty, in point of sincerity and in point of ability, you cannot have a substitute."

Patel wondered what the use was of talking about the fact that civil service officers were serving whilst Congress leaders were in jail. He had himself been arrested many times, "But that has never made any difference in my feeling towards people in the services." He continued: "I wish to place it on record in this House that if, during the last two or three years, most of the members of the services had not behaved patriotically and with loyalty, the Union would have collapsed." He asked, "Is there any Premier in any province who is prepared to work without the Services? He will immediately resign. He cannot manage." Patel reminded the Assembly that the administration had carried on despite the fact that it was "a broken Service" with half its members having left for Britain or Pakistan. He also reminded his fellow Assembly members that the Constituent Assembly was not a Congress platform, and that the Karachi Resolution of 1931 which committed to restricting civil service salaries was no longer relevant for "there is a long distance between Karachi and Delhi today." If members insisted on attacking the services they had to propose an alternative and take responsibility.

Patel then raised the idea of running the administration on a Gandhian philosophy with no army; "Tomorrow the whole of India will be run over from one end to the other, if you have not got a strong army." He noted that the Indian Police was functioning fairly efficiently across the country and was covered under the proposed article and asked "Are you going to put your Congress volunteers as captains? What is it that you propose to do?" He reminded the members of the fact that the guarantee was incorporated in the Indian Independence Act, had been circulated to the provinces, approved by Cabinet and passed by the Parliament with the Congress President Pattabhi Sitaramayya and Mohandas Gandhi in attendance and it was agreed to incorporate the guarantee into the new Constitution. Patel implored Assembly members to read their own history and fulfil their pledged commitments.

Patel then related an anecdote about a "senior Member of the Service" who had raised a loan to travel to England for university education and civil service training 25 years earlier. He had served the British Raj, and was now ably serving independent India- "His business is to serve the Government- that he is serving". This officer did have a sense of patriotism and "came into difficulties" when he had to carry out orders for the jailing of Congress workers, "But he could not go beyond a certain limit. Having spent so much on his education he was left with paltry savings and when he died his wife would get some money from a provident fund." Patel went on to argue for service officers' autonomy; they had to have the ability to offer their honest opinion to their ministers without fear of sanction for "That is what the Britishers were doing with the Britishers."

Patel framed the issue as a choice between a guarantee for the services or the potential dissolution of the nation; "The Union will go- you will not have a united India, if you have not a good all-India service which has the independence to speak out its mind, which has a sense of security that you will stand by your word and, that after all there is the Parliament, of which we can be proud, where their rights and privileges are secure." If members did not want the existing services they should just as well adopt a Congress Constitution or a R.S.S. Constitution, because "This Constitution is meant to be worked by a ring of Service which will keep the country intact." He repeated the phrase in his next sentence- "we shall have this model wherein the ring of Service will be such that

[it] will keep the country under control." Patel suggested that some Assembly members may not have been aware of the difficulties of running a government in 1947; "They do not know what would have happened. They do not even now know. Yet we have difficult times ahead. We are talking here under security kept in very difficult circumstances. These people are the instruments. Remove them and I see nothing but a picture of chaos all over the country." A Special Commission had selected new recruits to make up for the shortfall after the departure of the British and Muslim officers. The young recruits would have to be trained- "They will learn from these people."

Patel then told Assembly members to forget the past of conflict with the British, and invoked Gandhi; "What did Gandhiji teach us? ...But you come out of the jail and then say, 'These men put me in jail. Let me take revenge.', That is not the Gandhian way." The home minister then closed with an appeal to abstain from using the supremacy of Parliament to beat the services, and to be good on their word: "That is the way of administration."

***

Given the chaos which ensued around the time of Partition, the state could have collapsed if its officers had gone missing. They did not, and that was partly because staying at their desks was a matter of livelihood. But it was more than that, there was also a sense of vocation, what it meant to be a police officer or army officer or judge or civil servant. That sense of vocation was drawn from their training at the universities of England, Sandhurst and the Indian Military Academy, the Bar Associations and the Police Training Colleges, and the century old culture of their services which had been passed down by British and Indian senior officers alike. They had some sense of identity, pride in their cadre, in their role and rank, and so despite the exchange of population and the exodus of British and Muslim officers, they rose to the challenge and kept their offices and institutions functioning amidst the chaos of 1947.

Yet the officers of the services needed a patron, not only someone who would secure their interests and ensure continuity, but someone whom they could approach to take decisions and provide them with political support. It was Vallabhbhai Patel who was the Old Man in New Delhi, the captain steering India's ship of state. It was in his interaction with the officers of the services that he developed the high regard for them which he eventually spoke of on the floor of the Constituent Assembly. He was as reliant on them as they were on him; his job would have been impossible without them. It is not clear if the Indian Civil Service officer who he referred to in his speech was Hiralal Patel, but the description could just about fit. Whilst Hiralal initially approached Vallabhbhai as a potential new patron, during August and September 1947 it was Vallabhbhai who had to rely on Hiralal and his colleagues' competence and experience in bringing the situation in Delhi under control.

The criticisms of the Congressmen in the Constituent Assembly were not really about the competence of the officers of the services however, it was their loyalty which was suspect. They were considered fatcats, pampered with their high salaries and quick promotions, whilst the Congress leaders had sacrificed their careers and their prosperity and gone to jail. But again Patel stepped in and made an argument for dharma; they were doing their duty, in this case, their "business". There was a sense that whilst the previous government had gone and a new government had come, the eternal Indian state remained. The officers of the services served this state's government; "He served very ably, very loyally the then Government and later the present

Government." The current and future Indian Governments would expect the same loyalty from them as they had shown to the British. It was the exact reason why the Indian National Army soldiers and navy ratings had not been reinstated; they had been disloyal to their salt giver.

What emerged from Patel's intervention on the floor of the Constituent Assembly was his idea of India, one which would be obscured by the more poetic version found in Jawaharlal Nehru's *The Discovery of India*. Whilst Nehru wrote elegantly of India as a syncretic culture, absorbing cultural influences down through the centuries, layer upon layer, its genius being in its capacity for assimilation, Patel had a much more basic and practical vision of a "ring of Service" which would "keep the country intact". His speech prompted a historic reconciliation between the two divergent sections of the Indian middle class; the leaders of the Congress who had struggled against British rule, and the government officers who had remained loyal to the Raj. He saw the need for strong centrally controlled services which politicians would be able to call on in the event of threats to law and order and national security like those which occurred in 1947. The political class would need to rely on services which could draw on the best and brightest students, work towards a national ideal rather than a local one, and would follow orders no matter how difficult they were. In fact it has been this idea of 'Patelian statism', a strong central state backed by strong All India Services which has guaranteed the security of the Indian Republic since its establishment in 1950.

Afterword

The state has sometimes been compared to a vast and intricate machine which orders the lives of its citizens. However, the state is not a machine, it is a very human institution and only as good as the people who make it work. This idea was understood by the British from their earliest days in India. Before the question of Indians coming into the elite services of the state became so controversial at the end of the 19th century, they had spent many decades worrying over just who the ideal recruits from their own society were. The culture that the Englishman took with him as he administered the districts of the Raj was thought to be just as important as the rules and regulations and processes he had to abide by. There was a time in the late 19th century when the British felt that this culture of governance was not being sufficiently absorbed by intelligent but relatively lower class English boys and they began to fret about the calibre of the men that they were sending out to rule India. As Indians began to press their demands to enter the elite services of the state though, the British would claim that this culture of governance was a racial possession, only full blooded Englishmen could ever master it.

However, as the Indianisation process gathered pace and Indian officers came into the Indian Civil Service, the Indian Police and the Indian Army, and Indian judges began to sit on High Court benches across India, that old British racial claim would start to wither. When the Congress began to more forcefully challenge the state, in times of crisis Indians proved that the state was only as good as its officers. When law and order broke down at Sholapur in 1930 and the British fled and hid in their train carriages and Congress workers took up police duties it was Narayanrao Kamte who had to restore order. Likewise, in Monghyr in 1942 when the Quit India movement threatened to topple the Raj it was Nagendra Baksi who had to work with his British and Indian colleagues to improvise a way to maintain the authority of the state. When Lahore went to Pakistan, its Hindu judges were left without a court to sit in. A new one was created at the stroke of the viceroy's pen, and when the judges made it to India they did not yet have a building to sit in. Yet once things settled down and all the judges could be located, a remnant of the Lahore High Court continued on in India. As the fighting broke out in Kashmir Harbakhsh Singh was down with the flu in Ambala. He could have stayed in bed, but instead he got himself discharged and proceeded to Delhi to await further instructions from the new military leadership. When Delhi itself had been a picture of chaos in September 1947, Hiralal Patel and his colleagues had to hurriedly concoct an organisation to restore order and sanitation in the city. Time and again when buildings fell, communications broke down and officers became isolated, the state lived on because of their dedication, training, experience and commitment.

By 1947 the elite institutions of the state which had started as British institutions on Indian soil in the 19th century had become Indian. The work that these senior Indian officers did at the time of Independence is a testament to that. That process was initiated by the training which young Indian officers received from their British superiors in the 1920s. It was evident in Braj Nehru's interactions with Ivan Jones whilst inspecting the fields of Punjab. It was there in Joyanto Chaudhuri's time at Sandhurst, in Bishwa Nath Lahiri's attempt to survive the Officers' Mess in Moradabad and Narayanrao Kamte's training under William Herapath in Ahmadabad. Mahomedali Chagla even got a peek into a bygone era of the Bombay High Court when he observed John Inverarity during his last days of practice after World War I. But what helped to turn British institutions into Indian ones so quickly was what happened next. Indians who had been the understudies of

British officers then taught the next generation of Indian recruits the processes, procedures and culture of the services as early as the late 1920s. Astad Gorwala took Hiralal Patel out on camel back through the districts of Sind, Raghabendra Banerjee took Durgagati Bhattacharyya through the police station routine in a remote Bengal district in the late 1930s, and Harbakhsh Singh returned to the Indian Military Academy shortly after Independence to serve as deputy commandant. Even in the Indian Legislative Assembly Vithalbhai Patel held the sanctity of the office of president above his own party affiliations, setting an example for generations to come.

The elite institutions of the Indian state which had been Indianised were deeply constitutional and bureaucratic in their workings. Just as the quality of these institutions was initially dependent on the energy and sincerity of the Englishmen who brought them to India in the 19th century, their longevity in independent India depended on the Indians who staffed them from the 1920s. The deepening of constitutionalism could be seen throughout the Indian state structure. Braj Nehru met it when he joined the Finance Department in New Delhi in 1940 and was taught the system of files by the office superintendent. V.K.R. Menon literally carried it under his arm in the form of the *Bihar and Orissa Code*. Sankara Chettur sat in the Secretariat in Madras and learnt the hard way how long it would take to build a bridge in independent India. Eric Stracey learnt how to manage the never ending stream of petitioners in Erode by firing off the appropriate written instructions, and had to find a way to work within the law on non-cognisable offences. Even army officers, raised to be dashing men of action, had to learn how to dot their i's and cross their t's at Staff College and then navigate the established military protocols in New Delhi. The British barristers of the Bombay High Court had brought their great talent for nitpicking, and their commitment to legal principles in the 19th century, but by the 1940s it was a new

High Court deep in central India that was adjudicating over the precise level of officer required to inform the court of the detention of a political prisoner. And that most constitutional of all institutions, the Indian Legislative Assembly in Delhi, the maker of over 700 laws, would prove a training ground in parliamentary practices for three generations of Congressmen.

Most of the figures in *The Ring of Services* went on to successful careers after Independence. Mohammad Hidayatullah was appointed Chief Justice of India in 1968. He was Acting President of India for a brief period in 1969 and went on to serve as Vice President of India between 1979 and 1984. Harbakhsh Singh became a national hero during the India-Pakistan War of 1965. He led the Western Command and played a great role in reviving the spirits of an army which had been defeated by China just three years earlier. He rose to the rank of three star lieutenant general and received the Padma Bhushan, Padma Vibhushan and the Vir Chakra. Hiralal Patel served as a civil servant until 1959, and after his retirement became involved in politics. When Indira Gandhi was defeated at elections in 1977 Patel was appointed finance minister by the Prime Minister Morarji Desai, who had so liked to challenge the bureaucracy during his time as revenue minister in Bombay 40 years earlier. He would also be appointed home minister in 1979, following in the footsteps of Vallabhbhai Patel with whom he had worked so closely in 1947. K.P.S. Menon represented India as ambassador to the Soviet Union and China, whilst Mahomedali Chagla also turned to diplomacy after retirement, serving as India's ambassador to the United States and high commissioner to the United Kingdom before becoming external affairs minister in 1966. On the home front both Alakh Sinha and his son Mithilesh rose to the rank of inspector general of police in Bihar, as did Narayanrao Kamte in Bombay and Bishwa Nath Lahiri in Uttar Pradesh.

A study of the period of the Indianisation of the services shows that the 'transfer of power' which is generally thought to have taken place over a matter of months during the middle of 1947 actually took place over a period of 30 years from Edwin Montagu's August Declaration of 1917. The British had always understood their knowledge of statecraft as a type of power in itself. That declaration only handed over a small amount of governmental responsibility in the provinces, but if 'power' is defined as the ability to work and control the state, then a transfer had been taking place year after year through the 1920s and 1930s in the persons of the Indian officers who were coming in and learning to operate the courts, police stations, secretariats and army installations all over India. When the state was handed over to the Congress leadership in 1947 it was also handed an Indian officer class which had been trained in all aspects of statecraft for three decades.

Part of the reason for the continuity of the state was that Indian officers had done their jobs so creditably. Had Indian officers not performed so well in the War in Burma or in their posts in the districts of the Raj or managed to minimise violence in controlling political demonstrations and maintained their fidelity to the law, the future of the Indian state may have been very different and something new might have had to be built from scratch. In addition, from the time of the declaration of the goal of Complete Independence in Lahore in 1929, the Congress had not conceived of any specific alternative to the services of the British Raj. The Party did have a brief tilt with radicalism in the 1920s and 1930s but neither Mohandas Gandhi's anti-statist ideology nor Subhas Chandra Bose's hyper-statism prevailed and instead the Congress, always a bloc of moderate lawyers and liberal public men decided by the late 1930s to contest elections, form ministries and begin to work with the services rather than try to tear them down. The Party began a 'slow overhaul' of the state, which continues to this day. The

Congress spent much of the early 1940s immersed in communal issues and any prospect of reform of the services began to fall by the wayside. By the time that Vallabhbhai Patel spoke before the Constituent Assembly in October 1949 and rebutted the attacks on the services, he was able to point out that the Congress could not provide any reasonable alternative.

Patel passed away a little over a year after his speech on the floor of the Constituent Assembly, but the constitutional guarantee which he put in place would have a profound impact on the Indian state in the decades after Independence. He foresaw that governments would come and go, but the state would rely on the quality of its services. They had to be given security and the confidence to do their work and be able to speak the truth to their political masters. He wanted a 'ring of Service' to keep the country intact and under control and perhaps also sensed the threats to Indian unity which would emerge from religious and linguistic and ethnic separatism. Ultimately, he was proved right as time and time again the services have been brought in to keep India together when threats to law and order have emerged. Since the establishment of the Republic India's politicians have come to rely on their civil servants and police and army officers to restore order when events have spun out of control.

All the Indian services have played crucial roles in the development of the Indian state since 1950. The Indian Administrative Service which replaced the Indian Civil Service became involved in the Nehruvian economic project during the 1950s and 1960s. Its officers took up positions heading large public sector undertakings and increasingly directed India's economic life until the reforms of 1991. The Indian Army retains the structure of the pre-Independence army and has been called upon to defend India's frontiers in regular skirmishes, battles and wars with Pakistan and China, besides fighting insurgencies in Kashmir, Punjab, the North Eastern States and Naxal corridors in central India. Whilst neighbouring nations have faced the ever present prospect of army coups, the Indian Army has remained apolitical, subsumed to the civilian leadership even during periods of political instability. The upper judiciary has been, along with the army amongst the most respected institutions of the Indian state. Indians continue to look to the High Courts and the Supreme Court of India to interpret the Constitution, protect civil liberties, and control the power of the executive government. The criticisms which were made of the Indian Police in the 19th century still resonate today however. Despite drawing on a talented and capable officer cadre, the police continues to remain 'a weak point in the administration'.

Amazingly, the examinations for the services in 21st century India resemble the London examinations of the 19th century. They are amongst the most competitive in the world, and IAS coaching centres, similar to the crammers of 1870s London can be found in small towns and big cities across India preparing students for success in examinations which are based on merit. Much like for their English predecessors, these examinations can deliver young Indians a secure future of prestige and financial security. IAS probationers however, are worth significantly more than '£300 dead or alive' on the marriage market today.

The process of the Indianisation of the services which started in the 1920s is still ongoing, and will continue into the future. It was in 1968, more than two decades after Independence that the right of candidates to give their examinations in an Indian language was ensured, yet most students still write their examinations in English. Recent years have seen the rise of a new demographic coming into the services from smaller towns however, educated in Indian languages, bright boys and girls often from modest backgrounds. They will bring their experiences and perspectives to bear on the services, just as the services will shape them. And like generations past, they will serve the Indian state, the modern bearer of an ancient civilisation.

Notes

Chapter One: A Middle Class Quest

[i] B.B. Misra, *The Indian Middle Classes*, (London: Oxford University Press, 1961), 76.
[ii] Ibid.
[iii] Elmer H. Cutts, "The Background of Macaulay's Minute," *The American Historical Review* 58, 4 (1953): 839.
[iv] Ibid, 826.
[v] Ibid, 827.
[vi] Ibid.
[vii] Ibid.
[viii] Ibid.
[ix] D.H. Emmott, "Alexander Duff and the Foundation of Modern Education in India," *British Journal of Educational Studies* 13, 2 (1965): 161.
[x] Ibid, 162.
[xi] Lal Behari Day, *Recollections of Alexander Duff and of the Mission College which He Founded at Calcutta* (London: T. Nelson and Sons, 1878), 46.
[xii] Bentham to Col Young 28 December 1827, *The Works of Jeremy Bentham*, (Edinburgh: William Tait, 1843), Volume 10, 576.
[xiii] John Rosselli, *Lord William Bentinck: The Making of a Liberal Imperialist, 1774-1839* (London: Chatto & Windus 1974), 206.
[xiv] Suresh Chandra Ghosh, "Bentinck, Macaulay and the Introduction of English Education in India," *History of Education* 24, 1 (1995): 22.
[xv] Ibid, 21.
[xvi] Cutts, "The Background of Macaulay's Minute", 852.
[xvii] Thomas Macaulay, Speech to the House of Commons, 10 July 1833.
[xviii] Ibid.
[xix] Bentinck to Mancy, 1 June 1834. *Bentinck Papers* 2643/i. cited in Ghosh, "Bentinck, Macaulay", 23.
[xx] Anil Seal, *The Emergence of Indian Nationalism*, (Cambridge: Cambridge University Press, 1971), 124.
[xxi] Ibid., 122.
[xxii] Ibid., 357.
[xxiii] B.B. Misra, *The Indian Middle Classes*, 283.
[xxiv] Ibid.
[xxv] George Curzon, Presidential Address to Education Conference Simla, 6 September 1901 quoted in Misra, *The Indian Middle Classes*, 285.
[xxvi] Misra, *The Indian Middle Classes*, 288.
[xxvii] Ibid.
[xxviii] Lala Hansraj, 'Swami Dayanand and His Interpretation of the Vedas', *The Arya Samaj*, 34 cited in Sankar Ghose, *The Western Impact on Indian Politics* (Calcutta: Allied Publishers, 1961), 173.
[xxix] Kenneth Jones, *Socio-Religious Reform Movements in British India*, (Cambridge: Cambridge University Press, 1989), 98.

[xxx] Ghose, *The Western Impact*, 58.
[xxxi] Ibid., 6.
[xxxii] Ibid., 14.
Chapter Two: Insurmountable Distinctions?

[xxxiii] Thomas Macaulay, Speech to the House of Commons, 10 July 1833.
[xxxiv] John Beames, *Memoirs of a Bengal Civilian*, (New Delhi: Manohar, 1979), 64.
[xxxv] Ibid., 63.
[xxxvi] J. M. Compton, "Open Competition and the Indian Civil Service, 1854-1876" *The English Historical Review* 83 327 (1968): 265.
[xxxvii] Thomas Macaulay, Speech to the House of Commons, 24 June 1853.
[xxxviii] Bradford Spangenberg, "The problem of recruitment for the Indian Civil Service in the Late Nineteenth Century." *The Journal of Asian Studies,* 30 2 (1971): 344.
[xxxix] Ibid.
[xl] Ibid.
[xli] Thomas Macaulay, Speech to the House of Commons, 24 June 1853.
[xlii] Wood to Dalhousie, 24 November 1853, (India Office Library, Wood Papers) cited in J. M. Compton, "Indians and the Indian Civil Service 1853-1879: A Study in National Agitation and Imperial Embarrassment", *The Journal of the Royal Asiatic Society of Great Britain and Ireland*, 3 4 (1967): 99.
[xliii] Stafford Northcote, Speech to the House of Commons, 5 May 1868.
[xliv] Compton, 'Indians and the Indian Civil Service', 104.
[xlv] Argyll to Governor-General in Council, Public Despatch no. 113, 22 October 1872, *P.P.* 1878-9, LV, 310-11 cited in Anil Seal, *The Emergence of Indian Nationalism. Competition and Collaboration in the Later Nineteenth Century*, (Cambridge: Cambridge University Press, 1968), 138.
[xlvi] Surendranath Banerjea, *A Nation in Making*, (London: Oxford University Press, 1925).
[xlvii] India Public Letter, No. 9 of 1874, 6th February cited in Compton, "Indians and the Indian Civil Service," 105.
[xlviii] Government of Bengal to Government of India, 20th December, 1873, (Collection to Despatch No. 47) cited in Compton, "Indians and the Indian Civil Service," 105.
[xlix] Stephen to Lytton, 6 July 1876, Stephen Papers Add 7349 cited in Anil Seal, *The Emergence of Indian Nationalism*, 138.
[l] Lytton to Cranbrook, 30 April 1878, Lytton Papers, cited in Anil Seal, *The Emergence of Indian Nationalism*, 136.
[li] Note by Lytton, 30 May 1877, Notes in Home Department Public Proceedings cited in Anil Seal, *The Emergence of Indian Nationalism*, 139.
[lii] Lytton to Colonel Sir A. Clarke, 26 April 1878, Lytton Papers cited in Anil Seal, *The Emergence of Indian Nationalism*, 140.
[liii] Cranbrook to Lytton, 25 August 1878, LP (516/3) cited in Anil Seal, *The Emergence of Indian Nationalism*, 142.
[liv] Ripon to Kimberley, 4 April 1884, RP (B.M. I.S. 290/5) cited in Anil Seal, *The Emergence of Indian Nationalism*, 148.
[lv] Ripon to W. E. Forster, 26 May 1881, RP (B.M. I.S. 290/7) cited in Anil Seal, *The Emergence of Indian Nationalism*, 152.
[lvi] Baring to Mallet, 25 September 1882, enclosed in Baring to Ripon, 25 September 1882, RP (B.M. I.S. 290/8) cited in Anil Seal, *The Emergence of Indian Nationalism*, 156.
[lvii] Note by Mackenzie, 5 April 1882, RP Add MSS 43577 cited in Anil Seal, *The Emergence of Indian Nationalism*, 164.

lviii J.J. Keswick quoted in Judith Whitehead, "Bodies of Evidence, Bodies of Rule: The Ilbert Bill, Revivalism, and Age of Consent in Colonial India," *Sociological Bulletin*, 45 1 (1996): 37.
lix Quoted in Judith Whitehead, "Bodies of Evidence, Bodies of Rule", 37.
lx James Fitzjames Stephen, Letter, *The Times*, 1 March 1883.
lxi Ibid.
lxii Brajendranath De, "Reminiscences of an Indian member of the Indian Civil Service," *The Calcutta Review*, 132 2 (1954).
lxiii Letter Number 204 Commissioner of the Burdwan Division to the Secretary to the Government of Bengal, 7 May 1883 cited in Barun De, 'Brajendrananth De and John Beames - A Study in the Reactions of Patriotism and Paternalism in the ICS at the Time of the Ilbert Bill', *Bengal Past and Present*, 8 1 : 1 5 1 (1962): 21.
lxiv Resolution in the Home Department, 4 October 1886 cited in Anil Seal, *The Emergence of Indian Nationalism*, 180.
lxv Dufferin to Kimberley, 26 April 1886, DP 19 (Reel 517) cited in Anil Seal, *The Emergence of Indian Nationalism*, 185.
lxvi Kimberley to Reay, 30 July 1886, Kimberley Papers, D/26a cited in Anil Seal, *The Emergence of Indian Nationalism*, 185.
lxvii Maine to Dufferin, 2 June 1886, DP 37 (Reel 525) cited in Anil Seal, *The Emergence of Indian Nationalism*, 185.
lxviii Leonard Woolf, *Growing. 1904-1911* (London: Hogarth Press, 1961), 46.

Chapter Three: A Declaration of Intentions

lxix P.G. Robb, *The Government of India and Reform*, (London: Oxford University Press, 1976), 54.
lxx Memorandum by Craddock 16 September 1915 ACP 22/2 cited in Robb, *The Government of India and Reform*, 59.
lxxi Notes by Finance Member & Agriculture Member 26, 27 May 1916 CP17 cited in Robb, *The Government of India and Reform*, 59.
lxxii Chelmsford to Chamberlain 6 October 1916 CP2 cited in Robb, *The Government of India and Reform*, 60.
lxxiii Chelmsford to Chamberlain 31 January 1917 C51 cited in Philip Woods, *The Roots of Parliamentary Democracy*, (Delhi: Chanaykya Publications, 1996), 65.
lxxiv Chelmsford to Chamberlain 7 June 1917 CP3 cited in P.G. Robb, *The Government of India and Reform*, 65.
lxxv Chamberlain to Chelmsford 2 May 1917 CP3 cited in P.G. Robb, *The Government of India and Reform*, 66.
lxxvi Chelmsford to Chamberlain 18 May 1917 Telegram C51 cited in Philip Woods, *The Roots of Parliamentary Democracy*, 68.
lxxvii War Cabinet Papers, Minute No. 214(11), and Curzon Minute, 2 July 1917, *Curzon Coll.* 438 cited in Peter Robb, "The British Cabinet and Indian Reform 1917-1919," *The Journal of Imperial and Commonwealth History*, 4 3 (1976): 324.
lxxviii *Curzon Collection* 438 cited in Peter Robb "The British Cabinet and Indian Reform", 324.
lxxix Montagu to Chamberlain 15 August 1917 Chamberlain Papers, cited in Richard Danzig, "The Announcement of August 20th 1917", *The Journal of Asian Studies*, 28 1, (1968): 25.
lxxx Edwin Montagu, Speech to the House of Commons, 20 August 1917.
lxxxi P.G. Robb, *The Government of India and Reform*, 103.
lxxxii Chelmsford to Montagu 15 January, 12, 19, 16 February, 5 March 1919 CP3 cited in P.G. Robb, *The Government of India and Reform*, 104.

[lxxxiii] Chelmsford to Montagu 31 July 1919 CP5 cited in P.G. Robb, *The Government of India and Reform*, 105.
[lxxxiv] David C. Potter, "Manpower Shortage and the End of Colonialism The Case of the Indian Civil Service," *Modern Asian Studies*, 7 1 (1973): 49.
[lxxxv] Ibid., 50.
[lxxxvi] Ibid.
[lxxxvii] Ibid.
[lxxxviii] T.H. Beaglehole, "From Rulers to Servants: The I.C.S. And the British Demission of Power in India," *Modern Asian Studies*, 112 (1977): 238.
[lxxxix] Ibid.
[xc] Indian Civil Service Delegacy, Oxford to the India Office, 21 December 1920 cited in Potter, "Manpower Shortage", 52.
[xci] Beaglehole, "From Rulers to Servants", 239.
[xcii] F.C. Turner, Speech to the Central Provinces Legislative Assembly, 6 March 1922.
[xciii] David Lloyd George, Speech to the House of Commons, 2 August 1922.
[xciv] Beaglehole, "From Rulers to Servants", 242.
[xcv] Telegram of Secretary of State to Home Department 15 October 1931 cited in Potter, "Manpower Shortage", 60.
[xcvi] Ibid.
[xcvii] Potter, "Manpower Shortage", 62.
[xcviii] Beaglehole, "From Rulers to Servants", 243.
[xcix] Ibid.
[c] Philip Woodruff, *The Men Who Ruled India The Guardians*, (London: Jonathan Cape, 1963), 220.
[ci] Ibid., 224.

Chapter Four: New Sahibs

[cii] Home (Ests.) File No. 420 0f 1920 pp 1-5 cited in B.B. Misra, *The Bureaucracy in India*, (Delhi: Oxford University Press, 1986), 238.
[ciii] Home (Ests.) File No. 420 0f 1920 p 9 cited in B.B. Misra, *The Bureaucracy in India*, 239.
[civ] Home (Ests.) File No. 420 0f 1920 (Correspondence) pp 1-4 cited in B.B. Misra, *The Bureaucracy in India*, 241.
[cv] Home (Ests.) File No. 420 0f 1920 (Correspondence) pp 6-10 cited in B.B. Misra, *The Bureaucracy in India*, 242.
[cvi] Ibid.
[cvii] Neil Bruniat Bonarjee, *Under Two Masters*, (Calcutta: Oxford University Press, 1970).
[cviii] Jayavant Mallanah Shrinagesh, *Between Two Stools*, (New Delhi: Rupa & Co, 2007).
[cix] Kumar Padma Sivasankara Menon, *Many Worlds*, (London: Oxford University Press, 1965).
[cx] Shrinagesh, *Between Two Stools*.
[cxi] Bonarjee, *Under Two Masters*.
[cxii] Rabindra Chandra Dutt, *Imperialism to Socialism*, (New Delhi: Milind Publications, 1985).
[cxiii] Edward Nirmal Mangat Rai, *Commitment My Style*, (Delhi: Vikas Publishing House, 1973).
[cxiv] Hiralal Muljibhai Patel, Ed. Sucheta Mahajan, *Rites of Passage*, (New Delhi: Rupa & Co, 2005), Vadakke Kurupath Ramunni Menon, *The Raj and After*, (New Delhi: Har Anand Publications, 2000).
[cxv] Ronald Piedade Noronha, *A Tale Told By An Idiot*, (New Delhi: Vikas Publishing House, 1976).
[cxvi] Nagendra Baksi in Kewal L. Punjabi, *The Civil Servant in India*, (Bombay: Bharatiya Vidya Bhavan, 1965).
[cxvii] Shrinagesh, *Between Two Stools*.

[cxviii] Dharma Vira, *Memoirs of a Civil Servant*, (Delhi: Vikas Publishing House, 1975).
[cxix] Triloki Nath Kaul, *Reminiscences, Discreet and Indiscreet*, (New Delhi: Lancer Publications, 1982).
[cxx] Bonarjee, *Under Two Masters*.
[cxxi] Dutt, *Imperialism to Socialism*.
[cxxii] Rai, *Commitment My Style*.
[cxxiii] Braj Kumar Nehru, *Nice Guys Finish Second*, (New Delhi: Viking, 1997).
[cxxiv] Menon, *Many Worlds*.
[cxxv] Menon, *The Raj and After*.
[cxxvi] Kaul, *Reminiscences, Discreet and Indiscreet*.
[cxxvii] Nehru, *Nice Guys*.
[cxxviii] Bonarjee, *Under Two Masters*.
[cxxix] Rai, *Commitment My Style*.
[cxxx] Nehru, *Nice Guys*.
[cxxxi] Dutt, *Imperialism to Socialism*.
[cxxxii] Kaul, *Reminiscences Discreet and Indiscreet*.
[cxxxiii] Astad Dinshaw Gorwala, *The Role of the Administrator*, (Poona: Gokhale Institute of Politics and Economics, 1952).
[cxxxiv] Nehru, *Nice Guys*.
[cxxxv] Patel, *Rites of Passage*.
[cxxxvi] Sankara Krishna Chettur, *The Steel Frame and I*, (London: Asia Publishing House, 1962).
[cxxxvii] Kaul, *Reminiscences Discreet and Indiscreet*.
[cxxxviii] Rai, *Commitment My Style*.
[cxxxix] Nehru, *Nice Guys*.
[cxl] Ibid.
[cxli] Menon, *The Raj and After*.
[cxlii] Chettur, *The Steel Frame and I*.
[cxliii] Menon, *Many Worlds*.
[cxliv] Vira, *Memoirs*.
[cxlv] Baksi in *The Civil Servant*.
[cxlvi] Patel, *Rites of Passage*.
[cxlvii] Menon, *Many Worlds*.
[cxlviii] Nehru, *Nice Guys*.
[cxlix] Jawaharlal Nehru, *Towards Freedom*, (New York: The John Day Company, 1941), 35.
[cl] Menon, *Many Worlds*.
[cli] Rai, *Commitment My Style*.
[clii] Noronha, *A Tale*.

Chapter Five: War Veterans

[cliii] Ian Sumner, *The Indian Army 1914-1947*, (London: Osprey Publishing, 2001), 3.
[cliv] Ibid.
[clv] Gavin Rand & Kim A. Wagner, "Recruiting the 'martial races': Identities and Military Service in Colonial India", *Patterns of Prejudice*, 46 3-4 (2012): 234.
[clvi] Lieutenant General Sir George Chesney to General Sir Donald Stewart 22 January 1885 BL (OIOC) L/MIL/7/19019 cited in Chandar Sundaram, 'Reviving a Dead Letter': Military Indianization and the Ideology of Anglo-India 1885-1891 in *The British Raj and its Armed Forces 1857-1939* edited by Anirudh Deshpande & Partha Sarathi Gupta (New Delhi: Oxford University Press 2002), 52.
[clvii] Ibid., 53.

clviii Government of India, Army Department, Despatch 47 of 1885, 21 March 1885, BL (OIOC) L/MIL/3/133 cited in Deshpande & Gupta, *The British Raj and its Armed Forces*, 55.
clix Kimberley to Dufferin 15 May 1885, Dufferin Papers, BL (OIOC) Mss.Eur.F.1 30/3 cited in Deshpande & Gupta, *The British Raj and its Armed Forces*, 57.
clx General Sir Frederick Roberts, Memorandum on a Proposal of the GoI to Appoint Native Gentlemen to the Commissioned Ranks of the Indian Army in the Same Ranks as European Officers, 29 July 1886, BL (OIOC) L/MIL/17/5/1615 cited in Deshpande & Gupta, *The British Raj and its Armed Forces*, 63.
clxi General Sir Frederick Roberts, Memorandum on the Question of the Employment and Rank of Native Officers, 11 May 1887, cited in Deshpande & Gupta, *The British Raj and its Armed Forces*, 65.

clxii Deshpande & Gupta, *The British Raj and its Armed Forces*, 65.
clxiii Secretary of State for India Military Despatch No. 314 of 1887 30 November 1887, BL (OIOC) L/MIL/3/2122 cited in Deshpande & Gupta, *The British Raj and its Armed Forces*, 66.
clxiv Sir George Chesney, Military Education for the Natives of India, 23 January 1888, BL (IOCO) L/MIL/17/5/2202 cited in Deshpande & Gupta, *The British Raj and its Armed Forces*, 67.
clxv General Sir Frederick Roberts, Memorandum on Military Education for the Natives of India, 18 May 1888, cited in Deshpande & Gupta, *The British Raj and its Armed Forces*, 70.
clxvi Memorandum from General Kitchener, 9 September 1908, Birdwood Collection, BL/IOR, Mss.Eur.D.686/3,2. cited in Pradeep Barua, *Gentlemen of the Raj; The Indian Officer Corps 1817-1949*, (Westport: Praeger, 2003), 16.
clxvii Pradeep Barua, *Gentlemen of the Raj*, 17.
clxviii Ibid., 18.
clxix Memo by Cobbe 14 September 1921 IMR.17 CAB 16/38/2 cited in Omissi, *The Sepoy and the Raj*, (Basingstoke: Macmillan, 1994), 169.
clxx S.L. Menezes, *Fidelity and Honour: The Indian Army from the Seventeenth to the Twenty First Century* (New: Delhi; Viking, 1993), 324.
clxxi Secretary of State to Viceroy, 14 February 1922 IOR L/MIL/3 cited in Keith Jeffrey, *The British Army and the Crisis of Empire*, (Manchester: Manchester University Press, 1984), 107.
clxxii Shankarrao Pandurang Patil Thorat, *From Reveille To Retreat*, (New Delhi: Allied Publishers, 1986).
clxxiii Joyanto Nath Chaudhuri, *General J.N. Chaudhuri: an autobiography as narrated to B.K. Narayan*, (New Delhi: Vikas, 1978).
clxxiv Harbakhsh Singh, *In the Line of Duty: A Soldier Remembers*, (New Delhi: Lancer Publishers & Distributors, 2000).
clxxv Singh, *In the Line*, and Thorat, *From Reveille*.
clxxvi Ibid.
clxxvii K.V. Krishna Rao, *In Service of the Nation: Reminiscences*, (New Delhi: Viking, 2001).
clxxviii K.K. Tewari, *A Soldier's Voyage of Self Discovery*, (Auroville, 1995).
clxxix Pessie Madan, *An Odyssey: My Reminiscences*, (Delhi: Konark Publishers, 2008).
clxxx Singh, *In the Line*.
clxxxi Tewari, *A Soldier's Voyage*.
clxxxii Thorat, *From Reveille*.
clxxxiii Daniel Marston, *The Indian Army and the End of the Raj: Decolonising the Subcontinent*, (Cambridge: Cambridge University Press, 2014), 95.
clxxxiv Ibid.
clxxxv A.S. Naravane, *A Soldier's Life in War and Peace*, (New Delhi: A.P.H. Publishing Corp, 2004).
clxxxvi Onkar Kalkat, *The Far Flung Frontiers*, (New Delhi: Allied, 1983).

[clxxxvii] Singh, *In the Line*.
[clxxxviii] Anirudh Deshpande, *British Military Policy in India, 1900-1945: colonial constraints and declining power*, (New Delhi: Manohar, 2005), 90.
[clxxxix] Singh, *In the Line*.
[cxc] Thorat, *From Reveille*.
[cxci] Kalkat, *The Far Flung Frontiers*.
[cxcii] Madan, *An Odyssey*.

Chapter Six: Braving the Consequences

[cxciii] J.C. Curry, *The Indian Police*, (London: Faber & Faber, 1932), 25.

[cxciv] Removal of C.E. Berry, ASP Jhansi UP Appts F214/1904 UPSA cited in David Andrew Campion, *Watchmen of the Raj* (University of Virginia, 2002), 66.
[cxcv] Bengal to Government of India 9 January 1890, H D, Police Progs 115 240 cited in Anand Swarup Gupta, *The Police in British India: 1861-1947*, (New Delhi: Concept Publishing, 1979), 118.
[cxcvi] Gupta, *The Police in British India*, 119.
[cxcvii] Ibid., 120.
[cxcviii] Ibid.
[cxcix] Ibid.
[cc] Ibid.
[cci] Ibid.
[ccii] Ibid.
[cciii] Ibid., 125.
[cciv] Ibid., 123.
[ccv] Ibid., 125.
[ccvi] Ibid., 127.
[ccvii] Ibid., 131.
[ccviii] Ibid., 134.
[ccix] Quoted in Kirpal S. Dhillon, *Defenders of the Establishment*, (Shimla: Indian Institute of Advanced Study, 1998), 113.
[ccx] Ibid.
[ccxi] Ibid.
[ccxii] Gupta, *The Police in British India*, 156.
[ccxiii] Proposed recruitment of Asst District Superintendents in England." GOI, Home Dept, Police Proceedings, 94-130, Jan 1893. NAI. cited in David Andrew Campion, "Watchmen of the Raj", 67.
[ccxiv] Notes by His Excellency on Police Reform 23 October 1903 Curzon Collection Mss.Eur F111/281OIOC cited in Campion, "Watchmen of the Raj", 172.
[ccxv] Gupta, *The Police in British India*, 184.
[ccxvi] Dispatch No 28 1903 19 November 1903 cited in Gupta, *The Police in British India*, 234.
[ccxvii] Resolution 248-259 H.D. Police 21 March 1905 cited in Gupta, *The Police in British India*, 241.
[ccxviii] Duties of the Deputy Superintendents UP. Appts. F.398/1908 UPSA cited in Campion "Watchmen of the Raj", 184.
[ccxix] Alakh Kumar Sinha, *Thirty Two Years in the Police and After*, (Patna: Sanjivan Press, 1952).
[ccxx] Government of India Letter to Secretary of State Finance Department No 213 of 1919 18 June 1919 cited in Gupta, *The Police in British India*, 364.
[ccxxi] Gupta, *The Police in British India*, 368.
[ccxxii] B.N. Lahiri, *Before and After*, (Allahabad: Chugh Publications, 1974).

ccxxiii Narayanrao Marutirao Kamte, *From Them to Us*, (Bombay: Kamte Agencies, 1981).
ccxxiv Ibid.
ccxxv D.G. Bhattacharyya, *Random Reminiscences of a Police Officer Under Two Flags*, (New Delhi: Gyan Publishing House, 2003).
ccxxvi Kamte, *From Them to Us*.
ccxxvii Eric Stracey, *Odd Man In*, (New Delhi: Vikas, 1981).
ccxxviii Lahiri, *Before and After*.
ccxxix Kamte, *From Them to Us*.
ccxxx Sinha, *Thirty Two Years*.
ccxxxi Mithilesh Sinha, *In Father's Footsteps*, (Delhi: Vanity Books, 1981).

Chapter Seven: High Traditions

ccxxxii Despatch of the Secretary of State, 14 May 1862 cited in B.S. Chowdhury, *Studies in Judicial History of British India*, (Calcutta: Eastern Law House, 1970), 74.
ccxxxiii Phirozshah Bejanji Vachha, *Famous Judges, Lawyers, and Cases of Bombay*, (Bombay: Tripathi, 1962), 125.
ccxxxiv Ibid.
ccxxxv Ibid., 114.
ccxxxvi Ibid.
ccxxxvii Ibid., 115.
ccxxxviii Ibid., 116.
ccxxxix Ibid.
ccxl Ibid., 118.
ccxli Ibid., 199.
ccxlii Ibid., 201.
ccxliii Ibid., 202.
ccxliv Ibid., 203.
ccxlv Ibid., 206.
ccxlvi Ibid.
ccxlvii Ibid., 208.
ccxlviii Home Judicial Proceedings 29 September 1862 No. 23-32App 1-9 cited in Mahua Sarakar, *Justice in a Gothic Edifice: the Calcutta High Court and Colonial Rule in Bengal*, (Calcutta: Firma, 1997), 98.
ccxlix *The Hindu Patriot*, 29 July 1867 cited in Mahua Sarkar, *Justice in a Gothic Edifice*.
ccl Quoted in Mahua Sarkar, *Justice in a Gothic Edifice*, 107.
ccli Mehr Chand Mahajan, *Looking Back*, (Bombay: Asia Publishing House, 1963).
cclii Mahomedali Currim Chagla, *Roses in December: an Autobiography*, (Bombay: Bharatiya Vidya Bhavan, 1973).
ccliii Pralhad Balacharya Gajendragadkar, *To the Best of my Memory*, (Bombay: Bharatiya Vidya Bhavan, 1983).
ccliv W.S. Krishnaswami Nayudu, *My Memoirs*, (Madras: Krishnaswami Nayudu, 1977).
cclv Mohammad Hidayatullah, *My Own Boswell*, (New Delhi: Arnold-Heinemann, 1980).
cclvi Bhuvaneshwar Prasad Sinha, *Reminiscences and Reflections of a Chief Justice*, (Delhi: B.R. Publishing Corporation, 1985).

cclvii Chagla, *Roses*.
cclviii Gajendragadkar, *To the Best*.
cclix Hidayatullah, *My Own Boswell*.
cclx Mahajan, *Looking Back*.
cclxi Nayudu, *My Memoirs*.
cclxii Hidayatullah, *My Own Boswell*.
cclxiii Chagla, *Roses*.
cclxiv Gajendragadkar, *To the Best*.
cclxv Mahajan, *Looking Back*.
cclxvi Sinha, *Reminiscences*.
cclxvii Hidayatullah, *My Own Boswell*.
cclxviii Nayudu, *My Memoirs*.
cclxix Chagla, *Roses*.
cclxx Gajendragadkar, *To the Best*.
cclxxi Hidayatullah, *My Own Boswell*.
cclxxii Chagla, *Roses*.
Chapter Eight: An Immovable Bloc

cclxxiii Gandhi to V.S. Srinivasa Sastri, 18 July 1918 cited in Judith Brown, *Gandhi's Rise to Power*, (Cambridge: Cambridge University Press, 1972), 150.
cclxxiv Jayabrata Sarkar, "Power, Hegemony, and Politics: Leadership Struggle in Congress in the 1930s", *Modern Asian Studies* 4 2 (2006): 334.
cclxxv Ibid.
cclxxvi Quoted in Jayabrata Sarkar, "Power, Hegemony and Politics", 336.
cclxxvii Ibid.
cclxxviii Ibid.
cclxxix Ibid.
cclxxx Rani Shankar Vasudevan, "Why the Congress Accepted Office in 1937" *Studies in History*, 4 1 & 2 (1988): 49.
cclxxxi Nehru Press Statement Allahabad 8 March 1937 cited in Rani Shankar Vasudevan, "Why the Congress Accepted Office in 1937", 49.
cclxxxii Speech by Sitaramayya at Meeting of Anti-Ministry Committee Bombay 27 July 1936 *Bombay Chronicle* 28 July 1936 cited in Rani Shankar Vasudevan, "Why the Congress Accepted Office in 1937", 48.
cclxxxiii K.M. Munshi "Office Acceptance: A Survey of the Problem" cited in Rani Shankar Vasudevan, "Why the Congress Accepted Office in 1937", 53.
cclxxxiv Rajendra Prasad to S.K. Sinha 4 March 1938 Rajendra Prasad Ms 3-B/38 cited in Rani Shankar Vasudevan, "Why the Congress Accepted Office in 1937", 53.
cclxxxv Collected Works of Mahatma Gandhi, (New Delhi: Publications Division Government of India, 1999),Volume 15, 151.
cclxxxvi Ibid., Volume 16, 118.
cclxxxvii Ibid., 119.
cclxxxviii Ibid., 123.
cclxxxix Ibid., Volume 18, 184.
ccxc Ibid., Volume 26, 250.
ccxci Ibid., Volume 30, 159.
ccxcii Ibid., 276.
ccxciii Ibid., Volume 32, 378.

ccxciv Ibid., Volume 42, 362.
ccxcv Ibid., 405.
ccxcvi Ibid., Volume 46, 123.
ccxcvii Ibid., Volume 48, 168.
ccxcviii Ibid, Volume 67, 334.
ccxcix Ibid., Volume 71, 152.
ccc Subhas Chandra Bose, *The Indian Struggle*, (London: Wishart & Company, 1935).
ccci Ibid., 344.
cccii Ibid.
ccciii Ibid., 283.
ccciv Quoted in Sulekha Das, *Congress at the Helm: Bihar ,1937-1939*, (New Delhi: Bahri Publications, 1986), 12.
cccv Rani Dhavan Shankardass, *The First Congress Raj: provincial autonomy in Bombay*, (Delhi: Macmillan, 1982), 37.
cccvi Brabourne to Linlithgow, Report No. 2, 16 October 1937, Mss. Eur. F.125/113 cited in Rani Dhavan Shankardass, *The First Congress Raj*, 65.
cccvii Quoted in Rani Dhavan Shankardass, *The First Congress Raj*, 66.
cccviii Press Note, Director of Information, Government of Bombay, 26 August 1937, Kher Papers File No.5 cited in Rani Dhavan Shankardass, *The First Congress Raj*, 67.
cccix Rani Dhavan Shankardass, *The First Congress Raj*, 67.
cccx Quoted in Rani Dhavan Shankardass, *The First Congress Raj*, 72.
cccxi Rani Dhavan Shankardass, *The First Congress Raj*, 181.
cccxii Note of Home Minister 11 November 1938 S.R.O Bombay Political & Reforms Department File No. 2728-34-B-1938 cited in Rani Dhavan Shankardass, *The First Congress Raj*, 184.
cccxiii Quoted in Rani Dhavan Shankardass, *The First Congress Raj*, 227.
cccxiv Sulekha Das, *Congress at the Helm*, 36.
cccxv Ibid., 37.
cccxvi Ibid., 39.
cccxvii Quoted in Sulekha Das, *Congress at the Helm*, 39.

Chapter Nine: A Little Parliament

cccxviii Quoted in Anil Chandra Banerjee, *The Constitutional History of India Volume Two*, (Delhi, Macmillan, 1978), 157.
cccxix Henry Grey, Speech to the House of Commons, 26 April 1861.
cccxx Quoted in Subhas Kashyap, *The History of the Parliament of India*, (New Delhi: Centre for Policy Research, 1994), 33.
cccxxi Ibid.
cccxxii Ibid.
cccxxiii Charles Wood, Speech to the House of Commons, 6 June 1861.
cccxxiv Henry Grey, Speech to the House of Lords, 9 July 1861.
cccxxv Quoted in Subhas Kashyap, *The History of the Parliament of India*, 39.
cccxxvi Quoted in Salil Kumar Nag, *Evolution of Parliamentary Privileges*, (New Delhi: Sterling, 1978), 103.
cccxxvii Quoted in Subhas Kashyap, *The History of the Parliament of India*, 49.
cccxxviii Gilbert Elliot-Murray-Kynynmound, Speech to the Imperial Legislative Council, Delhi, 27 March 1907.
cccxxix John Morley, Speech to the House of Commons, 6 June 1907.

cccxxx Minto, Speech to the Imperial Legislative Council, Delhi, 25 January 1910.
cccxxxi John Morley, *Recollections*, (London, 1917) Volume 2, Book 5, 172.
cccxxxii "Bombay Elections: Mr Mody's address", *The Times of India*, 12 November 1920.
cccxxxiii "Assembly Candidates: Two More Manifestos", *The Times of India*, 8 October 1923.
cccxxxiv "To the Voters: Sir C H Setalvad's Appeal", *The Times of India*, 12 November 1923.
cccxxxv "Nationalists to the Assembly: Mr Jinnah's Manifesto", *The Times of India*, 20 September 1923.
cccxxxvi "Mr Jinnah's Candidature: A Plea for Unity", *The Times of India*, 12 November 1923.
cccxxxvii "Democracy Comes to Stay", *The Times of India*, 15 November 1923.
cccxxxviii "Uphold Hindu Cause: An Election Cry Independent Party's Campaign", *The Times of India*, 21 September 1926.
cccxxxix "Swaraj Rout: Pandit Nehru's Apologia", *The Times of India*, 13 December 1926.
cccxl Vithalbhai Patel, Speech to the Indian Legislative Assembly, 20 January 1927.
cccxli Quoted in Subhas Kashyap, *The History of Parliament in India*, 173.
cccxlii "An Agitation Will Kill the Award Pandit Malaviya Urges Support to his Party", *The Times of India*, 19 September, 1934.
cccxliii M. Rashiduzzaman, *The Central Legislature in British India*, (Dacca: Mullick Brothers, 1965), 151.
cccxliv "Big Issues at Stake: Mr Jinnah's Plea to Muslims for Support", *The Times of India*, 1 November 1945.
cccxlv "Political Standard of Country Lowered": Pandit Nehru on League Leadership, *The Times of India*, 12 November 1945.
cccxlvi "Mr Jinnah's Pakistan Plan Impracticable": Mr V. Patel's View, *The Times of India*, 19 November 1945.

Chapter Ten: An Idea of India

cccxlvii Peter Heehs, "India's Divided Loyalties", *History Today*, July 1995, 22.
cccxlviii Quoted in Peter Heehs, "India's Divided Loyalties", *History Today*, July 1995, 22.
cccxlix Quoted in Maybritt Jill Alpes, "The Congress and the INA Trials, 1945-1950: A Contest Over the Perception of 'Nationalist' Politics", *Studies in History*, 23 1 (2007): 143.
cccl Nehru, Press interview, Delhi 29 August 1945, cited in Kuracina, "Sentiments and Patriotism, The Indian National Army, General Elections and the Congress' Appropriation of the INA Legacy", *Modern Asian Studies*, 44 4 (2010): 841.
cccli *Bombay Chronicle* 1 November 1945 cited in Kuracina, "Sentiments and Patriotism", 841.
ccclii Nehru's speech at Subhas Chandra Bose's birthday celebrations in Delhi, 23 January 1946 cited in Kuracina, "Sentiments and Patriotism", 849.
cccliii AICC resolution on 'Indian National Army', Bombay, 23 September, 1945 cited in Kuracina, "Sentiments and Patriotism", 846.
cccliv Quoted in Deepak Kumar Das, *Revisiting Talwar: A Study in the Royal Indian Navy Uprising of February 1946* (Delhi: Ajanta Publications, 1993), 211.
ccclv Quoted in Deepak Kumar Das, *Revisiting Talwar: A Study in the Royal Indian Navy Uprising of February 1946*, 220.
ccclvi Ibid.
ccclvii Patel to Bishwanath Das 5 January 1946 cited in Kuracina, "Sentiments and Patriotism", 855.
ccclviii Nehru to Baldev Singh 25 December 1946 cited in Kuracina, "Sentiments and Patriotism", 855.
ccclix Letter by Nehru, 23 February 1948, cited in Maybritt Jill Alpes, "The Congress and the INA Trials 1945-1950: A Contest over the perception of 'Nationalist' Politics", 154.

ccclx Letter by Nehru on 11 March 1948 to Baldev Singh, Gopal 1984 Volume 5 438 cited in Maybritt Jill Alpes, "The Congress and the INA Trials 1945-1950: A Contest over the perception of 'Nationalist' Politics", 154.
ccclxi Deepak Kumar Das, *Revisiting Talwar: A Study in the Royal Indian Navy Uprising of February 1946*, 277.
ccclxii Hiralal Muljibhai Patel, Ed. Sucheta Mahajan, *Rites of Passage*, (New Delhi: Rupa & Co, 2005).
ccclxiii D.G. Bhattacharyya, *Random Reminiscences of a Police Officer Under Two Flags*, (New Delhi: Gyan Publishing House, 2003).
ccclxiv Mehr Chand Mahajan, *Looking Back*, (Bombay: Asia Publishing House, 1963).
ccclxv Harbakhsh Singh, *In the Line of Duty: A Soldier Remembers*, (New Delhi: Lancer Publishers & Distributors, 2000).
ccclxvi Joyanto Nath Chaudhuri, *General J.N. Chaudhuri: an autobiography as narrated to B.K. Narayan*, (New Delhi: Vikas, 1978).
ccclxvii Home (Establishments) File No. 30/12/46 p13 cited in B.B. Misra, *The Bureaucracy in India*, (Delhi: Oxford University Press, 1986), 299.
ccclxviii Home Department File No. 32/46 Ests (R) Minutes of the Conference cited in B.B. Misra, *The Bureaucracy in India*, 301.
ccclxix Patel to Nehru Letter 27 April 1948, in David Potter, *India's Political Administrators, 1919-1983*, (New York: Oxford University Press, 1986), 147.

Index

A Passage to India, 103-06, 112
Abdullah, Sheikh, 473-82, 490
Aiyer, Alladi Krishnaswamy, 322, 328
Aiyer, P.S.. Sivaswamy, 185-86
All India Congress Committee, 354, 358-59, 361, 445
Ambedkar, Bhimrao, 434
Article 314 (Indian Constitution), 499
Arya Samaj, 36-40
Asaf Ali, Aruna, 446-47
Auchinleck, Claude, 227, 446, 451
August Declaration 1917, 92-93, 117, 185, 514
Ayyangar, M. Ananthasayanam, iv, 502-504
Baksi, Nagendra, 129, 155-59, 169, 511
Banerjea, Surendranath, 41-45, 61-62, 304-05, 408, 437
Banerjee, Raghabendra, 266-68, 284, 512
Bardoli, Gujarat, 354, 357, 366, 368
Beames, John, 55, 70, 243
Beaumont, John, 332-33, 340
Bentinck, William, 22-27
Besant, Annie, 86-88, 90
Bhagalpore Police Training School, 251
Bhattacharyya, Durgagati, 265-68, 462-69, 512
Blagden, John, 342, 346
Blavatsky, Helena, 39-43
Bombay Bar Association, 289-93
Bombay High Court, 289-300, 305, 308, 332-33, 339, 346-47, 389, 511-12
Bonarjee, Neil, 120-21, 126, 130, 134
Bose, Subhas Chandra, x, 216-17, 349-50, 362-65, 369-76, 382, 392-94, 442-44, 448, 514
Bourke, Richard (Earl of Mayo), 27
Brahmo Samaj, 32-36, 39
Brett, Reginald (Viscount Esher), 184
British East India Company, v-vi, 12-43, 54-56, 171, 175, 290
Brodrick, William (Earl of Midleton), 249, 297
Brown, Hilton, 107-08
Bucher, Roy, 490-94
Bulwer-Lytton, Robert (Earl of Lytton), 63-65, 79, 399
Burke, Edmund, 46, 394
Burma, 209, 216, 218-28, 233, 442-43, 514
Calcutta High Court, 289, 300-04, 395
Cambridge, University of, ix, xi, 57, 98, 124, 126-29, 134-35, 168, 306, 369
Campbell, George (Duke of Argyll), 60, 64
Chagla, Mahomedali, 305-09, 313, 326, 332-33, 339-42, 346, 511, 513
Chaliha, Kuladhar, 503
Chamberlain, Austen, 88-91, 183
Chauri Chaura, Gorakhpur, 257, 354, 366

530

Chaudhuri, Joyanto, 195-97, 233, 449, 490-96, 511
Chaudhuri, Rohini, iv, 501
Chesney, George, 72, 177-82
Chettiar, O. Thanikachallam, 310
Chettur, Sankara, 141-42, 148-49, 512
Chetwode, Philip,198
Chetwode Committee, 198-99
Chungking, China, 162-63
Civil Disobedience, 114, 167, 169, 237, 273-77, 354-55, 359-60, 363, 365-75, 326, 428-30
Cobbe, Alexander, 187-90
Cobbe Committee, 187-88
Communal Award, 360, 430-31
Congress (Indian National Congress), iv-x, 43-48, 84-88, 95-96, 111, 131, 155, 169-70, 180, 199-200, 233-34, 247, 256-57, 273-76, 348-94, 396-97, 400, 416, 428-37, 440-49, 505, 510, 514-15
Congress Ministries 1937, 167, 337, 349-50, 364, 376-92
Congress Socialist Party, 349, 361-62
Constituent Assembly, iv, x-xi, 431, 442, 499-508, 515
Constructive Programme, 365-76, 392-93
Corkran, Charles, 195
Council Entry, x, 348,-65
Cross, Richard, 72, 180, 243
Curzon, George, 30-31, 47-48, 91, 182, 247-49, 403
Das, Chittaranjan, 351-55, 370, 415, 437
De, Brajendranath, 69
Desai, Bhulabhai, 309, 431, 437
Desai, Morarji, 385-86, 513
Deshmukh, Panjabrao, v, 501-02
Dhillon, Gurbakhsh, 444-46
Dhillon, Mahabir, 212-13
Dismiss!, 107
Dharma, 169, 285, 508
Dominion Status, 84, 94, 185, 357-58, 374, 416-419, 430
Duff, Alexander, 18, 33, 120
Duke, William, 88-90
Durbars (British), 81
Dutt, Balai, 446
Dutt, Rabindra, 130-31, 135
Dyarchy, vii, 89-95, 351, 356
El Edroos, Syed, 491-96
Elliot-Murray-Kynynmound, Gilbert (Earl of Minto), 403
English education, v-vi, 12-48, 50, 63, 74, 119, 122, 177, 181
Esher Committee, 184-86
Farran, Charles, 291-93, 299
Federal Court of India, 327-28, 345, 470
Fergasson, James, 65, 294
Fernandes. D.C., 295-96
Forster, E.M., 103, 112
Forty One Years in India, 175-76

Forward Bloc- It's Justification, 375
Freeman-Thomas, Freeman (Lord Willingdon), 87-88, 93, 307
Frere, Henry, 398

Gajendragadkar, Prahlad, 305-06, 314-16, 333, 340-41, 346
Gandhi, Mohandas, iv, x, 96, 256, 278, 348-94, 469, 505, 514
Gascoyne-Cecil, Robert (Marquess of Salisbury), 62-63
General Committee on Public Instruction, 23-26
George, David Lloyd, 91, 100, 133
Goddard, Eric, 490-92
Gorwala, Astad, 137-40, 168, 450, 456, 512
Gour, Hari Singh, 414, 429, 439
Government of India Act 1919, 80, 94-95, 115, 117, 347, 351, 409, 415, 418, 431
Government of India Act 1935, 349, 363, 386, 431
Grant, Charles, 21-22
Grey, Henry, 395
Griffith, Francis, 264-65
Grille, Frederick, 329, 331, 336, 343-44
Gokhale, Gopal Krishna, 402-07, 436
Gupta, Behari Lal, 67, 450
Haileybury, 54-55
Hamilton-Temple-Blackwood, Frederick (Marquess of Dufferin), 70-72, 79-80, 180-81, 400-03
Harries, Trevor, 334
Herapath, William, 264-65, 204, 511
Hidayatullah, Mohammad, 306, 312, 316-17, 326-32, 336-37, 342-45, 513
Hind Swaraj, 374
Hindu Mahasabha, 379, 434
Home Rule League 379, 434, 83, 86-87, 90, 307
Hans Raj, Lala, 37-38
Hume, Allan, 42-43
Ilbert Bill, 66-70, 300
Independent Congress Party, 357, 419-21
India as I knew it, 109-10
Indian Army, vii-viii, 27, 82, 171-234, 235-36, 253, 286, 348, 406, 443, 448-49, 480, 482, 484, 492, 494, 510, 515-16
Indian Civil Service, iv-viii, 13, 27, 42, 45, 48, 49-81, 85, 97-102, 106-12, 113-70, 184, 235-38, 245-46, 250, 255, 263-66, 281, 286, 289, 298, 351, 406, 450, 497-509, 510, 515
Indian Councils Act 1892, 72, 80, 400-02, 436
Indian Councils Act 1909, 80, 404
Indian High Courts Act 1861, 288-89
Indian Legislative Assembly, 93-95, 100, 111, 116-17, 173, 185-86, 188-91, 198, 253, 356, 359, 361, 395-439, 512-13
Indian Military Academy, 173, 199-202, 212, 228-33, 507, 512
Indian National Army, 212-17, 435, 440-49, 508
Indian National Party, 419-421
Indian Police, iv-ix, 235-85, 286, 348, 466-69, 505, 516
Indian Railways, 207

Indianisation, vii-xi, 94, 112, 114, 116-18, 172-73, 183-91, 198-99, 202, 230, 232-34, 236, 253, 256, 264, 287, 305, 348, 406, 441, 450, 510, 514, 516
Inverarity, John, 291-92, 308-09, 511
Isaacs, Rufus (Earl of Reading), 116-17, 188-89, 194, 354, 415
Islington Commission, 115, 253-54
Jacob, Claude, 190, 196
Jacob Committee, 190-92
Jallianwala Bagh, 96, 109, 125, 166, 279, 351-52, 500
Jayakar, Mukund, 198, 355, 357, 419-23
Jinnah, Mohammad Ali, 191-92, 198, 233, 306-08, 326, 351, 408, 417-23, 429, 431, 434-35, 475, 477, 480
Judicial Commissioner's Court Nagpur, 312, 316, 344
Jung, Zain Yar, 494-95
Justice Party, 326, 338
Kalkat, Onkar, 228-29, 231
Kamte, Narayanrao, 261-65, 268-70, 274-77, 283-85, 510-13
Kanga, Jamshedji, 309
Kania, Harilal, 313, 340, 342, 346
Kaul, Triloki, 130, 133, 135-37, 142-43
Khan, Mir Osman Ali (Nizam of Hyderabad), 164, 494-96
Khan, Mohammad, 447
Khan, Shah Nawaz, 443-44
Khan, Zafarullah, 162, 328
Khare, Narayan, 480-82
Kher, Balasaheb, 380, 385-86
Khilafat movement, 96, 352, 354
Kim, 77-79, 103
Kipling, Rudyard, 74-80, 236
Kitchener, Herbert, 171-72, 182
Knight, Henry, 275-76
Kolhapur (Princely State), 295-96
Krishna Rao, K.V., 207
Lahiri, Bishwa Nath, 258-60, 273-74, 283, 511, 513
Lajpat Rai, Lala, 200, 353, 357, 419-23
Lal, Ram, 470-72
Lee Commission, 101, 118, 255-56
Lentaigne, Walter, 228-29
Liberals (British), 23, 40, 42, 49-56, 58, 63-65, 69, 72, 79, 83-84, 108, 177
Macaulay, Thomas, 24-25, 30, 53, 56, 59, 63
Madan, Pessie, 208-09, 231-32
Mahajan, Mehr, 305, 317-21, 326, 334, 470-82
Maharishi, Sri Ramana, 322-26
Malaya, 209-17, 230-31
Malaviya, Madan Mohan, 90, 254, 351, 355, 357, 406, 408, 418-21, 429-30
Mangat Rai, Edward, 128, 131, 134, 143-44, 167
Martial Races, 64, 73, 110, 172-77, 179, 187, 233, 243
Mayhew, Charles, 290-91
Meerut Conspiracy Case, 427

Menon, K.P.S., 124-25, 128, 132, 149-54, 162-67, 513
Menon, V.K.R., 129, 132-33, 147-48, 512
Menon, V.P., 453, 456, 474, 479-81, 493, 496
Middle Class (Indian), vii-viii, 12-48, 71, 80, 110-12, 128, 131, 178, 182, 192, 199, 363, 397, 409, 436, 509
Mill, James, 22, 52, 55
Mill, John, 52
Minute on Education 1835, 25, 53
Mishra, Dwarka, 378, 380-82
Missionaries, 13, 16-24, 32-34, 37-38, 51-52, 120, 391
Mitter, Dwarkanath, 302-03
Monghyr, Bihar, 155-59, 391, 510
Montagu, Edwin, 90-96, 106, 116-18, 189, 230, 254-55, 348, 514
Montagu-Chelmsford Reforms,vii, x, 93, 95, 98-99, 103, 108-09, 111, 113, 115, 172, 253, 348, 350-52, 396, 409, 413, 415-16, 436
Moradabad Police Training School, 258-60, 283, 511
Morley, John, 403-04
Mudaliar, T. Ethiraja, 309-10
Muddiman Committee 418
Munshi, Kanaiyalal, 329, 363, 379-80, 387-88, 394, 494-96, 500
Mountbatten, Louis, 218, 453, 470, 474, 490
Muslim Conference, 475
Muslim League, 88, 326, 383, 433-35, 444, 466
Mutiny, 1857, 42, 51, 122, 172-79, 239, 396
Mutiny (Navy), 1946, 435, 440-50, 470
Nair, Chettur Sankaran, 254-55
Naoroji, Dadabhai, 43-46, 406-07, 437
Naravane, Anant, 228
Nariman, Khurshed, 380
Nasik Police Training School, 261-63, 283
National Conference, 475, 479, 490
National Demand, 418-420
National Liberal Federation, 96, 413
Nayudu, W. Krishnaswamy, 306, 309-11, 317, 321-26, 337-38
Nehru, Braj, 131-34, 138, 144-47, 165, 511-12
Nehru, Jawaharlal, x, 131-32, 166, 200, 349, 358, 362, 371, 377, 394, 435, 440, 444-48, 452, 471, 479, 498, 508
Nehru, Motilal, 132, 192, 352-58, 415-27, 437
Niyogi, Bhiwani, 336-37, 342-44
No Changers, 355, 357, 360
Non-cognisable offences 272-73, 512
Non-cooperation, iv, viii, x, 96, 125, 236-37, 256-57, 278-79, 284, 348-56, 365, 370-71, 412-20, 437
Norris, John, 304
North West Frontier, 74-77, 162, 172, 179-80, 202-05, 254, 409, 475-76
Noronha, Ronald, 129, 167
O'Dwyer, Michael, 109-12
Olcott, Henry, 39-40
Open Competition, 27, 50, 54-66

Operation Polo, 490-94
Orientalists, 20, 23-24, 52
Oxford, University of, vii, xi, 56-57, 62, 98, 124-28, 130, 133-34, 166, 305
Pandit, Sambhu Nath, 301-02
Pandharpur, Bombay, 269, 275-78
Pant, Govind, 155, 364, 383, 431, 437, 497
Partition of Bengal, 1905, 166, 401-03
Partition of India, 1947, 453-96, 507
Patel, Hiralal, 129, 139-40, 160-62, 168, 450-62, 493, 508, 511-13
Patel, Vallabhbhai, v, x, 335, 338, 360-62, 377, 379-81, 387, 424, 431, 435, 440-509, 513, 515

Patel, Vithalbhai, 405, 408, 416, 419, 424-28, 437-38, 512
Patronage, 49, 54-56
Peacock, Barnes, 301-04, 395
Peel, William, 99, 101, 118
Petty-Fitzmaurice, Henry (Marquess of Lansdowne), 246
Phansalkar, Balkrishna, 275-78, 285
Playfair, Harold, 275-76
Police Commission 1904, 248-50
Prasad, Brajeshwar, 502-03
Prasad, Rajendra, 158, 279, 360-63, 377-78, 389
Premiers' Conference, 1946, 441, 496-98
Proclamation, of Queen Victoria, 1858, 43-44, 63-64, 70, 109, 403
Prohibition, 359, 387-89
Public Service Commission, 1886, 71, 239-40, 245
Purna Swaraj Declaration, 1929, 200, 358
Quit India movement, 155-59, 169, 327-32, 345, 444, 510
Rahim, Abdur, 429
Rahman, Abdul, 324-326
Rajagopalachari, Chakravarti, 355, 360, 467
Rawlinson, Henry, 187-90, 209
Rawlinson Committee, 187-88
Razakars, 494-96
Responsive Co-operation Party, 419
Roberts, Frederick, 175-82, 202, 230
Robinson, George (Marquess of Ripon), 42, 65-71, 79
Robinson, William, 244
Round Table Conferences, 173, 198, 232, 359-60
Rowlatt Acts, 1919, 96, 408
Roy, Ram Mohun, 18, 22, 32-33
Sahgal, Prem, 444-445
Salt March, 1930, 359
Sandhurst, Royal Military College, ix, xi, 173, 183-85, 190-200, 232-33, 245-46, 507, 511
Sapru, Tej Bahadur, 90, 130, 186, 198, 408
Sarda, Har Bilas, 439
Sardah Police Training College, 266
Sargent, Charles, 294, 298
Satyagraha, iv, 154, 256, 365-68

535

Satyamurti, Sundara, 360, 431
Satyartha Prakash, 36-37
Saxena, Shibban, 503
Self-government, vii-x, 83-91, 111, 183, 187-89, 351, 365, 374, 394, 416, 420, 430, 437
Sen, Keshab Chandra, 34-35
Sen, Lionel, 223, 487-89
Setalvad, Chimanlal, 340, 413, 416
Shae, John, 188
Shae Committee, 188-92
Shah, Agha, 476-77
Shukla, Ravi, 378-82
Skeen, Andrew, 192
Skeen Committee, 192-93, 198
Sholapur, Bombay, 268-69, 274-78, 490-91, 510
Shrinagesh, Jayavant, 122-27, 129
Shrinagesh, Satyavant, 122, 449, 494
Sheshadri, Shripat, 19-20
Shuddhi, 38
Sidhwa, Rustom, 501
Simon Commission, 358, 371, 423, 428
Singapore, 209-17, 442
Singh, Baldev, 473, 479, 487-88, 492
Singh, Bhagat, 200, 438
Singh, Gurbakhsh, 213-17
Singh, Harbakhsh, 199-206, 209-18, 229-31, 482-90, 511-13
Singh, Hari (Maharaja of Kashmir), 473-82, 489-90
Singh, Karan, 472-73
Singh, Kulwant, 488-89, 494
Singh, Mohan, 212-13, 442
Singh, Ramnarayan, v, 503-04
Sinha, Alakh, 251-53, 278-82, 284-85, 513
Sinha, Bhuvaneshwar, 306, 311-12, 335-37
Sinha, Mithilesh, 278, 281-83, 513
Sinha, Nirsu, 311-12
Sinha, Satyendra, 84, 278-79
Sinha, Sri Krishna, 158, 335-36, 497
Sitaramayya, Pattabhi, 351, 362-64, 505
Slim, William, 218, 443
Spens, Patrick, 327-28
Spinning (Khadi), 356, 366-67
Staff College, Quetta, 137, 172, 227-28
Stephen, James, 62-63, 69
Stodart, James, 324-26
Stone, Leonard, 333, 340-42, 346
Stracey, Eric, 270-73, 512
Swami Dayanand (Mul Shanker), 36-40
Swaraj, 354-55, 366-70, 374-75, 393-94, 413, 416
Swaraj Party, x, 96, 349, 355-60, 367, 371, 415-21, 437, 439

Utilitarians, 13, 22-24
Tagore, Debendranath, 33-36
Tara Devi (Maharani of Kashmir), 472-73
Tayler, William, 302-05
Tewari, Krishna, 207-08, 218-22
The City of Dreadful Night, 74-75, 79
The Head of the District, 75-77, 79, 149
The History of British India, 52
The Lost Dominion, 107-08
Theosophical Society, 39-43, 87
Thesiger, Frederick (Viscount Chelmsford), 84-96
Thimayya, Kondandera, 222-24, 228
Thorat, Shankarrao, 194-95, 202-06, 222-27, 231, 233
Tilak, Bal Gangadhar, 87-88, 293, 351, 353
Tirupati Devasthanam, 318, 321-22
Tottenham, Alexander, 108-09
Trivedi, Chandu, 470-71, 474
Tyagi, Mahavir, 500-01
Vellore Police Training College, 271
Victoria, (Queen of the United Kingdom of Great Britain & Ireland), 43-44, 57, 81
Vincent, William, 115-16, 254
Vira, Dharma, 129-30, 154-55
War Cabinet, 83, 90-91, 183
Westropp, Michael, 290, 294
Wodehouse, John (Earl of Kimberley), 71-72, 179-80
World War I, iv, vii, xi, 80-81, 82-83, 97, 103, 122, 124, 126, 171-73, 183-84, 236, 253, 278, 287, 305, 319, 352, 450
World War II, ix, xi, 207, 209-28, 233, 320, 331, 435, 442, 490
Wray, John, 295-96
Writers (English), 12, 22
Wood, Charles, 59, 288, 395, 398
Wylie, Francis, 381-82
Zhob, Baluchistan 149-54
Zuhoorun, Musammat, 302